INCLUSION AND SCHOOL REFORM

INCLUSION AND SCHOOL REFORM
TRANSFORMING AMERICA'S CLASSROOMS

BY

DOROTHY KERZNER LIPSKY, PH.D.
NATIONAL CENTER ON
EDUCATIONAL RESTRUCTURING AND INCLUSION
THE GRADUATE SCHOOL AND UNIVERSITY CENTER
THE CITY UNIVERSITY OF NEW YORK
NEW YORK

ALAN GARTNER, PH.D.
THE GRADUATE SCHOOL AND UNIVERSITY CENTER
THE CITY UNIVERSITY OF NEW YORK
NEW YORK

·P A U L·H·
BROOKES
PUBLISHING C⁰

Baltimore • London • Toronto • Sydney

Paul H. Brookes Publishing Co.
Post Office Box 10624
Baltimore, Maryland 21285-0624

Typeset by Barton Matheson Willse & Worthington,
Baltimore, Maryland.
Manufactured in the United States of America by
The Maple Press Company, York, Pennsylvania.

Permission to reprint the following materials is gratefully acknowledged:
Quotations from *National Study of Inclusive Education*. (1994, 1995).
    New York: National Center on Educational Restructuring and
    Inclusion.
Pages 102–103: *Creating schools for all our children: What 12 schools have to
    say.* (1995). Reston, VA: Council for Exceptional Children.
Pages 212–213: Burello, L. (1995, July 18). *School changes which facilitate
    inclusion.* Paper presented at the Inclusive School Institute on
    "Changing Paradigms: Educating Students with Disabilities in
    Regular Classrooms." Fairfield, NJ.

Library of Congress Cataloging-in-Publication Data

Lipsky, Dorothy Kerzner.
    Inclusion and school reform : transforming America's classrooms /
Dorothy Kerzner Lipsky, Alan Gartner.
        p.   cm.
    Includes bibliographical references and index.
    ISBN 1-55766-273-8 (pbk. : alk. paper)
    1. Inclusive education—United States.   2. Mainstreaming in educa-
tion—United States.   3. Handicapped children—Education—United
States.   4. Educational change—United States.   I. Gartner, Alan.   II. Title.
LC1201.L56   1997
371.9\046\0973—dc21
                                                                    96-37325
                                                                         CIP

British Library Cataloguing in Publication data are available from the
British Library.

CONTENTS

ABOUT THE AUTHORS

Dorothy Kerzner Lipsky, Ph.D., National Center on Educational Restructuring and Inclusion, The Graduate School and University Center, The City University of New York, 33 West 42nd Street, New York, NY 10036

Dr. Lipsky is Director of the National Center on Educational Restructuring and Inclusion. She brings a unique combination of experience and expertise to her work: as a theoretician and a researcher, as a translator of research into practice, as a school administrator, as a manager of national and international projects, as an advocate for students with disabilities, and as the parent of a child with a disability.

Dr. Lipsky's research has been funded by federal and state agencies, local school districts, and private foundations. Projects include those in general and special education, transition, family support issues, and international reviews of services for students with special needs. She was honored in 1985 by the International Exchange of Experts and Information program of the World Rehabilitation Fund and in 1987–1988 by the National Institute on Disability and Rehabilitation Research as a Mary E. Switzer Distinguished Fellow.

Alan Gartner, Ph.D., The Graduate School and University Center, The City University of New York, 33 West 42nd Street, New York, NY 10036

Dr. Gartner is Dean for Research and University Programs at The Graduate School and University Center. He has played leadership roles in a wide range of organizations, each concerned with providing opportunity and equity: Chair, Boston CORE, Community Relations Director, national CORE; Executive Director, antipoverty program in Suffolk County, New York; Director, New Careers Training Laboratory; Executive Director, Division of Special Education, New York City Public Schools; Director, Center for Advanced Study in Education; and Executive Director, New York City Districting Committee.

Dr. Gartner has authored and edited more than 20 books concerning social policy, humanpower programs, self-help mutual aid, education, and disability. With Dorothy Kerzner Lipsky, he has written two books and more than a score of articles concerning inclusive education and school restructuring. His and Dr. Lipsky's 1987 *Harvard Educational Review* article was included in the *Review's* reprint of seminal articles in contemporary special education and was cited in the circuit court's decision in *Oberti*.

PREFACE

Every time a child is called mentally defective and sent off to special education for some trivial defect, the children who are left in the regular classroom receive a message: No one is above suspicion; everyone is being watched by the authorities; nonconformity is dangerous.

—Granger & Granger (1986, p. xii)

The history of educating students with disabilities in the United States parallels that of other groups in our society that have been excluded from services, including women, students from ethnic groups, and those of "minority" religions. The historical stages in the treatment of these groups have comprised, first, exclusion, by law or regulation; followed by formal programs based on judicial and/or legislative requirements; and, finally, progress toward defining the nature of the inclusive policies and practices. In the third stage of inclusion, as typified in the 1990s, issues of law, attitudes, and pedagogy are entwined, for it is society's valuing of people with disabilities that determines the "place" given to them, as expressed not only in law but also in policies and programs.

This book examines the education of students with disabilities based on these three historical stages, in the course of which are addressed attitudes about people with disabilities, the purpose(s) of schooling, and the nature of society. The questions raised include the following: Who belongs and who does not? Whom and what do we value? What kind of people are we? How does the education system represent the attitudes and beliefs of the people of the United States? And how can the polity affect the education system?

Equity in education is a phrase commonly used in discussing equal opportunities for racial and language minorities, women, and the poor. Generally, the phrase has not been used in reference to students with disabilities. In part, this reflects society's overall attitude toward disability, in which disability typically is viewed within a medical framework. One consequence of that perspective has been a special and separate education system.

Funk (1987), a founder of the Disability Rights Education and Defense Fund (DREDF), recognized the linkage between these factors.

> Organized society, its decision makers, and program and policy implementers do not understand the concepts of integration and equal opportunity as [they] relate to the inclusion and participation of disabled adults and children in the social, political, and economic mainstream. This unwillingness or inability to understand and utilize these concepts as they apply to disabled adults and children is rooted in the overriding influence of the persisting images of disabled people as deviant, incompetent, unhealthy objects of fear who are perpetually dependent upon the welfare and charity of others; and the resulting inability of society to view the confirmed exclusion, segregation, and denial of equal opportunity as unlawful and harmful discrimination.
>
> The myriad of disability-specific programs and policies, the segregation of disabled people, the inability to gain access to organized society, to experience an integrated and adequate education, to obtain meaningful employment, and to socially interact and participate [have] resulted in a politically powerless and diffuse class of disabled people who are unable to coalesce with other groups of disabled people on common issues, to vote, to be seen or heard. This class has accepted the stigma and cause of second-class citizenship and the incorrect judgment of social inferiority. (pp. 23–25)

The authors of this book strongly support Funk's assertion of the connection between society's attitudes concerning people with disabilities and their treatment within the society. Throughout this book, attention is given to the importance of weaving together school reform with broader societal developments.

This book is organized into five broad sections: Section I describes the separate special education system; Section II examines efforts toward inclusive education; Section III discusses school restructuring and the ways in which it has (and has not) included students with disabilities; Section IV addresses broader societal issues, which are both a cause and a consequence of the ways in which people with disabilities are treated in schools and by society; and Section V comprises a series of chapters that amplify the issues.

The seven chapters in Section I review the separate special education system, its structure, and the students served. Information on the results of and the response to the special education system is presented; together, the findings provide the impetus for change. Chapter 1 describes the separate special education system, based primarily on the annual reports of the U.S. Department of Education to Congress on the implementation of the Individuals with Disabilities Education Act (IDEA) of 1990 (PL 101-476). The chapter gives particular attention to the growth in the number of students served and placement patterns of service, highlighting differences in placement across disability categories, age groups, and the states.

Chapter 2 reviews the outcomes for students served in the special education system. Using data from Department of Education annual reports, as well as longitudinal studies, the chapter details the limited outcomes in terms of student learning, dropout rates, graduation rates, postsecondary education and training, employment, and community living.

Chapter 3 focuses on issues of race, language, and gender, describing the continuing differential treatment of and limited outcomes within special education for students from various minority groups, female students, and those whose native language is not English. It also addresses the harmful consequences of the evaluation system, not only for students from minority groups and female students but also for students in general.

Chapter 4 examines the costs and funding of special education and describes reform efforts designed both to reduce the separation of special and general education and to contain costs. Chapter 5 describes the roles of parents within special education and their advocacy in seeking both greater involvement for themselves and more effective outcomes for their children. Chapter 6 places the experience of students with disabilities into the broader context of disability rights. The disability rights movement offers a challenge to the "medical," or deficit, model of disability. Chapter 7, the closing chapter of Section I, examines proposals for renewing IDEA as a basis for summarizing the state of special education in the 1990s and the limits of reform proposals.

The eight chapters in Section II present information about inclusive education efforts and the challenge that they represent to the separate general and special education systems. Chapter 8 provides historical background, beginning with the earliest program for students with disabilities. Chapter 9 summarizes federal court decisions that have provided a key impetus for the development of inclusive education. Chapter 10 contains an overview of inclusive education, nationally as well as a summary of major state initiatives.

Chapter 11 describes local school district implementation of inclusive education programs, including program initiation, the extent of inclusive education, staffing and school organization, staff attitudes, professional development activities, parental responses, fiscal issues, and the responses of students. A key data source is the *National Study of Inclusive Education*, conducted in 1994 and again in 1995 by the National Center on Educational Restructuring and Inclusion (NCERI) at The City University of New York. The only such national studies, the reports contain information from more than 1,000 school districts concerning their efforts to implement inclusive education, in addition to personal accounts from teachers, administrators, parents, and students themselves regarding their experiences.

Chapter 12 focuses on classroom supports and instructional strategies, again using data from the *National Study of Inclusive Education* for 1994 and 1995, as well as reports from other sources. Chapter 13 reports on the attitudes of organizations, both educational and disability focused, toward inclusive education. It is based on the NCERI's original survey of organizations. Chapter 14 presents research data on the outcomes of inclusive education, based on studies conducted by school districts, states, university researchers, and others. Chapter 15, the final chapter in Section II, presents an "Inclusion Talkback," a recapitulation of the differing views of critics and advocates of inclusive education.

The three chapters in Section III address the need for school restructuring. Chapter 16 describes the limits of current restructuring efforts in terms of their inclusion of students with disabilities. Chapter 17, drawing from the NCERI *National Study of Inclusive Education* for 1994 and 1995 and an NCERI survey of national educational reform efforts, describes restructuring efforts that include all students. Chapter 18 proposes a paradigmatic shift in education, one that re-creates school practice, pedagogy, and policy to serve *all* students well.

Chapter 19, the single chapter in Section IV, relates emerging changes in U.S. society with those necessary for the inclusive education of all students.

The eight chapters in Section V amplify key issues presented in the volume's earlier sections. Chapter 20, by Thomas K. Gilhool, discusses the history of PL 94-142, the Education for All Handicapped Children Act of 1975, and the continuing importance of the law's provisions. Chapter 21, by Thomas B. Parrish, discusses fiscal issues concerning special education inclusion. Chapter 22, by Diane Lipton, provides detail on the "full inclusion" court cases from 1989 to 1994. Chapter 23, by Harlan Hahn, describes needed educational changes from a disability rights perspective. Chapter 24, by Harvey Pressman and Sarah Blackstone, challenges traditional thinking about the uses of technology and promotes technology as a tool for inclusion. Chapter 25, by Jenifer Goldman and Howard Gardner, applies Gardner's multiple intelligences theory to the education of students with disabilities. Chapter 26, by Robert E. Slavin, describes inclusive education as incorporated into the Success for All and Roots and Wings school reform efforts. Chapter 27, by Henry M. Levin, describes inclusive education as incorporated into the "Accelerated Schools" school reform effort.

Authors' note: All quotations included in the book are presented in their original form; no wording has been changed to reflect the authors' or publisher's preference for person-first language.

REFERENCES

Funk, R. (1987). Disability rights: From caste to class in the context of civil rights. In A. Gartner & T. Joe (Eds.), *Images of the disabled: Disabling images* (pp. 7–30). New York: Praeger.

Granger, L., & Granger, B. (1986). *The magic feather.* New York: E.P. Dutton.

Individuals with Disabilities Education Act (IDEA) of 1990, PL 101-476, 20 U.S.C. § 1400 *et seq.*

National Study of Inclusive Education. (1994). New York: City University of New York, National Center on Educational Restructuring and Inclusion.

National Study of Inclusive Education. (1995). New York: The City University of New York, National Center on Educational Restructuring and Inclusion.

ACKNOWLEDGMENTS

We are grateful to the chief state school officers, teachers, administrators, parents, and students in school districts across the United States who have helped us learn the finer and difficult aspects of what is necessary to create a unitary school system that educates well all students together.

Our many colleagues at The Graduate School and University Center, The City University of New York, have been extremely supportive of the work of the National Center on Educational Restructuring and Inclusion (NCERI) and have shared their scholarship willingly. President Frances Degen Horowitz, by her leadership and example, has made The Graduate School and University Center a place that encourages such collaboration. For that we are most appreciative. Others at the Graduate Center whom we wish to thank are Laura Ciavarella-Sanchez, Hilry Fisher, Carlene Fowler, Anne Kanelloupoulous, Bonnie Moses, and Arlene Richards.

At Paul H. Brookes Publishing Co., we thank Melissa Behm and Scott Beeler, who have our respect for their knowledge and sensitivity to issues of disability, which they generously shared with us, and Molly Ruzicka for her editing of the manuscript.

Without the support of The Annie E. Casey Foundation, the work of the NCERI would not have gone forward as it has; we are grateful to Doug Nelson and Tony Cippolone.

Many of our colleagues have long fought for inclusive education. They have taught us and have saved us from many errors. From our families, we have learned much that we continue to build on. To Danny, we will be forever grateful for the lessons that he has taught us about disability and how to live a full and happy life. For the remaining gaps in learning, we retain responsibility.

To our families,
especially the newest members:
Alexa, Eleanor, John-John, and Simon

In every child who is born, under no matter what circumstances, and of no matter what parents, the potentiality of the human race is born again.

—James Agee

INCLUSION AND SCHOOL REFORM

I

THE SEPARATE SPECIAL EDUCATION SYSTEM

Outcomes of youth with disabilities exiting public schools have not improved significantly during the last decade. Both historical and current data indicate that this population of individuals continues to drop out of school at a rate ranging from 30–80% and to experience low levels of full-time employment.
—P.D. Kohler (1993)

Section I begins by describing the status of the separate special education system; successive chapters then address major factors promoting change—the limited outcomes for students with disabilities, equity and rights issues, the costs of special education, parental advocacy, and the disability rights movement. The section concludes with a consideration of major proposed changes in the renewal of the Individuals with Disabilities Education Act (IDEA) of 1990.

1

THE CURRENT SYSTEM

Special programs for students with disabilities have been supported by states and individual school districts since the mid-1800s. Not until 1975, however, did the U.S. Congress enact PL 94-142, a law that in effect requires each state (and its local school districts) to educate all children with disabilities. Indeed, Congress summarized the purpose of PL 94-142 when, using the language of the day, they titled the law the Education for All Handicapped Children Act.

In many ways, PL 94-142 has been an extraordinary success. The act and its reauthorization, PL 101-476, the Individuals with Disabilities Education Act (IDEA) of 1990, have ensured that with few exceptions all eligible students with disabilities have access to publicly supported education. Special education programs serve more than 5 million students, with costs exceeding $20 billion in federal, state, and local funds. Since 1975, there have been two major developments:

- The number of students served has increased by more than 1.4 million, an extraordinary achievement in terms of access.
- The placement pattern for students with disabilities has remained largely identical to the one in effect when PL 94-142 was first implemented. Approximately one third of the students are served in general classes, one third attend "pull-out" resource rooms, and one third are members of special classes or are in other, more restrictive, placements. This familiar pattern has persisted despite that the greatest increase in the number of students served has been among those labeled as having learning disabilities.

STUDENTS SERVED UNDER IDEA

A federal report for the 1993–1994 school year indicated that 5,373,077 students were served under IDEA (U.S. Department of Education, 1995). After limited year-to-year percentage increases during the 1980s, the percentage increase in students with disabilities served under IDEA from 1992–1993 to 1993–1994 was 4.2%, the greatest increase since the passage of PL 94-142. This followed increases of 3.6% and 3.9% in the 1991–1992 and 1990–1991 school years, respectively. The increase between the 1992–1993 and 1993–1994 school years exceeded the growth rate in the total number of children through age 21, as well as the growth in the total number of school children. Although children ages 5 years and younger represented only 10% of the students with disabilities receiving special education services, one third of the increase was attributable to the growth in the number of these children receiving special education services.

The disabilities of more than 90% of the students ages 6–21 being served under IDEA in the 1993–1994 school year fall into four categories: specific learning disabilities, 51.1%; speech or language impairments, 21.1%; mental retardation, 11.6%; and serious emotional disturbance, 8.7%. According to the U.S. Department of Education (1995), no other category of disability identified in IDEA accounts for more than 4% of the students served.

PATTERNS OF PLACEMENT: STATE AND DISABILITY VARIATIONS

Between 1990 and 1995, general classroom placements increased over previous years by almost 10% (reaching 38.9% in 1993–1994)[1], and the use of resource rooms decreased by a similar percentage (to 31.7% in 1993–1994), while other, more segregated, placements remained stable (29.4% in 1993–1994) (U.S. Department of Education, 1995). Placement patterns varied widely based on student age, disability, and state practices.

---

[1]Changes in data collection procedures, especially in large states such as California, Indiana, Minnesota, and New York, may account, according to the Office of Special Education Programs (OSEP) for much of the increase. In California, for example, an almost 100% increase in students in general classrooms was reported between 1991–1992 and 1992–1993 ("OSEP Finds," 1995). Such changes were made known by states' self-reports.

Placement Based on Student Age

The youngest students, ages 6–11 years, were more likely to attend general education classes (almost 50% attended inclusive classrooms), compared with 30% of students ages 12–17, and 23% of students ages 18–21 (U.S. Department of Education, 1995). These variations among age groups have several likely explanations. The greater likelihood of younger students to attend inclusive classrooms may be a consequence of a smaller gap between their achievements and their perceived capacity in relation to those of their peers without disabilities, whereas the greater likelihood of older students to be educated in more segregated settings may be a result of the growing gap between their achievements (at least as measured by traditional measures) and those of their peers without disabilities. An additional factor is that a growing number of school districts are reluctant to assign a disability label prior to a child's enrollment in second grade. When children are in the primary grades, school districts and parents increasingly are likely to want to address educational concerns in general education classroom settings. The data suggest that many of the older students attend specialized vocational programs or other transition programs outside of the general school building.

Placement Based on Disability

In terms of disability, more than three quarters (81.8%) of students labeled as having speech or language impairments attended general education classes, whereas two thirds (66.1%) of those labeled as having mental retardation attended separate classes or other, more restrictive, environments. Among those students with learning disabilities, one third (34.8%) attended general education classes, whereas one fifth (21.3%) attended separate classes or other, more restrictive, environments. Among those students with serious emotional disturbance, one fifth (19.6%) attended general education classes, whereas more than half (53.7%) attended separate classes or other, more restrictive, environments (U.S. Department of Education, 1995).

Placement Among States

Even greater than the variability patterns within and among age and disability category ranges was the variability among the states. The following examples are indicative of this range of state practices:

- Iowa placed 0.93% of its students with specific learning disabilities in general classes, whereas Vermont placed 94.98% of its students with such disabilities in general classes.

- West Virginia placed 2.27% of its students with speech or language impairments in general classes, whereas Indiana placed 99.89% of its students with such impairments in general classes.
- New Jersey placed 0.28% of its students with mental retardation in general classes, whereas Vermont placed 74.70% of its students with such impairments in general classes.
- The District of Columbia placed 1.48% of its students with serious emotional disturbance in general classes, whereas Vermont placed 73.87% of its students with such impairments in general classes (U.S. Department of Education, 1995).

Such variations exist despite a federal law that defines disability categories and imposes on all states a common requirement for placing students in the least restrictive environment (LRE). Given the different population makeup of the various states, one would not expect absolute uniformity. An analysis by the Center for Special Education Finance reports that demographics, such as population density, influence the selection of special education settings. For example, the center reported that the more populous a state, the more its schools tend to use separate placement ("Geography Plays," 1996).

Although differences in professional judgment will likely result in variations in classification and placement decisions, the reasons for the variability in placement are more complex. Indeed, the wide range of differences suggests both that states' policy and program decisions vary sharply in the extent to which they honor federal requirements, and that federal monitoring efforts have not proved effective. In its annual report to Congress, the Office of Special Education Programs (OSEP), U.S. Department of Education, in noting the overall increase in inclusive placements, suggested that five sets of activities need to continue: demonstration projects to build a cadre of model inclusive schools, outreach projects to help schools address problems during implementation of inclusive programs, state-level projects to address policy barriers, training projects, and systemic projects ("OSEP Finds," 1995). Beyond these recommendations, however, OSEP did not cite the need for more rigorous monitoring or for sanctions for a state's failure to honor the law's 20-year-old LRE requirements.

Placement of Students with Mental Retardation

The Arc has conducted annual studies of the placement of students with mental retardation (Davis, 1994, 1995). The organization's 1995 report, covering the 1992–1993 school year, stated, "On the eve of the 20th anniversary of the Individuals with Disabilities Education Act, [for children with mental retardation] . . . placement in segregated educational environments continues to be the rule of the land" (Davis, 1995, p. i).

Throughout the United States during the 1992–1993 school year, only 7.1% of students with mental retardation were educated in general classrooms.[2] This represents a 0.4% increase over the previous 3 years. Only one state, Vermont, served more than half of its students with mental retardation in general classrooms. Five other states served more than 20% of their students with mental retardation in general classes. Eight states served 2% or fewer of their children with mental retardation in general classes. The Arc's study reported that as students age, the percentage served in general classes drops. For example, in the 1992–1993 school year, 8.5% of students with mental retardation ages 6–11 years, 5.9% of students with mental retardation ages 12–17 years, and 4.6% of students with mental retardation ages 18–21 years attended general classes (Davis, 1995).

Approximately 60% of U.S. students with mental retardation were served in the 1993–1994 school year in separate classrooms; an additional 9% of students with mental retardation were served in more segregated settings. In 23 states, 5% or fewer of the students with mental retardation were educated in general classrooms (U.S. Department of Education, 1995). That some states can educate significant numbers of students with mental retardation in general classrooms suggests that other states' failure to do so is less a function of the students and more one of state (and local school district) policies and practices, rooted in attitudes that restrict opportunities for students with disabilities. Such attitudes are reflected not only in placement patterns but also in the instruments that have been used by the federal government to collect data, as discussed next.

FEDERAL DEFINITION OF MENTAL RETARDATION

The U.S. Department of Education's Office of Civil Rights (OCR), in collecting data concerning mental retardation, has demonstrated limited vision and expectations for students with mental retardation. In terms of the educational placement of students with mental

---

[2]Davis (1995, p. 21) noted that this figure is exceeded by the percentage of students served in totally separate day and residential schools (8.7%).

retardation (what the form ED-102 [1992, p. 2] calls "Program Status"), the department offers only two options: 1) "full-time in special education" and 2) "part-time in special education." By failing to include the option of full-time in general education with appropriate services and supports, this federal form reflects a negative bias concerning the potential of students with mental retardation.

The form ED-102 (1992) displays further bias in its definitions of degrees of mental retardation, worded as follows:

- *Mild retardation*: Children capable of becoming self-sufficient and learning academic skills through the upper elementary grades.
- *Moderate retardation*: Children who are not able to profit from regular instruction or from instruction for the mildly retarded.
- *Severe retardation*: Children who are significantly subaverage in intellectual functioning and who have concurrent deficits or impairments in adaptive functioning. This is a developmental disorder whose onset occurs before the age of 18. (p. 3)

The preceding federal definitions of *retardation* use a deficit model based on the student's capacity to perform in an educational setting. Such a model defines what the child is *not* able to do and implies that educational activities should be limited. The definition also inappropriately restricts the levels that a child with mental retardation can attain (i.e., a child with mild mental retardation is presumed unable to learn academic skills beyond the upper elementary grades,[3] and the descriptions of *moderate* and *severe retardation* ignore the potential of such children to function in general educational settings).

CONCLUSION

Ralph Waldo Emerson asserted that a foolish consistency is the hobgoblin of little minds. Likewise, rigid uniformity in educational practices for children with disabilities is mindless. The extraordinary range of placement patterns among states, as well as ongoing findings of states' failure to implement the LRE requirements, suggests that states are exercising more than appropriate flexibility. This was highlighted by OCR and OSEP reports in 1995. In Maryland, the OCR found that schools failed to consider general education as an option for students with disabilities when determining placement. In Louisiana, central office staff members made placement

---

[3]In the 1992–1993 school year, of the students 14 years of age and older who exited educational programs, 5.4% of those with mental retardation did so with a high school diploma, and an additional 4.8% exited with a high school certificate (U.S. Department of Education, 1995).

decisions for children without considering less-restrictive alternatives ("OSEP Monitors," 1995). In California, OSEP reported that scores of students were unlawfully placed in separate classes without ever being considered for general education placement. For example, in the Los Angeles Unified School District, only 13 of its 3,455 students with mental retardation were in settings that allowed for contact with general education students; all others were in self-contained classes. In the San Francisco Unified School District, all 446 students with mental retardation and all 211 students with severe emotional disturbance were in self-contained classrooms. In the San Diego Unified School District, not one of 862 students with mental retardation was in a general education classroom placement ("California Earns," 1996). And in North Carolina, rather than placement decisions being based on students' needs, placement decisions were based on disability labels, the availability of services, and parental preferences ("North Carolina," 1995).

Research indicates that negative attitudes toward people with disabilities serve to define and limit expectations for children with disabilities and continue to influence special education practices and placement patterns. Although the reasons are multifaceted, the consequences of these attitudes and practices are found in the limited outcomes for students served in the separate special education system, as discussed in the following chapter.

PL 94-142 and PL 101-476 were passed to ensure all eligible students with disabilities a "free appropriate public education" (FAPE), holding out promise of a pathway for the educational improvement for all students. A number of factors provide both compelling justification and impetus for supporting a paradigmatic shift in education and a restructured unitary school system. These factors, as addressed in subsequent chapters in this section, include

- Continuing limited outcomes for special education students (Chapter 2)
- Equity and rights issues (Chapter 3)
- The high costs of special education (Chapter 4)
- Increasing parental advocacy and litigation (Chapter 5)
- Intensified advocacy in the area of disability rights (Chapter 6)

REFERENCES

California earns poor grade in IDEA monitoring report. (1996, February 15). *Education Daily*, 1, 3.

Davis, S. (1994). *1994 update on inclusion of children with mental retardation*. Arlington, TX: The Arc.

Davis, S. (1995). *1995 report card on inclusion in education of students with mental retardation*. Arlington, TX: The Arc.

Education for All Handicapped Children Act of 1975, PL 94-142, 20 U.S.C. § 1400 *et seq.*

Geography plays strong role in separate placements. (1996, January 5). *Education Daily*, 1, 3–4.

Individuals with Disabilities Education Act (IDEA) of 1990, PL 101-476, 20 U.S.C. § 1400 *et. seq.*

Kohler, P.D. (1993). Best practices in transition: Substantiated or implied? *Career Development for Exceptional Individuals, 20*(5), 107–121.

North Carolina falling short on least restrictive setting. (1995, October 13). *Education Daily*, 1, 3.

OSEP finds inclusive practices spreading across nation. (1995). *Inclusive Education Programs, 2*(12), 1, 5.

OSEP monitors emphasize least restrictive settings. (1995, December 12). *Education Daily*, 1, 3.

OSEP: Regular classroom becoming placement of choice. (1995). *Special Educator, 11*(8), 4.

U.S. Department of Education. (1995). *Seventeenth annual report to Congress on the implementation of the Individuals with Disabilities Education Act*. Washington, DC: Author.

2

LIMITED OUTCOMES
FOR STUDENTS

The progress of students in special education programs is not systematically measured, either by the states or by the federal government. There are sufficient data, however, to conclude that the outcomes for students who participate in the separate special education system are severely limited. This is true across a variety of metrics discussed in this chapter: dropout rates, graduation rates, postsecondary education and training, employment, and residential independence. The widespread failures that are documented in the special education system provide a strong basis for change. As this chapter emphasizes, one of the areas most in need of restructuring to improve student outcomes is that of personnel preparation programs for educators.

STUDENT OUTCOMES

Dropouts

During the 1991–1992 school year, nearly one quarter of the students with disabilities who exited school dropped out. In addition to the 22.4% who dropped out, it is likely that a significant portion of the 18.3% whose reason for leaving was reported as "status unknown" also dropped out (U.S. Department of Education, 1994).

Comparisons with the general education student population are confounded by differences between the categories used by the Office of Special Education Programs (OSEP) of the U.S. Department of Education and those used for general education. Based on a pilot study, "29 percent of all students in the NCES [National Center on Educational Statistics] pilot test will drop out over the course of their high school careers, [whereas] the percentage of students with disabilities who will drop out, based on the same definition of a dropout, will be 38 percent" (U.S. Department of Education, 1993, p. 35).

Graduation Rates

During the 1991–1992 school year, fewer than half of the students with disabilities (43.9%) exited the educational system with a regular diploma. An additional 13.5% exited with a certificate of completion, certificate of attendance, modified diploma, or completion of an individualized education program (IEP). The range among disabilities varied greatly. For the four largest categories of disabilities represented, the percentages of those who graduated with a regular diploma were specific learning disabilities, 49.7%; speech or language impairments, 43.9%; mental retardation, 36.1%; and serious emotional disturbance, 28.1% (U.S. Department of Education, 1994).

Owing to revisions in the way in which the U.S. Department of Education has collected data on students with disabilities exiting educational programs, the data collected for the 1992–1993 school year are not comparable to those collected for the 1991–1992 school year (or previous years). In the 1992–1993 school year, of the students with disabilities 14 years of age or older exiting educational programs, 7.2% graduated with a diploma, and an additional 2.4% graduated with a certificate. Despite the difficulties in making year-to-year comparisons, however, the Department reported in 1995 that "the graduation rate for students with disabilities as a whole has been essentially unchanged over the past five years" (U.S. Department of Education, 1995, p. 22).

Postsecondary Education and Training

"Only 14.6 percent of students with all types of disabilities who have exited special education take courses from any postsecondary institution" (Kohler, 1994, p. 5). Barely half of those attend a 2- or 4-year college. This compares with the more than half of youths without disabilities who are enrolled in postsecondary education (Wagner, 1989). Similarly, when participation in postsecondary education is compared for youth who have been out of school for 3–5 years, there is a substantial gap between those with disabilities and those without: 27% for the former and 68% for the latter (Blackorby & Wagner, 1996, p. 406).

The National Longitudinal Transition Study of Special Education Students (NLTS) examined the relationship between time spent by students with disabilities in general education high school classes and their postschool outcomes. The students studied attended secondary school programs between 1985 and 1990, at a time when there were only limited supplementary aids and support services for students with disabilities who were served in general education classrooms. Nonetheless, the NLTS found that "across a number of analyses of postschool results, the message was the same: those who spent more time in regular education experienced better results after high school" (U.S. Department of Education, 1995, p. 87). The implications of this finding require more study; however, the report noted that it is possible that the most competent students with disabilities enrolled in more general education classes and that these same competencies or strengths helped the students when they left school. An equally reasonable assumption, according to the report, is that increased time in general education classes enhanced student abilities and provided better preparation for adulthood.

Employment

The rate of unemployment for people with disabilities is the highest of any population subgroup. Two thirds of people with disabilities are not working, whereas 20% work full time and 13% work part time. Eight of 10 who do not work say that they would like to work; this is up from 2 of 3 in 1986. A quarter of those not working say that they would not need special equipment or technology in order to work. Although one third of the general population live in households with total incomes of less than $25,000, 59% of people with disabilities live in such households (*Persons with Disabilities*, 1994). According to a 1995 study by John Tierney, approximately 30% of men with disabilities worked or actively sought work (i.e., were in the labor force) in 1993, down 3 percentage points from the previous year. Among women with disabilities, the rate dropped 1 percentage point—from 28 to 27—during the year. Despite legislation such as the Americans with Disabilities Act (ADA) of 1990 (PL 101-336), the likelihood of employment among people with disabilities dropped during 1985–1995, according to Tierney (cited in "Employment Among," 1995, p. 4).

Residential Independence

One third of youths in the general population were living independently less than 2 years after secondary school (i.e., living alone, with a spouse or roommate, in a college dorm, in military housing), compared with 13% of youths with disabilities (Blackorby & Wagner, 1996, p. 40). For youths 3–5 years after secondary school, the comparable figures were 60% for those in the general population and 37% for youths with disabilities.

Longitudinal research on young people with disabilities indicates that they are not faring as well as their counterparts in the general population along a number of axes. According to the NLTS, a comparison of 15- to 20-year-old youths with disabilities with youths in the general population who were in secondary school or who had been out of school for less than 2 years indicates that

- More exiters with disabilities left secondary school by dropping out.
- Fewer dropouts with disabilities completed general equivalency diplomas (GEDs).
- Fewer graduates with disabilities attended postsecondary schools, although about the same percentage of graduates with and without disabilities attended postsecondary vocational schools.
- Fewer youths with disabilities had paid jobs, both during and after secondary school.
- More employed youths with disabilities worked part time and in low-status jobs.
- Fewer out-of-school youths with disabilities achieved residential independence.
- More youths with disabilities were arrested. (cited in Marder & D'Amico, 1992, p. 47)

A further follow-up to the NLTS reported comparative employment data for students with disabilities and those in the general population, up to 2 years out of high school and 3–5 years out of school. In both sets of comparisons, the students with disabilities lagged significantly behind their counterparts in the general population. The employment rate for those less than 2 years out of high school was 46% for students with disabilities and 59% for students without disabilities; among students 3–5 years out of school, the employment rates were 57% for students with disabilities and 69% for students without disabilities (Blackorby & Wagner, 1996).

Summarizing the data from the NLTS, Blackorby and Wagner (1996) reported the following:

Despite strong progress made by many youth with disabilities in the four outcome areas [employment, wages, postschool education, and residential independence], the NLTS found substantial gaps between youth with disabilities and their peers in the general population. A particularly important difference relates to the lower level of educational attainment of many youth with disabilities, which does not bode well for their long-term economic future. . . . [T]he gap in employment and earning between youth with disabilities and youth in the general population can be expected to widen in the future. (p. 410)

The NLTS furthermore found important differences in employment in terms of gender and ethnicity between youths with disabilities and those without:

> Although young women in the general population were closing the gap in employment between the sexes, the gap continued to widen among youth with disabilities.
>
> [T]he gap between white and minority youth with disabilities on measures of effective transition that was observed in the early years after high school largely was sustained in the subsequent 3 years. . . . [T]hese findings suggest that minority status may present further obstacles to successful transitions beyond those that youth experience because of disability alone. (Blackorby & Wagner, 1996, p. 410)

Noting the national educational goal of increasing the percentage of students who graduate from high school, Blackorby and Wagner (1996) pointed out that "even among high school graduates, however, those with disabilities were lagging behind their peers in the general population" (p. 410). A high school diploma alone, they noted, "does not mean that graduates with disabilities are playing on a level field relative to their peers without labeled disabilities" (p. 411).

PERSONNEL PREPARATION

PL 94-142, the Education for All Handicapped Children Act of 1975, enjoins states to develop personnel preparation programs that require "state-of-the-art" practices (Gilhool, 1989). There is a marked gap between understanding of "best practices," however, and their implementation (Williams, Fox, Thousand, & Fox, 1990). Although special education practice has improved—in both design and implementation—there continues to be substantial inadequacy in teacher education programs, both preservice and in-service. Teacher training programs and licensing continue to perpetuate a dual system in education as evidenced in new proposals such as the "Model Standards for Beginning Teacher Licensing and Development," developed by the Interstate New Teacher Assessment and Support Consortium (*Model Standards*, 1996) and the proposed "International Standards for the Preparation and Certification of Special Education Teachers" (*What Every*, 1995). Such proposals do nothing to break down the barrier between the separate systems, and they continue to "limit the scope of instructional methodology" (Mercer, Lane, Jordan, Allsop, & Eisele, 1996, p. 234) available to all teachers. With general education teacher preparation programs focusing on whole class instruction and special education teacher preparation programs focusing on meeting individual needs, the dilemma of meeting the needs of the whole class versus meeting the needs of individual students is not addressed (Vaughn et al., 1995).

At the early childhood level, Miller (1992) has described teacher training programs as "immoral and inefficient" (p. 39):

> Teachers must be prepared to meet children's needs along a broad continuum of development and personal characteristics. Only then will integration and the optimal positive outcomes for typically developing and atypically developing children occur. The debate is over and the decision is in. How long will the children and families have to wait for educators to do what is right? (pp. 50–51)

Syracuse University, one of the few teacher training programs to address these issues systematically, has announced the merger of its Special Education and Teaching and Leadership departments ("Syracuse Univ.," 1994). In 1994, the first class of its "Inclusive and Elementary Special Education Program" graduated. A parallel step has been taken by the Lawrenceburg (Indiana) Community Schools, whose hiring agreement now stipulates that a teacher must become dually certified within 3 years of hiring ("Dual Licensing," 1994).

CONCLUSION

The historical rationale for a dual educational system in which special education students are educated separately from general education students is that the service model is "special," and, as a result, it produces special benefits for the students served.

Algozzine, Morsink, and Algozzine, in a 1986 review of special education efficacy studies, stated the following:

> When one looks at attempts to study special education effectiveness, one is struck by the apparent completeness with which the topic has been addressed. There are efficacy studies [the authors cite six studies], studies of efficacy studies [the authors cite nine studies], and studies of efficacy study studies [the authors cite two studies]. Despite all the study, the general conclusion from most of the effort tends to be similar to that of Tindall (1985). "The only conclusion that can be made at this time is that no conclusion is yet available about special education efficacy." (pp. 214–215)

In 1996, a decade since the Algozzine et al. (1986) review, although further studies have been conducted of special education efficacy and outcomes, the reports are no more positive. The chapter following returns to these issues and examines gender and race in special education.

REFERENCES

Algozzine, K.M., Morsink, C.V., & Algozzine, B. (1986). Classroom ecology in categorical special education classrooms: And so, they counted the teeth in the horse! *Journal of Special Education, 20*(2), 209–217.

Americans with Disabilities Act (ADA) of 1990, PL 101-336, 42 U.S.C. § 12101 *et seq.*

Blackorby, J., & Wagner, M. (1996). Longitudinal postschool outcomes of youth with disabilities: Findings from the National Longitudinal Transition Study. *Exceptional Children, 62*(5), 399–413.

Dual licensing a must in Indiana district. (1994). *Inclusive Education Programs, 1*(10), 3.

Education for All Handicapped Children Act of 1975, PL 94-142, 20 U.S.C. § 1400 *et seq.*

Employment among disabled people lags despite ADA, study says. (1995, February 19). *Education Daily,* 4.

Gilhool, T.K. (1989). The right to an effective education: From *Brown* to PL 94-142 and beyond. In D.K. Lipsky & A. Gartner (Eds.), *Beyond separate education: Quality education for all* (pp. 243–253). Baltimore: Paul H. Brookes Publishing Co.

Kohler, P.D. (1994). *Serving students with disabilities in postsecondary education settings: A conceptual framework of program outcomes.* Unpublished manuscript, University of Illinois, Urbana-Champaign.

Marder, C., & D'Amico, R. (1992). *How well are youth with disabilities really doing? A comparison of youth with disabilities and youth in general.* Menlo Park, CA: SRI International.

Mercer, C.D., Lane, H.B., Jordan, L., Allsop, D.H., & Eisele, M.R. (1996). Empowering teachers and students with instructional choices in inclusive settings. *Remedial and Special Education, 17*(4), 226–236.

Miller, P.S. (1992). Segregated programs of teacher education in early childhood: Immoral and inefficient practice. *Topics in Early Childhood Special Education, 11*(4), 39–52.

Model standards for beginning teacher licensing and development: A resource for state dialogue. (1996). Washington, DC: Council of Chief State School Officers.

Persons with disabilities lag behind other Americans in employment, education, and income. (1994). Washington, DC: National Organization on Disability.

Syracuse Univ. blurs lines between regular, special ed. (1994). *Inclusive Education Programs, 1*(10), 2.

The transition experiences of young people with disabilities. (1993). Menlo Park, CA: SRI International.

U.S. Department of Education. (1993). *Fifteenth annual report to Congress on the implementation of the Individuals with Disabilities Education Act.* Washington, DC: Author.

U.S. Department of Education. (1994). *Sixteenth annual report to Congress on the implementation of the Individuals with Disabilities Education Act.* Washington, DC: Author.

U.S. Department of Education. (1995). *Seventeenth annual report to Congress on the implementation of the Individuals with Disabilities Education Act.* Washington, DC: Author.

Vaughn, S., Schumm, J., Elbaum, B., Saumell, L., Cohen, P., Caballero, K., Duryea, J., & Gonzales, M. (1995, March) *Effective inclusion practices: From implementation to evaluation.* Paper presented at the annual meeting of the Learning Disabilities Association of America, Orlando, FL.

Wagner, M. (1989). *The transition experiences of youth with disabilities: A report from the National Longitudinal Transition Study.* Menlo Park, CA: SRI International.

What every special educator must know: The international standards for the preparation and certification of special education teachers. (1995). Reston, VA: The Council for Exceptional Children.

Williams, W., Fox, T.J., Thousand, J., & Fox, W. (1990). Level of acceptance and implementation of best practices in the education of students with severe handicaps in Vermont. *Education and Training in Mental Retardation, 27*(2), 120–131.

3

Racial, Social, and Gender Inequities

Inequities based on race, gender, and language permeate U.S. society, especially in public education. Nowhere are these inequities more magnified than in special education. Indeed, it is fair to suggest that the separate special education system, if not designed to relieve the mainstream system of such pressures, nonetheless serves that function. This chapter examines special education issues of student identification and placement, first in terms of discriminatory treatment of children by race and gender, and then more broadly. The chapter closes with a look at the consequences of such a dual system of treatment for students without disabilities.

RACE ISSUES IN STUDENT IDENTIFICATION AND PLACEMENT

Nationwide, African Americans are twice as likely as Caucasians to be enrolled in special education programs.[1] "In 39 states, according to a *U.S. News & World Report* analysis of Department of Education data, black students are overrepresented in special education programs, compared with their percentage of the overall student

---

[1]A study conducted by the National Association of State Directors of Special Education (NASDSE) pointed out that "there is no Federal mandate to collect special education enrollment data by race/ethnicity" ("Disproportionate Representation," 1994, p. 3).

population" ("Separate and Unequal," 1993, p. 48). Based on comparisons of the total percentage representation of the African American student population with the percentage of African American students in special education programs, the largest discrepancies were found in Delaware (29% versus 41%, respectively); South Carolina (42% versus 51%); Connecticut (14% versus 22%); Louisiana (46% versus 53%); North Carolina (33% versus 40%); and Nevada (12% versus 19%).

Similar disparities are evident in the percentages of students from different racial groups receiving various disability labels:

- Retarded: Black, 26%; white, 11%; Hispanic, 18%
- Learning-disabled: Black, 43%; white, 51%; Hispanic, 55%
- Emotionally disturbed: Black, 8%; white, 8%; Hispanic, 4%
- Speech-impaired: Black, 23%; white, 30%; Hispanic, 23% ("Separate and Unequal," 1993, p. 54)

The data indicate that more than one third of African American students in special education have the stigmatizing labels of "retarded" or "emotionally disturbed," compared with fewer than one fifth of Caucasian students. Conversely, four fifths of Caucasian students in special education are more benignly labeled as "learning disabled" or "speech impaired," compared with two thirds of African American special education students who are so labeled. To the already heavy burden that race imposes in U.S. society, the special education system further segregates and denigrates students from various ethnic groups.

Kirkpatrick (1994) pointed out that mental retardation can be caused by poverty conditions; however, "the greater number of black children in special education cannot be explained solely by socioeconomic factors" (p. 2). The inability of schools to be successful for African American students, especially males, is a significant factor in special education. Ysseldyke, a national expert on referral and assessment,[2] has stated: "Studies show teachers refer kids who bother them, and we've been able to demonstrate that specifically African American males demonstrate behavior that bothers teachers" (cited in Richardson, 1994, p. B7).

U.S. Department of Education Office of Civil Rights (OCR) investigations have uncovered discriminatory practices resulting in the overrepresentation of students from ethnic groups in special education. These include differences in

---

[2]For a comprehensive survey of the literature on referral and assessment, see Ysseldyke (1987).

- Prereferral interventions[3] (e.g., districts with predominantly Caucasian students have more extensive prereferral programs than do the schools with predominantly African American students)
- Reasons for referrals for special education evaluations (e.g., for African American students, there is greater emphasis on behavioral reasons as opposed to academic reasons for referral for special education)
- The factors used in the evaluations (e.g., greater reliance is placed on IQ tests in the evaluation of African American students)
- Placement in more restrictive settings (e.g., a disproportionate number of African American students are labeled as having mental retardation, the category in which students are most likely to be in separate settings) ("OCR: Numbers," 1995)

The OCR found sufficient disparities to make wrongful assignments of students from ethnic groups to special education a priority in its investigations:

- In Rock Island, Illinois, where African American students represent 29.3% of the district's population, such students comprised 36.5% of the students in special education.
- In Bismarck, North Dakota, school officials relied heavily on scores from standardized tests in making placement decisions, failing to heed test makers' cautions about using such tests for students with such limited English proficiency (LEP) and for students from ethnic groups.
- In Alton, Illinois, where African American students represented 33.1% of the district's overall enrollment, they comprised 44.6% of the students in special education. The OCR found that the district used varying standards for student referral.
- In Albuquerque, New Mexico, the OCR faulted the district for ignoring cultural and linguistic differences among children ("Schools Struggle," 1995).

An additional study of a medium-size school district in Maryland found that "more males and African Americans were in dis-

---

[3]Prior to a student being referred for a formal evaluation to consider special education certification, a number of school districts have initiated prereferral interventions to support the learning of a student having difficulty. The prereferral interventions are designed to keep a student out of special education whenever possible. Such services vary widely and often are dependent on the philosophy and financial resources of the local district. They may include tutoring, counseling, special assistance, and technology.

trict special education programs than proportionately in either state or district general education enrollments" (Haigh & Malever, 1993–1994, p. 13).

Discrepancies across states in labeling students as retarded are particularly revealing. Five states label more than one third of their African American special education students as retarded: Alabama, 47%; Ohio, 41%; Arkansas, 37%; Indiana, 37%; and Georgia, 36%. Yet five states label fewer than one tenth of their African American special education students as retarded: Nevada, 9%; Maryland, 8%; Connecticut, 7%; New Jersey, 6%; and Alaska, 3% ("Separate and Unequal," 1993). These discrepancies exist even with a common national law, the Individuals with Disabilities Education Act (IDEA) of 1990 (PL 101-476), which provides a single national basis for the classification of students. The problem arises from state (and local district) practices that fail to honor the law. The remedy is in stricter enforcement of the law by the states and the federal government.

The foregoing disparities in the national data are reflected in local districts and are especially magnified where special education students from ethnic groups are overrepresented in more restrictive settings, producing, in effect, double segregation. In the New York City public schools, for example, 84% of students in separate special education classes were African American and Hispanic, whereas 73% of the overall student population comprised these two groups. Conversely, Caucasian students, who comprised 20% of the school system's population, accounted for 37% of the special education students placed in general education settings while receiving support services (Richardson, 1994).

GENDER ISSUES IN IDENTIFICATION AND PLACEMENT

Gender issues have been addressed in studies of special education referral and placement for several decades. Many studies report an overreferral and overcertification of males (Haigh & Malever, 1993–1994; Kos, 1993; Leinhardt, Seewald, & Zigmond, 1982; Norman & Zigmond, 1980; Weinstein, 1993–1994). Lichtenstein's (1996) findings provide a case in point:

> More than two thirds (68.5%) of all secondary students with disabilities were male, which in large part is a function of the high proportion of males in the high-incidence categories of learning disabilities (73.4%) and serious emotional disabilities (76.4%). Only in the category of deaf-blind (49.5%) was the proportion of males approximately the same as in the general population. (pp. 7–8)

Several years prior to the Lichtenstein (1996) study, the National Longitudinal Transition Study of Special Education Students (NLTS) reported that

> females in secondary special education represented a different combination of abilities and disabilities than males. As a group, females were more seriously impaired; even among males and females with the same disability category, females had marginally greater functional deficits than males. (cited in Wagner, 1992, pp. 33–35)

While attempting to disentangle the sources of these gender differences, it is pertinent to note that in the area of emotional disturbance, boys are more likely to act out, whereas girls are more likely to be passive. Each type of behavior may be of equivalent consequence for the student, but it is the former that is more likely to disrupt the class and lead to a referral for special education services. In seeking to explain the discrepancy in educators' reports on students with reading disabilities, which classified four times more boys than girls as having reading disabilities yet which determined that there were no significant differences by sex, researchers at Yale Medical School Center for the Study of Learning and Attention suggested that educators might be targeting disruptive boys and overlooking girls who sit quietly and get pushed along from grade to grade even though they are not learning to read (cited in "Reading Disabled Girls," 1995).

As with variation in placement patterns discussed in Chapter 1, uniformity is to be neither expected nor desired. However, as also suggested in that chapter, the wide range of findings cited here suggests something more than appropriate flexibility at work: namely, negative attitudes and racially discriminatory practices in a number of states and local school districts and dereliction on the part of the federal authorities in meeting their monitoring responsibilities.

RACE AND GENDER IN SPECIAL EDUCATION IDENTIFICATION AND PLACEMENT

A review of data from Connecticut provides a case study of discrepancies in the labeling and placement of students, in terms of race and gender (Nerney & Conroy, 1994). For the 1990–1991 school year, Nerney and Conroy reported the following:

- Of all females from ethnic groups certified as "handicapped," 18% were labeled as having mental retardation. This compares with 2% of Caucasian males and 5% of Caucasian females.

- Thirty percent of males from ethnic groups were labeled as having social or emotional disturbances. This compares with 20% of Caucasian males and 12% of females from ethnic groups so labeled.

In terms of prevalence rates, African American students were twice as likely to be labeled as having social and emotional disturbances as were Caucasian students; they were half as likely to be labeled as having speech or language impairments; and were three times as likely to be labeled as having mental retardation. Female African American students were half as likely to be labeled as having learning disabilities as were Caucasian females, were one third as likely to be labeled as having social and emotional disabilities, and were half as likely to be labeled as having speech or language impairments.

Concerning discrepancies in placements in Connecticut, Nerney and Conroy (1994) reported the following:

- Forty-three percent of males from ethnic groups and 42% of females from ethnic groups were in "separate classes," whereas the comparable figure for Caucasian students, male and female, was 22%.
- Among those students labeled as "LD" (learning disabled), more than one third of the students from ethnic groups were placed in "separate classes" (36% for males and 34% for females), whereas the comparable figure for Caucasians, both males and females, was less than half that, at 15%.

The availability of these data is owed to Nerney's energetic pursuit of equity issues. Although specific to Connecticut, there is no reason to believe that the conditions are unique to that state.

UNEQUAL PLACEMENT OF STUDENTS WITH LEP

Students who have limited English proficiency (LEP) face similar discrepancies as do those typed by race and gender. The Bilingual Special Education Training Program at the University of Texas (Austin) reported the following pattern of variation: "It appears that the district in which a culturally and linguistically diverse student attends school is a major determinant in whether the student receives special education services and in which disability category he or she is identified" (Robertson & Kushner, 1994, p. 1). Robertson and Kushner further reported that according to the latest OCR studies, students with LEP are served in categories of specific learning disabilities and trainable mental retardation more often than their counterparts without LEP and less often in categories of speech impairment and serious emotional disturbance (Robertson & Kushner, 1994). Again, these discrepancies go beyond expected and reasonable variations and suggest that students with LEP are being stereotyped and, as a result, harmed.

Psychological and language assessment research documents the difficulty that teachers and clinicians have in distinguishing between a language difference and a language disability (Baca & Almanza, 1993). The use of a standardized language assessment approach has proved inadequate in assessing the dual language abilities of bilingual students. Some have challenged school psychologists to initiate a major paradigmatic shift to avoid continuing to engage in what some consider to be malpractice (Figueroa, 1989). Others have pointed to the item and norm biases in standardized tests (e.g., Duran, 1988). Rather than replace such tests with criterion-referenced instruments, Duran (1989) called for a dynamic assessment approach, which establishes a strong link between testing and teaching. At the same time, inadequacies of assessment instruments for Native American students, for example, and the limited likelihood that they will be improved has led several researchers to emphasize the need for prereferral interventions for these students (Dodd, Nelson, & Spint, 1995).

EVALUATION AND CERTIFICATION PROCESSES

The previous sections of this chapter have addressed the disproportion in certification and placement for students who are members of "minority" groups. This section discusses fundamental flaws in the processes of evaluation and certification to enable students to obtain special education services. An increasing number of professionals and parents believe that the evaluation and certification system is psychometrically and pedagogically flawed as the "gatekeeper" into or out of special education and as the prescriptor for the student's educational program. The system leads to numerous students being inappropriately identified as having a disability and in need of special education services, classified in an inaccurate specific disability category, and served in self-contained classrooms rather than in the least restrictive general education classroom. In addition, the classification and evaluation system does not lead to individualized education programs (IEPs) that provide useful guidance for the classroom teacher.

For parents, the system often forces them to deal with a tangled bureaucratic process in seeking access for their children to the appropriate education that the law ensures. The conceptualization that was expressed in the Education for All Handicapped Children Act of 1975 (PL 94-142) and continued in IDEA was that parents would be partners with the school system on behalf of their children in developing programs that would provide an appropriate education. The reality, however, is far different. Parents report that rather than a partnership, they are placed in an adversarial position whenever they disagree with the professionals, especially in the evaluation process. They report that often they feel intimidated and are not provided enough or appropriate information to ask the "essential" questions.

The evaluation and classification process validates one type of knowledge—that developed by professionals—and disdains another—that of the parents. As Engel (1993) stated,

> Professional knowledge about the child is grounded in insights obtained through brief, intensive, controlled, diagnostic encounters between child and professional. Often the professional is a stranger to the child: knowledge of the child outside the evaluation context is not necessary to administer the battery of tests on which the CSE [IDEA-mandated Committee on Special Education] typically rely. (p. 807)
>
> Parents' practical experiences with their own children provide a fund of knowledge and information that the CSE professionals . . . simply lacked. In this sense, then, parents are able to portray themselves as *more* [emphasis in original] knowledgeable than the professionals, not less. Further, [parent reports] provide a basis for asserting that the knowledge system of the professionals must be supplemented—or countered—by a different kind of knowledge system not based on science but on their own experiences and common sense. (p. 810)

Since the implementation of PL 94-142 in 1975, there has been little change in parental views about the process and usefulness of evaluation. Testimony in 1995 before the National Council on Disability captured current attitudes:

- Families complain of evaluations that are done in places that . . . their child is unfamiliar [with], rather than in their home or familiar child care settings.
- I had one psychologist tell a parent, "Well, you don't need to know what's wrong with your child. You just need to do what we tell you to."
- Parents believe they were not valued as equal participants in the evaluation process.
- Over and over again, parents testified about being shut out of the assessment and evaluation process. (pp. 42–43)

A student, Julie Farar, described her experience:

> I can't tell you how many IQ tests and psychological evaluations I went through every year with someone I had never met before. In an hour, they were going to decide my psychological status, my IQ, and my abilities, and that was used for my educational plan. (National Council on Disability, 1995, p. 43)

Of most significance to teachers is that the evaluation process has not proved useful in developing and implementing an instructional program. In 1982, the National Academy of Sciences Panel on Placement of Students in Special Education concluded that the focus should not be on classification and placement but on appropriate instructional interventions (Heller, Holtzman, & Messick, 1982).

In a comprehensive review in 1987 of the evaluation and classification practices, James Ysseldyke summarized the system as follows:

1. There is currently no defensible psychometric methodology for reliably differentiating students into categories. Yet, school personnel in all but two states [Massachusetts and South Dakota] are required by law to use indices of pupil performance on psychometric measures to classify and place students.
2. There is no evidence to support the contention that specific categories of students learn differently. Yet, students are instructed in categorical groups on the notion that these groups of students learn differently.
3. With the exception of sensorily impaired students, categorically grouped students do not demonstrate a set of universal and specific characteristics—or, for that matter, even a single universal and specific characteristic. There is no logic to current practice.
4. The current system used by public schools to classify exceptional children does not meet the criteria of reliability, coverage, logical consistency, utility, and acceptance to users. (p. 265)

Ysseldyke (1987) furthermore called for the disbanding of the present "gatekeeping" system:

> I firmly believe that we know very well what stance we ought to take in regard to the practice of classifying exceptional children: the practice makes very little sense, and it is time to disband efforts to find new and better ways to classify children. (pp. 268–269)

Since 1987, recommendations for redesigning the special education evaluation and certification system have been advanced by professional and parent groups and policy makers. In 1996, the U.S. Senate Disability Policy Subcommittee of the Education and Labor Committee proposal for the renewal of IDEA, S. 1578, would have eliminated the requirement that a student be labeled with a particular impairment to qualify for federal special education funding. Along with this change, the proposed bill would have eliminated the federal division of data into 13 disability categories ("Senate Bill," 1996). As the 104th Congress failed to act on the renewal of IDEA, these and other changes await action of the 105th Congress. (See Chapter 7 for a discussion of the IDEA renewal process.)

Moving classification and labeling from a test basis to one based on curriculum and instruction is the thrust of a recommendation from the National Research Council (NRC). It calls for curriculum-based measurement (CBM) for students suspected of having learning disabilities. This would involve brief weekly assessments of a child's progress in several subject areas, to be conducted by the general education teacher. A key goal of the NRC recommendations is to replace the extensive reliance on IQ tests ("Report Offers," 1996).

Additional recommendations include the following:

- Instruments must not be used unless they have been appropriately validated for the purposes and subjects involved.
- Parents' knowledge and rights must be recognized and honored.
- Personnel must be trained to do the work undertaken.
- Racial and cultural bias, insensitivity, and discriminatory practices must be eliminated.
- The evaluation must be sensitive to the range of capacities and strengths (i.e., multiple intelligences) of all children.
- Evaluations must be conducted in the settings in which the child learns, not in the artificial setting of the tester's office.

The preceding recommendations have been developed in the context of improving the present dysfunctional evaluation and certification system, which is inherent in the current dual education system. However, to bring about a reconceptualized education system in which all children are educated in inclusive classrooms, more fundamental questions about evaluation and certification must be addressed:

- Why must children suspected of having a disability undergo a costly, lengthy, and intrusive process in order to receive public education services similar to ones that their peers without disabilities receive without such procedures?
- Why must parents of children with disabilities be denied opportunities available to parents of children without disabilities to choose the neighborhood school, or "magnet," or "school of choice" program?
- Why must some children be certified to enter a special education system if all children are entitled to a free public education that prepares them effectively to participate in and contribute to the society of which they are a part?

- Why must parents and their children in need of special education services lose substantial free-choice opportunities to gain procedural rights? Are the gains worth the cost?

DIFFERENTIAL OUTCOMES BY RACE AND GENDER

Limited postschool outcomes by race and gender have been documented for students with disabilities. For example, according to the NLTS,

> during secondary school, poorer school performance was noted for students with disabilities [who] were male, African American, or from low-income or single-parent households.
>
> For example, controlling for other differences between them, male students with disabilities were significantly more likely than females to receive failing grades in school and to drop out. Similarly, African American students were significantly more likely than their white peers to be absent from school and to receive failing grades. Significantly higher absenteeism also was noted for students from low-income and from single-parent households, independent of other differences between students.
>
> The effects of these factors separately understate their actual influence because these demographic factors often clustered together. For example, 62% of students with disabilities who were poor also came from single-parent households, making them subject to the detrimental effects on school performance of both factors. (*The Transition Experiences*, 1993, p. 1-4)

As with school performance, the NLTS reported that demographic factors influenced postschool outcomes for youths from ethnic groups:

> Controlling for other differences, African American youth with disabilities were significantly less likely than white youth to find competitive jobs. When they did work, they earned significantly less than white workers. They were also significantly less likely to be living independently and to be fully participating in the community (i.e., being productively engaged outside the home, residentially independent, and socially involved).
>
> Similarly, students from low-income households were significantly less likely to have enrolled in either colleges or postsecondary vocational programs after high school. Although they found jobs at about the same rate as wealthier peers, their jobs paid significantly less. Because poor youth were not upgrading their skills through postsecondary education and were not well paid for the jobs they found, economic disadvantage is likely to continue for these young people.
>
> Full community participation also was less common for poor youth than for those from wealthier households.[4] (*The Transition Experiences*, 1993, p. 1-4)

---

[4] Particularly disturbing is the finding that "few youths who were not fully independent were receiving services that would help them become so" (*The Transition Experiences*, 1993, p. 5-1).

Comparative data on experiences by gender of students with disabilities are more limited. The NLTS reported that "young women with disabilities had a pattern of experience in the early years after secondary school that differed significantly from [that of] men" (cited in Wagner, 1992, p. 2). Specifically, the NLTS noted that young women were

> less involved outside the home than their male counterparts with disabilities. Less involvement in employment and other productive activities outside the home and less social involvement raise concerns about the long-term prospects of females with disabilities becoming financially independent and personally satisfied with their adult lives. (cited in Wagner, 1992, p. 33)

Further analyses of the NLTS data point to the fact that these limited outcomes may be a function of girls' "lower rate of participation in programs designed to facilitate the transition from school to adult life" (Lichtenstein, 1996, p. 9). For example, the NLTS documents that girls are significantly less likely to receive occupationally oriented vocational education (Wagner et al., 1991), which has the potential to facilitate the transition from school to employment. This confirms the findings of several statewide studies in Vermont (Hasazi, Gordon, & Roe, 1985; Hasazi, Gordon, Roe, Hull, et al., 1985; Hasazi, Johnson, Hasazi, Gordon, & Hull, 1989).

In his extensive review of gender differences in education and employment of young adults, Lichtenstein (1996) asserted that the special education field "has been slow to recognize these differences and slower to respond with educational and training strategies and interventions" (p. 17):

> Perhaps the lack of attention directed toward issues of gender in special education is a consequence of its separateness from general education. This separateness has contributed to shaping our attitudes and expectations for students served in special education. Unfortunately, systems with separate instructional and curricular approaches run the risk of establishing separate (and diminished) norms, outcomes, and expectations. For the most part, this has been the case with special education. (p. 17)

SOCIOECONOMIC STATUS AND FAMILY

Meadmore (1993) has asserted that "race, gender, and class intersect in discrimination and social injustice" (p. 2). Such discrimination and prejudice are evident in special education practices. For example,

- Approximately 4 in 10 secondary students in the general population came from households with annual incomes of less than

$25,000; this compares with 68% of secondary students with disabilities.

- At the time they were secondary school students, one fourth of youth in the general population were living in single-parent families; 37% of youth with disabilities had a single parent. (*The Transition Experiences*, 1993)

Teachers' personal efficacy has been reported to be a significant factor in the referral of children from families of low socioeconomic status (SES). Podell and Soodak (1993) found that teachers with high personal efficacy were more likely than those with low personal efficacy to consider a general class placement for students with mild disabilities from low-SES families. Podell and Soodak concluded the following: "Low-SES students may be at greater risk for referral because of teacher, rather than student, factors. In other words, teachers' decisions about poor children are susceptible to bias when teachers perceive themselves as ineffectual" (p. 251).

Standardized tests play a major role in special education referrals. Beyond cultural bias and its role in the overreferral of students from ethnic groups, such tests are based on an erroneous understanding of intelligence as a fixed and largely heritable characteristic that can be precisely measured and provides an accurate predictor of success in life and school.

Sternberg (1994), in his review of *The Bell Curve*, linked the testing practices of an earlier period with the continuing salience of the "race factor" in the 1990s. He noted that in 1904, when Alfred Binet developed the first IQ test,

> the goal . . . was to ensure that children whom a teacher found merely disagreeable were not, as a result of their intransigence, relegated to classes for the retarded where the teacher would not have to deal with them anymore. Perhaps little has changed: Ethnic and other groups that do not conform to the desired behavioral patterns of society still seem to be targets for labels of mental inferiority. (p. 12)

Echoing the words of the late Ron Edmonds, the major initiator of school effectiveness research, Richard L. Green has stated, "The essential problem comes from the structure and attitudes of those in public education today who simply are not overly concerned as to whether or not minority kids learn" (cited in Richardson, 1994, p. B7).

CONSEQUENCES FOR STUDENTS WITHOUT DISABILITIES

It is not only students from racial minority groups or others referred for special education evaluation, however, who are harmed by the dual system concept that undergirds the special education system. Parents of a Caucasian child labeled as having a learning disability in suburban Chicago stated,

> Special education plays a sorting role, both for those consigned to it and for those students who remain in general education.
> Children of Special Education are children of Small Expectations, not great ones. Little is expected and little is demanded. Gradually, these children—no matter their IQ level—learn to be cozy in the category of being "special." They learn to be less than they are. (Granger & Granger, 1988, p. 26)

As a result, asserted Granger and Granger (1988), children without disabilities are harmed as well.

> Every time a child is called mentally defective and sent off to the special class for some trivial defect, the children who are left in the regular classroom receive a message: No one is above suspicion; everyone is being watched by the authorities; nonconformity is dangerous. (p. xii)

A mother of a kindergarten student without disabilities provided another perspective (Minnesota State Education Department, 1993). At a conference with her son's teacher, the mother was told that two students with physical disabilities would be in his class. The teacher " 'quickly added that there would be a full-time paraprofessional so their presence would not take away time from other students. This statement was made with the best of intentions—for my son' " (p. 4). When the mother picked up her son at the end of the first day, he pointed to an adult and said, " 'That lady is for the wheelchair people' " (p. 4). The mother further commented,

> Today I thought, "What was Charlie going to learn about people with physical disabilities and other differences that carry the perception of not normal?" He could learn that people with disabilities are not competent and need another person to be with them, that they cannot communicate for themselves, that they remain together as a subculture within a larger community, that they are always the recipients of help from caregivers." (p. 4)
> The presence of children with physical disabilities in my son's class represents just one of many kinds of diversity in today's classrooms and schools. Physical proximity is the start of what could be invaluable and positive learning about and appreciating differences. I believe that children with disabilities do not take away from other children. They do not diminish the community. I believe, instead, that these two children, currently known as the "wheelchair people," have the potential to contribute enormously to my son's learning and growth—but only if the environment and people take advantage of this opportunity. (p. 5)

CONCLUSION

The negative consequences of the separate special education system are greater for students from racial minority groups and for those with LEP. The fundamental premises of the dual system are that there are two types of children, those with disabilities and those without disabilities, and that assessment systems can make valid and reliable distinctions between the two. The system's consequent design—that the two groups are best served in separate systems, general and special education—harms all children, majority and minority, those with disabilities and those without disabilities.

The benefits for *all* of the alternative, a unitary system, have been delineated by Barth (1993):

> I would prefer my children to be in a school in which differences are looked for, attended to, and celebrated as good news, as opportunities for learning. The question with which so many school people are preoccupied is, "What are the limits of diversity beyond which behavior is unacceptable?" . . . But the question I would like to see asked more often is, "How can we make conscious, deliberative use of differences in social class, gender, age, ability, race and interest as resources for learning?" . . . What is important about people—and about schools—is what is different, not what is the same. (pp. 220–221)

REFERENCES

Baca, L.M., & Almanza, E. (1993). *Language minority students with disabilities.* Reston, VA: CEC-ERIC.

Barth, R.S. (1993). Reflections on a conversation. *Journal of Personnel Evaluation in Education, 7*(3), 212–221.

Dodd, J.M., Nelson, J.R., & Spint, W. (1995). Prereferral activities: One way to avoid biased testing procedures and possible inappropriate special education placement for American Indian students. *Journal of Educational Issues of Language Minority Students, 15,* 107–122.

Duran, R. (1988). Testing of linguistic minorities. In R. Linn (Ed.), *Educational measurement* (3rd ed., pp. 303–316). Austin, TX: PRO-ED.

Duran, R. (1989). Assessment and instruction of at-risk Hispanic students. *Exceptional Children, 56,* 154–159.

Education for All Handicapped Children Act of 1975, PL 94-142, 20 U.S.C. § 1400 et seq.

Engel, D.M. (1993). Origin myths: Narratives of authority, resistance, disability and law. *Law & Society Review, 27*(4), 785–826.

Figueroa, R. (1989). Psychological testing of linguistic-minority students: Knowledge gaps and revelations. *Exceptional Children, 56,* 145–153.

Granger, L., & Granger, B. (1988). *The magic feather: The truth about "special education."* New York: E.P. Dutton.

Haigh, J.A., & Malever, M.C. (1993–1994). Special education referral practices by gender, ethnicity, and comparison to state and district enrollments. *CASE in Point, 8*(11), 13–24.

Hasazi, S., Gordon, L., & Roe, C. (1985). Factors associated with the employment status of handicapped youth exiting high school from 1979 to 1983. *Exceptional Children, 51*, 455–469.

Hasazi, S., Gordon, L., Roe, C., Hull, M., Finck, K., & Salembier, G. (1985). A statewide follow-up on post–high school employment and residential status of students labeled as "mentally retarded." *Education and Training of the Mentally Retarded, 20*, 222–234.

Hasazi, S., Johnson, R., Hasazi, L., Gordon, L., & Hull, M. (1989). Employment of youth with and without handicaps following high school: Outcomes and correlates. *Journal of Special Education, 23*, 243–255.

Heller, K.A., Holtzman, W., & Messick, S. (1982). *Placing children in special education: A strategy for equity.* Washington, DC: National Academy Press.

Individuals with Disabilities Education Act (IDEA) of 1990, PL 101-476, 20 U.S.C. § 1400 *et seq.*

Kirkpatrick, P. (1994). Triple jeopardy: Disability, race, and poverty in America. *Poverty & Race, 3*(3), 1–2, 8.

Kos, R. (1993). Karen: An interaction of gender role and reading disability. In R. Donmoyer & R. Kos (Eds.), *At-risk students* (pp. 111–117). Albany: State University of New York Press.

Leinhardt, G., Seewald, A., & Zigmond, N. (1982). Sex and race differences in learning disabilities classrooms. *Journal of Educational Psychology, 74*, 835–843.

Lichtenstein, S. (1996). Gender differences in the education and employment of young adults: Implications for special education. *Remedial and Special Education, 17*(1), 4–20.

Meadmore, D. (1993). Divide and rule: A study of two dividing practices in Queensland Schools. In R. Slee (Ed.), *Is there a desk with my name on it? The politics of integration* (p. 27–38). London: Falmer Press.

Minnesota State Education Department. (1993). Will our children learn to value diverse community members? In *Inclusive education in Minnesota: What's working?* (pp. 4–5). Minneapolis: Author.

National Council on Disability. (1995). *Improving the implementation of the Individuals with Disabilities Education Act: Making schools work for all of America's children.* Washington DC: Author.

Nerney, T., & Conroy, J.W. (1994). *Special education labeling: Policy analysis of state-level data on discriminatory practices.* Unpublished manuscript.

Norman, C., & Zigmond, N. (1980). Characteristics of children labeled and served as learning disabled in school systems affiliated with child service demonstration centers. *Journal of Learning Disabilities, 13*, 16–21.

OCR: Numbers don't lie for minorities and special ed. (1995). *Special Educator, 10*(20), 308–309.

Podell, D.M., & Soodak, L.C. (1993). Teacher efficacy and bias in special education referrals. *Journal of Educational Research, 86*(4), 247–253.

Reading disabled girls overlooked, research says. (1995, December 28). *Education Daily*, 3–4.

Report offers alternatives to IQ tests for LD students. (1996, March 5). *Education Daily*, 1–2.

Richardson, L. (1994, April 6). Minority students languish in special education system. *New York Times*, A1, B7.

Robertson, P., & Kushner, M.I. (1994). An update on participation rates of culturally and linguistically diverse students in special education. *Perspective*, *14*(1), 1–9.

Schools struggle with policies on special ed for minorities. (1995, June 19). *Education Daily*, 1, 3.

Senate bill would lift labeling under IDEA. (1996, February 29). *Education Daily*, 2–3.

Separate and unequal. (1993, December 13). *U.S. New & World Report*, 46–60.

Sternberg, R.J. (1994). *For whom does* The Bell Curve *toll? It tolls for you.* Unpublished manuscript.

The transition experiences of young people with disabilities. (1993). Menlo Park, CA: SRI International.

Wagner, M. (1992, April). *Being female—A secondary disability? Gender differences in the transition experiences of young people with disabilities.* Paper presented at the annual meeting of the American Education Research Association, San Francisco.

Wagner, M., Newman, L., D'Amico, R., Jay, E.D., Butler-Nalin, P., Marder, C., & Cox, R. (Eds.). (1991). *Youth with disabilities: How are they doing? The first comprehensive report from the National Longitudinal Transition Study of Special Education Students.* Menlo Park, CA: SRI International.

Weinstein, D.F. (1993–1994). Special education referral and classification practices by gender, family status and terms used: A case study. *CASE in Point*, *8*(1), 25–36.

Ysseldyke, J. (1987). Classification of handicapped students. In M.C. Wang, M.C. Reynolds, & H.J. Walberg (Eds.), *Handbook of special education: Research and practice: Vol. I. Learner characteristics and adaptive education* (pp. 253–272). New York: Pergamon Press.

4

COSTS OF SPECIAL EDUCATION

Special education, as organized and conducted in the 1990s, is an expansive and complicated enterprise, complicated by virtue of the fact that special education programs are funded from federal, state, and local district resources. With the substantial increase in the number of students identified for special education services over the decade 1984–1994 (up 1 million over the 1982–1983 school year), there is great concern at state departments of education and in local school districts regarding continued funding of services for children with disabilities.

FEDERAL FUNDING OF SPECIAL EDUCATION

The Individuals with Disabilities Education Act (IDEA) of 1990 (PL 101-476) is the driving force behind the federal government's education programs. The federal contribution, however, represents only a small portion of the overall cost of special education. When enacted in 1975, the Education for All Handicapped Children Act (PL 94-142, the predecessor to IDEA) provided for a gradually increasing percentage of federal aid, beginning with 5% of the national average per pupil expenditure (APPE) in FY 1978 and rising to 40% of APPE in FY 1982 and thereafter. In practice, however, federal support has never exceeded 12% (Verstegen, 1994).

The basic source of federal support is IDEA, Part B, which in FY 1994 amounted to $2,149,686,000 to the states—an allocation of $413 per child (U.S. Department of Education, 1995). Federal funding also included Chapter 1 state formula grants of $116 million in FY 1994—an allocation of $387 per eligible pupil. This represents 8% of APPE. The remaining funding for special education—more than 90% of the total—consists of state and local district funds.

Federal funds have been allocated in two different ways. From 1970 to 1975, federal funding as a result of PL 91-230, the Education of the Handicapped Act, was based on the total number of children ages 3–21 in a state. This is called a population-based formula. A new formula was adopted in 1975 with passage of PL 94-142; the new formula was a flat grant based on the number of students identified for special education services—up to 12% of the total student population. This is called an identification-based formula. Some have argued that the federal entitlement program causes states to lose money; for example, the average cost of assessment, which is necessary to identify students, is $1,206, whereas the average federal Part B allocation is $411 (Tucker, cited in Behrmann, 1994). There are now proposals to change the federal funding formula, based on IDEA, to a more neutral system, in effect returning to the federal funding formula used prior to 1975.

The identification-based system has numerous faults. A study by the Office of Inspector General, U.S. Department of Education (*ED Can Allocate*, 1994, p. 1) pointed to a number of factors indicating that the count of students provides an unreliable basis for allocating special education funds:

- States report widely divergent proportions of children in each disability category.
- Local school districts report widely divergent proportions of children in each disability category.
- States' enrollment of students in special education is inconsistent with other statistics on the number of people with disabilities.[1]

Not only are there substantial differences among the states in categorizing special education students (e.g., Rhode Island classifies 66% of its special education students as having a specific learning disability, whereas Georgia classifies 32% in that category), but also the states vary widely in the percentage of students identified as having disabilities. The range among residents with disabilities, ages 3–17, is from 11.8% in Massachusetts to 2.1% in the District of Columbia. Thirty-one of the states classify 8% or more of their resi-

---

[1]Comparing the state's rank based on work-related disabilities with its rank based on the number of students with disabilities, the difference in ranking in 19 of the states is greater than 15 places (*ED Can Allocate*, 1994).

dents, ages 3–17, as having disabilities, whereas the remaining states so classify 7.9% or fewer residents (*ED Can Allocate*, 1994). Whereas precise uniformity is not to be expected, the range among the states of people identified as having disabilities suggests substantial unreliability in the figures. It is, therefore, inappropriate to use such data as a basis for allocating resources.[2]

Parrish (1993), codirector of the federally funded Center for Special Education Finance, summarized the arguments for and against funding formula changes. Arguments for change include that it is more cost-effective to work outside of special education; some students will be better served outside of special education; overidentification is now the major issue that needs addressing; and procedural safeguards would remain in place. Arguments against change include that an altered system would not be fair to states and districts with higher incidence rates; procedural safeguards cannot be maintained if students are not identified; a retreat from the traditional federal role of fostering and promoting special education services would occur; fiscal accountability would be jeopardized; and levels of special education funding would be threatened.

Reverting to population-based funding of special education would cause dramatic changes among the states: Fourteen states would experience funding gains or losses exceeding 15% of their federal special education allocation, according to an analysis by the Center for Special Education Finance (*IDEA: Fiscal policy issues*, 1994). In light of such dramatic consequences, Parrish (1993) has proposed a waiver procedure to allow states to develop specific reform efforts.

STATE FUNDING OF SPECIAL EDUCATION

The key issues in fiscal reform concern state funding, as mentioned previously, because more than 90% of special education funding comes from sources other than the federal government. A study

---

[2]A 1995 report to Congress on the implementation of IDEA included similar data, using a slightly different base. Looking at students ages 6–21, during the 1993–1994 school year, Georgia classified 2.25% as having a disability, whereas Massachusetts classified 7.17% as having a disability. For the same school year and age group, the range of students classified as having mental retardation was from 0.29% in New Jersey to 2.55% in Alabama, an eightfold difference; and for students classified as having serious emotional disturbance, the range was from 0.06% in Arkansas to 1.48% in Maine, a twenty-fivefold difference (U.S. Department of Education, 1995).

conducted by the National Association of State Directors of Special Education (NASDSE) found that

> state special education funding programs have the capacity, inadvertently or intentionally, to influence programs at the local level, as they can affect the number and type of children served as handicapped, the type of programs and services provided by local school districts, the duration of time students spend in special education programs, the placement of students in various programs, and class size and caseloads. (O'Reilly, 1989, p. 8)

A survey among the states concerning practices regarding inclusion reported: "The most frequently cited barrier to inclusion, as reported by 14 states, was their existing state special education funding formula" (Katsiyannis, Conderman, & Franks, 1995, p. 283). A Center for Special Education Finance study, while confirming the importance of funding formulas on the implementation of LRE policy, also cited the importance in this regard of geographic features of states, such as region and population density (O'Reilly, 1995).

The Illinois Planning Council on Developmental Disabilities commissioned a comprehensive study of special education funding, focusing on the disincentives to educating students in their home schools (*The Identification of Financial Disincentives*, 1993). The report pointed out that "in special education the funding structure is not separate from, but was created with, and is an integral part of, the whole special education system" (p. 1). The authors stressed several key points:

> Funding and the institutional structure that it gives life to are an integrated whole. They exist and change together. If there are disincentives to inclusion in the funding system, they only reflect and reinforce the disincentives to inclusion that are found in the larger structure of special education as it exists today. (p. 127)
>
> The personnel and reimbursement system is disability based. It is designed on the assumption that special education is carried out separately from regular education and has its own administrative and service delivery structure. Although inclusion can be forced into this established role, it is not a natural fit. Local school districts have to be "creative" in the way they describe and report inclusion expenditures. Inclusive practices take on the cover of segregated reporting categories. (p. 131)

Such categorical funding is tied to particular kinds of expenditures (e.g., personnel, transportation, room and board), to particular kinds of placements (e.g., private schools, orphanages), to excess costs, and to certain children. The Illinois Planning Council study stated: "To the extent that dollars are attached to specific, limited kinds of expenditures, or to specific, limited kinds of placements, school districts are limited in the range of programming that can be incorporated into Individual Educational Plans" (*The Identification of Financial Disincentives*, 1993, p. 102).

The Center for Special Education Finance reported in 1993 that 18 states implemented some type of special education finance reform in the 5 years previous and that 28 states were considering major changes in fiscal policy ("Flurry of Reform," 1993). In 1995, the center reported that 30 states were actively considering special education finance reform ("Most States Grappling," 1995). Although particulars of funding formulas vary, only four states—Massachusetts, Montana, Pennsylvania, and Vermont—provide funding based on total district enrollment. California is considering using total district enrollment as its funding base for special education. Given the size of its program, which serves more than half a million students, such a shift would have a significant effect nationally ("California Pondering," 1996). The remaining states provide funding that in one way or another depends on the number of students identified and served. As of 1996, each of these states uses one of four funding formulas, as follows:

1. Pupil weights, expressed as a multiple of regular education aid
2. Resource-based funding based on specific education resources (e.g., teachers, classroom units)
3. Percentage reimbursement, funding based on a percentage of allowable or actual expenses
4. Flat grant, a fixed amount of funding per student or per unit

According to O'Reilly (1995), "states that are low users of separate placements tend to use a funding formula that is not explicitly linked to student placement" (p. 21). Conversely, "no single type of funding formula was found for states that rank highest in their use of separate placements for students with disabilities" (p. 21). This confirms the finding of Hasazi, Johnston, Liggett, and Schattman (1994) that many factors influence where students with disabilities receive special education services.

A shift in the funding formulas could promote inclusion and reduce expenditures. In testimony before the National Council on Disability, Kane (1993) stated that Illinois spends annually $110 million to transport pupils away from their home schools. He projected that if Illinois were to use a building-based cost model, similar to that used in Pennsylvania—where 10%–15% of the students in a building are considered eligible for special education services, 1% of those children have severe disabilities, and there is state support for unusual cases—then Illinois still would spend only 60% of its 1993 expenditure. The remaining 40%, he said, could be reallocated for additional supports, aids, and curricular adaptations. (See also discussion in Freagon & Kachur, 1994.)

A Study Group on Special Education, convened by the National Association of State Boards of Education (NASBE), described the characteristics of a funding structure that would be supportive of inclusive education (*Winners All*, 1992):

- Funding must not be triggered by the labeling of students.
- The level of funding must not depend on the placement of students or who provides the programs.
- Funding should be oriented toward outcomes for students and not inputs for programs.
- Funding for special education should be linked with funding for general education to minimize competition for dollars.
- Funding should be focused on the local school district, and all special education funds should flow through the local district.

LOCAL FUNDING OF SPECIAL EDUCATION

It is at the local school district where the consequences of funding decisions at the federal and state levels play themselves out. Local school districts are both the objects of funding decisions at other governmental levels and participants themselves in funding special education services. Nationwide, local governments provide approximately half of the funding for services to students with disabilities. In addition, the local school district is the locus for taxpayer concerns regarding the costs of education.

Local funding issues are only part of the equation in the movement to adopt inclusive education. As Kane (1993) has emphasized, funding patterns and program decisions are intimately linked:

> As school districts now try to change the structure of special education and integrate children with disabilities into regular classrooms the funding structure which was designed to support a separate system and reimburse the costs of that system becomes an impediment. The funding structure itself, with its rules, its forms, its identification of "allowable" reimbursable costs, becomes a disincentive to change, an incentive to maintain a separate segregated system. (p. 2)

The charge that districts may be adopting inclusive education for the sole purpose of cutting costs does not appear to be warranted. Stating that "initial implementation of inclusion can require additional resources," McLaughlin and Warren (1994) pointed out that

> when the costs of providing services in home schools are examined *relative* [emphasis in original] to the costs of transportation and edu-

cational services in cluster programs or specialized schools, inclusion appears to be less expensive. However, in order for districts to realize these savings, dollars would have to follow the students into the new program. (p. 25)

CONCLUSION

Unless special education financial reforms become part of the financing of educational reform in general, school districts will not have the required flexibility to develop quality programs for all children. In addition, unless financial reform is carried out, increased special education needs will eventually "break the bank." It is fiscally impossible—and programmatically undesirable—to continue to place children out of the general education program in inclusive education settings one at a time. At a time of increasing taxpayer opposition to public expenditures, increases in spending for special education will not be supported.[3]

REFERENCES

Behrmann, J. (1994). Including everyone. *Arizona School Boards Association Journal, 24*(2), 6–8.

California pondering special ed funding changes. (1996, February 9). *Education Daily*, 1, 3.

ED can allocate special education funds more equitably. (1994). San Francisco: U.S. Department of Education, Regional Inspector General for Audit, Region IX.

Education for All Handicapped Children Act of 1975, PL 94-142, 20 U.S.C. § 1400 *et seq.*

Education of the Handicapped Act (EHA) of 1970, PL 91-230, 20 U.S.C. § 1400 *et seq.*

Flurry of reform in special education finance. (1993). *The CSEF Resource, 1*(2), 1–3.

Freagon, S., & Kachur, D.S. (1994). *Thoughts, perspectives, and ideas presented at the Illinois Deans of Colleges of Education symposium on inclusive education of students with disabilities.* Springfield: Illinois Planning Council on Developmental Disabilities.

Hasazi, S.B., Johnston, A.P., Liggett, A.M., & Schattman, R.A. (1994). A qualitative policy study of the least restrictive environment provision of the Individuals with Disabilities Education Act. *Exceptional Children, 60*(6), 491–507.

---

[3]Based on data from nine school districts that represent a cross-section of the nation, a study reported that programs for students with disabilities accounted for 38% of new, inflation-adjusted school spending between 1967 and 1991. During the same period, special education costs rose from 3.7% of the districts' spending to 17% (*Where's the Money Gone?* 1995).

IDEA: Fiscal policy issues and alternatives. (1994). Palo Alto, CA: Center for Special Education Finance.

The identification of financial disincentives to educating children with moderate to severe and multiple developmental disabilities in their home schools. (1993). New Berlin, IL: Program Analysis.

Individuals with Disabilities Education Act (IDEA) of 1990, PL 101-476, 20 U.S.C. § 1400 *et seq.*

Kane, D. (1993, August 13). *Testimony on financial disincentives to inclusive education in Illinois.* National Council on Disability hearings on making inclusive education work, Chicago.

Katsiyannis, A., Conderman, G., & Franks, D.J. (1995). State practices on inclusion: A national review. *Remedial and Special Education, 16*(5), 279–287.

McLaughlin, M.J., & Warren, S.H. (1994). *Resource implications of inclusion: Impressions of special education administrators at selected sites.* Palo Alto, CA: Center for Special Education Finance.

Most states grappling with special ed formulas. (1995, October 18). *Education Daily*, 1–2.

O'Reilly, F.E. (1989). *State special education finance systems, 1988–89.* Alexandria, VA: National Association of State Directors of Special Education.

O'Reilly, F.E. (1995). *State special education funding formulas and the use of separate placements for students with disabilities: Exploratory linkages.* Policy Paper 7. Palo Alto, CA: Center for Special Education Finance.

Parrish, T. (1993). Federal policy options for funding special education. *CSEF Brief, 1*, 1–4.

U.S. Department of Education. (1995). *Seventeenth annual report to Congress on the implementation of the Individuals with Disabilities Education Act.* Washington, DC: Author.

Verstegen, D.A. (1994). *Fiscal provisions of the Individuals with Disabilities Education Act: Historical overview.* Palo Alto, CA: Center for Special Education Finance.

Where's the money gone? Changes in the level and composition of education spending. (1995). Washington, DC: Economic Policy Institute.

Winners all: A call for inclusive schools. (1992). Washington, DC: National Association of State Boards of Education.

5

PARENTAL ADVOCACY

Parental advocacy was a key factor in the passage of PL 94-142, the landmark Education for All Handicapped Children Act of 1975, as well as in protecting the law from Reagan administration efforts to gut it. The law provides both programmatic entitlements for children with disabilities and procedural rights for such children and their parents.

IDEA AND DUE PROCESS RIGHTS FOR PARENTS

The Individuals with Disabilities Education Act (IDEA) of 1990 (PL 101-476), which reauthorized PL 94-142, includes a panoply of due process rights for parents, including requirements that school districts keep parents informed, that parents give consent to initial evaluations, and that parents be invited to participate in the development of their child's individualized education program (IEP).

In the years since passage of PL 94-142, Congress has added a number of features that increase parental roles. The Part H provisions of the law (PL 102-119)—the IDEA Amendments of 1991 that added the program for infants and toddlers—established a requirement for individualized family service plans (IFSPs), in recognition that the "client" being served was the family, not the child alone (Mallory, 1995). During the transition phase from early intervention to preschool programs, the regulations emphasize "Congress's desire to create a seamless relationship between the Part H provisions and those for preschool services and to extend the family focus to preschool programs" (Brown, 1994, p. 4-1). The 1991 amendments also require that plans be developed, with parental and student involvement, for the transition from school-age programs to adult services no later than age 16.

Although lacking the requirements of other federal programs for parental involvement in policy making, such as those of Head Start and Follow Through, IDEA envisions a genuinely collaborative decision-making process. Nonetheless, parents' participation in educating their children with disabilities has been reported as more passive than active (Turnbull & Turnbull, 1990). Such findings are the consequence of professional attitudes, which both view disability through a deficit perspective (see Chapter 6) and treat families as if they too were "disabled" and in need of professional services:

> The child with a handicapping condition needs help—a role for the professional; the parents of the child are incapable of making major decisions—no interference for the professional; the parents need help to combat psychological stress—another role for the professional. Additionally, the belief that parents displace their anger onto the professional is a kind of "Catch 22." That is, whenever the parent disagrees with or confronts the professional, that behavior can be dismissed as an expression of inadequate adjustment, frustration, displaced anger, or a host of psychological problems. Any interpretation is possible other than that the parent is correct! (Lipsky, 1985, p. 616)

The major arena for parent–professional engagement is the student evaluation process, conducted by the multidisciplinary body required by IDEA:

> From the perspective of the participants in the CSE [Committee on Special Education] process, there is a tension between the statutory model of cooperative planning envisioned by the congressional drafters and the more familiar model of expert recommendation and parental consent that is, perhaps, a product of the traditional culture of professional-client relationship. Parents tend to experience this tension as exclusion from the decisionmaking process. (Engel, 1993, p. 805)

Harry, Allen, and McLaughlin (1995) studied parental involvement among African American families with children with disabilities:

> Findings of even greater passivity among minority families is [sic] often interpreted as reflecting numerous parental difficulties, such as lack of knowledge of their rights, or of system procedures and policies; difficulties with transportation, child care or work; unquestioning trust in, or deference to, school authorities. Such interpretations view the responsibility for participation as essentially belonging to the parents. (pp. 364–365)

Although Harry et al.'s (1995) study focused on African American families, their findings apply to parental participation more broadly.

For example, based upon 10 regional hearings and testimony from more than 400 witnesses, most of whom are parents or other family members of students with disabilities, the National Council on Disability, a presidentially appointed advisory body, reported that

> in spite of provisions mandating parent participation in decision making, parents in many parts of the country still feel largely left out of the process. Many parents reported that they arrived at IEP planning meetings only to be presented with a completed plan. (1995, p. 11)

This fact—of parents being presented with a completed IEP without their involvement—is symbolic of the larger issues of professional treatment of parents. In their concluding comments, Harry et al. (1995) presented four issues for practitioners to consider: 1) the untapped potential of parents as partners in decision making; 2) the impact of labeling on both parents and children; 3) the implication that even when professionals adhere to the letter of the law regarding parental participation, several practices may communicate to parents that low priority is placed on parental input; and 4) perhaps most important, the implication that as professionals identify with the culture of the school bureaucracy, most become entrenched in a "we–they" posture by which parents are seen as potential adversaries. In special education, the due process specifications make this even more likely.

At stake are not simply issues involving the relationship between parents and professionals, but, more fundamentally, how each of these individuals views the child with a disability. Engel (1993) has underscored the dichotomy:

> Whereas parents tend to perceive the whole child and to emphasize capabilities, the professionals tend to perceive the child in terms of "defects"—those aspects of the child that deviate from the norm and justify the child's classification as "handicapped" or "disabled." The defects are the basis for professional intervention; the defects are the raison d'être of the CSE meeting, and the CSE committee itself; the defects are the reason the law requires "special" education and remediation. (pp. 811–812)

Parents and professionals also differ in status and in the power to control resources:

> There is an asymmetry to the IEP conference that arises not only because parents and professionals speak different languages and view the world through different lenses, but also because their status at the conference table is fundamentally different. In the CSE meeting, one party enters the discussion with control over resources while the other only has needs and rights. The party with control over resources—the CSE—has no needs or emotions to "share" or trade, just

as the party with needs and emotions—the parents—has no resources to offer in the negotiations. The negotiating process for the parents is, therefore, a matter of attempting to bargain for resources by citing needs—a frustrating and sometimes humiliating process. (Engel, 1993, pp. 820–821)

For the professionals to behave differently would challenge the essence of both their work and their professional training. As Harry et al. (1995) have pointed out,

For professionals to take parental concern into account would [be] to question the assumption that a real dividing line exists between students with disabilities and those without and should be used to separate even the youngest students—by program, by curriculum, by location. A system structured on classifying and separating students could not afford to be challenged by these parents' charges of inappropriate placement, even though the responsibility for appropriateness is one of the cornerstones of the law. This speaks directly to the need for a unified system of education, in which all students' needs can be identified and addressed without their having been designated "disabled." (pp. 373–374)

COMMON PARENTAL CONCERNS

Increasingly many families of children with disabilities have embraced a unified system of education, insisting on placement for their children in general education classrooms, with the necessary supplementary aids and support services. This was a theme at hearings of the National Council on Disability in 1994, during which more than 400 witnesses testified at 10 field sites nationwide (cited in "Parents, Advocates," 1994, p. 2). Among common concerns voiced by parents throughout the hearings were the following:

• Far too many school buildings remain physically inaccessible to students with disabilities, thereby denying these students placement in general education settings.[1]
• The system of identifying students as eligible for special education encourages the harmful labeling of children, fails to identify some needy students as eligible, overidentifies children from minority backgrounds as having disabilities, and often employs assessment criteria that are inappropriate for students or insensitive to their cultural and communication backgrounds.

---

[1]A 1995 survey by the U.S. General Accounting Office reported that although accessibility to programs and activities in public school facilities has been required by federal law since 1973 (Section 504 of the Rehabilitation Act of 1973 [PL 93-112], now strengthened by the Americans with Disabilities Act [ADA] of 1990 [PL 101-336]), accessibility remains an unachieved mandate (*School Facilities*, 1995).

- There is great variability in the quality of IEPs required under IDEA.
- In spite of provisions requiring placement in the least restrictive environment, placement in a regular school building is simply not an option offered in many school districts. In fact, there are financial incentives to place students in separate facilities (see discussion in Chapter 4). Virtually all of the parents who had gained inclusive placements for their children reported that they had to fight for these placements, sometimes through legal proceedings. Nevertheless, these parents universally stated that these inclusive placements were far superior to segregated placements.
- The field of special education needs to undergo a paradigm shift from its current status as a system apart from general education to one that is an integral part of general education, providing an array of supports and services within the context of general education programs and facilities. Services and supports should come to students, not the other way around (National Council on Disability, 1995).

These parental concerns are fueling a growing movement for fundamental change, especially one directed toward ending the dual system of special and general education. Particularly active in pursuit of inclusive placements are families of young children who benefited from IDEA's preschool programs in integrated settings. They are insisting that those same options be made available for their children in the public schools. Furthermore, parent organizations and advocacy groups are becoming increasingly vocal in support of inclusion and the training of parents regarding their rights. Chapters of SAFE (Schools Are For Everyone) are emerging across the United States, and the PEAK Parent Center in Boulder, Colorado, funded by the Office of Special Education Programs (OSEP), U.S. Department of Education, has been designated as a national resource to support parental involvement in inclusive education.

The increasing number of court cases in which parents are seeking inclusive placements for their children in the face of resistant school districts is another indication of parental advocacy. In the 1990s, four federal circuit courts have issued similar decisions supporting inclusion. The cases involve an 11-year-old with Down syndrome, a 9-year-old labeled as having mental retardation, a kindergarten student with severe behavior problems, and a student with mental retardation requiring extensive supports and physical disabilities (see Chapters 9 and 22 for further discussion of these cases).

CONCLUSION

Parental advocacy is powered by two realities. The first is parents' belief that their children with disabilities are being denied services to which they are entitled by law. The second is parents' belief that their children with disabilities are entitled to participate fully in society—in schools, in work, and in the community. The separate special education system, which reinforces the norms of professional dominance and privilege, both supports that denial and fetters the fulfillment of those rights.

REFERENCES

Brown, W. (1994). *Early intervention regulations: Annotation and analysis*. Horsham, PA: LRP Publications.

Education for All Handicapped Children Act of 1975, PL 94-142, 20 U.S.C. § 1400 *et seq.*

Engel, D.M. (1993). Origin myths: Narratives of authority, resistance, disability, and law. *Law & Society Review, 27*(4), 785–826.

Harry, B., Allen, N., & McLaughlin, M. (1995). Communication versus compliance: African-American parents' involvement in special education. *Exceptional Children, 61*(4), 364–377.

Individuals with Disabilities Education Act (IDEA) of 1990, PL 101-476, 20 U.S.C. § 1400 *et seq.*

Individuals with Disabilities Education Act Amendments of 1991, PL 102-119, 20 U.S.C. § 1400 *et seq.*

Lipsky, D.K. (1985). A parental perspective on stress and coping. *American Journal of Orthopsychiatry, 55*(4), 614–617.

Mallory, B.L. (1995). The role of social policy in life-cycle transitions. *Exceptional Children, 62*(3), 213–223.

National Council on Disability. (1995). *Improving the implementation of the Individuals with Disabilities Education Act: Making schools work for all of America's children*. Washington, DC: Author.

Parents, advocates rail against schools that thwart education and inclusion. (1994). *Inclusive Education Programs, 1*(12), 2–3.

Rehabilitation Act of 1973, PL 93-112, 29 U.S.C. § 701 *et seq.*

School facilities: Accessibility for the disabled still an issue. (1995). Washington, DC: U.S. General Accounting Office.

Turnbull, A.P., & Turnbull, H.R. (1990). *Families, professionals, and exceptionality*. Columbus, OH: Charles E. Merrill.

6

DISABILITY RIGHTS MOVEMENT

The special education system, operating as it does from a deficit model (i.e., a model premised on the perceived "deficits" of people with disabilities), incorporates too few meaningful roles for adults with disabilities. Increasingly, these adults are challenging the premises of such a system and calling for its reconceptualization. The disability rights movement has played a crucial role in heightening awareness of the significant contributions that adults with disabilities can make as integral participants in the redesign process.

DISABILITY RIGHTS AND DISABILITY CULTURE

The appointment of people from the disability rights movement to key leadership positions in government provides evidence of the movement's historical achievements and support for further change. Among these individuals are, in the U.S. Department of Education, Judith Heumann,[1] assistant secretary for Special Education and Rehabilitative Services; and Frederick K. Schroeder,[2]

---

[1]In 1970, Judith Heumann was denied a license to teach in the New York City public schools. She had failed the physical examination administered by the Board of Examiners, which licensed teachers, on the grounds that her lack of mobility in emergencies would endanger the students. A federal court order rejected the board's claim. Following several years as a teacher, she served an internship with the U.S. Senate Subcommittee on the Handicapped, where she participated in writing what became PL 94-142, the Education for All Handicapped Children Act (Berkowitz, 1987). At the Department of Education, she is responsible for administering the Individuals with Disabilities Education Act (IDEA) of 1990.

[2]Fred K. Schroeder sued the training certification body that refused to certify him as a mobility trainer of blind youth because he was blind. Schroeder is responsible for administering the federal rehabilitation system.

commissioner, Rehabilitation Services Administration. Both were appointed in 1995.

Tracing the background of the disability rights movement in the United States, Brannon (1995) has attributed the movement's growth to "improved medical success in treating disabling conditions" (p. 4) as well as to the influence of other civil rights movements, including the African American civil rights movement, the feminist movement, and the anti–Vietnam War effort.[3] The efforts of students at the University of California, Berkeley, led by Ed Roberts, to gain access to the university's services in the early 1960s generally is seen as the starting point of the disability rights movement. The establishment of the Center for Independent Living provided the first institutional base for the movement. In 1971, the first cross-disability group, Disabled in Action, was founded in New York City. The passage of the Rehabilitation Act of 1973 (PL 93-112), with its Section 504 modeled after the Civil Rights Act of 1964, provided an organizing focus for the new movement, which gained momentum when the Johnson administration delayed implementing the regulations (Scotch, 1984). Sit-ins in 1977 at the headquarters of the U.S. Department of Health, Education & Welfare, Washington, D.C., and at the agency's San Francisco regional office propelled the issuance of the regulations and gave the movement a sense of its strength. The White House Conference on Handicapped Individuals, in 1977, heralded the new interest in disability issues and provided a mobilizing opportunity as well. Increasingly, people with disabilities were advocating a paradigmatic shift in society's attitudes toward and treatment of people with disabilities, expressed in the title of the 1986 National Council on Disability monograph, *Towards Independence*. The report called for a civil rights law that would guarantee equal protection for people with disabilities. Two years later, Senator Lowell Weicker (R-Conn.), whose son has Down syndrome, introduced such a bill in Congress; in 1990, the Americans with Disabilities Act (ADA) (PL 101-336) became law.

Just as the civil rights and women's movements provided impetus for the development of African American and women's studies, so "the emerging disability rights movement provided the critical framework in which disability culture emerged" (Brannon, 1995, p. 6). At the 1984 conference of the Association on Handicapped Student Service Programs in Post-Secondary Education, David Phieffer and Andrea Schien addressed the question, "Is there a dis-

---

[3]See Shapiro (1993) for historical perspective on the disability rights movement.

ability culture?" Two years later, the *Disability Rag* reported on Carol Gill's presentation on disability culture at a meeting of the California Association of the Physically Handicapped. The *Disability Rag* provided an important forum for the emerging discussion, which drew not only upon anthropology (Phieffer and Schien) but also sociology (Schien), psychology (Gill), and the new voices of political scientist Harlan Hahn and historian Paul Longmore. The establishment in 1983 of the Society for Disability Studies by Irving Kenneth Zola, a sociologist at Brandeis University, provided a further base for the evolving disability culture. Simi Linton, an emerging leader in the disabilities studies community, has proposed a shift in the discourse on disability from a medical/treatment model to a social/cultural/political paradigm. Gill (1995) has identified the following core values of the disability culture[4]:

1. An acceptance of human differences;
2. A matter-of-fact orientation towards helping. An acceptance of human vulnerability and interdependence;
3. A tolerance for lack of resolution, for dealing with unpredictable[s] and living with unknowns or less-than-desired outcomes;
4. Disability humor—the ability to laugh at our oppressor and our situations;[5]
5. Skill in managing multiple problems, systems, technology, and assistants;
6. A sophisticated future orientation;
7. A carefully honed capacity for closure in interpersonal communication; and
8. A flexible adaptive approach to tasks, a creativity stimulated by both limited resources and experience with untraditional modes of operating. (pp. 17–18)

DISABILITY RIGHTS PERSPECTIVES ON EDUCATION

Consequences of Exclusion

Hahn (1994) has argued for "the need to alter the educational environment rather than to pursue continuous efforts to modify the functional characteristics of disabled students" (p. 9). Echoing the language of race relations, he further stated: "Since separation on the basis of disability is apt to leave an enduring imprint on the hearts

---

[4]See Brown (1995a) for a bibliography on disability culture.

[5]Similarly, Ralph Ellison (1952) has described the character he strove to create in *The Invisible Man*:

I decided that it would be one who had been forged in the underground of American experience and yet managed to emerge less angry than ironic. That he would be a blues-toned laugher-at-wounds who included himself in his indictment of the human condition. (p. 14)

and minds of disabled young people, desegregation or inclusion is a fundamental component of this process" (p. 9). Morris (1990) similarly contended that

> people's expectations of us are informed by their previous experience of disabled people. If disabled people are segregated, are treated as alien, as different in a fundamental way, then we will never be accepted as full members of society. This is the strongest argument against special schools and against separate provision. (p. 53)

The segregation of people with disabilities in the special education system has consequences not only for students with disabilities. According to Hahn (1994), the challenge facing teachers is to

> [relate] to the everyday experience of disabled individuals. Most educational theories have been formulated with little, if any, regard for disability; and most teachers are not disabled themselves. As a result, disabled students and their teachers may stare at each other daily in the classroom across a vast chasm produced by divergent understandings and lifestyles. Given the prevalence of paternalistic attitudes, teachers may sympathize rather than empathize with their disabled pupils; or they may have trouble in coping with barely conscious feelings of avoidance and aversion. Perhaps an increased appreciation of the strengths instead of the presumed deficiencies of disabled students might improve the attitudes of teachers whose negative perceptions of inclusion often seem to be based on the belief that they will be overwhelmed by an excessive need for attention and assistance. (p. 12)

Contributions of Adults with Disabilities

In this regard, adults with disabilities can provide—through their experience and advocacy—a strength-based understanding of disability to replace special education's deficit model. Two programs in particular address the gap between the experiences of children with disabilities and those of parents and teachers without disabilities. The National Federation of the Blind works with parents of blind children and their teachers, while "Through the Looking Glass," a California program, enlists adults with disabilities as expert advisors to parents of children with disabilities. Both programs recognize the valuable expertise that adults with disabilities can lend to the development of children who have disabilities.

Society's Vision of Disability

One area in need of heightened attention is that of creating awareness of the multitude of accommodations that society makes for its members without disabilities, some of which can be considered "normal" (i.e., appropriate), whereas others seem extraordinary or neglectful of the needs and rights of people with disabilities. With some irony, Hahn (1994) noted that

> chairs are an accommodation to the needs of nondisabled students; but they are of no value to many disabled persons, such as myself, who are considerate enough to bring our own chairs. Without chairs, nondisabled students would undoubtedly become fatigued from standing or sitting on the floor, they would probably be discouraged from attending classes, and their performance on tests and other evaluations might be adversely affected. (p. 10)

The principle of "equal environmental adaptations" is necessary, according to Hahn (1994), to provide commensurate advantages to people with or without disabilities. For example, such benefits for students with disabilities must extend beyond providing accessible restrooms, widening the aisles between library stacks, and installing ramps or elevators for wheelchair users:

> The objective of this concept . . . is simply to establish parity, or commensurate benefits, for disabled and nondisabled school children. . . . [A]t a minimum . . . disabled students should not be forced to bear the stigma of a segregated school system; and mastery of the *existing* [emphasis in original] environment should not be considered a necessary prerequisite to exercising the rights of citizenship. (p. 17)

Society's myopic vision of disability is reflected in the response of Christopher Nolan, author of *Under the Eye of the Clock*, to a reporter. Nolan has been immobilized with severe cerebral palsy since birth. When asked by a reporter, "What is the first thing you would do if you could leave your wheelchair?" Nolan replied, "Get right back in" (cited in Minow, 1990, p. 155). As Minow (1990) noted, this response "affords a glimpse into the strikingly different experience of this young man and into his perspective, which challenges the assumption that he could still be who he is out of the wheelchair" (p. 155). She goes on to point out that Nolan's answer rejects, first, the view that people with disabilities lack something that people without disabilities have; and, second, the assumption that because people with disabilities differ in some respects from those without disabilities, they differ in all respects. This point has been expanded on by Temple Grandin, a biologist who has autism: "She [Grandin] thinks that she and other autistic people, though they unquestionably have great problems in some areas, may have extraordinary, and socially valuable, powers in others— *provided they are allowed to be themselves, autistic*" [emphasis added] (Sacks, 1995, p. 290).

Being oneself is the theme of Longmore's (1995) argument that people with disabilities must move from a focus on disability rights to disability culture. The author pointed to the merging disability consciousness of a younger generation of people with disabilities. Citing a 1986 Louis Harris survey of adults with disabilities, Longmore noted that although a minority of adults with disabilities over 45 years of age regarded people with disabilities as a "minority group" like African Americans or Hispanics, 54% of those ages 18–44 agreed with that perspective. Whereas majorities in every age group believed people with disabilities needed legal protection from discrimination, the largest percentage of respondents who held this view was among the youngest age group, those 18–30 years of age:

> The younger generation has spurned institutionalized definitions of "disability" and of people with disabilities. At its core, the new consciousness has repudiated the reigning medical model, which defines "disability" as physiological pathologies located within individuals.
>
> In the place of the medical model, activists have substituted a sociopolitical or minority-group model of disability. "Disability," they have asserted, is primarily a socially constructed role. For the vast majority of people with disabilities, prejudice is a far greater problem than any impairment: discrimination is a bigger obstacle for them to "overcome" than any disability. The core of the problem, in the activists' view, has been historically deep-seated, socially pervasive and powerfully institutionalized oppression of disabled people. (pp. 5–6)

The lives of people with disabilities, especially of children, are not set in fixed, immutable arcs but are open to a range of opportunity, limited less by their impairments than by societal attitudes that result in a lack of supports for them and their families. The evolution of these attitudes is a consequence of the way people regard others, including those with disabilities. Goffman (1963) captured this view, stating, "Society establishes the means of categorizing persons and the complement of attributes felt to be ordinary and natural for members of each of these categories" (p. 2). Edgerton (1990) also made the point succinctly: "Any social system can make any behavior into a social problem" (p. 525). More specific, according to Stone (1984), academic disciplines frame *disability* according to their particular perspectives:

> Psychological analyses tend to regard it [disability] as an individual experience, with an eye to understanding how physical and mental limitations interact with personality development. Economic analyses treat disability as a social position with its own income stream, much like a job, and seek to explain the extent to which individual choice determines the assumptions of the disabled role. Sociological analyses focus on the institutions that treat, house, and manage disabled people—including families, schools, hospitals, and rehabilitation clinics—and above all, they examine disability as a stigmatized

social status, exploring the means by which stigma is created, maintained, and resisted.

A political approach . . . explore[s] the meaning of disability for the state—the formal institutions of government, and the intellectual justifications that give coherence to their activities. . . . Why does the state create a category of disability in the first place, and does it design a workable administrative definition? (pp. 3–4)

These are nuanced distinctions. More recently, disability rights scholars, many finding a forum in the Society for Disability Studies, have challenged the traditional premises of academia, in much the same way that scholars have challenged disciplines for ignoring the experiences and perspectives of women and African Americans.[6] Longmore (1995), in calling for a second phase of the disability rights movement, asserted the necessity of self-definition:

People with disabilities . . . affirm the validity of values drawn from their own experience. Those values are markedly different from, and even opposed to, nondisabled majority values. They declare that they prize not self-sufficiency but self-determination, not independence but interdependence, not functional separateness but personal connectedness, not physical autonomy but human community. This values-formation takes disability as the starting point. It uses the disability experience as the source of values and norms. (p. 9)

There is a parallel between the views of Sacks (1995), who found that "defects, disorders, diseases . . . can play a paradoxical role, by bringing out latent powers, developments, evolutions, forms of life, that might never have been, or even be imaginable, in their absence" and thus have their own "creative" potential (p. xvi), and those of Longmore (1995), who saw accommodations such as architectural modifications, adaptive devices and services as merely "different modes of functioning" (p. 6). Longmore saw these differing modes as "not inherently inferior" (p. 6), and Sacks (1995), writing in much the same vein, contended that the different states of being "are no less human for being different" (p. xx).

Cutter (1994), recipient of the National Federation of the Blind's Distinguished Educator of Blind Children Award, noted the "disturbing sighted bias and erroneous assumptions about blindness" expressed in the first sentence of *First Steps* (Blind Children's Center, 1993), a book about teaching children who are blind: "The world of children with visual impairments is very different from ours." Cutter's response to this statement was, " 'How so?' Are the authors

<hr />

[6]A special issue of *Disabilities Studies Quarterly* provides an insider's view of the status of disability culture (see Brown, 1995a, 1995b).

implying that blind children are fundamentally different from sighted children? I don't believe it [that those with visual impairment are different], and the evidence doesn't support it. *We all live in the same world*" [emphasis in original] (p. 20).

As these views express, there is nothing "natural" or even inevitable about responses to impairments; rather, they are culturally determined. Describing the African American community's response to sickle cell anemia as one that "neither exaggerates nor minimizes the consequences of the condition," Asch (1988) asked, "Suppose Down syndrome, cystic fibrosis, or spina bifida were depicted not as an incalculable, irreparable tragedy but as a fact of being human?" (p. 87). Just as disability is only one dimension of a person, impairment is a human constant. What varies—over time and different cultures—is how "societies have defined what did and did not constitute a disability and a handicap" (Scheer & Groce, 1988, p. 23).

A notable exception to the pattern of negative attitudes toward people with disabilities occurred on Martha's Vineyard, Massachusetts, from the 17th through the early 20th centuries, when the island was the home of the largest concentration of people in the United States who were deaf. Community members purposefully integrated people with deafness into all realms of its life by learning sign language, thus addressing the impairment—absence of hearing—and not allowing it to become a handicap. Groce (1985) noted that

> although we can categorize the deaf Vineyarders as disabled, they certainly were not considered to be handicapped. They participated freely in all aspects of life in this Yankee community. They grew up, married, raised their families, and earned their living in just the same manner as did their hearing relatives, friends, and neighbors.
>
> Perhaps the best description of the status of deaf individuals on the Vineyard was given . . . by an island woman in her eighties, when . . . asked about those who were handicapped by deafness when she was a girl: "Oh," she said emphatically, "those people weren't handicapped. They were just deaf." (pp. 4–5)

Kenneth Jernigan (1985), in his presidential address at the annual convention of the National Federation of the Blind, made a similar point:

> Sight is enjoyable; it is convenient. But that is all that it is—enjoyable, useful, convenient. Except in imagination and mythology it is not the single key to human happiness, the road to knowledge, or the window to the soul. Like the other senses, it is a channel of communication, a source of pleasure, a tool—nothing less, nothing more. . . . [I]t is certainly not the essential component of human freedom. (p. 387)

Culture affects how others view disability and treat people with disabilities, and it affects the way people with disabilities perceive themselves. Bogdan (1980) interviewed people who had been labeled "retarded" who nonetheless said, "I'm not retarded." One person he interviewed said, "I have never really thought of myself as retarded. I never had that ugly feeling deep down" (p. 78).

Response of Educational and Child Development Communities

By and large, the educational and child development communities have little attended to the profound debates within the disability community and about the nature of disability. Instead, they continue to view disability through a deviation analysis. This is not simply a matter of ignorant prejudice; rather, it is the intellectual root of traditional scholarship. In this connection, Gliedman and Roth's (1990) critique of Erik Erikson's typology of human development remains pertinent. If we are to apply the typology to people with disabilities, pointed out Gliedman and Roth, then we must "approach disability by means of a deviance analysis, looking at the problems of the handicapped by identifying specific areas of potential deviance for each stage." This requires, however, that we "prejudge precisely those developmental questions about handicap which, above all others, require painstaking investigation" (p. 106). Gliedman and Roth stated, for example, that Erikson's formulation that the child's mastery of body functions, which is central to resolving issues of autonomy versus shame and doubt, remains an open issue for the adult with a disability who either lacks bladder control or is dependent on an attendant (or family member). Thus, quoting Erikson, "'There is an "infantile" quality to the way he [the adult with a disability] must assert mastery over his body. Like the young child who must call his mother for help, the physically handicapped person must sometimes relate to his own body by means of another (able-bodied) person'" (Gliedman & Roth, 1980, p. 107). Gliedman and Roth (1980) asserted that one cannot approach the development of a child with disabilities "on terms spelled out in advance by personality theories developed for able-bodied children and adults" (p. 113). Such an approach would be akin to studying the development of stages of people's moral growth with data drawn solely from males. The point is that before assuming "facts" and drawing conclusions about a group, one must examine the reality of the group members' lives.

CONCLUSION

Disability rights advocates, particularly adults with disabilities, have much vital knowledge and insight to contribute toward the reconceptualization of educating children with disabilities. Among the numerous potential benefits of their participation in this process are the following:

- Defining a strength-based model and challenging the traditional deficit model
- Offering a positive life perspective for people with disabilities and challenging one that equates difference with deviance
- Expanding the notions of "normal" and "capable" and challenging the notion that disability means being unable
- Bringing the insights and experiences of people with disabilities into the education field and challenging the present paradigm
- Creating an energy force for change that will challenge the status quo

Parental advocacy, combined with that of the disability rights movement, could provide a powerful force for change in educating students with disabilities, change that recognizes students' capacities and rights.

REFERENCES

Americans with Disabilities Act (ADA) of 1990, PL 101-336, 42 U.S.C. § 12101 et seq.

Asch, A. (1988). Reproductive technology and disability. In S. Cohen & N. Taub (Eds.), Reproductive laws for the 1990's. Clifton, NJ: Human Press.

Berkowitz, E.D. (1987). Disabled policy: America's programs for the handicapped. Cambridge, MA: Cambridge University Press.

Bernstein, R. (1995, December 20). Black identity, racism and a lifetime of reflection. New York Times, A19.

Blind Children's Center. (1993). First steps: A handbook for teaching young children who are visually impaired. Los Angeles: Author.

Bogdan, R. (1980). What does it mean when a person says, "I'm not retarded"? Education and Training of the Mentally Retarded, 15, 74–79.

Brannon, R. (1995). The use of the concept of disability culture: A historian's view. Disability Studies Quarterly, 15(4), 3–15.

Brown, S.E. (1995a). A celebration of diversity: An introductory, annotated bibliography about disability culture. Disability Studies Quarterly, 15(4), 36–55.

Brown, S.E. (1995b). Disability culture: Here and now. Disability Studies Quarterly, 15(4), 2–3.

Civil Rights Act of 1964, PL 88-352, 20 U.S.C. § 241.

Cutter, J. (1994). Parents: Blind children's first mobility teachers. Braille Monitor, 13(4), 11–23.

Edgerton, R.B. (1970). Mental retardation in non-Western societies: Toward a cross-cultural perspective on incompetence. In H.C. Haywood (Ed.), *Social-cultural aspects of mental retardation* (pp. 523–559). New York: Appleton-Century-Crofts.

Education for All Handicapped Children Act of 1975, PL 94-142, 20 U.S.C. § 1400 *et seq.*

Ellison, R. (1952). *The invisible man.* New York: Random House.

Gill, C.J. (1995). A psychological view of disability culture. *Disability Studies Quarterly, 15*(4), 16–19.

Gliedman, J., & Roth, W. (1980). *The unexpected minority: Handicapped children in America.* New York: Harcourt Brace Jovanovich.

Goffman, E. (1963). *Stigma: Notes on the management of spoiled identity.* Englewood Cliffs, NJ: Prentice Hall.

Groce, N.E. (1985). *Everyone here spoke sign language: Hereditary deafness on Martha's Vineyard.* Cambridge, MA: Harvard University Press.

Hahn, H. (1994, April 28–May 1). *New trends in disability studies: Implications for educational policy.* Paper presented at the National Center on Educational Restructuring and Inclusion invitational conference on inclusive education, Racine, WI.

Individuals with Disabilities Education Act (IDEA) of 1990, PL 101-476, 20 U.S.C. § 1400 *et seq.*

Jernigan, K. (1985, August–September). Presidential address. *Braille Monitor,* 387.

Longmore, P.K. (1995, September/October). The second phase: From disability rights to disability culture. *Disability Rag and Resource,* 4–11.

Minow, M. (1990). *Making all the difference: Inclusion, exclusion, and American law.* Ithaca, NY: Cornell University Press.

Morris, J. (1990). Progress with humanity? The experience of a disabled lecturer. In R. Reiser & M. Mason (Eds.), *Disability, equality in the classroom: A human rights issue.* London: ILEA.

National Council on Disability. (1986). *Towards independence.* Washington, DC: Author.

Nolan, C. (1987). *Under the eye of the clock: The life story of Christopher Nolan.* New York: Dell Publishing.

Rehabilitation Act of 1973, PL 93-112, 29 U.S.C. § 701 *et seq.*

Sacks, O. (1995). *An anthropologist on Mars.* New York: Alfred A. Knopf.

Scheer J., & Groce, N. (1988). Impairments as a human constant: Cross-cultural and historical perspectives on variation. *Journal of Social Issues, 44*(1), 23–37.

Scotch, R.K. (1984). *From good will to civil rights: Transforming federal disability policy.* Philadelphia: Temple University Press.

Shapiro, J. (1993). *No pity: People with disabilities forging a new civil rights movement.* New York: Times Books.

Stone, D.A. (1984). *The disabled state.* Philadelphia: Temple University Press.

7

IDEA
Renewal and a Summary View

During 1995 and 1996, Congress deliberated the renewal of the Individuals with Disabilities Education Act (IDEA) of 1990 (PL 101-476) and its Amendments of 1991 (PL 102-119). The 104th Congress expired without action. With the core of the law (Part B) permanently authorized, the failure of Congress to act does not affect the basic entitlement of students with disabilities. The 104th Congress did address aspects of Part B, and it is likely that the 105th Congress will reexamine it. The Special Purpose Funds, Parts C–H, have been extended and will be the subject of consideration in the 105th Congress. Although Congress did not act on the reauthorization, it did increase federal support of state special education programs from $2.3 billion in FY 1996 to $3.1 billion for FY 1997.

Many concerns with the law have been expressed by various groups, including organizations of people with disabilities, advocacy groups, parent organizations, educators, and state and local school district officials. The numerous proposals for change were reflected in testimony before the congressional committees and in the protracted debate within the committees and between the leadership of the two chambers. Some of these are matters of pervasive concern and have been discussed in previous chapters. These include the relationship between general and special education, the negative consequences of the dual system, outcomes for students in special education programs, and issues of parental involvement and funding formulas. Other topics are of more temporal concern. These include the issue of disciplinary procedures toward students with disabilities, attorney fees, and mandated mediation of disputes.

This chapter reviews the Clinton administration's major recommendations for change and then examines responses to the proposed changes. The merits of specific changes in IDEA are inhibited by the continuing fundamental dualism of general and special education. Unfortunately, the recommendations for renewing IDEA fail to provide the needed paradigmatic shift for educating children with disabilities as an integral part of school restructuring efforts. In that regard, the recommended changes are little more than tinkering at the margin.

CLINTON ADMINISTRATION'S RECOMMENDATIONS

Six key principles in the Clinton administration's proposed legislation (H.R. 1986 and S. 1075) were identified by Richard W. Riley, secretary of the U.S. Department of Education, in his 1995 testimony before Congress:

> The first principle is that IDEA needs to connect with the many efforts at the state and local levels to improve teaching and learning. . . . [T]his means we really need to stop thinking about special education as a separate program and a separate place and start thinking about special education as the supports and services that children need in whatever setting that helps them learn.
>
> This quite naturally leads to a second principle regarding high expectations, achievement and access to the general curriculum. . . . [W]e propose two related strategies for promoting high expectations.
>
> First, we believe that when schools assess students with disabilities and report the results, they will focus more on the teaching and learning aspects of IDEA. . . . [O]ur second strategy is to improve the individualized education program.
>
> [O]ur third principle addresses the issue of categorization. The heart of IDEA is individualized approaches. But too often we label a child by [his or her] disability and lump all the children with the same disability together without regard to the educational and social abilities of each child.[1]

---

[1]A communication from the U.S. Department of Education, Office of Special Education Programs, in response to a congressional letter, reaffirmed that IDEA does *not* require states and local districts to label individual children:

> According to OSEP, although the definitions of children with disabilities which are set forth at 34 CFR 300.7 [the regulation derived from the language of IDEA] must be used by states to prepare annual data reports for the Department of Education regarding the numbers of children served, a state may use different categories of disabilities than those specified in that regulation, or, in the alternative, they may use a noncategorical approach provided that those students are appropriately identified and served. ("Part B Does Not," 1996, pp. 15–16)

[W]e want to allow schools to use their IDEA funds to pay for special education services in the regular classroom without having to track the costs of any benefits to non-disabled students. . . . [Also w]e are proposing that the federal funding formula be changed to allocate to states all new funding above their fiscal year 1995 grants . . . based on the total number of children in the state.

[W]e propose to give states more flexibility to decide how to identify students—while ensuring that students who are eligible under current law remain eligible.

[T]he fourth principle is focused on the family and teachers. We want parents more involved in where a child is educated, and we believe that we can reduce unnecessary law suits by expanding mediation services to all states.

[O]ur fifth principle again comes back to what happens in the classroom [regarding] the twin issues of safety and discipline.

[O]ur sixth and final principle is focused on early intervention for infants and children up to age two. (June 20, 1995)

Specific recommendations from the Department of Education for renewing IDEA include the following:

- Replacing IDEA's 13 eligibility categories with a single broad definition of *disability* (The proposed language would define an eligible child as one "who has a physical or mental impairment and who, by reason of that impairment, needs special education and related services.")
- Changing the system of funds distribution to the states from one based on the number of students with disabilities to the overall student population[2] (This change would apply to funds above the FY 1995 level.)
- Extending the maximum time period that school districts may suspend a student with disabilities who brings a gun or dangerous weapon to school from 10 to 45 days[3] and modifying the "stay put" rule[4] to permit action by hearing officers

---

[2]The Center for Special Education Finance has reported that such "census-based" funding schemes have been adopted by a number of states (including Massachusetts, Montana, Pennsylvania, and Vermont) and are being considered in many others (Parrish, 1995).

[3]The "Jeffords" amendment (Section 314 of the "Improving America's Schools Act") modified IDEA's discipline procedures to allow schools to move students with disabilities who bring weapons to school to an alternative placement for 45 days. If parents seek to implement their due process rights during this period, the "stay put" rule was modified to apply to the alternative placement rather than revert to the student's previous in-school placement.

[4]The "stay put" rule requires that if during the alternative placement period a school district adhering to the due process procedures of IDEA seeks to change a student's placement over parental objection, then the child "stays put" in her or his placement. According to IDEA, only a court order allows for such a change.

- Requiring states and school districts to offer mediation to parents in order to settle disputes without litigation
- Requiring the inclusion of students with disabilities in general state and districtwide assessments
- Allowing the use of funds to provide special education in the general education classroom without having to document whether such spending benefits students without disabilities
- Revising the individualized education program (IEP) to require a "transition plan" at age 14 (2 years earlier than specified in the 1990 act); to describe services and accommodations needed for a student's participation in general education classrooms; and to cover the entire school day
- Requiring that notices sent to parents by school districts be written in clear, understandable language

The Clinton administration's bill excludes language that had been in the law since its initial passage as the Education for All Handicapped Children Act of 1975 (PL 94-142), pledging support to the states for each pupil served in the amount of 40% of the national average cost. Although this figure never has been achieved—federal spending has never exceeded 12% and was 7% in 1995—advocates believe that its promise should nevertheless remain ("IDEA Funding," 1995, pp. 3–4).

RESPONSES TO PROPOSED CHANGES

Various interest groups have responded to the administration's recommendations. The presidentially appointed National Council on Disability proposed replacing the mandated "continuum" of placements with an array of services designed to educate students with disabilities in general education classrooms. It also recommended "placement neutral" funding and that increases in funding to the states be based on improved student outcomes. These include increases in students receiving special education services in general education classrooms, higher graduation rates for students with disabilities, higher rates of special education students included in standardized district and state assessment programs, and higher rates of adult employment for students who had received special education. The council further recommended better monitoring and enforcement activities by the Department of Education regarding the implementation of the least restrictive environment (LRE) requirement and overall IDEA implementation ("NCD Suggests," 1995, p. 3).

Disability advocates argued that the expanded authority concerning the "stay put" rule would limit inclusion and that before new procedures are allowed, the current ones should be applied ("Riley Proposes," 1995, p. 3). An opposite viewpoint was expressed by the National School Boards Association (NSBA), which argued that the Department of Education's proposals do not give schools enough flexibility to remove students who pose a danger to others.[5] A coalition of national educational organizations (including the National Education Association, the American Association of School Administrators, the American Federation of Teachers, the National Association of Elementary School Principals, and the National Association of Secondary School Principals) joined in the NSBA's criticism of the changes in the "stay put" rule.

The NSBA (along with the other members of the educational organization coalition), while endorsing the department's requirement that mediation be offered, proposed limiting the recovery of fees to cases that go to court. In addition, they criticized the department's recommendation of a single definition of *disability* and its failure to declare that its policy letters could not make new rules but could only clarify existing ones ("Education Groups," 1995, p. 3). The Learning Disabilities Association asserted that eliminating labels would blur distinctions among children and hamper the ability of educators to teach them ("IDEA Proposals," 1995, p. 3).

The House of Representatives and Senate committees put forward proposals for IDEA changes. Although differing in particulars, there are broad areas of commonality among the Clinton administration's proposals and those of the two chambers. All of the proposals include the following:

- Provide new attention to improving results and the quality of education provided (i.e., going beyond a focus on student access).
- Propose changing the IEP to enhance parental roles, to describe how the child's disability affects progress in the general education curriculum, and to require the participation of the general education teacher in developing the IEP when the child will participate in general classroom activities.
- Require the establishment of a state mediation system, designed to reduce litigation.
- Expand parental notification requirements.

---

[5]The NSBA would expand the "Jeffords" amendment restriction (see note 3), which applies to bringing a gun to school, and the Education Department's recommendation to include "dangerous weapons" to students who engage in "dangerous behavior."

The proposed changes in IDEA respond, at least in part, to failures in special education practice evident in the mid-1990s. Yet one cannot but suggest that Skrtic's (1991) critique of special education reformers applies as well to IDEA's revisers. "Their criticism," contended Skrtic, "stops at the level of special education practices . . . [without] questioning the assumptions in which these practices are grounded" (p. 150). Skrtic summarized these presuppositions as follows:

- Disabilities are pathological conditions that students have.
- Differential diagnosis is objective and useful.
- Special education is a rationally conceived and coordinated system of services that benefits diagnosed students.
- Progress results from rational technological improvements in diagnostic and instructional practices. (p. 152)

The formulation presented by Skrtic (1991) challenged the premises that undergird IDEA:

> In organizational terms, student disability is neither human pathology nor an objective distinction; it is an organizational pathology, a matter of not fitting the standard programs of the prevailing paradigm or a professional culture, the legitimacy of which is artificially reaffirmed by the objectification of school failure as a human pathology through the institutional practice of special education. (p. 169)

IDEA AND CIVIL RIGHTS

Understanding special education in the way presented by Skrtic (1991) makes clear that the changes necessary are more than mere tinkering. The inclusive education debate presents the question of whether inclusion is a matter of civil rights, as Funk (1987) and other disability rights advocates have asserted. American Federation of Teachers president Albert Shanker has demurred on the subject: "I see no basis for the civil rights [analogy]," he stated. "Black youngsters were eager to learn. That's different from a youngster who is yelling and screaming and so forth." At the heart of the segregation issue, said Shanker, was merely the color of a child's skin, which "was totally irrelevant of [her or his] education. These are two very, very different motivations" (cited in "Teachers Union President," 1994, p. 174).

Frank Laski, a leading special education attorney, challenged Shanker's viewpoint. In a 1994 article commemorating the 40th anniversary of *Brown v. Board of Education,* Laski argued the common ground that people with disabilities have with African Americans and other oppressed minorities. Laski cited the argument made by John Davis, chief lawyer for the defendants, in response to Thurgood Marshall, chief lawyer for the plaintiff, in *Brown:*

> I think if [Marshall's construction of the Fourteenth Amendment] should prevail here, there is not doubt in my mind that it would catch the Indian within its grasp as much as the Negro. If it should prevail, I am unable to see why a state would have any further right to segregate its pupils on the ground of . . . mental capacity. (cited in Laski, 1994, p. 4)

Laski also cited Marshall in his capacity as associate justice of the Supreme Court. After surveying the extensive record of social exclusion of people with disabilities, Marshall concluded that a regime of state-mandated segregation of such people emerged that "in its virulence and bigotry rivaled and indeed paralleled the worst excesses of Jim Crow" (cited in Laski, 1994, p. 4).

The transformative nature of the issues of social justice and equity that are encapsulated in inclusion/integration was powerfully stated by Branson and Miller (1989):

> Integration must be . . . oriented toward its own destruction, aiming to destroy the very categories which are seen as needing to be "integrated" into the "normal" world. If the disabled are "normal," so much an accepted part of our world that we take their presence, their humanity, their special qualities for granted, then there can be no "integration" for there is no "segregation," either conceptually, in terms of categories, taxonomies, or actually, in terms of institutional separation. (p. 161)

CONCLUSION

What is needed, then, is not tinkering at the margins of IDEA but rather a fundamental change of the existing dual, failing, and costly special and general education systems. Such change involves redirecting the focus of the IDEA debate toward the broader matters of educating students with disabilities in a unitary system that will prepare them to participate in society. What is required is reconfiguring IDEA to support a strategically altered educational paradigm—one that more equitably addresses disability, student learning, and the nature and purposes of schooling in a democracy preparing for the 21st century.

REFERENCES

Branson, J., & Miller, D. (1989). Beyond policy: The deconstruction of disability. In L. Barton (Ed.), *Integration: Myth or reality?* London: Falmer Press.

Brown v. Board of Education, 347 U.S. 483 (1954).

Education for All Handicapped Children Act of 1975, PL 94-142, 20 U.S.C. §1400 et seq.

Education groups pummel ED's IDEA recommendations. (1995, July 21). *Education Daily*, 1, 3.

Funk, R. (1987). Disability rights: From caste to class in the context of civil rights. In A. Gartner & T. Joe (Eds.), *Images of the disabled, disabling images* (pp. 7–30). New York: Praeger.

IDEA funding goal missing from House, ED proposals. (1995, August 17). *Education Daily*, 3–4.

IDEA proposals. (1995, July 27). *Education Daily*, 3.

Improving America's Schools Act of 1994, PL 103-382, 108 *Statutes at Large* 3518.

Individuals with Disabilities Education Act (IDEA) of 1990, PL 101-476, 20 U.S.C. §1400 et seq.

Individuals with Disabilities Education Act Amendments of 1991, PL 102-119, 20 U.S.C. §1400 et seq.

Laski, F. (1994). On the 40th anniversary of *Brown v. Board of Education:* Footnotes for the historically impaired. *TASH Newsletter, 20*(5), 3–4.

NCD suggests IDEA reforms. (1995, September 21). *Education Daily, 1,* 3.

Parrish, T.B. (1995, Fall). What is fair? Special education and finance equity. *CSEF Brief,* 7.

Part B does not require states to label students by disability. (1996). *The Special Educator, 11*(11), 15–17.

Riley proposes to modify "stay put" provision. (1995, June 21). *Education Daily*, 1, 3.

Riley, R.W. (1995). Testimony before Congress, June 20, 1995. Washington, DC: U.S. Department of Education.

Skrtic, T.M. (1991). The special education paradox: Equity as the way to excellence. *Harvard Educational Review, 61*(2), 148–207.

Teachers union president calls inclusion a "fad." (1994). *Special Educator, 9*(12), 173–174.

II

INCLUSIVE EDUCATION

[Inclusion] is part of our total belief and practice. It goes part and parcel with the idea that our responsibility is to all children. If inclusion is only used as a way to deal with special education students, it will never accomplish anything.
—*Ontario School District, Oregon,*
cited in "National Study" (1995)

Historically, the assurance written into the Education for All Handicapped Children Act of 1975 (PL 94-142) that each student with disabilities is entitled to a free appropriate public education (FAPE) was seen as balancing the requirement that education be provided in the least restrictive environment (LRE). Whatever the merit of that balancing act in an earlier period, it does not serve the needs of students with disabilities today. This is evidenced in court rulings (see Chapter 9), program evaluation research (see Chapter 14), the law's requirements that states ensure that students receive "an education reasonably calculated to yield real educational benefits" and that schools adopt "promising practices and materials" (Gilhool,

1989, p. 252), and the need to respect the humanity of students. To meet the standard of appropriateness (FAPE), the education of students with disabilities should occur with their age peers in the general education classroom, with the necessary supplemental aids and support services. Anything other than full inclusion denies the students' rights to an appropriate education.

The first chapter in this section explores the historical background and current developments in inclusive education. Major court cases that have supported inclusive education's rapid expansion are presented in the chapter following. Successive chapters provide a national overview of inclusive education, a more detailed look at its implementation and classroom supports, a description of the views of various organizations, evaluation and research on inclusive education, and a review of critical comments and positive responses to inclusion.

REFERENCES

Education for All Handicapped Children Act of 1975, PL 94-142, 20 U.S.C. § 1400 *et seq.*

Gilhool, T.K. (1989). The right to an effective education: From *Brown* to PL 94-142 and beyond. In D.K. Lipsky & A. Gartner (Eds.), *Beyond separate education: Quality education for all* (pp. 243–253). Baltimore: Paul H. Brookes Publishing Co.

National Study of Inclusive Education. (1995). New York: The City University of New York, National Center on Educational Restructuring and Inclusion, Graduate School and University Center.

8

HISTORICAL BACKGROUND
OF INCLUSIVE EDUCATION

The issue in the United States of where students with disabilities should be educated has been inextricably intertwined with the issues of whether and how they should be educated. Indeed, since the mid-1800s, the nation has struggled to accord to the public the responsibility for educating children with disabilities. This chapter first examines the hard-fought battle to ensure educational opportunities for students with disabilities, culminating in 1975 with the passage of the Education for All Handicapped Children Act (PL 94-142). The chapter then turns to the implementation of that law and to its successor, the Individuals with Disabilities Education Act (IDEA) of 1990 (PL 101-476).

FROM SEPARATE STATE SCHOOLS
TO A FEDERAL RESPONSIBILITY

Special education began in the United States in 1823 with the establishment of a state school in Kentucky for people who were deaf. In 1852, Massachusetts enacted the nation's first compulsory education law, which explicitly permitted the exclusion of children with handicaps from required attendance. The congressionally authorized Columbia Institution for the Instruction of the Deaf and Dumb, and the Blind, opened in 1857, in Washington, D.C.; it is now Gallaudet University. Public school education for people with disabilities began in 1869 in Boston with a school for students with hearing impairment. A separate class for pupils with mental retardation was established in Providence, Rhode Island, in 1896. By 1905, New York City established its first nonresidential school for truants, delinquents, and "incorrigible" children; part of the rationale for this school was that removing these students from the regular school would benefit those who remained. A decade later, Cleveland began an innovative program, a "sight saving class," in which students with visual impairments spent a portion of the day with sighted peers and the remainder in a special class. In 1945, a panel at the Council for Exceptional Children convention recommended that children with educable mental retardation be included in general school settings. Then, in the 1960s, several studies were published questioning the benefit of special classes for children with mental retardation. Key among these studies was L.M. Dunn's 1968 study, summarized by Hocutt, Martin, and McKinney (1991) as follows:

- No available evidence suggested that the academic progress of children with mental retardation in special, separate classes was better than the academic progress of such children in general classrooms.
- Labels accompanying special class placement were stigmatizing.
- General education was capable of providing effective individual instruction to slow pupils or to those with mental retardation.
- Self-contained classes for children with mental retardation also tended to segregate African American children from Caucasian children, as the former were disproportionately enrolled in special education as a result of virtually complete reliance on IQ testing for placement decisions.

The issue of racial disproportionality was the subject of several court suits in California (e.g., *Diana v. Board of Education* in 1970, *Larry P. v. Riles* in 1972). These cases resulted in injunctions against group testing and in requirements that tests be developed and standardized for different cultural and language subgroups and that parents' permission be obtained before placing students in special education.

In 1966, Congress added Title VI to the landmark Elementary and Secondary Education Act of 1965 (PL 89-10), passed the previous year. Title VI established a program to aid states to educate students with disabilities, as well as a Bureau of Education for the Handicapped (BEH) in what was then the U.S. Office of Education. In 1970, Title VI was supplanted by the Education of the Handicapped Act (EHA) (PL 91-230), which continued the new bureau and its state grant program and added support for equipment, school construction, personnel preparation, and research and demonstration programs.

Congressional efforts in the early 1970s to extend the EHA failed, at least in part because there had been insufficient time for the EHA initiatives to show results. Coincidentally, however, developments across the country forced Congress's hand. Court suits in two different circuits—*Pennsylvania Association of Retarded Citizens (PARC) v. Pennsylvania* (1972) and *Mills v. Board of Education* (1972)—established the right of children with disabilities to a free public education. In the Pennsylvania court suit, the consent agreement stipulated that children could not be denied admission to school and that schools could not change a student's placement without due process. The consent agreement furthermore expressed a preference for integration over more restrictive placements.[1] In the District of Columbia case, the federal district court held not only that the Washington, D.C., public schools must educate students with disabilities but also that they could not deny these students that right because of financial limitations any more than they could deny such a right to students without disabilities. Legislatures across the country (most notably in Massachusetts with the passage of Chapter 766 in 1972, which took effect in 1974) responded to parental and community pressure. A BEH grant to the Council for Exceptional Children helped to draft model state statutes.

In 1973, disability advocates won a major victory with the passage of the Rehabilitation Act (PL 93-112), including its civil rights component in Section 504. It took 2 years to promulgate the regulations implementing Section 504. The combination of support from the Office of Civil Rights staff and demonstrations by advocates on the outside (including weeks-long sit-ins at the U.S. Department of Health, Education & Welfare [HEW] in Washington, D.C., and at the department's San Francisco regional office) finally led HEW Secretary Joseph Califano to issue the regulations (Scotch, 1984).

In part to bring some uniformity to developments across the United States and to relieve states of the fiscal burden of educating children with disabilities, bills were introduced in Congress (H.R. 7217 by Congressman John Brademas on May 21, 1974, and S. 7 by Senator Jennings Randolph on January 15, 1975). At issue in the congressional debate were which students were to be covered (their

---

[1]Thomas K. Gilhool, (former counsel for the plaintiffs in *Pennsylvania Association of Retarded Citizens [PARC] v. Pennsylvania* [1972]), testified in Congress in 1995 on activities in the states prior to *PARC* and on the impact of the case on the passage of PL 94-142. Gilhool's text is presented in Chapter 20 of this volume.

ages and the percentage of the total student population, as well as the number and percentage of students with the then-new designation of "learning disabled"), the nature of the programs to be offered, the balance between the roles of states and local school districts, total funding, and the method of fund allocation. With resolution of these issues, Congress enacted PL 94-142, the Education for All Handicapped Children Act of 1975. On August 23, 1975, following a statement criticizing the legislation for its high cost, for raising false expectations among advocates, and for the federal government's intrusion on the proper roles of states and localities, President Gerald R. Ford signed the act into law.

Like many groups at one time or another in U.S. history—females, non-Caucasians, those of the "wrong" (i.e., not the majority's) religion, the poor, the non–English-speaking—people with disabilities had long been barred from the public school system. Over the course of nearly 2 centuries, the legal exclusion of each of these groups, except for children with disabilities, had been abolished. With passage of PL 94-142, the exclusion of students with disabilities was ended as well. As its title stated, the new law mandated "education for all handicapped children."

EDUCATION FOR ALL
HANDICAPPED CHILDREN ACT OF 1975

PL 94-142 is both a funding law and a law that provides substantive rights. An early federal court decision, *Smith v. Robinson* (1984), identifies both of these features:

> The [law] was an attempt to relieve the fiscal burden placed on States and localities by their responsibility to provide education for all handicapped children. At the same time, however, Congress made clear that the [law] is not simply a funding statute. . . . [T]he Act establishes an enforceable substantive right to a free appropriate public education.

Walker (1987), a key Senate staff member in drafting PL 94-142, identified nine basic objectives of the law:

1. Establish the right of access to public education programs;
2. Require individualization of services to alter automatic assumption about disability;
3. Establish the principle that disabled children need not be removed from regular classes;
4. Broaden the scope of services provided by the school;
5. Establish a process for determining the scope of services;
6. Establish general guidelines for identification of disability;
7. Establish principles for primary state and local responsibility;

8. Clarify lines of authority for educational services; and
9. Move beyond staffing and training personnel [a reference to the primary focus of prior law, the Education of the Handicapped Act of 1970]. (pp. 99–100)

In discussing Principle 3, Walker (1987) stated,

> Congress was interested in the normalization of services for disabled children, in the belief that the presence of a disability did not necessarily require separation and removal from the regular classrooms, or the neighborhood school environment, or from regular academic classes. (p. 99)

IMPLEMENTING THE LAW'S LRE REQUIREMENT

Assessing the status of what has come to be referred to as the least restrictive environment (LRE) principle a decade after the implementation of PL 94-142, Walker (1987) wrote,

> If the law has been massively successful in assigning responsibility for students and setting up mechanisms to assure that schools carry out those responsibilities, it has been less successful in removing barriers between general and special education. Pub. L. No. 94-142 and other public policies of the time did not anticipate the need to take special steps to eliminate turf, professional, attitudinal, and knowledge barriers within public education. It did not anticipate that the artifice of delivery systems in schools might drive the maintenance of separate services and keep students from the mainstream, that the resource base for special education and other remedial services would be constrained by economic forces, or that special education might continue to be dead-end programs in many school districts. Nor could it anticipate how deeply ingrained were our assumptions about the differences between students with learning problems and those without, and the substantial power of high (or, unfortunately, low) expectations in learning. (p. 109)

In the early years of implementing PL 94-142, LRE was expressed through the concept of *mainstreaming*. A term not found in the law, mainstreaming emphasized the place in which special education took place; it assumed the existence of two separate systems—general and special education—and was applicable to those students who were considered to be most like "normal." Educational services were to be delivered along a "continuum" of locations, each matched to the student's "deficit" and disability; the phrase *cascade of services* also was used. In the 1980s, some advocates began to use the term *integration,* which borrowed a civil rights focus from race relations and viewed students with disabilities as targets of discrimination and disenfranchisement (Gliedman & Roth, 1980). These formulations, although well meaning and an advancement over practices of the past, suffered from the same fundamental flaw that is inherent in the LRE. As Taylor (1988) has pointed out, the LRE principle

- Legitimates restrictive environments. Although it incorporates a presumption favoring less restriction, it also implies the acceptability of a more restricted and segregated setting for at least some students.
- Confuses segregation and integration on the one hand with the intensity of services on the other. The clear implication is that students who need more intensive services must receive them in more restrictive settings.
- Is based on a "readiness" model. That is, students must prove their readiness for an integrated setting rather than presume such a setting as the norm. Not only is this morally unacceptable, but also the evidence is that more restrictive settings do not prepare people for less restrictive ones.
- Directs attention to the physical settings rather than to the services and supports that people need to be integrated into the community.

In the early 1980s, in response to a growing concern about the effectiveness of separate special education programs, Madeleine Will, then assistant secretary, U.S. Department of Education, called for general and special educators to share responsibility for students with learning problems. Will's efforts, labeled the "Regular Education Initiative" (REI), were limited to students with mild impairments. The initiative was based on prior educational research—especially the work of Reynolds and Wang (1983)—which indicated a lack of success for students in special education programs. The REI created a furor. Many special educators responded defensively, both denigrating the need for change and arguing that general education would be neither willing nor able to serve students with disabilities. (See Lloyd, Singh, & Repp [1991], especially chapters by Hocutt, Martin, & McKinney; Kauffman; Gottleib, Alter, & Gottleib; and Fuchs & Fuchs. See also Stainback & Stainback [1992], especially chapters by Adelman; Clark; Fuchs & Fuchs; Heller; Leiberman; and Vergason & Andregg.) As the first major challenge to the separate special education system from within the federal government, the REI served to "break the ice" and thus provided an opening for substantive change.

In response to the limits of the REI, a number of researchers and practitioners challenged the fundamental design of two separate systems. These included Stainback and Stainback (1984), who called for the "merger" of general and special education; Biklen (1985), who called for "integrating" special and general education; and Gartner and Lipsky (1987), who called for going "beyond special education" to a unitary and "refashioned mainstream." Biklen, Lehr, Searl, and Taylor (1987) proposed "purposeful integration," whereby all students with disabilities, regardless of severity, would be educated in general classrooms, with necessary supports. The authors emphasized that this did not mean doing away with "special services" or failing to provide necessary support services to the child and teacher to make integration work. More a conceptual model than an actual program, the "purposeful integration" design elevated the discussion to broader systemic issues.

Nisbet (1995) has summarized these reform efforts:

> These initiatives departed from earlier reform attempts of mainstreaming and integration in their appreciation of the need for broader structural reform. Rather than adding on a new service, creating a new specialist, or identifying a new category of disability, these initiatives challenged underlying assumptions about students' learning and the established relationship between general and special education. They became the precursors to a movement that suggests that, rather than ever separating students on the basis of disability, all students should be included from the beginning of their schooling careers, by right, in the opportunities and responsibilities of public schooling. Inclusion requires restructuring of both the assumptions and the organization of public education in this country. (p. 152)

States struggling to reform their general education systems in the 1980s increasingly began questioning the effectiveness of special education as well. Among the concerns were the following:

- A disproportionate number of students from ethnic backgrounds were being placed in special education.
- Too many students overall were being placed in special education.
- Students were unnecessarily labeled in order to "fit" into the system.
- Labeling was leading to educating students in overly segregated settings.
- Special education had evolved into a separate system.
- In lean budgetary times, the escalating costs of special education were beginning to eat into the general education program.
- Educators did not regularly provide substantially different methods of instruction depending on individual students' needs.
- Students' curricular options were being limited based on their disability label. (Roach, 1995, p. 6)

Addressing the consequence of the dual system for students with disabilities, Pugach and Warger (1993) have written, "The curriculum that special education has enacted over the years, and the whole school context in which special education takes place, have interacted to disenfranchise students from access to a broad, rich, and meaningful education" (p. 135).

Summarizing the changes that have occurred since 1975 for people with disabilities in the United States, Valerie Bradley (1994), then–vice chairperson of the President's Committee on Mental Retardation, wrote,

> The initial metamorphosis began in the late 1960s and is frequently described as a shift from the medical model of care to the developmental model or from the custodial model to the rehabilitation model. This transition was the first inkling of . . . a paradigm shift. . . .
> [T]his evolutionary process can be broken into three distinct stages. In the first stage, the era of institutionalization, dependence and segregation (ending roughly in the mid-1970s), the governing norms were primarily medical and the objective was to separate people who were designated sick and vulnerable from the rest of the society. This era ended with the advent of the developmental model and a growing body of research showing the inadequacies of institutional care. This ushered in the second stage, the era of deinstitutionalization and community development (beginning in the mid-1970s), which was marked by the creation of group homes and sheltered workshops that were physically integrated in the community but that emphasized the provision of specialized services in socially segregated settings. The third and emerging stage is the era of community membership, which is marked by an emphasis on functional supports to enhance inclusion and quality of life as defined by physical as well as social integration.

Although the demarcation of stages is blurred, Table 8.1 provides a synopsis of the evolution of a service paradigm as described by Bradley (1994).

CONCLUSION

Since the passage in 1975 of the landmark PL 94-142, the central issue in educating students with disabilities has moved from establishing entitlement and access to providing quality outcomes for students with disabilities. Historically, the changes brought about by the law represent a great achievement in access. For the future, an equally great challenge has yet to be met to achieve equitable and quality educational outcomes.

Table 8.1. Evolution of services and supports

Focal questions	Era of institutions	Era of deinstitutionalization	Era of community membership
Who is the person of concern?	The patient	The client	The citizen
What is the typical setting?	An institution	A group home, workshop, special school, or classroom	A person's home, local business, neighborhood school
How are services organized?	In facilities	In a continuum of options	Through an array of supports tailored to the individual
What is the model?	Custodial/medical Care	Developmental/behavioral Programs	Individual support Supports
What are the services?	A plan of care	An individualized rehabilitation plan	A personal futures plan
How are services planned?			
Who controls the planning decision?	A professional	An interdisciplinary team	The individual
What is the planning context?	Standards of professional practice	Team consensus	A circle of friends
What has the highest priority?	Basic needs	Skill development, behavior management	Self-determination, relationships
What is the objective?	Control or cure	Changed behavior	Changes in environment and attitudes

Adapted from Bradley (1994).

REFERENCES

Biklen, D. (Ed.). (1985). *The complete school: Integrating special and general education.* New York: Teachers College Press.

Biklen, D., Lehr, S., Searl, S.J., & Taylor, S.J. (1987). *Purposeful integration . . . Inherently equal.* Boston: Technical Assistance for Parents Project.

Bradley, V.J. (1994). Evolution of a new service paradigm. In V.J. Bradley, J.W. Ashbaugh, & B.C. Blaney (Eds.), *Creating individual supports for people with developmental disabilities: A mandate for change at many levels* (pp. 11–32). Baltimore: Paul H. Brookes Publishing Co.

Dunn, L. (1968). Special education for the mildly retarded: Is much of it justifiable? *Exceptional Children, 35,* 5–22.

Education for All Handicapped Children Act of 1975, PL 94-142, 20 U.S.C. § 1400 *et seq.*

Education of the Handicapped Act (EHA) of 1970, PL 91-230, 20 U.S.C. § 1400 *et seq.*

Elementary and Secondary Education Act of 1965, PL 89-10, 20 U.S.C. § 6301 *et seq.*

Gartner, A., & Lipsky, D.K. (1987). Beyond separate education: Toward a quality system for all students. *Harvard Educational Review, 57*(4), 367–395.

Gilhool, T.K. (1995, May 9). Testimony before the Joint Subcommittee Hearings on the Events, Forces, and Issues that Triggered Enactment of the Education for All Handicapped Children Act of 1975.

Gliedman, J., & Roth, W. (1980). *The unexpected minority: Handicapped children in America.* New York: Harcourt Brace Jovanovich.

Hocutt, A., Martin, E., & McKinney, J.D. (1991). Historical and legal context of mainstreaming. In J.W. Lloyd, N.N. Singh, & A.C. Repp (Eds.), *The Regular Education Initiative: Alternative perspectives on concepts, issues, and models* (pp. 17–28). Sycamore, IL: Sycamore Publishing Co.

Individuals with Disabilities Education Act (IDEA) of 1990, PL 101-476, 20 U.S.C. § 1400 *et seq.*

Larry P. v. Riles, 495 F. Supp. 926, (N.D. Ca. 1979); 83–84 EHLR DEC. 555:304, California.

Lloyd, J.W., Singh, N.N., & Repp, A.C. (Eds.). (1991). *The Regular Education Initiative: Alternative perspectives on concepts, issues, and models.* Sycamore, IL: Sycamore Publishing Co.

Mills v. Board of Education, 348 F. Supp. 866 (D.D.C. 1972).

Nisbet, J. (1995). Education reform: Summary and recommendations. In *The national reform agenda and people with mental retardation: Putting people first* (pp. 151–165). Washington, DC: President's Committee on Mental Retardation.

Pennsylvania Association of Retarded Citizens (PARC) v. Pennsylvania, 334 F. Supp. 1257 (E.D. Pa. 1972), and 343 F. Supp. 279 (E.D. Pa. 1972).

Pugach, M.C., & Warger, C.L. (1993). Curriculum considerations. In J.I. Goodlad & T.C. Lovitt (Eds.), *Integrating general and special education* (pp. 125–148). Columbus, OH: Charles E. Merrill.

Rehabilitation Act of 1973, PL 93-112, 29 U.S.C. § 701 *et seq.*

Reynolds, M.C., & Wang, M.C. (1983). Restructuring "special" school programs: A position paper. *Policy Studies Review, 2*(1), 189–212.

Roach, V. (1995). *Winning ways: Creating inclusive schools, classrooms, and communities.* Alexandria, VA: National Association of State Boards of Education.

Scotch, R.K. (1984). *From good will to civil rights: Transforming federal disability policy.* Philadelphia: Temple University Press.

Smith v. Robinson, 468 U.S. 992, 1009, 1010 (1984).

Stainback, W., & Stainback, S. (1984). A rationale for the merger of regular and special education. *Exceptional Children, 51,* 102–112.

Stainback, W., & Stainback, S. (Eds.). (1992). *Controversial issues confronting special education: Divergent perspectives.* Boston: Allyn & Bacon.

Taylor, S. (1988). Caught in the continuum: A critical analysis of the principle of least restrictive environment. *Journal of The Association for Persons with Severe Handicaps, 13*(1), 41–53.

Walker, L. (1987). Procedural rights in the wrong system: Special education is not enough. In A. Gartner & T. Joe (Eds.), *Images of the disabled/disabling images* (pp. 97–116). New York: Praeger.

9

COURT DECISIONS REGARDING INCLUSIVE EDUCATION

A measure of the centrality of the least restrictive environment (LRE) issue within inclusive education is the lawsuits brought to delineate its parameters. From 1980 to 1994, the annual percentage of special education lawsuits focusing on the LRE has ranged from 6% to 21%; the figures for 1993 and 1994 were 10.4% and 9.3%, respectively ("Analysis," 1995). Moreover, since the late 1980s, a series of court cases (discussed in detail in Chapter 22) has emphasized the concept of LRE; as a group, they have been called the "full inclusion cases." These and the other cases examined in this chapter express the growing desire of individual parents for inclusive education opportunities for their children and set a new standard for what schools are obliged to provide for all children.

APPELLATE COURT DECISIONS

This section of the chapter examines a number of crucial appellate court decisions since the late 1980s that have helped to clarify the intent of legislation with respect to inclusive education.

In 1989, the Fifth Circuit Court of Appeals developed a standard for determining when placing full time a child with a disability in a general education class with supplementary aids and services is appropriate and when removal to a special education class is educationally justified. *Daniel R.R. v. Board of Education* (1989) involved a child with mental retardation. The first step in determining the appropriate placement for a child, the court stated, is to "examine whether the state [i.e., the local school district] has taken the steps to accommodate the handicapped child in regular education." Basically, the court held that the school district must provide supplementary aids and support services and modify the general education program to meet the needs of the student. If the district fails to meet its obligations, then it is in violation of the law. The court set forth two limits for the school district in making these accommodations. First, the general education teacher is not required to devote all or most of his or her time to the child with a disability; and second, the general education program need not be modified beyond recognition.

The next step, the court held, is to determine whether the child with a disability will benefit from this modified general education program. The benefits to be examined include academic achievement but are not limited to it. The court declared that "integrating a handicapped child into a nonhandicapped environment may be beneficial in and of itself." Thus, the court identified both social and academic benefits as matters to consider in determining the appropriateness of an inclusive placement. Attention to both types of benefits were to be addressed by school districts as they considered inclusive placements. Finally, the court stated that school districts may examine the effect of the presence of a child with a disability on other children; the standards for this examination were narrowly drawn.

In another case, *Greer v. Rome City School District* (1991), Christy Greer was a kindergarten student with severe cognitive disabilities whose parents sought an inclusive placement for her despite the school district's refusal. In *Greer*, in the first appellate court citation of *Daniel R.R.*, the 11th Circuit Court of Appeals in 1991 held that the case turned on the first prong of the *Daniel R.R.* test; that is, whether education in the general education classroom can be achieved satisfactorily with the use of supplementary aids and support services. The court stated, "Before the school district may conclude that a handicapped child should be educated outside the regular classroom, it must consider whether supplemental aids and services would permit satisfactory education in the regular classroom." More than any other issue, the nature and extent of supplementary aids and support services to be provided has become the central issue as school districts have been challenged to provide inclusive placements for children.

The school district may consider the cost of such services, the court held; however, mere incremental additional costs are not a sufficient basis to deny the child placement in the general education class. Only when such costs "would significantly impact upon the education of other children in the district" may such a placement be denied the child with a disability.

In a case in 1993, Rafael Oberti was an 8-year-old boy with Down syndrome whose parents wanted him placed in a general classroom despite the school district's refusal. In *Oberti v. Board of Education* (1993), the 3rd Circuit Court of Appeals in 1993 emphasized that the burden of proving compliance with the law's requirement rests squarely on the school district. The court placed heavy emphasis on the use of supplementary aids and support services as a means of accommodating the child with disabilities. The use of these services, the court held, was the key to resolving any tensions between the presumption in the Individuals with Disabilities Education Act (IDEA) of 1990 (PL 101-476) in favor of general placement and providing an individualized program tailored to the specific needs of each child with disabilities. The court stressed that many of the special education techniques used in separate classes can be successfully imported into a general classroom and that the general classroom teacher could be trained to apply these techniques. It also pointed to the "reciprocal benefits of inclusion to the nondisabled students in the class." This was the first time that a court at the appellate level had focused on the benefits to students without disabilities. Previous cases had addressed potential harm to such students.

In considering the potential disruptive effect of the child with disabilities in the classroom, the court in *Oberti v. Board of Education* held that were the school district to provide the appropriate services, there was no reason to believe any behavior problem could not be addressed in the general classroom. Affirming this decision, the court of appeals stated, "Inclusion is a right, not a privilege of a select few." It went on to note: "We construe IDEA's mainstreaming requirement to prohibit a school from placing a child with disabilities outside of a regular classroom if educating the child in the regular classroom, with supplementary aids and support services, can be achieved satisfactorily."[1]

In the fourth "full inclusion case" to be discussed here, Rachel Holland was an 8-year-old with mental retardation requiring limited supports whose parents wanted her placed in a general educa-

---

[1]Despite their victory in *Oberti v. Board of Education*, Rafael's parents decided that the school district would not provide the inclusive education that Rafael needed. His parents thus transferred him to an inclusive program in a private school (Schnaiberg, 1996a).

tion classroom despite the school district's refusal. In *Sacramento City Unified School District v. Rachel H.* (1994), the 9th Circuit Court of Appeals found that the goals and objectives of Rachel's individualized education program (IEP) could be achieved in the general education class, with curriculum modification and supplementary aids and services. It also found that Rachel derived significant nonacademic benefits from a general educational class placement. It held that the school district had failed to meet its burden of showing that the special education class was at least equal or superior to the general class in providing academic benefit. In terms of cost, the court held that the district failed to present any persuasive or credible evidence that educating Rachel in a general classroom with appropriate services would be significantly more expensive than educating her in a separate class.

The U.S. Supreme Court refused to review the circuit court's decision in *Sacramento v. Rachel H.*; this suggests that with circuits in agreement, these decisions are likely to stand as the benchmarks for other court cases. Subsequent district court decisions have reaffirmed that each case will be decided based on its factual circumstances.

Individually and as a group, these four appellate court decisions delineate the meaning of the law's "least restrictive environment" principle. They emphasize that 1) school districts must consider placement in general education for all students with disabilities, regardless of the degree of the disability; 2) such consideration must be more than rhetorical and is best done in actual practice; 3) "inclusion" is not "dumping" but rather placing students with disabilities in the general education setting with the individually necessary supports and supplementary aids; and 4) although issues such as the consequence of inclusion for the other students in the class, the amount of teacher time required to implement it, and the costs to the school district of doing so each are matters for consideration, the standard for denying a student with disabilities such an opportunity is very high.

OTHER COURT DECISIONS

In most subsequent cases, the courts have affirmed the holdings of the four appellate decisions cited in the previous section and ordered school districts to honor parental requests for an inclusive placement with the necessary classroom supports. In other cases, district court judges have found exceptions, within the context of the appellate decisions (e.g., that the changes in the general classroom curriculum were so extreme as to go beyond what was warranted, that an inclusive placement with supports had been tried and had not succeeded, that the child's needs were so great that the supports necessary were beyond what a school district was obliged to provide). Some of these cases involved older children, whereas the affirmed appellate cases all concerned elementary-level students.

Among other significant court cases, *Mavis v. Sobol* (1994) involved a 14-year-old student with mental retardation requiring extensive supports. The district court held that a New York school district's proposal to place the student in a special education classroom and to mainstream her in nonacademic subjects violated the LRE standard. The school district's failure to attempt to provide services in the general classroom with supplementary aids and services was a fatal flaw in its defense.

Unlike *Mavis*, in which the parents supported inclusion against the school district's opposition, in *Norma P. et al. v. Pelham School District* (1995), a New Hampshire school district fought the parents of a teenager with Down syndrome who opposed an inclusive placement. Ruling in a case that spanned 6 years, the judge, who upheld the school district, stated that, "there has been a major turnaround in the past few years where mainstreaming a student is now deemed more beneficial to the handicapped student as they respond to their peers" (cited in "Court OKs," 1995, p. 198).

In *Hall v. Shawnee Mission School District* (1994), the district court rejected the parents' claim for placement of their son in a residential setting, based on behavior problems that he was exhibiting at home; at the time, the child was attending a general classroom for a significant portion of the schoolday. The court found that the student's academic achievement was at grade level and that his behavior problems at school were minor; thus, the court saw no obligation to provide a residential placement. The court stated, "Had the district considered residential placement for a child who was by all accounts performing well at school and who was being mainstreamed for increasing percentages of his school day without incident, the district might have run afoul" of the LRE mandate (cited in "Home Behavior Problems," 1994, p. 99).

School districts' obligations do not end with development of an appropriate IEP; the IEP must be implemented as well. In a matter involving a Muscogee County (Georgia) school district, the U.S. Office of Civil Rights held that the frequent absence of a paraprofessional (and the failure of the school district to provide a substitute) denied a student with mental disabilities her entitlement to community-based training ("Paraprofessionals' Absence," 1995).

In *MR v. Lincolnwood Board of Education* (1994), the district court supported a hearing officer's determination that a student's placement in a self-contained classroom for children with behavior disorders, which also included some general education classes, had resulted in a deterioration of the student's behavior. Thus, the court supported the Illinois district's assignment of the 13-year-old to a therapeutic day program.

In *Clyde K. and Sheila K. v. Puyallup School District* (1995), the court supported a Washington state school district's decision to remove from general classes a 15-year-old boy with Tourette syndrome—a compulsive-obsessive disorder—and attention-deficit/hyperactivity disorder (ADHD) and place him in a separate program. The student had assaulted a school staff member, frequently disrupted his classes by taunting other students, made vulgar and insulting remarks to teachers, and directed sexually explicit remarks at female classmates. Applying the previously mentioned *Daniel R.R. v. State Board of Education* four-part test, the court held that the student was not receiving academic benefit from the general class placement; that nonacademic benefits were, at best, only minimal; and that his "dangerously aggressive" behavior had a negative effect on the teacher and other students and were disruptive. The student's placement was changed to his neighborhood high school in a combination general class and resource room program.

In *Poolaw v. Parker Unified School District* (1994), the district court in Arizona ruled that a Native American student who was deaf and living on a reservation should be placed in the state's School for the Deaf, despite the parent's preference for an inclusive placement. The 13-year-old boy had been educated in several school districts, some of which provided mainstreaming opportunities, and had acquired almost no language. The district argued that he was at a critical stage in his language development and that placement in the state school was required. A part of the parent's argument was that the local school would provide an opportunity for the child to develop a sense of his Native American heritage.

In *Kari H. v. Franklin S.S.D.* (1995), a federal judge in Tennessee upheld an administrative law judge's ruling that the appropriate placement for a 14-year-old student with mental retardation requiring extensive supports was a separate special education class with some mainstreaming for nonacademic subjects, not the fully inclusive placement that the parents sought. (The student had been in an integrated placement in her previous school in Minnesota.) Unlike *Oberti v. Board of Education*, in which the district had alleged that inclusion was inappropriate without even attempting it, in *Kari H. v. Franklin,* the Tennessee district had tried a general class placement and claimed that it had failed, both in terms of benefit for the student and in her disruption of the class.

In the same circuit, the court ruled that the academic and physical needs of a fourth-grade student with multiple disabilities could not be met in the general classroom and that the student required placement in a comprehensive development class (*McWhirt by McWhirt v. Williamson County School* [1995]). As in the *Poolaw v. Parker* and *Keri H. v. Franklin* cases, the court supported separate placement of a child who was older and had severe disabilities, and the school districts had provided a general class placement that, they asserted, had failed.

In *Hudson v. Bloomfield Hills School District* (1995), a federal district court in Michigan upheld the placement of a 14-year-old student, classified as "trainable mentally impaired" under the state's special education law, in a separate classroom, despite the mother's wish that the child be educated in an inclusive placement. The hearing officer, whose decision the court upheld, apparently was impressed by the student's failure to benefit from a placement that had been agreed to as a compromise between the school district and the mother. The placement involved a special education classroom in the morning and parallel instruction in a general education classroom in another school in the afternoon.

In *D.F. v. Western School Corp.* (1996), a federal district court judge in Indiana ruled that the general education curriculum would have to be modified beyond recognition to fit the needs of a 13-year-old with multiple disabilities. The judge found that the student, who was functioning socially at the level of a 2-year-old and whose IQ was tested at 23, would gain no academic or nonacademic benefits from a general education placement. Thus, he upheld the school district's argument that a special education placement was, for this boy, the least restrictive environment.

Contrary to the findings in other cases that emphasized the benefit to students with disabilities of being in classes with students without disabilities, two 1996 federal district court rulings held that such placements were undesirable, upholding parental wishes. In a New York case, *Evans v. Board of Education* (1996), involving a 15-year-old boy with dyslexia, the judge ordered the development of an IEP that ensures that the student will attend classes with students who have similar disabilities. The school district had provided placement in a general education class with daily 40-minute pull-out sessions with a reading and writing instructor. A witness for the parents, a doctoral student, said that students such as this boy were emotionally fragile and benefit from being with other students who have dyslexia so that they know they are not alone in their struggle ("Judge Orders," 1996).

In *Fort Zumwalt School District v. Board of Education* (1996), a federal district court judge found that the school district had erred in placing a third-grade student with learning disabilities in a general education class. "The reasoning: The child's self-esteem and behavior problems were aggravated by having to associate with students from whom he felt 'different,' and, consequently, his academic progress suffered" ("Court: LRE," 1996, p. 8). In commenting on the case, the editors of *Inclusive Education Programs* described the decision as "a highly unusual interpretation of the LRE requirement of the IDEA," pointing out that

> most would argue that mainstreaming makes children with disabilities feel the same as their nondisabled peers, not different. To date, one premise underlying inclusion has been that, given optimal opportunities to interact with nondisabled peers, students experience increased self-esteem and a variety of other social benefits.
>
> Most have viewed removal from the regular education environment as making a student with a disability feel inadequate and carrying with it the threat of negative effects on morale. This premise would seem even more valid where disabilities were less severe and the child had a greater awareness of those differences in educational treatment.
>
> But the court in this case said the opposite. The judge noted that although the school increased the student's participation in the regular education classroom when he experienced feelings of being different, it never helped him accept and understand his learning disabilities. ("Court: LRE," 1996, p. 8)

In a broader-based case, *Chanda Smith v. Los Angeles Unified School District* (1995), a class-action lawsuit challenged the entire special education system of the nation's second largest school district, serving some 65,000 students with disabilities. The suit was brought against the school district because, in the words of a consultant, "The district suffers from a pervasive, substantial, and systemic inability to deliver special education services in compliance with special education laws" (Schnaiberg, 1996b). A proposed consent decree, agreed to by the school district and the American Civil Liberties Union on behalf of the plaintiff class, reorganizes the special education administration, emphasizes the LRE requirement of the law, ensures access for special education students to all district schools, introduces general education programs in the district's 18 special education schools, centralizes and computerizes all student records, and requires extensive and ongoing staff development ("L.A.

Looks," 1995; Schnaiberg, 1996b, 1996c; "Tentative Agreement," 1995).

A suit of similar breadth is *Gaskin v. Commonwealth of Pennsylvania* (1995). Brought initially by 12 students with disabilities, their parents, and 11 state and regional advocacy groups, the district court certified class status on behalf of at least 98% of the 282,340 children enrolled in Pennsylvania's special education programs. In addition to the plaintiffs' claim that local school districts failed to provide adequate personnel development and supplementary aids and support services to students placed in general education classes, the suit charged that the state department of education had failed to monitor local school districts' compliance with IDEA ("Class Certified," 1995).

In 1996, in another case with a potentially broad urban impact, a consent decree involving the Boston public schools and requiring districtwide implementation of inclusive education awaited the initiatives of the district superintendent.

Whether honoring the law's requirement for LRE necessarily means the "neighborhood school" was the subject of a 10th Circuit Court of Appeals decision in *Tyler Murray v. Montrose County School District* (1995). The court held that although there was a preference for the neighborhood school in the IDEA regulations, there was no legal requirement to place a student in the neighborhood school in order to meet the law's LRE mandate. "While [IDEA] clearly commands schools to include or mainstream disabled children, as much as possible, it says nothing about where, within a school district, that inclusion should take place" (cited in "Court: LRE," 1995, p. 356). The decision in *Murray* reinforces a previous decision, *Urban v. Jefferson County School District* (1994), in which the federal district court in Colorado held that the statutory preference for the neighborhood school was not a mandate. The 10th Circuit Court's decision is in line with previous decisions in the 4th and 8th Circuit Courts.

Part H of IDEA, enacted in 1985, requires the provision of services for infants and toddlers with disabilities. In the first federal decision concerning Part H, a district court judge (Northern District of Illinois) held that the state had been "dragging its feet" on the implementation of the law (*Marie O. v. Edgar*, 1995). He ruled that the state must accelerate its provision of services. The costs of the Part H program led the Pennsylvania governor to propose that the state withdraw from the program. A similar proposal was made in Connecticut in 1995, but parents, advocates, and school administrators collaborated to kill the plan in the legislature ("Pa. Governor," 1996). A New York City case (*Ray v. Anthony*, 1995), challenged the city school system's practices in terms of student placement in the least restrictive environment. Commenting on the placement of one of the plaintiffs, federal district court Judge Eugene Nickerson stated that the school system "appears more concerned with issuing recommendations [for placement] according to available services rather than recommending and finding the most appropriate setting" (cited in "New York City," 1995, p. 3). During the 1991–1992 school year, over 90% of preschool special education students in New York City were placed in segregated programs, ranging from separate classes to private residential facilities. The national average that year was 54%.

Although there has been some debate as to whether the special education legislation (IDEA) is a matter of civil rights, there is no question that the Americans with Disabilities Act (ADA) of 1990 (PL 101-336) is a civil rights law, as is Section 504 of the Rehabilitation Act of 1973 (PL 93-112).[2] In *Peterson v. Hastings (Neb.) Public Schools* (1994), the court accepted the argument that the ADA supplements IDEA (cited in *"Peterson* Ruling," 1994). Because the ADA requirements in some areas go beyond those of IDEA, the civil rights perspective concerning inclusion gains impetus. A further factor is that under ADA, private schools are included as public accommodations and, thus, are bound by its provisions (42 U.S.C. § 1218 [7] [J]). Conversely, in a policy letter, the Office of Special Education Programs has declared that parents who choose to enroll their child in a private school cannot hold the public school responsible for the appropriateness of the services. Students voluntarily enrolled in private schools need not receive all of the benefits that public schools offer (cited in "School's Role," 1996).

Reporting on a South Dakota federal district court decision, *Yankton School District v. Schramm* (1995), Zirkel (1996) emphasized the blurring of the lines between IDEA, the ADA, and Section 504:

---

[2]These laws also provide protection for school employees with disabilities. In a case in New York, a teacher sued a school district for failing to provide her with an aide. The Court of Appeals for the Second Circuit ruled that a teacher who sued her employer, the Valley Central (New York) School District, for failing to provide her with reasonable accommodations necessary to perform her job has an appropriate cause of action pursuant to Section 504 of the Rehabilitation Act of 1973 (PL 93-112); thus, the appeals court overturned the district court's dismissal of *Borkowski v. Valley Central School District* and ordered a trial on the teacher's claim ("Teacher May Sue," 1995).

The *Yankton* decision and the underlying OSEP [Office of Special Education Programs] interpretation leave school districts in a confounding circle. In trying to meet the needs of students under Section 504 and the ADA, districts may be helping to establish eligibility under the IDEA. (p. 6)

The personal liability of educators has been emphasized in court decisions in the 1990s. In *Doe v. Withers* (1995), a high school general education teacher refused to provide the oral testing accommodation established in a student's IEP. A jury held the teacher personally liable for $15,000 in compensatory and punitive damages, as well as for the parents' attorney fees. Perry Zirkel, an attorney and professor at Lehigh University, pointed out that the decision to hold the teacher personally liable came from a lower state court and that, in general, courts have held that individuals cannot be held personally liable under IDEA. Zirkel stated, however, that it could be a different matter under Section 504 or under the ADA:

> My bet is that when situations [such as the facts in *Doe v. Withers*] are tested in courts with more clout and sophistication, the result will be rough sledding for the student under IDEA, but significantly better odds under Section 504. And, where won, the damages and attorneys' fees are bound to be higher in such courts. (cited in "Regular Education," 1995, p. 10)

Also of interest in this connection is a federal court of appeals decision that allowed a lawsuit to go forward, one that seeks damages against both a school district and several individual educators for failing to properly evaluate and educate a student with a disability. In *W.B. v. Matula*, the 3rd Circuit Court of Appeals overruled the district court's summary judgment in favor of the local officials of the Mansfield Township, New Jersey, school district and ordered a trial to go forward. Among the defendants were general educators, a principal, and two teachers. This decision is the latest phase in a 4-year dispute regarding the eligibility of a child for special education services and the appropriate classification. The district initially determined that the child had ADHD but was not entitled to services under IDEA because he was performing at or above grade level. The parents' independent evaluator determined that the child had Tourette syndrome as well as ADHD. A settlement between the parents and the district included classifying the boy as neurologically impaired. The matter before the court was whether the settlement precluded the suit for damages; the court of appeals decision held that it did not ("Third Circuit," 1996).

CONCLUSION

The court cases described in this chapter concerning "inclusion" have followed IDEA's requirement that school districts design programs that meet the individual needs of students with disabilities, with the understanding that there is no single "one size fits all" standard for all children. During the 1990s, however, courts have increasingly found that an inclusive placement, with necessary supplemental aids and support services, is appropriate for a wider range of students.

Reflecting on the ways in which the law will have an impact on educational placements, two educators, Osborne and Dimattia (1995), have stated,

> An inclusionary setting must be the placement of choice. Today a school district's decision to place a student in a segregated setting will be upheld only if school officials can show that their good faith effort at inclusion has failed or if they have strong evidence to support a contention that an inclusionary setting will not be satisfactory. This is not the way it was in the early LRE cases. . . . [C]ourts will no longer wait for school officials to act. Judges are telling us that the time to fully implement the LRE provision has arrived. We believe that in the future, courts will not defer to educators who "think" a segregated setting might be best. (p. 583)

REFERENCES

Americans with Disabilities Act (ADA) of 1990, PL 101-336 42 U.S.C. § 12101 *et seq.*

Analysis of IDEA litigation. (1995, April 4). *Education Daily,* 1, 3.

Borkowski v. Valley Central School District (2nd Cir. 1995).

Chanda Smith v. Los Angeles Unified School District, 93-7044.

Class certified in Pennsylvania inclusion lawsuit. (1995). *Inclusive Education Programs,* 2(12), 7.

Clyde K. and Sheila K. v. Puyallup School District, 21 IDELR 664 (Wash. 1996).

Court: LD student better served in private placement. (1996). *Inclusive Education Programs,* 3(8), 8.

Court: LRE not always in the neighborhood. (1995). *Special Educator,* 10(22), 346, 356.

Court OKs inclusion placement over parental objections. (1995). *Special Educator,* 10(13), 198.

Daniel R.R. v. State Board of Education, 874 F.2d 1036 (5th Cir. 1989).

D.F. v. Western Sch. Corp., 23 IDELR 1121 (Ind. 1996).

Disabled students' parents eye neighborhood schools. (1995, November 21). *Education Daily,* 1, 3.

Doe v. Withers, 20 IDELR 411 (1995)

Evans v. Board of Education, (95 CV 10102, New York, 1996).

Federal judge faults Illinois for early intervention delay. (1996, February 21). *Education Daily*, 1, 3.

Fort Zumwalt School District v. Missouri State Board of Education, 24 IDELR (Mo. 1996).

Gaskin v. Commonwealth of Pennsylvania, 23 IDELR 61 (Pa. 1995).

Greer v. Rome City School District, 950 F.2d 688 (11th Cir. 1991).

Hall v. Shawnee Mission School District, (Kan. 1994).

Home behavior problems not school's duty, court says. (1995). *Special Educator, 10*(7), 93, 99.

Hudson v. Bloomfield Hills School District, 23 IDELR 612 (E.D. Mich. 1995).

Individuals with Disabilities Education Act (IDEA) of 1990, PL 101-476, 20 U.S.C. § 1400 *et seq.*

Keri H. v. Franklin S.S.D., 23 IDELR 538 (M.D. Tenn. 1995).

L.A. looks down a long, hard—and expensive—road. (1995). *Special Educator, 11*(13), 5.

Marie O. v. Edgar, 94-C-1471 (Ill. 1995).

Mavis v. Sobel, 20 IDELR 1125 (N.D.N.Y. 1994).

McWhirt by McWhirt v. Williamson County School, 23 IDELR 509 (6th Cir. 1995).

MR v. Lincolnwood Board of Education, 20 IDELR 1323 (N.D. Ill. 1994).

New York City special ed suit targets preschoolers. (1995, June 7). *Education Daily*, 3.

Norma P. et al. v. Pelham School District, 21 IDELR 919 (N.Y. 1995).

Oberti v. Board of Education, 995 F.2d 1204 (3rd. Cir. 1993).

Osborne, A.G., Jr., & Dimattia, P. (1995). IDEA's LRE mandate: Another look. *Exceptional Children, 62*, 582–584.

Pa. governor proposes quitting IDEA's Part H. (1996, February 20). *Education Daily*, 1, 3.

Paraprofessionals' absence interfered with training of student. (1995). *Special Educator, 11*(7), 13.

Peterson ruling raises troubling questions on ADA. (1994). *Special Educator, 10*(4), 49, 59–60.

Peterson v. Hastings (Neb.) Public Schools, (Neb. 1994).

Poolaw v. Parker Unified School District, 21 IDELR 1 (D. Ariz. 1994).

Provision of aide for after-school program was not undue hardship. (1996). *Special Educator, 11*(12), 16.

Ray v. Anthony, (N.Y. 1995).

Regular education. (1995). *Special Educator, 11*(1), 9.

Rehabilitation Act of 1973, PL 93-112, 29 U.S.C. § 701 *et seq.*

Sacramento City Unified School District v. Rachel H., 14 F.3d 1398 (9th Cir. 1994).

Schnaiberg, L. (1996a). Educating Rafael: When a child has Down syndrome, who decides what kind of education is "best"? *Education Week, 15*(17), 18–26.

Schnaiberg, L. (1996b). In wake of suit, L.A. moves to revamp spec. ed. system. *Education Weekly, 15*(16), 6.

Schnaiberg, L. (1996c). L.A. board backs overhaul of special education system. *Education Weekly, 15*(26), 11.

School districts prevailing in cases involving older, involved students. (1995). *Individualized Education Programs, 3*(2), 3.

School's role limited when parents pick private special ed. (1996, March 6). *Education Daily*, 3.

Self-contained classroom was LRE for 14-year-old with severe MR. (1995). *Special Educator*, *11*(13), 9.

Shanker, A. (1994). Full inclusion is neither free nor appropriate. *Educational Leadership*, *52*(2), 18–21.

6th Circuit upholds special education classroom as LRE. (1995). *Special Educator*, *11*(13), 9–10.

Teacher may sue for right to an aide, appeals court says. (1995, August 23). *Education Daily*, 3.

Tentative agreement struck in L.A. special ed dispute. (1995, December 21). *Education Daily*, 1, 3.

Third Circuit: You can be liable for punitive damages under IDEA. (1996). *Special Educator*, *11*(11), 1, 8.

Tyler Murray v. Montrose County School District, (1995).

Urban v. Jefferson County School District, 21 IDELR 985 (Colo. 1994).

W.B. v. Mutula, (3rd Cir. 1996).

Yankton School District v. Schramm, 23 IDELR 42 (S.D. 1995).

Zirkel, P.A. (1996). More blurring of the line: Just what is "special education" anyway? *Special Educator*, *11*(13), 1, 6.

10

NATIONAL OVERVIEW
OF INCLUSIVE EDUCATION

This chapter begins by defining inclusive education and identifying those factors necessary for successful inclusion programs. Following a national overview of inclusion programs, the chapter surveys activities in individual states.

DEFINING INCLUSIVE EDUCATION

There is no legal definition of *inclusion* or *inclusive education*; however, the National Center on Educational Restructuring and Inclusion (NCERI) consulted with educational leaders to develop the following working definition of *inclusive education*:

> Providing to all students, including those with significant disabilities, equitable opportunities to receive effective educational services, with the needed supplementary aids and support services, in age-appropriate classrooms in their neighborhood schools, in order to prepare students for productive lives as full members of society. (*National Study*, 1994)

Addressing the definition from an institutional perspective, an *inclusive school* has been defined as

> a diverse problem-solving organization with a common mission that emphasizes learning for all students. It employs and supports teachers and staff who are committed to working together to create and maintain a climate conducive to learning. The responsibility for all students is shared. An effective, inclusive school acknowledges that such a commitment requires administrative leadership, on-going technical assistance, and long-term professional development. Within in-

clusive schools, there is a shared responsibility for any problem or any success for students in the schools. (*Creating Schools*, 1995, p. vii)

A 1995 Delphi investigation[1] predicted major trends in educating students with disabilities, based on a survey of 37 leaders in the field:

> The movement toward inclusion will continue, and the belief will predominate that people with disabilities have the right to full participation in integrated settings and activities. Indeed, panelists agree with the prediction that society as a whole will recognize the benefits of integrated education. (Putnam, 1995, p. 572)

Based on NCERI studies of inclusion programs in the United States, the movement toward inclusion indeed appears to be a reality (*National Study,* 1994, 1995). The results of these studies indicate that inclusive education programs are being implemented across the nation. The NCERI reported that

- Inclusion programs are being conducted in every state. Between 1994 and 1995, the number of school districts reporting inclusive education programs tripled.
- Inclusion programs are taking place in a wide range of locations— urban, suburban, and rural school districts, as well as large and small school districts.
- Inclusion programs are occurring at all grade levels, involving students across the entire range of disabilities.
- Inclusion programs are being initiated by administrators, teachers, parents, university faculty, state departments of education, and as a result of court orders.
- Inclusion programs are being evaluated in terms of implementation, outcomes, and financing.

FACTORS IN SUCCESSFUL INCLUSION PROGRAMS

The NCERI (*National Study*, 1994, 1995) reported that several factors emerged as necessary for inclusion to be successful:

1. *Visionary leadership* The statement of a Vermont special education director underscores the importance of this component:

> Some years ago, we came to view inclusion as a subset of the restructuring of the entire educational system. From this perspective, we no longer view special education as a means to help students meet the demands of the classroom, but as a part of the classroom services

---

[1]A Delphi investigation is a technique used to determine consensus among a group of respondents.

that must be available to accommodate the learning needs of all children in a restructured school. (*National Study*, 1994)

Villa, Thousand, Meyers, and Nevin (1993), based on a study of 32 school sites (in Arizona, Illinois, Michigan, New York, Ontario, and Vermont) that were implementing inclusive educational opportunities for students, reported that among both general and special educators the *degree of administrative support* emerged as the most powerful predictor of positive attitudes toward full inclusion.

2. *Collaboration* Reports from school districts indicate that the achievement of inclusive education presumes that no one teacher can be—or ought to be—expected to have all of the expertise required to meet the educational needs of all students in the classroom. Rather, individual teachers must have available to them the support systems that provide collaborative assistance and that enable them to engage in cooperative problem solving. Building planning teams, scheduling time for teachers to work together, recognizing teachers as problem solvers, conceptualizing teachers as front-line researchers—these tools were all reported as necessary for collaboration.

The type of collaboration needed to achieve a "full learning membership for students with severe disabilities" is captured by Ferguson, Meyer, Jeanchild, Juniper, and Zingo (1992):

> [It] requires teachers, regardless of their official labels, to provide all students with three crucial supports (teaching support, prosthetic support, and interpretive support), by flexibly working within three inclusion parameters (curriculum infusion, learning inclusion, and social inclusion), through the development of two teacher relationships (collaborative and consultative) in order to accomplish one schooling outcome. *The purpose of schooling is to enable all students to actively participate in their communities so that others care enough about what happens to them to look for a way to include them as part of that community* [emphasis in original]. (p. 226)

3. *Refocused use of assessment* Traditionally, student assessments have been used as screening devices—to determine who gets into which slot. In special education, numerous studies have documented the inadequacy of this screening (e.g., Ysseldyke, 1987). Inclusive education schools and districts are reporting moving toward more "authentic assessment" designs, including the use of portfolios of students' work and performances, and generally working to refocus assessment.

4. *Supports for staff and students* Two support factors are essential for successful inclusive education programs: systematic staff development and flexible planning time for special education

and general education teachers to work together. From the vantage point of students, supports for inclusion often mean supplementary aids and support services. Districts report that these include assigning school aides—full or part time, short or long term; providing needed therapy services integrated into the general school program; peer support; "buddy systems" or "circles of friends"; and effectively using computer-aided technology and other assistive devices.

5. *Appropriate funding levels and formulas* Special education funding formulas often favor restrictive placements for students in special education. Changes in funding to allow funds to follow the students are essential to the success of educational restructuring and inclusion. Districts report that, in general, inclusive education programs are no more costly than segregated models ("Does Inclusion Cost More?" 1994; McLaughlin & Warren, 1994). (See Chapter 11 for further discussion.)

6. *Effective parental involvement* Inclusive schools report encouraging parental participation through family support services, as well as the development of educational programs that engage parents as co-learners with their children. Programs that bring a wide array of services to children in the school settings report at least two sets of benefits—direct benefits to the children and opportunities for parents and other family members to become involved in school-based activities.

7. *Curricula adaptation and effective instructional practices* Classroom practices that have been reported as supporting inclusive education include cooperative learning, multilevel instruction, activity-based learning, mastery learning, use of instructional technology, peer support, and tutoring programs.

In a 1994 "Working Forum on Inclusive Schools," convened by 10 national organizations,[2] the following factors were identified as characterizing inclusive schools (cited in *Creating Schools*, 1995):

- *A sense of community.* An inclusive school has a philosophy and a vision that all children belong and can learn in the mainstream of school and community life. Within an inclusive school, everyone

---

[2]The 10 organizations included American Association of School Administrators, American Federation of Teachers, the Council for Exceptional Children, the Council of Great City Schools, National Association of Elementary School Principals, National Association of Secondary School Principals, National Association of State Boards of Education, National Association of State Directors of Special Education, National Education Association, and National School Boards Association.

belongs, everyone is accepted, and is supported by peers and the adults in the school.

• *Leadership.* The principal plays a critical role in an inclusive school by actively involving and sharing responsibility with the entire school staff in planning and carrying out the strategies that make the school successful.

• *High standards.* Within inclusive schools, all children meet high levels of educational outcomes and high standards of performance that are appropriate to their needs.

• *Collaboration and cooperation.* An inclusive school encourages students and staff to support one another with such strategies as peer tutoring, buddy systems, cooperative learning, team teaching, co-teaching, teacher–student assistance teams, and other collaborative arrangements.

• *Changing roles and responsibilities.* An inclusive school changes the old roles of teachers and school staff. Teachers lecture less and assist more, school psychologists work more closely with teachers in the classroom, and every person in the building is an active participant in the learning process.

• *Array of services.* An inclusive school offers an array of services—health, mental health, and social services—all coordinated with the educational staff.

• *Partnership with parents.* Parents are embraced as equal and essential partners in the education of their children.

• *Flexible learning environments.* Children in an inclusive school are not expected to move in lock steps, but rather they follow their individual paths to learning. Groupings are flexible, and material is presented in concrete, meaningful ways that emphasize participation. Although there is less reliance on programs that pull children out of classrooms, there are still opportunities for children to receive separate instruction if needed.

• *Strategies based on research.* Research into how people learn is providing new ideas and strategies for teachers, and an inclusive school incorporates those ideas. Cooperative learning, curriculum adaptation, peer tutoring, direct instruction, reciprocal teaching, social skills training, computer-assisted instruction, study skill training, and mastery learning are some of the practices that have emerged from the latest research and are applied in inclusive schools.

• *New forms of accountability.* An inclusive school relies less on standardized tests, using new forms of accountability and assessment to make sure that each student is progressing towards his or her goal.

• *Access.* An inclusive school ensures that students are able to participate in school life by making necessary modifications to the building and by making available appropriate technology that makes participation possible.

• *Continuing professional development.* An inclusive school enables staff to design and obtain professional development on an ongoing basis so that there is continuous improvement in the knowledge and skills that they can employ to educate students. (pp. 17–20)

STATE-LEVEL ACTIVITIES

IDEA places responsibility for education services for students with disabilities at the state level. Some states have passed new laws to support inclusive education. Other states have adopted policy statements and guidelines that promote inclusive education, and/or have conducted federally supported demonstration projects. Katsiyannis, Conderman, and Franks (1995) surveyed state education departments regarding their policies and activities concerning inclusion. Responses were received from 40 states. Although individual states were not identified, among respondents, 18 states[3] have state policies or guidelines on inclusion, 11 of which have been developed since 1990; 38 states indicated that they provide technical assistance and in-service training for local school districts; 16 states provide financial support for inclusion initiatives; 33 states reported state support for inclusion pilot projects; 14 states have developed procedures for monitoring compliance with federal and state requirements involving students with disabilities specific to inclusion; 6 states reported that they mandate inclusion-specific competencies for teacher certification; and 16 states reported that they are in the process of revising teacher certification requirements to address inclusion.

In testimony before the Subcommittee on Select Education and Civil Rights, Committee on Education, U.S. House of Representatives, a representative of the General Accounting Office reported on a study it conducted of inclusion in districts in California, Kentucky, New York, and Vermont (Morra, 1994):

> Parents, staff, and state officials perceived that the success of inclusion programs depends on attention being paid to creating and maintaining several key conditions: 1. a collaborative learning environment, 2. natural proportions of disabled students in their local education setting, 3. adequate support—including large numbers of aides and training—for classroom teachers, and 4. a philosophic reorientation—defining special education as a service, rather than a place.

Morra (1994) continued,

> For students with disabilities, having good peer role models and being exposed to a broad curriculum led to perceived gains in the areas of social interaction, language development, appropriate behavior, and self-esteem. Academic progress was also noted. For the non-disabled students, parents and teachers perceived them becoming, generally,

---

[3]Katsiyannis et al. (1995, p. 284) gently noted, "Although 18 states indicated the development of state inclusion policies, only 16 policies were available for review."

more compassionate, more helpful, and more friendly in relating to the disabled students.

Morra (1994) noted that districts were struggling with inclusion programs for some groups of students, based not on the severity or type of disability but, rather, on the individual needs of the student. Also, there were unanswered questions as to funding, access, equity, and the federal role.

Major developments regarding the progress of inclusion in a number of individual states are discussed in the pages following.

Vermont

The most extensive state legislation on inclusion of any state to date is Vermont's Act 230, passed in 1990. The goal of the act was to increase the capacity of schools to meet the needs of all students. It seeks to accomplish this through staff development and changes in the special education funding system to increase flexibility and remove incentives for identifying students as eligible for special education and by encouraging each school to develop a more comprehensive system of education services. Key program components include the following:

1. The Homecoming Model, a collaborative statewide approach that uses teams to develop the support services needed to transfer students from regional special education programs and serve them in general education classrooms. A school board member, a parent, and general and special educators compose the team.
2. An instructional support system to ensure the early identification of students at risk and the capability of meeting their needs, through the establishment of instructional support teams for collaborative problem solving to assist teachers.
3. Project Wrap-Around, which provides intensive home- and school-based support services to families who have children at home who are at risk of being placed in an alternative residence. The program "wraps" services around the child, providing whatever is deemed necessary to keep the child at home and in an integrated educational setting.

A Vermont state evaluation of Act 230 reported that

- 82% of the students who came off IEPs were rated as successful by their special education and [general education] classroom teachers.
- 98% of the teachers interviewed felt full-time placement in the general education classroom was appropriate for these students.
- 79% of the students who came off IEPs were rated as successful by their parents in classroom performance, behavior in school, be-

havior in the classroom, friendships, and participation in after-school activities.

- 96% of these students reported that they liked school.
- 89% of these students reported that they felt successful in school.
- Grades indicated that these students' academic performance was the same when they came off of IEPs as it had been when they were on IEPs. (*Act 230 in Vermont*, 1995, p. 4)

The students who came off of IEPs had mild to moderate impairments; 84% had previously been identified as having either a learning disability or a speech and language impairment. Only 2% had been previously identified as having an emotional/behavioral disability (*Act 230 in Vermont*, 1995).

In 1996, the Department of Education asserted that success was endangered unless "adequate, predictable, and flexible funding" was provided. They noted that

if support is not able to be provided to those not eligible for special education, parents and schools will begin to identify more students. This will result in a huge step backward and in expensive increases in paperwork, meetings and evaluations. (*Vermont's Act 230*, 1996, p. 3)

Kentucky

Inclusive education is a facet of Kentucky's overall school restructuring efforts, the 1990 Kentucky Education Reform Act (KERA), perhaps the most comprehensive reform program of any state (*KERA Program Outline*, 1994). A major component is the Collaborative Teaching Model, which sustains students with a variety of ability levels in a general education setting, including those who have disabilities, are gifted, and/or are at risk of school failure. Collaborative teams work daily to plan, implement, and evaluate instructional strategies appropriate for each student to meet success. The model focuses on the interaction between the general education teacher and "strategic" teachers working together to educate students of all abilities in the general classroom. The teams consist at a minimum of a general education teacher, a strategic teacher, and a school administrator.

Based on interviews with 17 special education directors, drawn from a stratified random sample of districts, on the impact of KERA on special education funding and programs, Montgomery (1995) reported that the directors viewed the new funding system as an improvement over the previous mechanism. Improvements were noted not only in funding as such but also in program consequences for students with disabilities.

They perceived the new system as having greater incentives for inclusion and fewer incentives to label children than the previous system.

Most directors viewed increased spending flexibility at the district level, resulting from the blending of special and regular education funds, as a major strength of the funding system. This flexibility was particularly helpful in providing opportunities for staff development and in purchasing materials and supplies for school use. Many directors felt that the blending of funds was moving districts toward greater funding equity, and an increased ability to meet the needs of individual students. Due to more collaborative teaching practices, they perceived that decisions related to the placement of students with disabilities were being more carefully considered and examined. (p. 19)

Michigan

In 1992, the Michigan State Board of Education adopted a *Position Statement on Inclusive Education*, which defines *inclusive education* as

the provision of educational services for students with disabilities, in schools where nonhandicapped peers attend, in age-appropriate *general education classes under the direct supervision of general education teachers, with special education support and assistance as determined appropriate through the individualized educational planning committee* [emphasis in original]. (p. 1)

Based on this position statement, an Inclusive Education Recommendations Committee was established to develop specific recommendations for needed changes in policy, funding, and legislation. The committee's report included the following propositions:

1. Resident school districts must be responsible for the education of all of their students.
2. There is an emerging standard established by both case law and research on integration/inclusion, as well as an overriding standard based on effective educational practice, that holds that the preferred mode of operation is for all students to be educated together in local schools with support provided according to individual needs.
3. A continuum of services must be defined as full-time general education with support to full-time special education in a general education building.
4. School improvements in general education, as part of Public Act 25, must provide the umbrella effort for improving instructional practice for all students including those with disabilities. Dual and parallel systems must be merged in favor of a unified system.
5. All students have unique educational needs, and assessing functional disability is important to help identify the type and level of support that is necessary. The current practice of categorical labeling is largely irrelevant in determining educational support needs for individual students.
6. Funding systems must be designed to provide incentives for the development of inclusive schools, and current funding practices

that perpetuate the maintenance of separate programs and dual systems must be eliminated.

7. Inservice and staff development efforts must be focused at the building level. The emphasis must be on improving classroom instruction so that students and staff are learning together and effective education practices are implemented.

8. Teacher training at the preservice level must be integrated and must prepare teachers who can demonstrate effective educational practices for all students including those with disabilities in general education classrooms. (*Final Report*, 1993, p. 35)

In 1993, the Michigan State Board of Education commissioned a study of characteristics considered necessary for educating students with disabilities in the 21st century (Frey, Bang, & Lynch, 1993). More than 200 people, representing the full range of constituency groups, were surveyed. Four requisites were identified as "fundamental":

1. Retain current due process protection for students with disabilities.
2. Address the functional needs of students.
3. Redesign school curriculums and assessment systems to accommodate the needs and learning styles of all students.
4. Provide transition services to all students with disabilities.

Beyond these four critical components, a number of other factors also were identified by Frey et al. (1993) as deserving of priority in education:

1. Special needs services available to all students should include community-based education and transition services.
2. Schools should meet different and individual needs of students.
3. Schools should communicate the full range of educational options available to students.
4. The purpose of special education should be to provide support to general education.
5. Special education and general education should function as a single entity with flexibility to provide needed services to all students.
6. Transition services and planning should be common practice.

Indiana

The Indiana LRE Statewide Task Force identified the following problems in the state's special education program: overreferral, stigmatization of students in special education, isolation of students in special education, programmatic disruption of the "pull-out" model, and dislocation from the students' home community (*Guidelines for*

Implementation, 1994). In implementing a new design, the task force specified four underlying assumptions:

1. The goals of schooling for all students—including those with disabilities—include more than academic achievement.
2. The characteristics of excellent schools and effective instruction are consistent across "general" and "special" education.
3. Students with disabilities are more like their typical peers than they are different, and the delivery of special education must reflect that similarity.
4. Implementing LRE provisions will require systems change.

New Mexico

In 1991, the New Mexico Department of Education issued an administrative policy on full inclusion (*Administrative Policy*, 1991):

> The New Mexico State Department of Education believes that all students must be educated in school environments which fully include rather than exclude them. School environments include all curricular, co-curricular, and extra-curricular programs and activities.
> Full inclusion means that all children must be educated in supported, heterogeneous, age-appropriate, natural, child-focused classrooms, school and community environments for the purpose of preparing them for full participation in our diverse and integrated society. [Emphasis in original.]

Describing the education system of the early 1990s as based on a "typical/atypical paradigm," the New Mexico policy states that in such an arrangement the

> central responsibility of teachers and schools . . . [is] find[ing] the dysfunctional students and arranging for someone else to educate them. Inability of children to measure up to an arbitrary and subjective idea of what is typical communicates to the child and others that the child is unable to perform and that something less is expected from the child. (*Administrative Policy*, 1991)

The vision of full inclusion, the policy asserted, incorporates high expectations for all students, understands that everyone learns cooperatively, and assumes that schools are both places of learning and social institutions.

Illinois

In a report prepared for the Illinois Planning Council on Developmental Disabilities, Cohen (1994) examined factors present in two states—Colorado and Vermont—that have extensively implemented inclusive education; these factors are not present in Illinois. Cohen identified two key variables:

First, each state has a funding formula [that] is essentially neutral [in relation] to the way children with disabilities are educated. What this means is [that] school districts do not receive any financial reward or incentive for serving children in more restrictive settings. Rather, funding is received independent of the location of services or the restrictiveness of programming. The second key variable in producing more inclusive programming was the emphasis on staff training. (p. 22)

Additional practices in Vermont that support inclusive practices included a clear definition of *inclusion* in the state's law (Act 230), the act's direct support for inclusive practices and tightened definition of eligibility for special services, the absence of segregated schools, a strong tradition of community responsibility for education, and the state education department's involvement of the teachers' union as inclusion plans were developed (Cohen, 1994). The report noted that in Colorado there has been extensive participation of parents in planning for inclusion, in the state's providing for substantial parental choice in the decision-making process, and in the shift from a deficit-based model of education (Cohen, 1994).

Comparing Illinois districts that were inclusive with those that were not, Cohen (1994) found that in the former, administrators evidenced a strong commitment to inclusion, supports were provided for teachers and students with disabilities in the general education environment, and significant in-service training was provided for general and special education teachers, leading to a high level of team teaching between general and special educators: "As an outgrowth of the above variables, these schools manifested a higher level of staff and community support for inclusion" (p. 27). In contrast, Cohen reported that in those districts that were "non-inclusive," administrators explicitly rejected inclusion as a desirable model for services to children with disabilities, a view reflected among school staff.

A number of other states have established inclusive education initiatives:

Arizona Arizona's systems change grant has placed special emphasis on preparing personnel working in rural areas to support inclusive education programs.

Connecticut In 1992, the Connecticut State Board of Education adopted a policy that "supports the concept that the goals of special education and the expectations for students with disabilities are the same as those outlined for all students in Connecticut's Common Core of Learning." That policy further states that "the Board presumes that these goals are best achieved in the school the student would attend if he/she did not have a disability."

Regional inclusive education resource/support teams, funded by the state's Developmental Disabilities Planning Council, support local districts and families of students with developmental and other disabilities interested in general classes in local public schools.

Delaware   The Delaware State Board of Education and the Department of Public Instruction have sponsored a study concerning the development of integrated intensive learning center programs in the general classroom.

Florida   The Florida State Department of Education's strategic plan for exceptional students includes a specific strategy on inclusion.

Georgia   The Governor's Council on Developmental Disabilities conducts a program, "Better All Together," that supports local school district efforts.

Iowa   The Iowa State Department of Education initiative, "Reorganizing the Delivery of Special Services," encourages local districts to develop new service delivery designs, in addition to supporting staff development and providing latitude in funding innovations.

Kansas   The Kansas Statewide Systems Change Project has developed a "checklist" for identifying characteristics of effective inclusion programs (*Kansas Checklist*, 1993), and the state has provided support to school district initiatives.

Louisiana   A Louisiana study has identified "barriers and bridges to inclusive education" in the state (Skrtic & Sailor, 1993). Among the "barriers" are the use of centralized pupil appraisal teams, which tend to diminish the will and capacity of building-level personnel to solve instructional and management problems, and the state's special education funding formula. Among the "bridges" are the state's program monitoring practices and plans to reconsider the funding formula.

Maine   The Maine LEARNS (Local Education for All in Regular Neighborhood Schools) project assists local school districts in developing inclusive schools for all students. It has developed a set of "guidelines" for such schools (*Guidelines for Inclusive Schools*, n.d.).

Massachusetts   An experimental grants program in Massachusetts, "Restructuring for Integration of All Students," provides support to seven districts for a 5-year period, with an explicit mandate to incorporate inclusion within school restructuring.

New Jersey   The New Jersey State Department of Education has established an inclusion network of 18 districts.

New York   The New York State Board of Regents has adopted a "Least Restrictive Environment Implementation Policy Paper."

The State Education Department has funded a score of districts as part of a statewide systems change project. In New York City schools, District 75[4] has taken the lead in developing inclusive education programs for students with severe disabilities, while some community school districts, such as District 1 in Lower Manhattan, have developed programs to include students with mild and moderate disabilities.

Ohio Ohio's Project Apex (Assistance for Principals Operating Experimental Models) provides in-service training, technical assistance, university credit, and other resources for building principals.

Oklahoma The closing of the Hisson Institute, a facility for people with severe disabilities, has sparked statewide efforts toward inclusion. A program quality checklist guides state activities.

Oregon Oregon offers three levels of training to school districts: general awareness, personnel training at school sites in which inclusion is being initiated, and specialized training for school personnel designed to institutionalize inclusion.

Pennsylvania Since 1990, instructional support teams (ISTs) have served as prereferral intervention groups linking all school resources in the state of Pennsylvania. To date, more than 1,400 elementary and middle schools in the state's school districts have initiated the IST approach. IST program evaluations report that the longer the school is involved in it, the more likely teachers are to use the process; in schools that are using the IST approach, referral rates for multidisciplinary evaluations are one third to one half of those of schools that have not yet implemented the process; and schools implementing the process have reduced retention rates by as much as 67% (Kovaleski, Tucker, & Stevens, 1996).

A 1995 circular from the Pennsylvania commissioner for elementary and secondary education stated that in the planning process, "consideration of the regular class *must* be the starting place for any decision-making about the placement of any special education student"; the directive emphasizes that "an inclusive placement is not dependent on a demonstration or prediction that there will be an incremental or additional benefit from inclusion.

---

[4]In the New York City Public Schools, for administrative purposes, students identified with severe impairments are assigned to District 75, which conducts programs in separate buildings and separate classes. Approximately 18,000 students are served by District 75. Students identified with mild and moderate impairments are served by the 32 community school districts and the High School Division. Approximately 130,000 students are served in these latter programs.

A child need not prove his or her way into a regular class or regular school building."

Rhode Island The Rhode Island State Department of Education used a request for proposal process to identify and support local districts that had an interest in implementing inclusion programs. The state Developmental Disabilities Planning Council has published a state *Guide to Inclusive Education in Rhode Island: Resource Persons and Promising Practices* (1993).

Texas The Texas State Education Agency has developed a paper, "A Leadership Initiative for Improving Special Education Services in Texas," which includes as one of its objectives developing the capacity to help districts "to fully include any student in regular education with necessary support to ensure student success." The state is funding a cost analysis and program evaluation of several pilot programs.

Washington The Washington State Center for Supportive Education works to increase the capacity of programs statewide to serve students with disabilities in typical settings and to minimize the use of segregated classroom or program placements. Statewide focus groups are addressing meeting the needs in inclusive settings of students with behavior problems or serious behavior disorders and are providing effective supports for students with disabilities who also are multicultural or bilingual.

West Virginia A 1992 "Integrated Educational Initiative Plan" guides activities, including systemic planning and collaborative efforts in West Virginia. School-based inclusion implementation teams have been formed at 14 pilot schools in the state.

Wisconsin A statewide inclusion initiative in Wisconsin committed $500,000 per year (starting in 1993) to developing and testing activities and assumptions related to inclusion.

CONCLUSION

This chapter's survey of the broad national developments concerning inclusive education, as well as the practices of selected states, reveals a number of common features in the movement toward inclusion: the importance of leadership, collaboration across the lines of general and special education, the need for changes in pedagogy and school staffing, and financial issues.

A set of central themes are expressed in a framework for state policies to promote educating all students in general education (Fisher et al., 1995). State policy goals for six key aspects of systemic reform are identified as follows:

Funding: Students with and without disabilities are financed under a single, unified funding system which supports the varied learning needs and abilities of all students.

Governance: Students with and without disabilities are effectively represented under a single administrative structure within the educational system at the state and local levels that serves all students, rather than a dual system for regular and special education.

Curriculum: Students with and without disabilities are educated under a single curriculum based on curriculum frameworks or guidelines that are sufficiently comprehensive to support the learning of all students.

Teacher education and licensure, and in-service professional development: The state has developed a comprehensive system of professional development through which all teachers, administrators, and staff collaborate to possess the capacity to work with a variety of students.

Assessment: Students with and without disabilities participate in a broad set of assessments, each aligned with state and local standards for curricula content and student performance. Students with all types of disabilities, including significant cognitive impairments, are provided alternative assessments, when necessary, along with the full range of accommodations.

Accountability: Students with and without disabilities are included in accountability systems in a consistent and equitable manner. (Fisher et al., 1995).

The chapter following describes inclusive education activities at the local school district level.

REFERENCES

Act 230 in Vermont: What's happening? (1996, March). Montpelier: Vermont Department of Education.

Administrative policy on full inclusion. (1991). Santa Fe, NM: Department of Education.

Cohen, M.D. (1994). *Overcoming barriers to the inclusion of children with disabilities in the local schools: A blueprint for change.* Report prepared for the Illinois Planning Council on Developmental Disabilities. Springfield: Illinois Planning Council on Developmental Disabilities.

Creating schools for all our students: What twelve schools have to say. (1995). Reston, VA: Council for Exceptional Children.

Does inclusion cost more? (1994). *Inclusive Education Programs, 1*(5), 4–5.

Ferguson, D.L., Meyer, G., Jeanchild, L., Juniper, L., & Zingo, J. (1992). Figuring out what to do with the grownups: How teachers make inclusion "work" for students with disabilities. *Journal of The Association for Persons with Severe Handicaps, 17*(4), 218–226.

Final report of the Inclusive Education Recommendations Committee. (1993). Lansing, MI: Department of Education.

Fisher, D., Tweit-Hull, D., Sax, C., & Rodifer, K. (1995, December 2). *Beyond teacher deals: School site collaboration and reform.* Paper presented at TASH Conference, San Francisco.

Frey, W.D., Bank, M., & Lynch, L. (1993). *Special education into the 21st century: A survey looking into the future of education for students with disabilities in Michigan.* Lansing, MI: Disability Research System.

Guide to inclusive education in Rhode Island: Resource persons and promising practices. (1993). Providence: Rhode Island Developmental Disabilities Council.

Guidelines for implementation of the Least Restrictive Environment provisions of the Individuals with Disabilities Education Act and Indiana's Article 7. (1994). Indianapolis: LRE Statewide Task Force.

Guidelines for inclusive schools. (n.d.). Orono: University of Maine, Center for Community Inclusion.

Individuals with Disabilities Education Act (IDEA) of 1990, PL 101-476, 20 U.S.C. § 1400 *et seq.*

The Kansas checklist for identifying characteristics of effective inclusion programs. (1993). Topeka: Kansas State Board of Education.

Katsiyannis, A., Conderman, G., & Franks, D.J. (1995). State practices on inclusion: A national review. *Remedial and Special Education, 16*(5), 279–287.

KERA program outline: Inclusion of students with disabilities in general education settings. (1994). Frankfort: Kentucky Department of Education.

Kovaleski, J.F., Tucker, J.A., & Stevens, L.J. (1996). Bridging special and regular education: The Pennsylvania initiative. *Educational Leadership, 53*(5), 44–47.

McLaughlin, M.J., & Warren, S.H. (1994). *Resource implications of inclusion: Impressions of special education administrators at selected sites.* Palo Alto, CA: Center for Special Education Finance.

Michigan State Board of Education. (1992). *Position statement on inclusive education.* Lansing, MI: Author.

Montgomery, D.L. (1995). *The impact of Kentucky Education Reform Act on special education programs and services: Perceptions of special education directors.* Palo Alto, CA: Center for Special Education Finance.

Morra, L.G. (1994). *Special education reform: Districts grapple with inclusion programs.* Washington, DC: U.S. General Accounting Office.

National Study of Inclusive Education. (1994). New York: The City University of New York, National Center on Educational Restructuring and Inclusion.

National Study of Inclusive Education. (1995). New York: The City University of New York, National Center on Educational Restructuring and Inclusion.

Putnam, J.W. (Ed.). (1995). *Cooperative learning and strategies for inclusion: Celebrating diversity in the classroom.* Baltimore: Paul H. Brookes Publishing Co.

Skrtic, T.M., & Sailor, W. (1993). *Barriers and bridges to inclusive education: An analysis of Louisiana special education policy.* Lawrence: Kansas University Affiliated Program.

Vermont's Act 230 and special education reform. (1996, Winter). Montpelier: Vermont Department of Education.

Villa, R., Thousand, J.S., Meyers, H., & Nevin, A. (1993). Regular and special education teachers and administrator perceptions of heterogeneous education. Unpublished manuscript.

Ysseldyke, J. (1987). Classification of handicapped students. In M.C. Wang, M.C. Reynolds, & H.J. Walberg (Eds.), *Handbook of special education: Research and practice: Vol. 1. Learner characteristics and adaptive education* (pp. 253–272). New York: Pergamon Press.

11

PROGRAM IMPLEMENTATION

As inclusive education programs have been implemented across the United States, a growing body of data and reports has focused on their implementation. These data come from local school districts, from state department of education reports, and from studies conducted by university researchers and professional and research organizations. Key among the latter are studies of the National Center of Educational Restructuring and Inclusion (NCERI) (*National Study of Inclusive Education* [henceforth, *National Study*], 1994, 1995), the National Association of State Boards of Education (NASBE) (*Winning Ways: Creating Inclusive Schools, Classrooms, and Communities*, by Roach, 1995), and the Working Group on Inclusive Schools (*Creating Schools for All of Our Students: What 12 Schools Have to Say* [henceforth, *Creating Schools*], 1994). Together, they reflect both the growth of inclusive education and its effectiveness.

In 1994 and 1995, the NCERI collected extensive national data on the implementation of inclusive education in school districts. In addition, the center collected personal accounts by teachers, administrators, parents, and students involved in inclusive education. To identify local school districts, the NCERI contacted each chief state school officer, seeking nominations of local districts conducting inclusive education programs. The school superintendents in these districts and in other school districts identified through federal projects and national organizations were contacted for information about the district's inclusive education programs and activities. The material in this chapter and in Chapters 12 (on classroom supports) and 14 (on program evaluation) is drawn extensively from the NCERI studies, with excerpts included from school district reports. This material is augmented by the NASBE and Working Group on Inclusive Schools reports and other research studies.

This chapter is organized into nine sections covering program initiation, the range of students involved, school staffing, changing personnel roles, staff attitudes, professional development and leadership, parental attitudes, fiscal issues, and student responses.

PROGRAM INITIATION

There is no single point of entry or even a general pattern of how inclusive education programs were first initiated in local school districts. Rather, programs were established in a variety of ways, through the efforts of parents; teachers, both general and special education; administrators, both school principals and district superintendents; clinicians and related services providers; state or district reform initiatives; federally funded systems change projects; and court decisions (see Chapter 9 for further discussion of the latter).

The National Association of State Boards of Education (NASBE), based on data from schools across the United States, has identified four ways in which districts typically initiate inclusive education programs: 1) a case-by-case evolutionary process; 2) pilot programs; 3) a comprehensive, phased-in approach; and 4) complete conversion to districtwide inclusion (Roach, 1995, pp. 15–17).

Commenting on the merits of each of these approaches, the NASBE report stated that the "case by case" approach has the disadvantage of being ad hoc in nature, is less likely to involve the board of education, and "does not force a district to consider how the *system* [emphasis in original] must be realigned to promote inclusion (i.e., how funding mechanisms, teaming and grading policies, teacher hiring and evaluation, and staff assignments must be adjusted)" (Roach, 1995, p. 15). The "pilot program" approach usually is initiated by the district special education director and is limited by being perceived as a special education initiative and as requiring additional funding, which districts often are unable to afford (Roach, 1995).

According to the NASBE report, the "comprehensive, phased-in approach" generally has been initiated by a superintendent, a strong supporter of inclusion, who has soon left the district. The superintendent then has been succeeded by a less-supportive successor; nevertheless, the inclusion initiative has been continued by supportive principals, who have maintained the effort on a school-by-school basis. In these districts, inclusion generally has been phased in grade by grade, starting with prekindergarten and kindergarten and adding one or two grades in each subsequent year.

> In these cases, all students start school in classrooms of diverse learners and continue in inclusive environments as they progress through their school careers. Teachers and administrators report that with this type of implementation, the general education students themselves become key elements in training teachers as they advance through the grades. (Roach, 1995, p. 17)

The fourth approach, "complete conversion to districtwide inclusion," occurs in "small or rural districts that are used to operating flexibly, have a small administrative staff, and have a very receptive staff and community" (Roach, 1995, p. 17).

The grade level at which inclusive education programs are first initiated varies widely across the United States. The *National Study* (1995) reported that although school districts initiate inclusion programs at *all* grade levels, from preschool through high school, programs most often are initiated at the early elementary level. Programs may first be established in single classrooms, across a grade level, buildingwide, and/or districtwide. When success is established or students move to another grade level, inclusive education programs often are initiated at that new level. In some school districts, the changes are instituted simultaneously at all levels as part of a larger restructuring effort and a new district philosophy. In a few instances, intermediate units have initiated the process, whereas in other cases they have responded to member district initiatives (*National Study*, 1995).

The question often is raised as to which category of disability generally is addressed first in an inclusive education program. The *National Study* (1995) found no single pattern. Initiation of inclusive education began with students with mild and moderate disabilities, as well as with students with significant impairments. Often, school districts that first initiated an inclusion program with students with mild or moderate impairments have emphasized the similarity of such students with students without disabilities and view their instruction as part of a broader blending. Conversely, districts that have first initiated inclusion programs with students with significant impairments have also reported success with that approach, owing, in part, to the additional resources that follow such students and to support from federal systemwide change projects. No single disability category lends itself to the initiation of inclusive education more successfully than another.

Although the data in NCERI's *National Study* (1994, 1995), the NASBE study (Roach, 1995), and the Working Forum on Inclusive Schools report (*Creating Schools,* 1994) are not strictly compa-rable, the findings on the relative advantage of program initiation approaches are similar. The limits of the case-by-case approach are confirmed in both the NCERI studies and in the Working Forum report, the latter of which reviewed a dozen school districts imple-menting inclusive education. Likewise, the benefits of the compre-hensive, phased-in approach are asserted in all three reports. School districts indicate that successful initiation of inclusion by whatever approach can lead to broader inclusion efforts. Data from all three reports indicate that to ensure successful *and* ongoing implementa-tion of inclusive education, the following systemic issues must be addressed: district policy, funding mechanisms, staff assignments and personnel utilization patterns, curricular redesign, testing, and grading policies.

The planning process in some school districts is informal. In oth-ers, it is comprehensive and ongoing. Following are excerpts of reports from district administrators surveyed in the *National Study* (1995).

> The school discussed the topic [inclusion], pro and con, and wrote a Site-Based Restructuring Plan. . . [that] called for inclusion of special education students full time into the regular education classroom. An aide would be hired for every 10 special education students, and the special education teacher would develop a schedule for her and the aide to assist [general] teachers and students. . . . [C]ollaborative planning was developed on a weekly basis and a substitute hired to allow the regular education teacher time to plan with the special edu-cation teacher. The school wrote into the pilot the need for software and computers and other audio aids for students. [These] were granted. (pp. 110–111)
>
> *Hammond Public Schools, Indiana*

> In 1990, a team of 30 individuals, representing a broad cross-section of staff and community members, developed 16 beliefs about educa-tion, general parameters for which the district will accomplish the mission, and . . . the district mission statement. This strategic plan-ning team merged with the framework for a comprehensive strategic plan, [which] has allowed the district to "create the future," not merely react to it. Many of the . . . strategies in this plan have a direct impact on the inclusion process. (p. 183)
>
> *Burnsville-Eagle-Savage Public Schools,*
> *Independent School District #191, Minnesota*

> The development of a plan for implementing inclusion is closely tied to Goals 2000. Inclusion was the first program to prompt the schools to such activities as developing vision and mission statements, institut-ing core teams to make recommendations at the school level, and un-dertaking large-scale staff development in the new direction. (p. 288)
>
> *Cumberland School Department, Rhode Island*

The [inclusion] process was [instigated by] a top-down directive for all to begin using inclusion practices district-wide. The inclusion practices were a part of a strategic plan to begin teaching all children, regardless of their needs, as individuals. Initially, the staff resisted the inclusive model; now, however, they say they would never go back to the "old" way. (p. 360)

Boyceville Public Schools, Wisconsin

DISABILITY CATEGORY AND GRADE LEVEL

Data from school districts across the United States indicate that students within each of IDEA's 13 categories of disability, at all levels of severity and in all grade levels, are effectively integrated in inclusion programs (*National Study*, 1995). A number of school districts provide inclusion opportunities at all schools in the district, at all grade levels, and serve students with all types of disabilities. Other districts, starting with one or more schools, have committed themselves to districtwide programs over time. Many districts include all students with a particular disability—most frequently those with mild impairments and, particularly, students identified as having learning disabilities. Many others have included all of the students at particular grade levels—most frequently in the elementary grades, on occasion at the middle school level, and rarely at the high school level.

Excerpts from school districts reports in the *National Study* (1995) on the extent of inclusive education program follow.

Deaf children are included in an inclusive model, with classes taught by a general education teacher and a deaf education teacher, both of whom sign; teachers who sign are given a "bilingual education" bonus. There is no isolation of the deaf students, in the classroom or playground. Hearing students sign. Indeed, at the eighth-grade graduation ceremony, the three hearing students who were chosen as speakers (the fourth was deaf) each signed their speech. (p. 39)

Burbank Unified School District, California

Canton Middle School operates as a full inclusion school with multiage, heterogeneously grouped classes of six, seventh, and eighth graders. The special needs students include 84 who are learning disabled, 37 language impaired, 11 seriously emotionally impaired, 6 moderately intellectually limited, 5 multi-handicapped, 3 other health impaired, 2 with traumatic brain injury, and 2 with hearing impairments. (pp. 150–151)

Baltimore City Schools, Maryland

Special needs students include those with mental retardation, spina bifida, cerebral palsy, profound retardation, autism, visual impairments, hearing impairments, and learning disabilities. (p. 167)

O'Hearn School, Boston Public Schools, Massachusetts

All children with an IEP [individualized education program] have been fully included across the grade levels. Handicapping conditions include L[earning] D[isabled], B[ehaviorally] D[isordered], O[rthopedically] H[andicapped], V[isually] I[mpaired], and EM[otionally] H[andicapped]. The self-contained and itinerant resource rooms have been eliminated. Support services are provided to the regular classroom teachers and other support staff to assure that all students have access to the core curriculum. (p. 195)

Kansas City School District, Missouri

Inclusion activities are currently in place at all levels in the district, from preschool through high school. Children with every disability are part of this process. (p. 199)

Helena School District #1, Montana

As a member of the Coalition of Essential Schools, we are fully inclusive: all students with disabilities are fully included in the mainstream of regular education. (p. 203)

Souhegan High School,
Souhegan School District, New Hampshire

Inclusion is now a full-blown activity for [kindergarten through eighth] grade. All of the students who are residents of this township attend their age-appropriate class, in their neighborhood school, and are assigned to regular education classrooms. (p. 205)

Clinton Township School District, New Jersey

We do not have any self-contained classes at any level, which results in all of our special education students being involved in classes with their grade-level peers. (p. 239)

Southern Cayuga Central School District, New York

All students with disabilities who live in the school district have the opportunity to be totally included in the regular classroom and the extracurricular activities of their school. The only criterion for a student to attend any of our six elementary schools, our middle school or our high school is that they must be breathing. Our school district does not view inclusion as a program. It is part of our total belief and practice. It goes part and parcel with the idea that our responsibility is to all children. If inclusion is only used as a way to deal with special education students, it will never accomplish anything. (p. 260)

Ontario School District, Oregon

High School–Level Inclusion

Emphasis on the mastery of content in high school, as well as the size and structure of schools at this level, have led some professionals to believe that inclusion in high schools is, at best, difficult. Other school professionals, however, believe that student peers at this stage can represent a valuable resource. This point has been strongly made by Flynn, who was superintendent of an inclusive school district, the Waterloo Region Catholic School System, Ontario, Canada (see Flynn & Innes, 1992; Flynn & Kowalczyk-McPhee, 1989).

Souhegan High School (New Hampshire) provides an instructive example. It is a fully inclusive school: All students with disabilities are totally included in the mainstream of general education. Inclusion has been part of the school's overall restructuring; reform efforts have included interdisciplinary planning teams, community-based instruction for all students, case management, and an Academic Support Center that is available to all students. There are three key program components in Souhegan's efforts:

1. *Collaborative planning time*, by both special and general education teachers
2. *Curriculm design characterized by planning backward* from expected outcomes and a final student exhibition to the details of lesson design
3. *"Essential questions"*—overarching questions (or statements) used to guide performance-based curriculum development (Jorgensen, 1994–1995, p. 52)

This last feature, "essential questions," is an aspect of the perspective of the Coalition of Essential Schools, a major national educational restructuring effort led by Ted Sizer at Brown University. This feature enables all students, regardless of their level, to participate in the responses. In developing an inclusive curriculum, teachers at Souhegan High School have found that students with disabilities can participate in many activities without modifications. When modifications are necessary, these may include support from an adult or a classmate; altered, adapted, or substitute materials; assistive technology; and changes in expectations, assignments, or assessment mode (Tashie et al., 1993).

In the excerpts following, a parent reports on the experiences of her son at a New York high school, and the science department chairperson at a Texas high school reports on the impact on students without disabilities (*National Study*, 1995).

> "K" walks through the halls of Brewster High School with his numbered sports shirt and his hat turned backwards. He's showing the world "he's one of the guys." He entered Brewster High School less than 2 years ago as a young ninth grader. It was difficult for "K," as he had not gone through the Brewster school system.
>
> Although the teenage years are both sensitive and demanding, "K" has managed to emerge as a fairly normal teenager, if there is a such a thing! It's been a team effort that makes "K's" school experience extremely rewarding. The whole team approach has proven to be a

huge success. His teachers, along with the special area teachers, are a cohesive group. They believe in the principle of inclusion in the student's everyday work effort. I am very pleased with "K's" progress. At present, he is on the honor roll.

Coach "B" is an excellent example of dedication to children who have disabilities. He worked diligently to organize the first baseball Challenge League. These teams are the first of their kind in the county. This activity sparks both pleasure and enthusiasm, as well as team discipline.

From a student's point of view, the feelings and opinions flow easily from my son's lips. He feels inclusion is beneficial and rewarding. Brewster High School has a Junior ROTC program of which "K" is a member. He stands for inspections, marches, and takes a class in U.S. Naval History.

To enhance his program further, the Brewster district is ordering a laptop computer. ["K"] will also continue a vocational program in conjunction with his regular studies . . . [which will] explore different avenues of employment suitable for [him]. "K" will also be included in a driver's ed program. Altogether, his whole school experience reflects the inclusion philosophy of the Brewster school district. (pp. 222–223)

Parent of a high school student,
Brewster Central School District, New York

I believe that regular education students benefit from inclusion, too. I am not sure we will be able to measure these benefits with TAAS [state test] scores; however, inclusion is providing students with positive life experiences. [As general education] students help the special students, they gain a sense of importance, and their own self-image seems to improve.

Academically, the regular education students gain because of the relearning that occurs as they teach concepts to "their student." In addition, because these students know that someone needs their help, they are more attentive; therefore, their behavior is improved. Finally, the special education co-teacher provides the regular education students with academic support by offering additional opportunities beyond those provided the regular education teacher. All persons in the inclusion classroom reap benefits from this arrangement. (pp. 337–338)

High school science department chairperson,
Texas City Independent School District

SCHOOL STAFFING

Many staffing models are used by school districts to support inclusive education (*National Study*, 1995). This section of the chapter describes several of those models. Briefly, the models include

- A co-teaching, or collaborative teaching, model, whereby a general education and a special education teacher share a classroom

- A consultant model, whereby the special education teacher serves as a "consultant" to one or more general education teachers
- A teaming model, whereby teachers on one grade level team with a special education teacher added by the district
- A "methods and resources teacher model" (first developed in New Brunswick, Canada), involving a special education teacher (a methods and resources teacher) whose students are placed full time in general education classes. This teacher works with general education teachers to support curriculum and material adaptations and to provide demonstration lessons.

In a number of national studies and reports on inclusion, co-teaching has been identified as the most widely used model of teacher collaboration ("Collaboration," 1996; *Creating Schools,* 1994; "Great Co-teaching," 1996; King-Sears & Cummings, 1996; Mercer, Lane, Jordan, Allsopp, & Eisele, 1996; *National Study,* 1995; Roach, 1995; Walter-Thomas, Bryant, & Land, 1996; Werts, Wolery, Snyder, & Caldwell, 1996). *Co-teaching* has been defined as "an educational approach in which general and special education educators or related service providers jointly plan for and teach heterogeneous groups of students in integrated settings" (Bauwens, Hourcade, & Friend, 1989, p. 19). Within this broad pattern, there are a number of designs:

- *One teacher, one support* One teacher leads the class while another circulates and provides individual support or observes to gather data.
- *Parallel teaching* The teachers divide the class into heterogeneous groups and teach them simultaneously.
- *Station teaching* Teachers divide content and students, unlike parallel teaching, where the content is essentially the same.
- *Alternative teaching* One teacher leads enrichment or alternative activities, while the second teacher reviews concepts with small groups needing reteaching.
- *Team teaching* The teachers work together to deliver the same material to the entire class. (Cooke & Friend, cited in "Great Co-teaching," 1996, p. 4)

Effective co-teaching requires planning between the teachers. It involves discussions and mutual consent around such issues as overall instructional philosophy, respective roles and responsibilities, instructional content, teaching strategies, discipline and other classroom management issues, outcomes for students, and evaluation. Teachers have identified conflict resolution skills and a sense of humor as important when working closely together (*National Study,* 1995).

The broader topic of supports for successful inclusion has been identified from the teachers' perspective in several studies. ("Great Co-teaching," 1996; Walter-Thomas et al., 1996). The *National Study* (1995) has found that teachers have identified the following classroom practices as supportive of inclusive education: multilevel instruction, cooperative learning, activity-based learning, mastery learning, use of technology, peer support, and tutoring programs. Based on an intensive survey in Pennsylvania and a national mail survey, Werts et al. (1996) found that three categories of support were ranked highest: training, support from a team of professionals, and having help in the classroom.

Kentucky, under its statewide Collaborative Teaching Model, has developed three designs for linking the general education teacher with the "strategic teacher" (e.g., the latter could be a special education teacher, a teacher of gifted students, a speech-language pathologist, Chapter 1 teachers, remediation teachers). These designs are

- *Complementary instruction*, whereby the general education teacher takes the main responsibility for the subject matter, and the strategic teacher works with the mastery of specific skills based on the subject matter
- *Role reversal teaming (dual certification)*, whereby both the general education teacher and the strategic teacher are certified in elementary education. Here the teachers jointly develop instruction and implement it according to their individual strengths and preferences.
- *Supportive learning style,* whereby both teachers share responsibility for planning. The general education teacher provides basic instruction on the essential content, and the strategic teacher designs and implements supportive and supplementary materials, activities, instruction, and so forth.

Collaboration between and among teachers is a key element in the success of inclusive education programs. The previously mentioned Working Group on Inclusive Schools assembled representatives of a dozen schools implementing inclusive education, all of which used an aspect of co-teaching. The Working Group report stated the following:

> General education teachers and special education teachers bring a tremendous amount of knowledge and skills to the task of teaching, and by being paired they pool their expertise. "When you put two teachers together, you get more than double," says one co-teacher.
>
> One of the benefits of co-teaching is that partners provide each other with evaluation and feedback. While one teacher teaches, the co-

teacher can act as an audience, sensing when some students are floundering and in need of further instruction. (*Creating Schools*, 1994, p. 21)

Beyond the work of individual pairs of teachers, general and special education teachers are teaming up increasingly in work groups to support inclusion of students with disabilities. Such groups provide support and suggestions to solve the educational and emotional problems that teachers encounter as they work to improve educational outcomes for all students. Ferguson (1994) cited three important features of these teacher work groups: 1) they are teacher directed, 2) they are outcome based, and 3) they focus on continuing evaluation and improvement.

Following are excerpted reports of staffing and organization models from some of the school districts in the *National Study* (1995). These reports illustrate the previously described models in practice, show how a variety of models can be successful, and give some sense of the range of activities across the United States.

The Full Inclusion programs [for students with severe impairments] are run with approximately the same staffing ratio as a Severely Handicapped Special Day Class, about 9–12 students, one teacher, and two instructional assistants. Fully included student [is] counted as one of the general education teacher's class caseload, not as an additional student (e.g., 1 of 30 students, not 30 plus 1 more student). In addition, a Memorandum of Understanding between the Napa Valley Educators Association and Napa Valley Unified School District has been written. It provides opportunities for the general education teacher to visit classrooms where full inclusion is taking place, to participate in staff development, and to have access to training funds. The general education teacher has the opportunity to review the IEP and, if appropriate, to participate in the development of a new IEP. The general education teacher and special education staff jointly plan for curriculum adaptation, level of support to be provided, safety issues, behavior interventions, and curricular modifications. A teacher support group has been established. (p. 52)
Napa Valley Unified School, California

The inclusion model at the Seven Springs Elementary School serves students with specific learning disabilities (SLD), grades 2–5, in integrated mixed-grade pods. Each pod is taught by a team of four teachers, with a specialized teacher in SLD serving as a fifth member of the team, . . . assisting both SLD and non-SLD students, as needed. Instructional planning and interventions are collaboratively decided upon by the teacher team. (p. 83)
District School Board of Pasco County, Florida

The cooperative [collaborative] model, which places an additional instructor in general education classes, has indeed been extremely supportive of inclusion. With two teachers providing instruction, far more student accommodations/adaptations can be provided. Opportunities for re-teaching are greater. Greater individualization of instructional materials can be achieved with cooperative teachers. (p. 114)

Marshalltown Community Schools, Iowa

[Canton Middle School] is a home-based community school [grades 6–8] with the number of special needs students being in proportion to those in the area. The school has been divided into five teams of 150 students with five general educators and two special educators. Each team has five classes with approximately 30 students per class, of which 6 students in each class have special needs. (p. 150)

Baltimore City Schools, Maryland

Special education students with severe disabilities have long been housed at P.S. 329, a general education school in southern Brooklyn. Based on the initiative of the special education administrators, an inclusion program has been developed for students with severe disabilities. The special education students, who had been in a class with one teacher and three paraprofessionals, are distributed across three general education classes (two students per class), along with an aide assigned full time to each class. The aide is not limited to working with the special education students. The special education classroom teacher serves now as a "methods and resources teacher," assisting the general education teacher through model lessons and direct classroom support, and encourages parental involvement. An inclusion facilitator assists the overall effort. Key to the success of the program is the active engagement of the building's general education principal. (p. 233)

New York City Public Schools, New York

Special education teachers in the district's two elementary and middle schools are part of a three- to four-person collaborative team with general education teachers. Team members share a common planning period daily. Students with disabilities are randomly assigned to heterogeneous home rooms. At the high school, special education teachers are part of each academic department. (p. 227)

Johnson City Central School District, New York

At the Reidsville Intermediate School, the speech teacher also utilizes the inclusion concept to serve her students. Although she occasionally provides individual therapy, she has found language therapy in the regular classroom to be the most successful for her students. (p. 244)

Rockingham County Consolidated Schools, North Carolina

At Dorseyville Middle School [grades 6–8], where 14% of the students are in special education, students are divided into teams and served by four general education teachers and one educational support specialist, [the latter of whom] works with the general education teachers in planning and teaching. This system has been effective not only for the special education students but for others as well who need additional assistance. The teams are also supported by aides and instructional assistants. (p. 276)

Fox Chapel Area School District, Pennsylvania

Special education self-contained resource classes were eliminated in the fall of 1994 and personnel reassigned. Four inclusion specialist positions were developed to help coordinate and support the needs of students in the inclusive classroom. They also instruct and co-teach. Each grade level, pre-K through 6, has an instructional assistant. The Chapter 1 [teacher] and speech therapist also teach in the general classroom. A NEWS Room (Nurturing Education with Support) has been created as an area where all students can go for extra assistance. (p. 325)

Elkhart Independent School District, Texas

PERSONNEL PRACTICES

Implementing inclusive education programs in a school district involves changes in personnel roles and responsibilities. Rather than special education personnel losing their jobs, the individuals may assume different and often more comprehensive responsibilities. For principals, it involves being responsible for all of the staff and students in the building, general and special education. For teachers, it involves working with a diverse group of learners, regardless of their general or special education status. For related services providers, often it means providing the service in general education classrooms and working with the classroom teacher to reinforce the desired student outcomes.

The following are excerpted reports on personnel practices from a sampling of school districts included in the *National Study* (1995):

The role of the principal changes from searching for outside solutions to greater use of building-based interventions, from more focus on behavior to more focus on intervention, from crisis orientation to prevention orientation, from little input into budgeting to greater responsibility for budgeting and expenditures, from limited involvement in programming to greater involvement, . . . from limited responsibility for the IEP development and implementation to increased responsibility, from limited responsibility for compliance to increased responsibility, from options to move the student elsewhere to limited options.

The role of the special education administrators and central office (CO) changes from the CO determining both the what and the how for special education to the building [i.e., the principal and the school staff] determining more of the how and the CO serving as a resource; from management of the special education budget to sharing management of the budget with the schools; from staffing allocations not being a part of the building formulas to allocation becoming a part of the regular planning process; from regular education curriculum supervisors having limited responsibility to greater responsibility. (p. 120)

Des Moines Public Schools, Iowa

Similar changes have occurred in other school districts:

- Boston Public Schools—Special education staff have been moved from the central office to area offices and individual schools.
- Kansas City Public Schools (Missouri)—The role of district special education director has been replaced by the creation of district coordinators.
- Ontario School District (Oregon)—The role of director of special education has changed from one of overseeing the program to acting as a quality control officer and technical assistance person.
- Pittsburgh Public Schools—The Division for Exceptional Children has been restructured. Formerly, special education and regular education were separate departments and were in separate buildings. Now, both come under the Unit of School Support.
- South Burlington School District (Vermont)—The special education director has been given new general education responsibilities.
- Winooski School District (Vermont)—The Pupil Personnel Services Department, a specialized department, has been dissolved, and its functions have become part of the general faculty.

In other noteworthy developments, related services—particularly speech and language therapy—increasingly are being provided in inclusive classrooms. Special educators have long talked about "transdisciplinary" services, whereby all those involved with the student (e.g., teachers, aides, therapists) collaborate on mutual goals. Thereby, as Freagon and Kachur (1993) have stated,

It is possible for a child's speech and language goals to be carried out all day long by each person who works with the child instead of three times a week for twenty minutes as was done in traditional therapy designs. . . . [T]his allows for the implementation of all therapy goals throughout the school day. (p. 19)

The term *role release* has been used to describe specialists working together, sharing their knowledge and skills. This model confronts traditional patterns of separation: specialists' fears that, in training general education teachers, they would eventually work themselves out of a job and general educators' concerns that learning these new skills would overburden them. A speech therapist stated, for example, "If we can show children that the adults can share and learn from each other, then they can learn to share and learn from each other" (*Creating Schools,* 1995, p. 23).

STAFF ATTITUDES

Staff attitudes about inclusive education range widely, from strongly advocating inclusion to strongly opposing it. In general, school districts report that when inclusive education programs have been initiated, staff attitudes have become more positive over time (*National Study,* 1995). Excerpts from some school districts' reports on attitudes toward inclusion follow. These reports provide insights into teachers' attitudes and also illustrate attitude changes over time.

> The transition from solo teaching to team teaching was met with mixed emotions and took some time and effort. As the year progresses, the teams feel more comfortable teaching together. (p. 36)
>
> *North Little Rock School District, Arkansas*

> The [general education] staff has moved beyond their initial concerns about whether they could adequately meet the needs of the special education youngsters. They now see [each] as simply one more student with a unique set of needs. . . . [F]ull inclusion benefits the regular classroom teacher in that the provision of services can often include a few other students that need the services but do not qualify for special education. (p. 40)
>
> *Colusa Unified School District, California*

> In terms of our special education teachers, we initially had staff that ranged from spearheading the inclusion movement to . . . passively agreeing. Our Leemore High School teachers have undergone an interesting "evolution." One of the most important skills they had to learn was how to work with general education teachers and in general education classes. All the veteran [special education] teachers have come to recognize that inclusive education does work. (p. 46)
>
> *Leemore Union High School District, California*

> The attitudes of staff members, both general and special educators, have changed dramatically. Most significantly, special education is no longer seen as something clearly separate and distinct from the larger mission of the school. The lines between general and special education are not as clear as they used to be, and the staff is now comfortable and accepting of this "parameter fusion." (p. 152)
>
> *Baltimore City Schools, Maryland*

> There is continued growth in "ownership" by the regular education staff, a loud cry for continued staff development, and a great unmet need for collaboration/joint planning time. There is still some feeling

among a few regular education staff that they must have an additional assistant/special education teacher with them at all times if students are placed in their class. For the most part, if some training is done with the regular education students and teacher, they are pretty open. (p. 187)

Eden Prairie Public Schools,
Independent School District #272, Minnesota

As a 19-year veteran special education teacher, the transformation from self-contained units to delivering services in a regular education environment required letting go. We were used to running our own little empires. Learning to share space with other teachers was a big adjustment; however, I enjoy teaching much more than I did when working with the traditional special education model. In the past, we instilled almost a learned helplessness in students with disabilities. We did a real disservice to students in special education when we did things for them; now they're learning to be responsible for their own learning. (p. 251)

Connotton Valley Union School District, Ohio

Inclusion has changed my life and career. I worked as an assistant and then a teacher for students with severe disabilities for 10 years. As a teacher, I felt I was doing the right things trying to prepare my students for life after school. But my students would go through the graduation process, move into the work world, and fail. They would end up sitting at home without any support, friendships, fun, or life because they weren't able to work and communicate with other people who didn't have that "special" training. I was looking for some other way to assist my students when I was asked to support a local school district to include a student with severe disabilities in a fifth grade class in the neighborhood school. The timing was perfect for me, even though I didn't know what I was doing. Luckily, my job changed quickly as more parents began to look at inclusion as the right place for their children. I'm sorry to admit, but I had an attitude toward people with disabilities that was mostly made up of charity and sorrow, rather than respect and admiration for who they are as individuals. Inclusion is about so much more than education; it's about friendship, respect, fun and just being a part of the community. It's about valuing people, all people. (p. 267)

Multnomah Education Service District, Oregon

Staff attitudes seem to be constantly improving. During the second year of implementation, there seems to be a significant difference in staff attitude. Basic education teachers seem to be more comfortable with other professionals in their classroom, and special education teachers seem to be adjusting to their new roles. (p. 279)

Hazelton Area School District, Pennsylvania

One example of a change in staff attitude that has pleased a middle school special education teacher is that regular staff no longer feel the need to "run to her" to solve or report every incident that affects one of her students. If a child misbehaves in the cafeteria during lunch, the child is sent to the office, like the other students are, and the special education teacher might not hear about it until the next day. Staff no longer feel that they must make exceptions for [special education] students' behaviors or have [the special educator] dole out the consequences. "That's progress," she reports. (p. 288)

Cumberland School Department, Rhode Island

The most identifiable change in the staff since we started inclusion is the commitment to all children in the classroom. There is no longer a "yours and mine" attitude. Responsibilities for children are shared rather than separated. Inclusion has built a tremendous sense of ownership and pride in the community of our school. The school environment is professional, with more of a sense of respect for one another. Inclusion has bolstered an entirely different working relationship among staff members. This is the best surprise of all. As the learning takes place casually and comfortably among us, we have become professional and personal friends. (p. 361)

Brillon Public Schools, Wisconsin

As the preceding excerpts reflect, teacher attitudes toward inclusive education are affected by the change in the traditional character of their schools that inclusion brings—that is, from an environment in which teachers often work in isolation to one typified by collaborative and collegial modes of instruction. The manner in which inclusion is introduced, the extent to which teachers are participants in—not objects of—the change process, has a critical effect on teachers' attitudes. Two studies of the same set of school districts in the southeastern United States that have been involved in restructuring for inclusive education describe the change process.

A source of resistance to integration stems from the fact that teachers work under conditions described by Goodlad (1984) as "autonomous isolation." That is, they are used to working and making decisions alone, with few links to other teachers. Therefore, teachers assume that any change will have to be accomplished independently, resulting in "double the workload" for them. However, when these general education teachers realize they had input into determining the pace and degree of integration, and also discovered the rewards of cooperative interaction with supportive, enthusiastic special education teachers, the resistance that stemmed from fears about integration's effect on their workload was quelled. (Janney, Snell, Beers, & Raynes, 1995, p. 18)

It is important to realize teachers' crucial roles not only in advancing new ideas but in bringing ideas to fruition. Moreover, a teacher's years of experience contribute a needed "practicality ethic" to proposals for change. In assessing restructuring for inclusion, Janney et al. (1995b) reported that "following their implementation experiences, teachers reevaluated the balance between the costs of teacher time and energy as compared to the benefits for students, and judged the integration effort successful" (p. 17). Teacher orientation played a key part in creating schools "where response to student diversity is individualization instead of pigeonholing. . . . [M]ost importantly, these teachers had developed a sense of their own efficacy in achieving these benefits" (Janney et al., 1993, p. 98).

PROFESSIONAL DEVELOPMENT AND LEADERSHIP

To implement successful inclusive education programs, the support of the superintendent of schools and school board members is critical. These individuals provide the framework for establishing a strong inclusive education policy and for engendering a districtwide approach to the needed changes (e.g., staff development, budget allocations). The role of the superintendent is to ensure that all new district personnel support inclusion and that current and new staff members have the necessary training (Roach, 1995). The San Francisco Unified School District superintendent, Waldemar Rojas, noted that the district worked for 2 years prior to the changeover in order to prepare teachers, administrators, and parents ("Road to Inclusion," 1995). The district's inclusion facilitator cited the superintendent's support as central ("Making Every Child Count," 1995), a finding supported by Irmsher's (1995) study of inclusion in Oregon.

How Principals Support Inclusion

Whereas the superintendent provides an overall leadership role in the district, the school building is the key locus of educational services. The central role of the principal as the school's leader has been extensively documented since publication of the school effectiveness studies by Edmonds (1979, 1982) and others in the early 1980s. Having the principal take responsibility for the education of *all* of the children and leadership of *all* of the staff members in the building is a critical variable in inclusive education. The growth of site-based management gives principals and other staff in the school the opportunity to make essential changes and to implement necessary restructuring. Principals can support inclusion through organizing and (re)deploying the staff; scheduling the necessary time for teachers to plan and to learn new skills; involving the parents of *all* of the children in school; ensuring access to needed staff development; and taking time to be involved with the outcomes of *all* of the students in the school.

Steven Levy, principal at the Surfside School (Brooklyn, New York) where students with significant impairments are educated in inclusive programs, has underscored the importance of turning rhetoric into reality:

> A good administrator develops ways of communicating things that are important and that he or she really wants to get done. Commitment means generating not only enthusiasm but following through with all the necessary supports and services to make the goals attainable. (1995, p. 26)

At the Lakeshore Alternative Elementary School, one of San Francisco's inclusion schools, Principal Sharon Guillestegui emphasizes the role of the students in achieving successful inclusion. "Children make it happen. Children can interpret for [students with disabilities], and help to foster belonging." ("Principal Perspective," 1995, p. 4). At Lakeshore, where developmentally appropriate curricula are guided by Gardner's (1983) multiple intelligences theories, class size has not been reduced to accommodate inclusion. Despite this and other challenges, Guillestegui says, "If I had to do it over, I wouldn't be fearful. Teachers probably picked up on [my fear]" ("Principal Perspective," 1995, p. 5).

The NASBE study (Roach, 1995) reported on several initiatives taken by school principals:

> In some schools principals pair teachers who do not have inclusion experiences with those who do. In other schools, principals sent interested teachers individually or in small groups to special training seminars sponsored by colleges or universities or by the district or state department of education. Some teachers are provided in-class support and training by teacher consultants who work in the classroom with the teacher on a day-to-day basis for a short period of time; and some districts are experimenting with including teacher inservice training as a support service on the child's IEP in order to ensure that the needed training is provided to the teacher. (pp. 20–21)

Based on the experience of the 12 schools involved in the Working Group on Inclusive Schools, key aspects of leadership for inclusive education were identified, including the need for site-based authority, sharing leadership, scheduling planning time, staff development, and redeploying resources (*Creating Schools*, 1994). Specifically, the Working Group report cited 16 ways in which principals could support inclusion. They included the following:

1. Organize a team of parents and staff members, including yourself, to help plan inclusive school strategies and practices.
2. Make sure teachers, paraprofessionals, substitute teachers, related services personnel, other building support staff, and parents get the ongoing training and support they need.

3. Make sure teachers and other staff get the planning time they need.
4. Arrange visits for teachers and other staff to inclusive schools.
5. Explore co-teaching with your staff.
6. Know the rights of students with disabilities and their families and the responsibilities of school personnel.
7. Use the same report card for all students.
8. Make sure all parents are full partners in your school.
9. Have a clear understandable policy on discipline so that every child and every adult knows what is expected.
10. Establish a school-wide behavior management plan so that the staff can be assured that support will be provided at critical times.
11. Make sure that the focus is always on what each child needs.
12. Provide teachers with a list of resources.
13. Monitor and assess constantly.
14. Engage the outside community in the work of the school.
15. Remember that [not everything] will work. Be willing to fail, re-group, and try a different approach. Let your staff know that failure is something to be learned from, not something to be punished for.
16. Empower and support your staff. (*Creating Schools*, 1994, pp. 44–45)

What Teachers Can Do to Support Inclusion

Teachers are the key educators of our children. Yet teacher training programs often have fallen far short of preparing teachers to meet the needs of diverse learners in restructured inclusive classrooms. Teachers of both general and special education have been educated, for the most part, in separate preservice programs[1]; therefore, ongoing professional development is an essential factor for successful inclusion programs. Training should include joint planning, collaboration, co-teaching, curricular adaptation, new instructional strategies, classroom management, and assessment. Such training must not be "one shot" but rather ongoing and on-call. Roach (1995), in the NASBE study commented, "Teachers who are successful in inclusive environments caution against overemphasizing preplacement training. . . . [S]uccessful inclusion teachers again and again point to the fact that each child is different, and so general training is of limited value" (p. 28).

---

[1]The Council for Exceptional Children (CEC) has developed a set of standards for the preparation of special educators. It will be used by the National Council for Accreditation of Teacher Education (NCATE) to modify its criteria for accrediting training programs. Although hailing the development of the standards as a positive step in a time of increasing teacher mobility, Diane Sydoriak, president of the National Association of State Directors of Special Education (NASDSE), objected to dividing teachers into eight categories at a time when special education is moving away from such labeling and divisions ("CEC Sets Standards," 1996).

The emphasis in professional development should be on situation-specific problem-solving sessions, training focused on instructional strategies and adapting curriculum, and training in the change process itself. Visits to restructured classrooms are helpful to general education teachers prior to having a child with a disability placed in their classroom. Just as students may need support to make inclusion work, the adults involved need support as well (Myles & Simpson, 1989; York & Vandercook, 1989; York, Vandercook, MacDonald, Heise-Neff, & Caughey, 1992; Ysseldyke, Thurlow, Wotruba, & Nania, 1990). Toward that end, a team of Colorado educators has developed a "toolbox" for supporting inclusive education, which organizes for each group of "stakeholders" (e.g., administrators, general education staff, special education staff, students) several types of support (e.g., beliefs and values, the *why* of inclusion; content, the *what* of instruction; method, the *how* of instruction; adult-to-adult interactions, the *who*) (Kronberg, Jackson, Sheets, & Rogers-Connolly, 1995). The "toolbox" serves as a useful hands-on resource.

Most general education teachers have a diverse student population in their classroom and are making accommodations and modifications for individual students. Thus, in most classrooms, including students with disabilities represents not a qualitative change but, rather, an expansion of the existing diversity. Freagon and Kachur (1993), who participated in an Illinois symposium on inclusive education, stated:

> Many general education teachers utilize effective instructional strategies which involve active participation of students, students working together and learning from one another, and meaningful and motivating instructional activities. These strategies are effective for all students, including those who have a disability. (p. 22)

Giangreco (1996) echoed this point: "Teachers who successfully teach students without disabilities have the skills to successfully teach students with disabilities" (p. 56). He recommended 10 strategies for general education teachers:

1. Get a little help from your friends.
2. Welcome the student in your classroom.
3. Be the teacher of all the students.
4. Make sure everyone belongs to the classroom community.
5. Clarify shared expectations with team members.
6. Adapt activities to the student's needs.
7. Provide active and participatory learning experiences.
8. Adapt classroom arrangements, materials, and strategies.
9. Make sure support services help.
10. Evaluate your teaching. (pp. 56–59)

Professional development for restructured and inclusive education involves a paradigmatic shift from traditional in-service and teacher training models. In the traditional model, the teacher, either general or special education, was a qualified professional who taught in his or her own classroom. Upgrading and/or expansion of the teacher's skills was based on the teacher's particular interest(s). In the new inclusive education classroom, special and general educators learn to rely on each other's skills and knowledge and to develop ways to work collaboratively as a team. During professional development, inclusion brings together teachers as peers, each as "trainee" and "trainer" of the other, collaborating to become quality teachers of all children.

A qualitative study of inclusion in a Minnesota school district that has been a leader in inclusive education demonstrated the respect for all individuals that the inclusion process brings. The authors (York-Barr, Schultz, Doyle, Kronberg, & Crossett, 1996) identified six major themes reflected in the St. Cloud Community Schools experience:

> The first theme, perspectives about students, was evident through descriptions of classroom practices, events, and people. Language and expression during the interviews suggested that all students were highly valued members of the classroom communities. Also evident was a view of the students with disabilities as individuals. Although special needs were recognized, children were viewed predominantly as whole people with needs more similar to than different from those of their classmates without identified disabilities. (p. 98)
>
> The second pervasive people theme related to how people viewed their supervisors and colleagues. A strong indicator of collegial interactions was that no one felt . . . alone. Everyone interviewed indicated feeling supported in his or her efforts. Classroom teachers respected and valued the special educators. Special educators were perceived as reliable in providing emotional and curricular support and as being an important link between school and home. (p. 100)
>
> A third theme emerging from the data revealed a common belief about people and the power of individual and collective personal effort. (p. 100)
>
> A fourth theme indicated that the professionals [in the St. Cloud schools] had a high sense of self-efficacy and worth. They were clear about their positive effect on children and the value of their work with all children. Without a doubt, these educators seem to be morally driven to accomplish social good. (p. 101)
>
> A fifth theme emerging among the teachers, parents, and administrators was their identification of individual people, including adults and children, who had a substantial impact on their lives. (p. 101)
>
> Finally, there were distinct, common themes among interviewees about advice they would offer to prospective educators, including guid-

ance for their professional preparation. The most salient message was that potential teachers must like (if not love) and believe in kids. (p. 101)

PARENTAL RESPONSES

For the most part, districts implementing inclusive education programs report a positive response from both special education and general education parents. Parental support for inclusion, however, is just the beginning of their involvement in the broader planning and policy issues of the school district. Districts that have effectively implemented inclusive education programs have involved parents in the initial planning—as part of study groups, in visiting other districts, in reviewing the research and the rationale for inclusion, and in developing the district's plan. This process includes parents of children with and without disabilities who want to know how changes may affect their children. It is important to share the research findings on outcomes for students with and without disabilities in inclusive classrooms (see Chapter 14), as well as identify the additional resources that inclusion brings to the general education classroom. As Roach (1995) has pointed out, "All students reap benefits from inclusion" (p. 20).

In the following excerpts from the *National Study* (1995), parents of a general education student provide evidence of such benefits.

As parents, we were skeptical of the inclusion concept at the beginning of the year; however, now we cannot say enough good things about this program. Our child has had the happiest, most successful year thus far in his education process. He shares with us a lot of what goes on in the classroom, and we have certainly been impressed with the overall ability of the teacher and her staff to cope with some of the difficult situations they are faced with daily.

We . . . feel the inclusion concept has definitely been a self-esteem booster for "C." When he could explain to us how good it made him feel to be able to help another student who was having difficulty with his work, and . . . to have the teacher express her appreciation and make comments about how he had helped another student succeed, we knew things were on the right track.

We were concerned that "C" might have a difficult time emotionally adjusting to the inclusion setting because of his sensitivity to the needs of others. Here again we were proven wrong. If anything, this made him more aware of the emotional needs of some of the students. We were afraid that the day-to-day interaction with physically handicapped students might be depressive. Here again, we learned he was very sensitive to [their] needs . . . but in a very positive way, even to the point of wondering what is going to happen to these students if they are not placed in an inclusion setting next year with other students to help them. "C" also commented on this being the first time in the handicapped students' lives that they have been allowed to be with "normal" children and to interact with them on a daily basis. "C" felt this was good and that [students with disabilities] should be mainstreamed so as not to be made to feel different.

This program has been very successful. We feel it has definitely given our child what he needed, both academically and socially. . . . We can now honestly say we were glad our child had this positive educational experience through inclusion. (pp. 245–246)

Parents of an elementary school student,
Rockingham County Consolidated Schools, North Carolina

Parents seeking inclusive opportunities for their children often have met with opposition from school officials. At a hearing of the National Council on Disability (NCD), Jane Swann, a parent and representative of The Arc of Montgomery County, Pennsylvania, described being "backed into a corner" when the district officials said that her child could not attend school in a general classroom because the school was not "ready." Again and again the district tried to discourage an inclusive placement, including refusing to have the general education kindergarten teacher included in the IEP meeting (cited in "Parents," 1994).

A parent from New York City reported a similar experience.

Well, the first thing the teacher said to me was, "It's fine if he's in this class but I'm not trained for this and I have no intention of getting trained for it either." I would just describe her attitude as not welcoming for him. And I know that rubs off on the other kids.

The teacher closed herself off from Ari. It's come down to the last few weeks of school where she has nothing at all to do with Ari except that she is present and he is present. She just ignores him, like he's an invisible child. (cited in Erwin & Soodak, 1995, p. 142)

Conversely, another New York City parent stated, "This was a really astute teacher. And the first thing she said to me was, 'I believe Timothy should be in a regular class'" (cited in Erwin & Soodak, 1995, p. 142).

Parents speaking at the previously mentioned National Council on Disability (1995) hearings reported other positive experiences:

Over the last year, I have learned that IDEA [the Individuals with Disabilities Education Act of 1990] works, and the least restrictive environment language in IDEA, in my opinion, is just fine as it is. I can tell you that supported inclusion, which entails support for students and parents, . . . works, period. I have a life. My kid has a life. And I can say to you honestly I . . . feel like now I have a child instead of a walking disability: walking Down syndrome. And a year later, I have those feelings corroborated by folks at the school, who say, "I wish we could have videotaped this child every day since he walked in the building, because no one would believe the progress." (p. 76)

Toni Robinson, Charlotte, North Carolina

For the first time, at age 16, Jay went out with friends. He went to a football game with some classmates. It's funny, we were always told that regular education kids just don't want anything to do with special education kids. The kids at the high school have been wonderful. Adults could learn a lot from them. He has friends. Now we have hope for his future. (p. 79)

Catherine Jortner, Boston, Massachusetts

My son, our family, his friends, and his school are all the beneficiaries of his inclusion of Columbine. I no longer fear for his future. His inclusion in school will ensure that he's included as an adult. There's no better feeling than to know that. Most important of all, he will learn about finding his place in the world, and his friends will learn about finding their place in the world. (p. 80)

Linda Frederick, Denver, Colorado

Summarizing the parents' view, the National Council on Disability (1995) reported,

A majority of witnesses who testified on the subject of least restrictive environment indicated strong support for integrated placements. Many parents of students with disabilities stated that their children made greater gains academically and socially in integrated settings than they had in segregated settings. Parents emphasized the friendships their children had made with nondisabled students that would not have occurred in segregated placements. Parents reported that their children were happier and were eager to be doing what their peers were doing. (p. 78)

A number of witnesses stated that a separate special education system could never be equal to the regular system. Some stated that children with mental retardation in segregated settings frequently miss out on academics and the positive behavior modeling of nondisabled peers. Others stated that segregation may encourage nondisabled students to maintain harmful attitudes, because segregation demonstrates that it is acceptable to treat some students under different rules and because nondisabled students do not have the opportunity to know students with disabilities as peers and as individuals. Several individuals stated that segregation itself creates further disability, perhaps worse than the original disabling condition. Thus, the supported integration of students with disabilities was described as not only producing better results for all students but as a positive instrumental method of reducing the historical prejudice that has been directed toward people with disabilities in our culture. (p. 82)

Parents who took the lead may become pathbreakers for others:

Many of the first parents to have their children included have subsequently spearheaded the effort in their district to organize other parents interested in having their children included in the regular program. These parents have run parent support groups, sat in IEP meetings with their peers, and made presentations to the school board when necessary. Some of these parents have worked through the district's special education advisory committee to have their voices heard, some have not. . . .

[U]nfortunately, some parents feel that they have to "keep up the fight" every new school year to keep their child included as he or she progresses through the grades. In many instances school administrators have provided staff with thorough and adequate training for the first year(s) a child is included, but have not maintained that level of training in the following years. In these districts, the struggle is especially great when the student progresses to the next [major] level of school. (Roach, 1995, p. 38)

The "struggle" becomes more bearable as increasing numbers of parents seek inclusion opportunities for their children and, in turn, support each others' efforts.

Just as inclusion benefits children with disabilities, there also are benefits for the family. Families of included students have higher aspirations for them (California Research Institute, 1992), and the parents themselves develop a wider range of friendships (Bailey & Winton, 1989). A report in the *National Study* (1995) quoted a district administrator who emphasized the experience of the mother ("J") of a student ("A") who has profound physical and cognitive disabilities:

"J" talks about the excitement, yet trepidation, she and the rest of the family felt the first time "A" received an invitation to a birthday party. She called the other child's mother and asked if she knew about "A." The other mother said, "Oh sure, my daughter has told me all about 'A,' even about her feeding tube." She assured "J" that they really wanted "A" to be part of the birthday party. "J" framed the birthday invitation. She took "A" to the birthday party, and for the first time sat down and visited with the other mothers while her little girl played with friends. (p. 94)

Gwinnett County Public Schools, Georgia

The experience of one set of parents, described in a letter of thanks to the Janet Berry Elementary School (Appleton Area School District, Wisconsin) describes both problems and successes.

We are a family with a difference because we have a child with a disability, and we often have found ourselves excluded and pushed away by schools, communities, and the public. This exclusion is born out of fear because people are afraid of things that are different. In fact, when our oldest daughter was diagnosed with a disability, we realized that *we* were afraid of *her* (and she was only 4 months old). We had no friends with disabilities; we could not even think of a person that we knew who had a disability. Where each of us had grown up, children with handicaps went to separate schools. And so did our daughter, in her early years.

Yet we came to realize as Rachel grew that she had many adults who loved her (parents, teachers, therapists, babysitters) but no one her own age, except her younger sister and brother, who could be her friend. Because Rachel went off on a school bus to a school outside of our neighborhood in San Diego, she didn't know the children in our own neighborhood. No one spoke to us when we played at the park or rode bikes up the street.

Then we decided to have Rachel attend our neighborhood school. She was the only child with severe special needs there. The adults were very difficult to work with, but the children were wonderfully accepting. Suddenly children appeared at our door, wanting to play, and they greeted us enthusiastically at the park. We felt as if we had been invited back into the human race. Still, the constant conflict with the unaccepting school administration was wearing on us. So we resolved to move to a place where the school would welcome us. And we certainly found that in Janet Berry.

Here in this community, everyone greets Rachel at school and in the neighborhood. Her classmates and PALS and neighbors show her friendship and concern. They are accepting and compassionate in a way that makes them mature beyond their years. The staff works tirelessly to have inclusion run smoothly for *all* the children, disabled and nondisabled. We are constantly amazed at the dedication and leadership . . . the teachers, staff, and principal display. Parents, too, have gone out of their way to be friendly to Rachel and to us. There are not enough words to express our gratitude. We are now not only members of the human race but members of a true community.

The Karches, May 20, 1994

Parents of special education students generally are very supportive of inclusive education programs, and parents of general education students have, for the most part, accepted them as part of school restructuring efforts and the value system of the district. Some general education parents report the positive social and academic benefits for their children as a result of involvement with people with disabilities and the increase in instructional supports in the classroom. The following reports of parental involvement and response are from schools districts included in the *National Study* (1995):

There have been no complaints from parents of students who have no disabilities. . . . [B]ecause of the support given to the teacher (i.e., a paraprofessional or a co-teacher), some parents see an additional benefit to having a special education student in the classroom. (pp. 63–64)
Ridgefield Public Schools, Connecticut

Parents of handicapped students have welcomed the opportunity to see their children educated with their age mates in nonexclusive settings. Parents of nonhandicapped students were cautious until they saw achievement results that were not depressed and a social milieu that was friendly and relaxed. (p. 177)

Hillsdale Community Schools, Michigan

There has been a positive response from parents that services will be brought to students within the regular classroom. Many do not want their student missing what is happening in the regular classroom, but they also want help for their student. With a recent change in the format of delivery of services for hearing impaired, many of the parents were very hesitant about their student being in a regular classroom, even when an interpreter would be provided. Now 4 months later, the parents are very pleased with the social interaction and the learning that is happening by [students] being with their peers. (pp. 214–215)

Roswell Independent School District, New Mexico

Initially the parents of special education students seemed concerned about two issues: 1) Would their child's specific needs for unique services really be met in the regular classroom? and 2) Would their child be only physically included in the class but be ignored, neglected, or resented? Often these same worried parents have become inclusion's most zealous supporters as they see their child really making friends and modeling peers in the classroom. However, this change in an ongoing process requires lots of meetings and collaborative problem solving. Likewise, parents of general education students tell us they approve of the compassion and tolerance they see in their children developing as a result of inclusion. Many of the same parents had worried initially that children with special needs would take away from the amount of teacher time their child would receive. (p. 259)

Bend LaPine Public Schools, Oregon

As the preceding excerpts attest, parental response to inclusion is not uniform. Parents want what is best for their children, whether or not they have disabilities. For the most part, parents of general and special education students indicate that when inclusive education is implemented successfully, they believe that the program is beneficial for their child(ren) (*National Study*, 1995; Roach, 1995).

FISCAL ISSUES

Data indicate that state funding formulas in the 1990s have supported segregation and have inhibited inclusion (see also Chapter 4). The National Council on Disability has described fiscal disincentives to inclusion in California, Florida, Illinois, Indiana, New Jersey, New York, and Rhode Island. In Illinois, for example, the NCD pointed to the following provisions that discourage inclusion:

- Allowing only large entities (i.e., intermediate unit), rather than school districts, to receive federal special education funds directly from the state. These entities, the council reports, are partial to segregated settings.
- Mandating that 12.5% of all federal special education dollars go to educating students with disabilities in private schools, which typically are segregated schools
- Reimbursing local districts for 80% of transportation costs so that when a district moves a student with disabilities to her or his home school, it loses dollars from the state
- The fact that the state pays a larger proportion of cost for students educated in out-of-district placements ("Council," 1995)

Several states have reported efforts to change the funding formulas to support inclusive education initiatives. For example, Florida is piloting a new funding system in 20 schools, using matrices to rate students by need rather than by label. In Iowa, the state has initiated a "hold harmless" provision, freezing funding at existing levels so that funds saved as a result of inclusion programs remain in the district. This is essential because changes in fiscal policy alone are not enough to effect reform (Parrish, 1995). "States reporting success with fiscal reform stress the need not only to remove disincentives for restrictive placements, but to provide a comprehensive system of professional development and [classroom] support" (Parrish, 1995, p. 1).

In other state initiatives, Vermont's Act 230 has reformed both the funding and the organization of services for students with disabilities (see also Chapter 10). A comprehensive evaluation of the implementation of the law concludes with a caution concerning the need for stable and adequate funding:

> If funding does not exist to provide services to students taken off IEPs or never identified for special education, then the only choice left to parents and educators to ensure services will be available is to identify students as eligible for special education. (*Vermont's Act 230*, 1993, p. 8)

Kentucky's comprehensive education reform (Kentucky Education Reform Act, KERA; see also Chapter 10) has streamlined special education funding. A survey of special education directors has reported that the reform has increased their control over funds, enhanced inclusion, and promoted collaboration among special educators and general education teachers (Montgomery, 1995). The opportunity to blend special education funds with other resources was reported as one of the new formula's major benefits.

A few school districts reported comprehensive studies of fiscal consequences. Two examples from the *National Study* (1995) are included here:

> A 1993 comparison of the costs of educating 168 students in traditional settings with those of inclusive settings indicates total costs of approximately the same magnitude ($1.047 vs. $1.059 million, respectively). State reimbursement provides $335,000 for the traditional settings and $616,000 for the inclusive settings; thus, a net savings to the district of $268,000 for the inclusive program. (p. 102)
>
> *West Chicago Elementary School District #33, Illinois*

> A longitudinal study of the financial consequences of inclusion compared the cost of the district's program in comparison with what costs would have been for the purchase of services from the region's B[oard] O[f] C[ooperative] E[ducational] S[ervices], where most of the Johnson City students had previously attended. The study reports that: 1) despite a 96 percent increase in adjusted local expenditures during the five year period under study, the average per pupil expenditures were considerably less than the projected costs in the BOCES programs, the differences ranging in the order of 50–60 percent; 2) despite a steady increase in the number of students receiving services, the proportion remained about 7 percent, which is much lower than most reported prevalence figures. This is explained as a function of the district's extensive prereferral interventions and services provided to nonclassified students; 3) there has been a substantial increase in the number of students with significant disabilities, which is interpreted as a function of the district's visibility and reputation for service provision; and 4) as a result of this increase in the number of students with significant disabilities, there has been a substantial increase in contractual related services and employment of paraprofessional aides. (pp. 227–228)
>
> *Johnson City Central School District, New York*

The Clark County (Indiana) Special Education Cooperative has conducted two analyses of their inclusion programs. In 1993, they reported a slight savings per pupil: $4,096 per pupil at the four inclusive elementary schools, as compared with $4,267 in traditional programming at the remaining schools. In a 1995 study, the inclusive education program cost $3,224 per pupil, representing an additional savings ("Indiana Districts' Fiscal Analysis," 1995; Roahrig, 1993, 1995).

A witness at a National Council on Disability (1995) hearing reported on the financial consequences of inclusion in the Oakland Unified School District, California:

> This year [the school district] will spend about $800 per inclusion student less than the cost of educating them in SDC [special day classes]. This is due largely to transportation savings ($2,300/student) offsetting additional costs due to staffing ($1,370/student), planning, and training.

As more students are included across the district and at all grade levels, there will be additional costs for equipment (about $20,000 per year districtwide), and reduced savings on transportation at the secondary level. However, any additional costs should be completely offset by projected savings from:

- Reduced escalation to more intensive services (e.g., about $32,000 per student per year not referred to nonpublic schools)
- Reduced legal fees associated with mediations and fair hearings (typically $2,000–$10,000 per case)
- Reduced need for expansion of facilities ($55,000 per classroom)
- Reduced facilities usage ($900 per class per year)
- The effects of economies of scale (e.g., potential for reducing staffing at $1,370 per student per year) (pp. 80–81)

The National Council on Disability (1995) summarized the cost issues as follows: "The costs associated with integration can be modest, with possible savings because of fewer due process hearings, fewer mediations, fewer referrals to special education, few non-public school placements, and lower transportation costs" (p. 80). When inclusion programs are implemented on a limited basis, however, the real cost consequences are skewed. For example, if a single child is included and an aide hired to work in the general education class, costs increase.

The pattern reported most frequently by school districts implementing inclusive education programs is that they support the restructuring by using the same fiscal resources previously used in separate special and general education, but they use them in a different manner. Roach (1995) summarized the financial practices of inclusion districts—where dollars previously used for students with disabilities in separate settings now follow the student into the general education classroom—as "improving the regular education setting as well, rendering better *value* [emphasis in original] for the special education dollar" (p. 21). Roach described the practices as follows:

> After implementing inclusion, districts report saving transportation costs, reduced administrative costs, fewer out-of-district tuitions for other public and private school placements, and savings in space and facility allocations. On the other hand, these costs are directly plowed back into personnel and programming in the inclusive environment. Many inclusive districts have increased the number of classroom aides in general education classes by using the savings gained from eliminating separate special education facilities and administrative structures. Savings reaped by eliminating dual systems have also been used to conduct evaluations of the efficacy of inclusion programs. (pp. 21–22)

Parrish (1995), summarizing the findings from the first 2 years (1993 and 1994) of the work of the federally funded Center for Special

Education Finance, has developed a set of guidelines for states attempting to revise their special education formulas to remove incentives for restrictive placements:

- First, fiscal incentives favoring restrictive and separate placements should be removed.
- Second, states must make decisions about the extent to which they wish to encourage private special education placements.
- Third, funding systems should be developed in which funds follow the students as they move to less restrictive placements.
- Fourth, states should enhance fiscal support for district training.
- Fifth, states could fund and encourage the use of appropriate interventions for all students. (U.S. Department of Education, 1995, p. 120)

Excerpts from reports from some school districts included in the *National Study* (1995) on the finances of inclusive education programs are included next.

For the most part, school staff are using the same special education resources in a different manner. (p. 34)

Kingman, Arizona

Funds have been reallocated from transportation and outgoing tuition to increase staff. Although there has been a significant staff increase, overall funds have been saved. (p. 61)

Milford Board of Education, Connecticut

Due to the number of students entering inclusive programs, the number of students within the self-contained program has dropped. This has led to the elimination of these classrooms. Excess staff had the option of changing roles and becoming inclusion facilitators for the district. (p. 129)

Shawnee Mission Public Schools
Unified School District 512, Kansas

The inclusion program has cost the district the expense of nine inclusion aides. There are small savings. Our special education buses no longer bring students from throughout the county into one central location, thus cutting down on transportation costs. More students are traveling on typical buses to their local schools. There are four elementary classrooms available for other uses. (p. 137)

Pulaski County Schools, Kentucky

Five years ago this district was spending $270,000 in [out-of-district] tuition costs; we are now spending in the ballpark of $60,000 for our two part-time students to maintain their out-of-district placements. The result has been that we have been able to provide additional staff to support our programs and . . . our students in school. (p. 207)

Clinton Township School District, New Jersey

Inclusion requires a new focus on training, which costs more up front but pays off in the end. . . . [W]e are able to stretch dollars further by bringing special education staff into the regular classrooms. (p. 256)
Bend LaPine Public Schools, Oregon

There have been no real fiscal changes on the school level. We have implemented inclusive programming in many sites without increased cost to the district. In a recent cost comparison of MOSAIC [Model Opportunities to Attend Inclusive Classrooms] and our segregated special education preschool, figures indicate no increased cost per pupil. (p. 283)
Pittsburgh Public Schools, Pennsylvania

THE VOICE OF STUDENTS

Students, of course, are both the object of and the rationale for inclusive educational programs. Thus, their reactions are of central importance. Students report overwhelmingly that they prefer being in inclusive education settings over separate special education classrooms.

One student's reaction follows:

Although I am blind, I spend my days in a regular classroom. For me, learning in a mainstream classroom has been a challenge. I have tried to demonstrate to "regular" educators that educating students with disabilities can be challenging and rewarding.

Integrating students with disabilities into the vast ocean of the mainstream society is often perceived as being complicated. I have fought the stereotype that I would be an "overly dependent" student. I strongly believe the confusing of disabilities and capabilities leads to negative perceptions about students with disabilities. I have a disability, but I am capable.

I don't live in an isolated society; I shouldn't learn in an isolated classroom. . . . [W]hen I go into the regular workforce, I will be required to complete the same tasks as every other worker.

[M]y parents had to be involved to insure that I would receive a proper education. And I learned from that example. I learned that the best advocate I have is me; I have to express my own needs. All students have to be aggressive; they have to be articulate. That's especially true for disabled students.

[O]ther students benefit from the insight I have. You've heard the expression, "When you lose one sense, you gain another." I guess that's true. In English class, I try to take a work of literature and translate that into what is happening now, take the work and expand its point of view. I can sometimes perceive things that other students miss. (McKeithan, 1995, p. 32)

Some districts included in the *National Study* (1995) provided the following reports from students, both with and without disabilities, in inclusive programs.

I hated to go to the "dummy room." I'm not dumb! (p. 144)
Student in Richland Parish School Board, Louisiana

I am a sophomore in high school and I am handicapped. The reason I like a regular school as opposed to a special school is that I like being treated as person without a handicap. People treat you different in a special school. . . . [B]eing treated like a regular person helps me more in my life. In the world we live in, it is not adapted for the handicapped. If I as a handicapped person learn to live and adapt to the regular world as I grow, it is better for me. In a special school, everything is done for you. While this is beneficial, it doesn't allow for doing normal tasks. I believe most handicapped kids should be able to attend regular schools to help them be successful in their life and to be happy. (p. 278)
Student in Hampton Township School District, Pennsylvania

I always used to make fun of handicapped people, not near them but when they were away. I would talk about them with my friends, or just to myself sometimes. I always tried to keep a distance away from them when they were nearby. When they left I would say things about them to myself like, "What a retard." But now things are different. I don't say things about them anymore, because I'm not afraid of them and am more mature. (p. 323)
Student in Deer Park Independent School District, Texas

You feel good when they [students with disabilities] do something right that [you've] helped them with. When they do things on their own they feel . . . they've made an achievement. You get to see that some people need help, and it's normal to need help. Even I need help sometimes.
They [students with disabilities] learn to do harder things . . . not baby things. It gives them a challenge, to be in a regular room. I help them when they need it and they help me when I need it. (p. 335)
Student in Santa Fe (Texas) Independent School District

I am thinking now that I did good to choose this peer assistant/tutor: special education class, because this is my first experience in working with students with disabilities. So it made me develop positive attitudes toward those with disabilities. . . . I am a Korean student, so did not even see this kind of special education class in Korea. Thus, this special education class is a very valuable experience for me. Also I cannot command of English very well, so I have some kind of disabilities like other disabled students. So I can feel and understand their feelings, emotions, and behavior very well.
[T]his is change my mental culture. Because, Korean students do not like to do this kind of job, which is helping a disabled student. Everyday I learn about quality of life by "RJ" and I learn [that] human beings . . . must respect each other even if . . . disabled . . . because we are all human beings in this society and we are all precious lives. . . .
High school peer assistant who emigrated from Korea,
Howard County Public School System, Maryland

This is a self assessment to see how I am doing in my class and how much I have learned. It's difficult for me to express what I have learned because Intensity Five Special Education [a program for students with significant disabilities] has changed me and changed my life for the better in a way that I can't communicate. When I signed up for this class, I took it because I needed an easy elective to pull up my GPA. I never guessed that I would end up working so much and so hard. I never guessed I could care so deeply about anyone or anything.

Before I became an aide, I came to school late every day. This is because I was so focused on being at every party, drinking as much as I could, and cruising around in my car faster than I should whenever possible. That was my life. I didn't care about school. Now, I have people who need me. And the work requires me to be alert and patient every minute. I've had to change my lifestyle. I want to go to college and major in special education now. Before, my parents wanted me to go to college, but I really didn't care. I really didn't think I was good enough to make it in college either. I have discovered that I can really make a difference in the lives of these kids. I felt a responsibility to be a better person, to work harder, and learn more. I'm not really sure I know how this happened to me. But I want to thank you for taking a chance on me. I know a lot of teachers think guys like me don't deserve to be an aide. They think it should be a job reserved for GT [gifted] people. I guess they don't believe all that stuff they preach about seeing people as a glass half full instead of a glass half empty. I'm starting to believe that stuff too. About the Intensity Five Students, and even about myself sometimes.

I have also discovered that I have guts I didn't know I had. When the guys use the word *retard* as an insult, I know now that it's a disability, not an insult. I feel so sick when they say that I can't just play along with the gag anymore. I have to speak up now. I've become an advocate just like you predicted I would. I'm not sure how this happened to me. It wasn't something I ever thought I could do.

I think having . . . students [with mental retardation] in regular classes has made our school a better place. I think it has made people think. One day "M" and "W" and I were talking with a bunch of our friends at lunch about what it would be like to have kids of our own. We all had our TV sitcom ideas about what it would be like. And when we thought about what it would be like if our kid was born with mental retardation. This was really heavy stuff to be talking about! Maybe it's normal for the smart honor student types to sit around and worry about real life, but for me and my dumb jock-type friends to get that serious is scary! This school is really different since Intensity Five came to town. It's made everybody . . . become better people than they were before the program. (pp. 158–159)

Eleventh-grade peer assistant,
Howard County Public School System, Maryland

CONCLUSION

Inclusion programs are being implemented in school districts throughout the United States. The programs serve students across the full range of disabilities, levels of severity, and grade levels. As teachers and support staff implement inclusive education programs, they become increasingly supportive and express a greater sense of professional and personal success. Generally, parents of children, both with disabilities and without, in inclusive classrooms report positive outcomes for their children. Data on the fiscal consequences of inclusive education over time are limited, but most school districts report that the overall cost of inclusive education is no greater than that of educating students in two separate systems and may produce cost savings as the program is implemented over time.

REFERENCES

Bailey, D.B., & Winton, P.J. (1989). Friendships and acquaintances among families in a mainstreamed day care center. *Education and Training in Mental Retardation, 24*(2), 107–113.

Bauwens, J., Hourcade, J.J., & Friend, M. (1989). Cooperative teaching: A model for general and special education integration. *Remedial and Special Education, 10*(2), 17–22.

California Research Institute. (1992). Educational practices in integrated settings associated with positive student outcomes. *Strategies on the Integration of Students with Disabilities, 3*(3), 1, 10.

CEC sets standards for special educators. (1996, January 18). *Education Daily, 1*, 3.

Collaboration: A key to effective inclusion. (1996, April). *Inclusive Education Reports.*

Council: States must ease inclusion's financial hurdles. (1995, June 24). *Education Daily*, 2–4.

Creating schools for all of our students: What 12 schools have to say. (1994). Reston, VA: Council for Exceptional Children.

Edmonds, R. (1979). Some schools work and more can. *Social Policy, 9*(5), 26–31.

Edmonds, R. (1982). Programs of school improvement: An overview. *Educational Leadership, 40*(3), 4–11.

Erwin, E.J., & Soodak, L.C. (1995). I never knew I could stand up to the system: Families' perspective on pursuing inclusive education. *Journal of The Association for Persons with Severe Handicaps, 20*(2), 136–146.

Ferguson, D.L. (1994). Magic for teacher work groups. *Teaching Exceptional Children, 27*(1), 42–47.

Flynn, G., & Innes, M. (1992). The Waterloo Region Catholic School System. In R.A. Villa, J.S. Thousand, W. Stainback, & S. Stainback (Eds.), *Restructuring for caring and effective education: An administrative guide to creating heterogeneous schools* (pp. 201–217). Baltimore: Paul H. Brookes Publishing Co.

Flynn, G., & Kowalczyk-McPhee, B. (1989). A school system in transition. In S. Stainback, W. Stainback, & M. Forest (Eds.), *Educating all students in the mainstream of regular education* (pp. 29–41). Baltimore: Paul H. Brookes Publishing Co.

Freagon, S., & Kachur, D.S. (1993). *Thoughts, perspectives, and ideas presented at the Illinois Deans of Colleges of Education symposium on inclusive education of students with disabilities.* Springfield: Illinois Planning Council on Developmental Disabilities.

Gardner, H. (1983). *Frames of mind: The theory of multiple intelligences.* New York: Basic Books.

Giangreco, M.F. (1996). What do I do now? A teacher's guide to including students with disabilities. *Educational Leadership, 53*(5), 56–59.

Great co-teaching starts before class begins—with planning. (1996). *Inclusive Education Programs, 3*(5), 4–5.

Indiana districts' fiscal analysis shows saving with inclusion. (1995). *Individualized Education Programs, 2*(12), 6–7.

Individuals with Disabilities Education Act (IDEA) of 1990, PL 101-476, 20 U.S.C. § 1400 *et seq.*

Irmsher, K. (1995). *Inclusive education in practice: The lessons of pioneering school districts.* Eugene: Oregon School Study Council.

Janney, R.E., Snell, M.E., Beers, M.K., & Raynes, M. (1993). Integrating students with moderate and severe disabilities: Classroom teachers' beliefs and attitudes about implementing an educational change. *Educational Administration Quarterly, 31*(1), 84–114.

Janney, R.E., Snell, M.E., Beers, M.K., & Raynes, M. (1995). Integrating students with moderate and severe disabilities into general education classes. *Exceptional Children, 61*(5), 425–439.

Jorgensen, C.M. (1994–1995). Essential questions—inclusive answers. *Educational Leadership, 52*(2), 52–55.

King-Sears, M.E., & Cummings, C.S. (1996). Inclusive practices of classroom teachers. *Remedial and Special Education, 17*(4), 217–225.

Kronberg, R., Jackson, L., Sheets, G., & Rogers-Connolly, T. (1995). A toolbox for supporting integrated education. *Teaching Exceptional Children, 27*(4), 54–58.

Levy, S. (1995). Inclusion demands top-down support for bottom-up implementation. *School Administrator, 52*(6), 26–27.

Making every child count: Top-down support helps San Francisco Unified triumph over urban issues. (1995). *Inclusive Education Programs, 2*(11), 1–6.

McKeithan, T.L. II. (1995, February 22). The best advocate I have is me. *Education Week,* 32.

Mercer, C.D., Lane, H.B., Jordan, L., Allsopp, D.H., & Eisele, M.R. (1996). Empowering teachers and students with instructional choices in inclusive settings. *Remedial and Special Education, 17*(4), 226–236.

Montgomery, D.L. (1995). *The impact of the Kentucky Education Reform Act on special education programs and services: Perceptions of special education directors.* Palo Alto, CA: Center for Special Education Finance.

Myles, B.S., & Simpson, R.L. (1989). Regular educators' modification preferences for mainstreaming mildly handicapped children. *Journal of Special Education, 22,* 479–489.

National Council on Disability. (1995). *Improving the implementation of the Individuals with Disabilities Education Act: Making schools work for all of America's children.* Washington, DC: Author.

National Study of Inclusive Education. (1994). New York: The City University of New York, National Center on Educational Restructuring and Inclusion.

National Study of Inclusive Education. (1995). New York: The City University of New York, National Center on Educational Restructuring and Inclusion.

Parents, advocates rail against schools that thwart education and inclusion. (1994). *Inclusive Education Programs, 1*(12), 2–3.

Parrish, T.B. (1995, Fall). Fiscal issues related to the inclusion of students with disabilities. *CSEF Brief, 7.*

Principal perspective: How one school adapts on a shoestring budget. (1995). *Inclusive Education Programs, 2*(11), 4–6.

Roach, V. (1995). *Winning ways: Creating inclusive schools, classrooms, and communities.* Alexandria, VA: National Association of State Boards of Education.

The road to inclusion can be smooth or hellish. (1995, April 2). *School Board News,* 5.

Roahrig, P.L. (1993). *Special education inclusion: Fiscal analysis of Clark County Schools inclusion site grant.* Terre Haute: Indiana State University.

Roahrig, P.L. (1995). *Special education inclusion: Fiscal analysis of Clark County Schools LRE study follow-up, 1994–95.* Greenwood, IN: Systems Management.

Tashie, C., Shapiro-Barnard, S., Schuh, M., Jorgensen, C., Dillon, A., Dixon, B., & Nisbet, J. (1993). *From regular to special: From ordinary to extraordinary.* Durham: University of New Hampshire, Institute on Disability.

U.S. Department of Education. (1995). *Seventeenth annual report to Congress on the implementation of the Individuals with Disabilities Education Act.* Washington, DC: Author.

Vermont's Act 230: Three years later. A report on the impact of Act 230. (1993). Montpelier, VT: Department of Education.

Walter-Thomas, C., Bryant, M., & Land, S. (1996). Planning for effective co-teaching: The key to successful inclusion. *Remedial and Special Education, 17*(4), 255–265.

Werts, M.G., Wolery, M., Snyder, E.D., & Caldwell, N.K. (1996). Teachers' perceptions of the supports critical to the success of inclusion programs. *Journal of The Association for Persons with Severe Handicaps, 21*(1), 9–21.

York, J., & Vandercook, T. (1989). A team approach to program development and support. In J. York, T. Vandercook, C. MacDonald, & S. Wolff (Eds.), *Strategies for full inclusion* (pp. 21–43). Minneapolis: University of Minnesota, Institute on Community Integration.

York, J., Vandercook, T., MacDonald, C., Heise-Neff, C., & Caughey, E. (1992). Feedback about integrating middle-school students with severe disabilities in general education classes. *Exceptional Children, 58*(3), 244–258.

York-Barr, J., Schultz, T., Doyle, M.B., Kronberg, R., & Crossett, S. (1996). Inclusive schooling in St. Cloud: Perspectives on the process and people. *Remedial and Special Education, 17*(2), 92–105.

Ysseldyke, J.E., Thurlow, M.L., Wotruba, J.W., & Nania, P.A. (1990). Instructional arrangements: Perceptions from general education. *Teaching Exceptional Children, 22*(4), 4–9.

12

Classroom Supports
and Instructional Strategies

This chapter begins by addressing the redesign of the individualized education program (IEP) in the context of inclusive education. It then provides details about the use of instructional strategies cited most often by school districts, describes some instructional strategies at the high school level, and concludes with reports from the National Center on Educational Restructuring and Inclusion (NCERI) *National Study of Inclusive Education* (1994, 1995) documenting these strategies.

School districts across the United States that are initiating inclusive education programs report that instructional strategies and classroom practices that support inclusion are, for the most part, similar to ones that teachers have found to be effective for students in general. Although this chapter's discussion is presented in the context of inclusive education, most of the approaches examined can be considered "best practices" in all classrooms, whether they are special education or general education.

IEP: TOOL FOR INCLUSION

A number of school districts have been reexamining their IEPs to determine how they can become more appropriate tools for inclusive education. For example, the Northeast Independent School District of San Antonio, Texas, has developed an adaptation checklist for the IEP. The checklist includes the following categories:

- *Pacing:* Extend time requirements; vary activity often; allow breaks; omit assignments requiring copy in timed situation; send home school texts for preview; supply a home set of texts/materials for preview/review

- *Environment:* Preferential seating; planned seating; alter physical room arrangement; define areas concretely; reduce/minimize distractions (visual, spatial, auditory, movement)
- *Presentation of subject matter:* Teach to student's learning style (e.g., linguistic, logical/math, spatial, bodily/kinesthetic, musical, interpersonal, intrapersonal, model experiential learning); utilize special curriculum; teacher provides tape lectures/discussions for replay; teacher provides notes; NCR [National Cash Register] paper for peer to provide notes; functional application of academic skills; present demonstrations/models; utilize manipulatives; emphasize critical information; preteach vocabulary; make/use vocabulary files; reduce language level/reading level of assignment; use total communication; use facilitated communication; share activities; use visual sequences
- *Materials:* Arrangement of material on page; taped texts and/or other classroom material; highlighted texts/study guides; use supplementary materials; note-taking assistance; type teacher material; large print; braille text; special equipment (e.g., electric typewriter, calculator, computer, braille reader/typewriter, tape-/videorecorder)
- *Assignments:* Give directions in small distinct steps (written/picture/verbal); use written backup for oral directions; lower the difficulty level; shorten assignment; reduce paper and pencil tasks; read or tape-record directions; use pictorial directions; give extra cues or prompts; allow students to record or type assignment; adapt worksheets, packets; avoid penalizing for spelling errors/sloppy; avoid penalizing for penmanship
- *Self-management / follow-through:* Visual daily schedule; calendars; check often for understanding/review; request parent reinforcement; have student repeat directions; teach study skills; use study sheets to organize material; design/write/use long-term assignment guidelines; review and practice in real situations; plan for generalizations; teach skill in several settings/environments
- *Testing adaptations:* Oral; taped; pictures; read test to student; preview language of test questions; application in real setting; test administered by a resource person; short answer; multiple choice; modify format; shorten length; extend time
- *Social interaction support:* Peer advocacy; peer tutoring; structure activities to create opportunities [for] social interaction; focus on social processes rather than end product; structure shared experiences in school/extracurricular; cooperative learning groups; use multiple/rotating peers; teach friendship skills/sharing/negotiation; teach social communication skills
- *Motivation and reinforcement:* Verbal; nonverbal; positive reinforcement; concrete reinforcement; planned motivating sequence of activities; reinforce initiation; offer choice; use strengths/interests often.

This extensive list provides a comprehensive view of potential adaptations. As Giangreco and Edelman (1995) cautioned, however, the services for students with disabilities in inclusive classes should be "only as special as necessary."

"BEST STRATEGIES" FOR INCLUSIVE EDUCATION

Teachers report that a precursor to inclusive programs is a belief in the benefits of heterogeneous classrooms. San Diego's AVID (Achieving Via Individual Determination) program, which places low-achieving students in college-preparatory classes, demonstrates the power of shifting "education policy for underachieving students away from a simplified or reduced curriculum toward a rigorous curriculum with increased support for low-achieving students" (Mehan, Hubbard, Lintz, & Villanueva, 1994, p. i). Mehan and colleagues (1994) pointed out that students placed in remedial tracks seldom catch up to their peers, rarely receive equivalent curriculum or instruction, and frequently experience the stigmatizing consequences of negative labeling; these factors are true as well for students placed in special education programs. The key elements in the AVID program—supports in the high track classroom, high expectations for the students, and advocacy on students' behalf by their teachers—are equally appropriate for students with disabilities. Students who participated in the AVID program had higher college enrollment rates than similar students who did not participate, and the "ethnic and linguistic minority students from low-income backgrounds who have been untracked do as well as or better than students from well-to-do backgrounds" (Mehan et al., 1994, p. 14).

Two key points made by reports from school districts are, first, that the adaptations appropriate for students with disabilities benefit all students; and, second, as indicated early in this chapter, that the instructional strategies used in inclusive education classrooms are practices recommended by educational researchers and reformers for general education students. Indeed, the most common statement from teachers was, "Good teaching is good teaching is good teaching."

Cooperative learning has been identified as the most important instructional strategy supporting inclusive education. In the *National Study* (1994, 1995), well over half of the districts implementing inclusive education reported using cooperative learning. Instructional strategies cited by a quarter or more of the districts include the following:

- Cooperative learning
- Curricular adaptations

- Students supporting other students
- Using paraprofessional/classroom aides
- Using instructional technology

Cooperative Learning

Cooperative learning involves students working together on a common or shared task. Inclusive education and cooperative learning have parallel goals and outcomes: improved social skills, greater communication skills, development of problem-solving skills, prosocial behaviors, and enhanced learning (Farlow, 1994). The use of cooperative learning has been extensively researched by Slavin and is an integral part of his "Success for All" program (described in Chapter 26). A growing literature including research articles and books describes how to facilitate cooperative learning in inclusive settings and the results of such efforts (Jakupcak, 1993; Lloyd, Crowley, Kohler, & Strain, 1988; Meyer & Henry, 1993; Nevin, 1993; Nevin, Thousand, & Villa, 1994; Putnam, 1993a, 1993b; Putnam & Spenciner, 1993; Sapon-Shevin, 1990; Sapon-Shevin, Ayres, & Duncan, 1994; Stevens & Slavin, 1991; Tateyama-Sniezek, 1990; Thousand, Villa, & Nevin, 1994; Williams, 1993).

Linking cooperative learning, inclusion, and broader school reform, Sapon-Shevin et al. (1994) stated,

> Cooperative learning is good for all students and . . . it is a part of comprehensive school reform efforts. To achieve this reform, teachers must work together to build networks within their school community. Teachers must also establish a cooperative classroom ethic that emphasizes overall community building, open communication about differences and classroom practices, and reciprocal helping relationships. Meaningful content in cooperative lessons is critical for the success of all students. For students to succeed within their groups, careful consideration regarding group heterogeneity must be given in conjunction with roles that ensure active, equal participation by all students. Creative assessment practices must be developed to document achievement of meaningful outcomes for students. All of these considerations require planning and structure in order for the teaching to be successful. (pp. 57–58)

Curricular Adaptations

Curricular adaptations are the technical strategies that support inclusive education. As a *Handbook for Inclusive Education* (n.d.), developed by the Napa Valley (California) School District, puts it, "Adaptations should make the difference between mere presence and meaningful participation" (p. 8). The handbook goes on to identify various curricular adaptation categories:

As is: Students are involved in the same lesson as other students with the same objectives and using the same materials.

Providing physical assistance: Assisting a student to complete activities by the actual manipulation of materials, equipment, or her/his body.

Adapting materials: Utilizing materials that allow for participation in age appropriate activities without having pre-requisite basic motor, communicative, or cognitive skills.

Multi-level curriculum: Students are working in the same subject area, but . . . at different levels of curriculum.

Curriculum overlapping: Students are involved in the same activity with other students but may have a goal for a different curriculum area.

Substitute curriculum: Students are involved in alternative activities that meet primary instructional needs when the team feels that the general education curriculum is not appropriate. These activities may occur within the classroom, school, or community, and can include general education peers. (pp. 9–10)

Whereas educators in other school districts may use different labels for these adaptations, this listing suggests the range of adaptations that a school district may consider.

Collaboration between general and special educators is shifting from a focus on adaptations for individual students "to making the curriculum accessible to a diverse group of students, including those with disabilities" (Warger & Pugach, 1996). According to Warger and Pugach,

The task becomes one of integrating knowledge about curriculum and new curriculum trends with expectations about how learners with diverse characteristics will interact with the content. Through such collaborative discussions—and, then, actions—teachers can shape what goes on in classrooms to the advantage of all students *before* [emphasis in original] presenting content—rather than after a student encounters difficulty. (1996, p. 62)

This is curriculum-based collaboration, using the curriculum as the starting point for redesigning classrooms to accommodate diverse learners. A proactive approach, it responds to the new norm of diversity in the classroom. Stated Warger and Pugach (1996), "The push for inclusive schools has moved away from excluding students who don't fit the mold to one of creating learning environments where all students can succeed" (p. 65).

"Scaffolding" is one of the ways of making the curriculum more accessible. This involves providing support to help learners bridge the gap between what they know and can do and the intended goal (Graves, Graves, & Braaten, 1996). Attending to students' reading styles is another strength-based approach to instruction (Carbo, 1996).

Students Supporting Other Students

Using peers as tutors or "buddies" has beneficial outcomes for all students. Many approaches have been researched, including students as tutors—cross-age and peer, in classwide dyadic programs and classwide teams; students as friends or buddies—individually or in circle of friends programs; and students as peer mediators (Forest & Pearpoint, 1990; Gartner & Lipsky, 1990; Harper, Maheady, & Malette, 1994; Harris, 1994; LaPlant & Zane, 1994; McNeil, 1994; Schrumpf, 1994; Stainback & Stainback, 1990).

Numerous studies have demonstrated the effectiveness of traditional tutoring programs; that is, ones in which older and/or more advanced students tutor those who are younger or in need of additional support. For the student being tutored, benefits accrue through individualization and additional time in instructional activities, including repetition, drill, and practice. Potentially more powerful are the benefits for tutors. The *Harvard Education Letter* reported that "tutors learn at least as much as the students they teach—and tutors who are far behind academically gain even more" ("Big Kids Teach," 1987, p. 2). Tutors learn by reviewing, reinforcing, and reformulating the material, as well as by seeing the learning from a different vantage point—that is, by observing the student being tutored learn. In the affective domain, tutors gain in self-confidence and self-esteem (Gartner & Lipsky, 1990).

For students with disabilities, opportunities to tutor other students—both with and without disabilities—as well as to be tutored, provide numerous benefits. As tutors, students with disabilities can learn new material, as well as reinforce previous learning; they can gain self-confidence as learners themselves and also as teachers of others; and—particularly when tutoring students without disabilities—they can alter the often limited views held about the capacities of students with disabilities by taking on the role of help giver rather than the traditional role of help receiver. (For a full discussion of programs in which students with disabilities play the tutor role, see Gartner & Lipsky, 1990).

ROLES OF PARAPROFESSIONALS

Paraprofessionals[1] have been used in classrooms to help implement instructional and related activities at least since the 1950s. In the 1970s, passage of the Education of the Handicapped Act of 1970

---

[1]Paraprofessionals have also been called aides, teacher aides, and instructional assistants. We use the more common term, *paraprofessional*.

(PL 91-230) and the Education for All Handicapped Children Act of 1975 (PL 94-142) led to major increases in the employment of paraprofessionals. Whereas initially paraprofessionals' roles focused on record keeping, preparing materials, monitoring students, or maintaining learning centers and equipment, increasingly they have become active participants in all components of the instructional process. New roles for paraprofessionals are a result of 1) efforts to integrate students with disabilities into general education programs; 2) the growing number of students with limited English proficiency; 3) the increasing number of students whose families are economically at a disadvantage or who experience other circumstances that may place them "at risk"; and 4) the continuing shortage of teachers, especially those from minority backgrounds (Pickett, 1996).

Paraprofessionals have played important roles in implementing inclusive education programs. The report from the Working Group on Inclusive Schools stated,

> In every school the paraprofessionals were a quiet key to success. They are both the continuity and support for students, staff, and families. As active participants of the team and of the school community, they are a critical element to both the planning and delivery of appropriate services to students. In many cases, paraprofessionals are a link to making inclusive schools work. (*Creating Schools*, 1994, p. 12)

Frequently, as a student with disabilities has been moved into an inclusive class, an individual paraprofessional has been assigned to that student. Increasingly it is being recognized, however, that this practice can prove detrimental to students both with and without disabilities:

> This practice, created in the early 1980s during the initial stages of the movement to unify general and special education, may inhibit rather than foster interaction between students with and without disabilities, and may increase reliance on an adult rather than helping the child to achieve independence. (Pickett, 1996, p. 47)

The paraprofessional "Velcroed" to the child, in effect, stands between the child and his or her peers without disabilities. The term *bubble children* has been used to describe students with disabilities who are placed in a general education class but who do not interact directly with the other children, interacting only with the assigned aide (Roach, 1995). Increasingly, school districts are assigning a paraprofessional to work with the general teacher and with all of the children in the class. This ensures that the teacher spends more direct time with the student(s) with disabilities; it enables the teacher–paraprofessional team to provide assistance to other students who may benefit; and it removes the barrier that may be created between students because of the constant presence of an adult—in this case, the paraprofessional.

As inclusive education programs increase, it is essential that the roles of paraprofessionals be updated and (re)defined. This includes developing programs of certification and career ladders, and educating and training paraprofessionals and teachers to their new roles and the nature of collaboration. Some states (e.g., Washington) have developed well-designed training programs for paraprofessionals, and Kansas has a systematic three-step design that allows paraprofessionals to move up a career ladder ("Paras's Expectations," 1995). Another noteworthy example is the "career ladder program" of the New York City Public Schools, the City University of New York, and the United Federation of Teachers (the collective bargaining agent for both the teachers and the instructional paraprofessionals), which has resulted in several thousand former paraprofessionals becoming certified teachers in the city's schools. Increasingly, colleges are developing training programs for paraprofessionals that focus on their role in inclusive classrooms.

USE OF INSTRUCTIONAL TECHNOLOGY

New developments in instructional technology provide extraordinary opportunities for all students, including those with disabilities. Increasingly, schools are identifying how to use technology to support inclusion. Examples of such applications include the following:

- Tape recordings of lessons for those students who find it difficult or impossible to take notes
- Taped books for students with visual impairments or learning disabilities
- Closed captioning for students who are deaf or have auditory learning disabilities
- Computer software that converts printed text into braille or voice transmission
- Computers that permit students who have difficulty writing, as well as those that help students with learning disabilities, [to] correct spelling and grammar
- Computers that have expanded keyboards or are switch or voice activated
- Computers that speak for students with visual impairments
- Photocopiers and computer printers that enlarge text
- Stereo-listening devices for students who are hard of hearing
- Computer networks that permit students (and teachers) to access information and communicate with others outside of the school

- Computer software that enables professionals to assess a student's mastery of the curriculum and design appropriate instruction and curricular modifications
- Computer software that permits students, individually or in groups, to master curricular goals by using computer programs that make maximum use of the students' learning styles and abilities, monitor progress, and provide interaction with the teacher
- Video disc, virtual reality, and other emerging technologies that empower students to learn from and explore the universe, regardless of their disability (*Creating Schools*, 1994, pp. 31–32)

The variety and sophistication of the technology present a danger as well. As Pressman and Blackstone point out in Chapter 24, the technology must not be allowed to become "an end in itself, rather than a tool that can enhance learning and participation within the regular classroom."[2] Construing technology as "diversity accommodation tools," the authors state: "Trying to make inclusion work without technology is like trying to win a fight with one hand tied behind your back. The core issue is *how* [emphasis in original] to use technology to promote as full and successful an inclusion situation as possible." This point is echoed by Linda Benton, technology coordinator with the Early Childhood Education Center, Albany, New York: "Technology can level the playing field for children with disabilities in regular classrooms and facilitate successful inclusive experiences" (cited in "Technology Helps," 1995, p. 5).

Often, technology developed for a student with a disability has benefits for other students in the class. For example, a high school student who is blind has described his own use of technology in this context:

> Technology has been essential to my success; I work with computers and other learning tools. If teachers are creative, they won't view "technology" as just a machine; it is another avenue to deliver special services in a regular classroom. My fellow students also benefit from this innovation. For example, in physics and health classes, my teachers constructed models of the human body so that I could learn by touch while my peers were learning visually. So although the model was for me, all of us learned from it. (McKeithan, 1995, p. 32)

(For various models of using technology to promote inclusive education, see Chapter 24.)

---

[2] A growing body of organizations and publications are expanding on the use of technology in the classroom. For example, the Alliance for Technology Access, the Foundation for Technology Access, *Alternatively Speaking, Augmentative Communication News, Computer Resources for People with Disabilities* (1994), the HarperCollins series *Integrating Computers in Your Classroom*, Male (1994), and Pressman (1995).

INSTRUCTION AT THE HIGH SCHOOL LEVEL

Attention both to student learning processes and to subject-area adaptations is a critical aspect of effective inclusion at the high school level. At the Center for Research on Learning, University of Kansas, Deshler and colleagues have developed a two-pronged approach to the inclusion needs of secondary school students with disabilities. Moreover, the approach has been noted to be successful for all students. The approach includes the following:

1. *Strategic learning:* For students to learn a large amount of content, they need to know how to use various learning strategies in thinking about, completing, and evaluating school tasks and assignments. . . . [T]hey need to learn to take stock of a classroom situation and then to use the appropriate strategies. Students can learn to be strategic learners in courses designed for that purpose or in their regular classes.

2. *Content enhancements:* Many emotionally or cognitively challenged students have difficulty organizing, understanding, and remembering the information presented during group instruction. Our research has shown that students' performance improves markedly when teachers enhance their delivery of the information to highlight critical features of the content.

   [W]hen students learn to be strategic learners and teachers use content enhancements, the instructional emphasis shifts from a "content" to a "process" focus. Consequently, the secondary teacher not only teaches the content but also the strategies required to make learning the content meaningful and transferable. In short, teachers organize content into a learner-friendly form, consider which strategies students need, and teach students how to use them by providing a "learning apprenticeship" in their classroom. (Schumaker & Deshler, 1994–1995, p. 50)

Farlow (1996) has emphasized the opportunities to use natural supports and to adapt the high school curriculum. Regarding the former, she has suggested allowing peers to facilitate learning, structuring classroom activities to make peer support available, priming students to be successful participants in inclusive classes, giving students valued roles, and utilizing existing expertise. In terms of adapting the curriculum, she proposes using independent prompts, varying the amount of work required of individual students, adjusting teacher information delivery modes, allowing students to express information in varied ways, and presenting alternative activities.

The transition from high school to life and work in the community is the focus of an education program for high school–age students with disabilities proposed by Sailor et al. (1989). As these authors make clear, "transition" is more than a plan for a student's post-IDEA future. It also entails opportunities for the student to learn in the community and, thereby, to prepare for life in the community—employment, living, and recreation. A transition curriculum involves the development of academic, vocational-technical, and work skills. Notable research studies in the 1990s have reported on the positive effects in terms of postschool outcomes of participation in vocational education and parental involvement (Gill & Edgar, 1990; Siegel et al., 1993; Wagner, Blackorby, Cameto, & Newman, 1993).

REPORTS FROM THE *NATIONAL STUDY OF INCLUSIVE EDUCATION*

Following are excerpted reports of instructional strategies and classroom supports from some school districts included in the *National Study* (1995). These reports reflect the range of instructional strategies used in implementing inclusive education programs as well as their common ties with many of the methods used in quality general education classrooms.

A research study of the middle school program [where cooperatively taught classes are used] found: 1) . . . general educators improved their perceptions of cooperative teaching process over time; 2) special needs educators held more positive views of cooperative teaching than general educators; 3) parents were generally positive about their children's educational experience and became more positive over time; 4) . . . special needs students became more positive about their school experience over time; 5) students in cooperatively taught classes have fewer incomplete assignments, [have] improved grades, were on-task more often, had more one-on-one instructor time, and were engaged in more individual work. Conversely, students in regular classes were more likely to receive large group instruction as opposed to students in cooperative classes. (p. 122)

Marshalltown Community Schools, Iowa

A study comparing the academic performance of ninth-grade students co-taught in general education classrooms with similar classrooms without co-teaching compared performance on the state's ninth-grade minimum competency tests and classroom grades. [Students in the co-taught classes and the comparison classes had similar academic profiles and backgrounds.] Results found that the co-taught classes, with a general educator and special educator working collaboratively with a heterogeneous group of special and general education students, can produce significantly better results than general education classrooms in achieving academic requirements for high school graduation. In particular, a significantly greater percentage of ninth-grade students from co-taught classes passed statewide minimum competency tests in three different content areas than students from content classes that did not include special education students and were not co-taught by a general educator and a special educator. The findings suggest that the combined effect of two teachers' capabilities, one strong in content and curriculum knowledge, the other in adaptive teaching strategies and classroom modifications, can in fact enable the general classroom to successfully address the learning needs of a diverse group of students, including mainstream special education students. Moreover, the results suggest that all students within a co-taught class benefit from this service delivery model and that school improvement plans should consider such collaborative models in developing education reform initiatives for all students. (p. 149)

Anne Arundel County Schools, Maryland

Since we began [inclusion] in the fall of the 1990–1991 school year, attitudes and processes have undergone many changes. Inclusion was not the only new initiative in our district at [that] time. Changes were underway in the Language Arts Process, and the adoption of a new student management program centered around Glasser's control theory/reality therapy. Teacher frustration was running high as [teachers] tried to internalize and implement all these programs at once. As each system was adopted by individual staff members for the "regular education" students, it became obvious to most that with very little modification, these practices were good for the included students also. Perhaps the biggest problem was that staff tried to make inclusion too hard by planning separate and distinct programs for their individual population instead of modifying their already existing programs to suit individual needs. The Writing Process, which is an integral part of our curriculum K–12, is an excellent program for included students also that makes them feel just like any other student as they are able, with help, to participate in all phases of the process from first draft to publication. As teachers became more familiar with each of these new concepts, attitudes also changed about their application for the included students. (p. 179)

Hillsdale Community Schools, Michigan

Whole Language in the elementary schools makes it possible for all students to participate in writing and reading experiences. The literature-based reading program provides a variety of options for reading (in groups, with a partner, listening to tapes). The activities that accompany the stories allow all students to be actively involved in some way. Math manipulatives and a focus on problem solving activities make it possible to include all children in math lessons. Current Events and the use of television and multimedia has become a part of the social studies curriculum, which has allowed all students, even nonreaders, to participate. Instructional supports such as Chapter I and Assurance of Mastery are provided in classrooms rather than pullout settings. The district has seen significant changes in classroom instructional settings. (p. 183)

Burnsville-Eagle-Savage Public Schools,
Independent School District #191, Minnesota

Many of the instructional strategies teachers use with "normal" children work well with children with disabilities. These can include modifying the curriculum, behavior interventions, assignment sheets, textbooks on tape or highlighted, more time allotment, shorter assignments, substitute written assignments, computer work *vs.* written work, special seating, study carrels, and many more. Supports include program or management assistants to help small groups or one-on-one, resource room time, and behavior specialists. This district also had an inclusion support group available in the elementary building to answer questions and to help with ideas. This group sponsors [meetings] during the school year that give parents, teachers, and other interested persons a chance to voice concerns and get answers. (p. 188)

Inver Grove Heights Public Schools, Minnesota

The Class Within A Class service delivery model has encouraged the placement of students with mild to moderate disabilities in the general education classroom. It is built upon the premise that special education students are capable of mastering the same challenging curriculum as their peers without disabilities when the resources of general education and special education are merged in a collaborative teaching model; [it is] supported by the strong alignment of curriculum, teaching, and assessment; and [it is] augmented with instruction in learning strategies for those children who do not possess efficient learning processes. (p. 197)

Frances Howell School District, Missouri

Learning to use the computer as a learning tool within the instructional program has proven very successful. Frequently teachers employ cooperative learning activities within the classroom. In addition, teachers allow students to select the types of projects that will demonstrate their knowledge—some present information in written reports, others through visuals, or oral reports. The learning styles of students are reflected in the presentations by the teachers. Teachers use manipulatives within all subjects and the calculator to assist in math. (p. 214)

Roswell Independent School District, New Mexico

Besides the obvious benefits to students across the board, another major benefit of inclusion I see is the overall improvement of instruction. Regular education teachers pass on tips for classroom management, keeping everyone occupied while dealing with various working speeds. The special education teachers pass on tips for modifications and learning strategies. Everyone is more enthusiastic. Each student gets discussed and reviewed more. (p. 294)

Lennox School District, South Dakota

Teachers are learning how to change a lesson so that all learners can benefit. The teachers who are teaching an inclusive classroom full of students are becoming more effective teachers. They are utilizing the multimodality approach to accommodate the various learning styles. Teachers have been noted to . . . become more student centered. . . . Now that the special education teacher or instructional assistant is involved in the activities, functions, and successes within the regular classroom, students have a better chance at immediate access to an adult for extra support and help. The teachers help everyone. There are no boundaries in the classroom in so far as who can work with whom. (p. 314)

Metropolitan Nashville Public Schools, Tennessee

East Ward [Elementary School] staff members create the interdisciplinary curriculum used throughout the school. Themes are designed to be relevant to the individual student and [to] develop as student interests are revealed. Students are able to explore areas of interest and to demonstrate knowledge through a variety of different products. Individual student growth is documented through use of authentic assessment. (p. 329)

Killeen Independent School District, Texas

"Jump Start" is a morning program, offered to all students, which involves previewing, preteaching, reviewing, and reteaching of classroom curricula. This enables students to get a "jump start" on the day to assure continuous academic success in the general education classroom. (p. 356)

Takhoma School District, Washington

Cooperative learning is one strategy that supports inclusion. Another is peer tutoring. . . . [W]here they are being used, inclusion is successful. The portfolio process also provides students with opportunities to demonstrate knowledge in unique ways, as does the emphasis on Gardner's [multiple] intelligences. For the first time, teachers in the district are allowing demonstration of skills in ways other than pen and pencil performance. This act in itself allows teachers to recognize unique intelligences and to catch students doing well who previously might not have been able to demonstrate success because of the limitations set. (p. 346)

Franklin Northeast Supervisory Union, Vermont

CONCLUSION

This chapter has described the instructional strategies most often used in inclusive classrooms. Whereas these strategies provide the classroom supports necessary for included special education students, they also represent the "best practices" of general educators. It is this confluence of instructional strategies that has the greatest potential for the success and expansion of inclusive education. The approach is reflected, for example, in Kentucky's "best practices recommendations" for implementation at the district, building, and classroom levels ("Best Practices," 1994). A key component of this process is the congruence between recommended practices at each level (i.e., district-level goals are reflected in classroom practices, while desired classroom practices are supported by district-level policies).

REFERENCES

Best practices. (1994). Frankfort, KY: Department of Education.

Big kids teach little kids: What we know about cross-age tutoring. (1987). *Harvard Education Letter, 3*(2), 1–4.

Carbo, M. (1996). Reading styles. *Educational Leadership, 53*(5), 8–13.

Creating schools for all of our students: What 12 schools have to say. (1994). Reston, VA: Council for Exceptional Children.

Education for All Handicapped Children Act of 1975, PL 94-142, 20 U.S.C. § 1400 *et seq.*

Education of the Handicapped Act (EHA) of 1970, PL 91-230, 20 U.S.C. § 1400 *et seq.*

Farlow, L. (1994, June 18). *Cooperative learning to facilitate the inclusion of students with moderate to severe mental retardation in secondary subject-area classes.* Paper presented at the annual conference of the American Association on Mental Retardation, Boston.

Farlow, L. (1996). A quartet of success stories: How to make inclusion work. *Educational Leadership, 53*(5), 51–55.

Forest, M., & Pearpoint, J. (1990). Supports for addressing severe maladaptive behaviors. In W. Stainback & S. Stainback (Eds.), *Support networks for inclusive schooling: Interdependent integrated education* (pp. 187–197). Baltimore: Paul H. Brookes Publishing Co.

Gartner, A., & Lipsky, D.K. (1990). Students as instructional agents. In W. Stainback & S. Stainback (Eds.), *Support networks for inclusive schooling: Interdependent integrated education* (pp. 81–93). Baltimore: Paul H. Brookes Publishing Co.

Giangreco, M.F., & Edelman, S.W. (1995, December). *Coordinating support services in inclusive classrooms.* Presentation at the TASH conference, San Francisco.

Gill, D., & Edgar, E. (1990). Outcomes of a vocational program for students with mild disabilities. The Pierce County vocational/special education cooperative. *Journal for Vocational Special Needs Education, 12*(3), 17–22.

Graves, M.F., Graves, B.B., & Braaten, S. (1996). Scaffolding reading experiences for inclusive classes. *Educational Leadership, 53*(5), 14–16.

Handbook for inclusive education. (n.d.). Napa, CA: Napa Valley School District.

Harper, G.F., Maheady, L., & Malette, B. (1994). The power of peer-mediated instruction: How and why it promotes academic success for all students. In J.S. Thousand, R.A. Villa, & A.I. Nevin (Eds.), *Creativity and collaborative learning: A practical guide to empowering students and teachers* (pp. 229–241). Baltimore: Paul H. Brookes Publishing Co.

Harris, T. (1994). Christine's inclusion: An example of peers supporting one another. In J.S. Thousand, R.A Villa, & A.I. Nevin (Eds.), *Creativity and collaborative learning: A practical guide to empowering stu-*

dents and teachers (pp. 293–301). Baltimore: Paul H. Brookes Publishing Co.

Jakupcak, J. (1993). Innovative classroom programs for full inclusion. In J.W. Putnam (Ed.), *Cooperative learning and strategies for inclusion: Celebrating diversity in the classroom* (pp. 163–179). Baltimore: Paul H. Brookes Publishing Co.

LaPlant, L., & Zane, N. (1994). Partner learning systems. In J.S. Thousand, R.A. Villa, & A.I. Nevin (Eds.), *Creativity and collaborative learning: A practical guide to empowering students and teachers* (pp. 261–273). Baltimore: Paul H. Brookes Publishing Co.

Lloyd, J.W., Crowley, E.P., Kohler, F.W., & Strain, P.S. (1988). Redefining the research agenda: Cooperative learning, prereferral, teacher consultations, and peer-mediated interventions. *Journal of Learning Disabilities, 21,* 43–52.

Male, M. (1994). *Technology for inclusion: Meeting the special needs of all students.* Needham, MA: Allyn & Bacon.

McKeithan, T.L., II. (1995, February 22). "The best advocate I have is me." *Education Week,* 32.

McNeil, M. (1994). Creating powerful partnerships through partner learning. In J.S. Thousand, R.A. Villa, & A.I. Nevin (Eds.), *Creativity and collaborative learning: A practical guide to empowering students and teachers* (pp. 243–259). Baltimore: Paul H. Brookes Publishing Co.

Mehan, H., Hubbard, L., Lintz, A., & Villanueva, I. (1994). *Tracking untracking: The consequences of placing low track students in high track classes.* Santa Cruz, CA: National Center on Cultural Diversity and Second Language Learning.

Meyer, L.H., & Henry, L.A. (1993). Cooperative classroom management: Student needs and fairness in the regular classroom. In J.W. Putnam (Ed.), *Cooperative learning and strategies for inclusion: Celebrating diversity in the classroom* (pp. 93–121). Baltimore: Paul H. Brookes Publishing Co.

National Study of Inclusive Education. (1994). New York: The City University of New York, National Center on Educational Restructuring and Inclusion.

National Study of Inclusive Education. (1995). New York: The City University of New York, National Center on Educational Restructuring and Inclusion.

Nevin, A. (1993). Curricular and instructional adaptations for including students with disabilities in cooperative groups. In J.W. Putnam (Ed.), *Cooperative learning and strategies for inclusion: Celebrating diversity in the classroom* (pp. 41–56). Baltimore: Paul H. Brookes Publishing Co.

Nevin, A.I., Thousand, J.S., & Villa, R.A. (1994). Creative cooperative group lesson plans. In J.S. Thousand, R.A. Villa, & A.I. Nevin (Eds.), *Creativity and collaborative learning: A practical guide to empowering students and teachers* (pp. 131–225). Baltimore: Paul H. Brookes Publishing Co.

Paras's expectations must change to accommodate the inclusive classroom. (1995). *Inclusive Education Programs, 2*(5), 1, 11–12.

Pickett, A. (1996, Winter). Paraeducators in inclusive education programs: The need for performance, professional development and management standards. *Impact,* 46–48.

Pressman, H. (1995). *Accommodating learning style differences in elementary classrooms.* New York: Harcourt Brace Jovanovich.

Putnam, J.W. (Ed.). (1993a). *Cooperative learning and strategies for inclusion: Celebrating diversity in the classroom.* Baltimore: Paul H. Brookes Publishing Co.

Putnam, J.W. (1993b). The process of cooperative learning. In J.W. Putnam (Ed.), *Cooperative learning and strategies for inclusion: Celebrating diversity in the classroom* (pp. 15–40). Baltimore: Paul H. Brookes Publishing Co.

Putnam, J.W., & Spenciner, L.J. (1993). Supporting young children's development through cooperative activities. In J.W. Putnam (Ed.), *Cooperative learning and strategies for inclusion: Celebrating diversity in the classroom* (pp. 123–143). Baltimore: Paul H. Brookes Publishing Co.

Roach, V. (1995). *Winning ways: Creating inclusive schools, classrooms, and communities.* Alexandria, VA: National School Boards Association.

Sailor, W., Anderson, J.L., Halvorsen, A.T., Doering, K., Filler, J., & Goetz, L. (1989). *The comprehensive local school: Regular education for all students with disabilities.* Baltimore: Paul H. Brookes Publishing Co.

Sapon-Shevin, M. (1990). Student support through cooperative learning. In W. Stainback & S. Stainback (Eds.), *Support networks for inclusive schooling: Interdependent integrated education* (pp. 65–79). Baltimore: Paul H. Brookes Publishing Co.

Sapon-Shevin, M., Ayres, B.J., & Duncan, J. (1994). Cooperative learning and inclusion. In J.S. Thousand, R.A. Villa, & A.I. Nevin (Eds.), *Creativity and collaborative learning: A practical guide to empowering students and teachers* (pp. 45–58). Baltimore: Paul H. Brookes Publishing Co.

Schrumpf, F. (1994). The role of students in resolving conflicts in schools. In J.S. Thousand, R.A. Villa, & A.I. Nevin (Eds.), *Creativity and collaborative learning: A practical guide to empowering students and teachers* (pp. 275–291). Baltimore: Paul H. Brookes Publishing Co.

Schumaker, J.B., & Deshler, D.D. (1994–1995). Secondary classes can be inclusive, too. *Educational Leadership, 52*(4), 50–51.

Siegel, S., Robert, M., Greener, K., Meyer, G., Halloran, W., & Gaylord-Ross, R. (1993). *Career ladders for challenged youths in transition from school to adult life.* Austin, TX: PRO-ED.

Stainback, W., & Stainback, S. (1990). Facilitating peer supports and friendships. In W. Stainback & S. Stainback (Eds.), *Support networks for inclusive schooling: Interdependent integrated education* (pp. 51–63). Baltimore: Paul H. Brookes Publishing Co.

Stevens, R.J., & Slavin, R.E. (1991). When cooperative learning improves the achievement of students with mild disabilities: A response to Tateyama-Sniezek. *Exceptional Children, 57,* 276–280.

Tateyama-Sniezek, K.M. (1990). Cooperative learning: Does it improve the academic achievement of students with handicaps? *Exceptional Children, 56,* 426–437.

Technology helps preschool inclusion succeed. (1995). *Inclusive Education Programs, 2*(6), 5.

Thousand, J.W., Villa, R.A., & Nevin, A.I. (Eds.). (1994). *Creativity and collaborative learning: A practical guide to empowering students and teachers.* Baltimore: Paul H. Brookes Publishing Co.

Wagner, M., Blackorby, J., Cameto, R., & Newman, L. (1993). *What makes a difference? Influences on postsecondary outcomes for youth with disabilities: The third comprehensive report from the National Longitudinal Transition Study of special education students.* Menlo Park, CA: SRI International.

Warger, C.L., & Pugach, M.C. (1996). Forming partnerships around curriculum. *Educational Leadership, 53*(5), 62–65.

Williams, D.R. (1993). Cooperative learning and cultural diversity: Building caring communities in the cooperative classroom. In J.W. Putnam (Ed.), *Cooperative learning and strategies for inclusion: Celebrating diversity in the classroom* (pp. 145–161). Baltimore: Paul H. Brookes Publishing Co.

13

ORGANIZATIONAL ATTITUDES TOWARD INCLUSIVE EDUCATION

During the 1990s, many organizations have adopted policy positions concerning inclusive education. This chapter surveys those policy stances. The positions of the presidentially appointed National Council on Disability are summarized first, followed by those of the two largest special education groups, the Council for Exceptional Children and The Association for Persons with Severe Handicaps (TASH). The viewpoints of groups focusing on individual disabilities, presented in descending order by the size of the student population they represent, are then described. Finally, the positions of several general education organizations are outlined, including the National Education Association (NEA) and the American Federation of Teachers (AFT).

POLICY POSITIONS OF NATIONAL ADVISORY AND OTHER SPECIAL EDUCATION GROUPS

In testimony in 1994 before the House Subcommittee on Select Education and Civil Rights of the Committee on Education, the National Council on Disability, an advisory body appointed by the president, challenged the least restrictive environment (LRE) conceptualization as the basis for special education programs ("NCD Calls," 1994). The council pointed out that the LRE conceptualization derived from prisoners' rights issues and is not appropriate to the education of students with disabilities. Instead of the concept of a continuum, which, on at least some occasions, requires students to be separated from their age peers to receive the services that they require (see Taylor, 1988), the council favored the concept of an "array of services." Special education, the council urged, "needs to evolve as a support to typical education, not as a way of supplanting it. Inclusion is the most promising way to achieve this end" ("NCD Calls," 1994, p. 3).

The Council for Exceptional Children (CEC), the largest professional organization of special educators in the United States, at its 1993 delegate assembly, adopted the following resolution:

> CEC believes that a continuum of services must be available for all children, youth, and young adults. CEC also believes that the concept of inclusion is a meaningful goal to be pursued in our schools and communities. In addition, CEC believes children, youth, and young adults with disabilities should be served whenever possible in general education classrooms in inclusive neighborhood schools and community settings. Such settings should be strengthened and supported by an infusion of specially trained personnel and other appropriate supportive practices according to the individual needs of the child. (Council for Exceptional Children, 1993a)

CEC's Division for Early Childhood (DEC) has issued its own position statement on necessary supports for inclusive practices. The DEC advocates

> (a) the continued development, evaluation, and dissemination of full inclusion supports, services and systems so that options for inclusion are of high quality; (b) the development of preservice and inservice training programs that prepare families, administrators, and service providers to develop and work within inclusive settings; (c) collaboration among all key stakeholders to implement flexible fiscal and administrative procedures in support of inclusion; (d) research that contributes to our knowledge of state of the art services; and (e) the restructuring and unification of social, education, health, and intervention supports and services to make them more responsive to the needs of all children and families. (Council for Exceptional Children, 1993b)

The Council of Administrators of Special Education (CASE) is the organization of local district special education administrators. In 1993, it adopted *CASE Future Agenda for Special Education: Creating a Unified Education System*, which incorporates five "policies" and proposes five "actions," as follows:

> *Policies*: 1. All stakeholders are responsible for the education of all students in a community; 2. A unified system of education must prevail to ensure quality, inclusive education for all students; 3. Accountability for all students is guaranteed through a system of unified outcomes; 4. All educators are prepared to educate all students; and 5. Funding systems that support a unified system emphasize shared resources for all students without label, penalty or prejudice.

Actions: 1. Site-based management is the means for building a community of learners responsible for one another; 2. A curriculum framework for a unified system is the means to dialogue about outcomes for planning and organizing schools into learning communities; 3. Staff development in a restructured workplace fosters ad hoc problem solving, shared resources and continuous improvement; 4. All students and their families have access to integrated community services at or near the school site; and 5. All students and staff have access to and training in appropriate technology that supports collaborative decision making. (1993, p. 2)

TASH has long been a proponent of inclusion. A 1988 resolution, as revised in 1993, reads, in part,

> TASH reaffirms a definition of inclusion that begins with the educational and moral imperatives that students with disabilities belong in general education classrooms and that they receive the supports and services necessary to benefit from their education in the general education setting. Inclusion proceeds to and is fully defined by a new way of thinking based upon current understandings about how *all* children and young people are educated—a new way of thinking that embraces a sociology of acceptance of *all* [emphasis in original] into the school community as active, fully participating members; that views diversity as the norm and maintains a high quality education for each student by assuring effective teaching, powerful pedagogies, and necessary supports to each child in the general education setting.
>
> [T]ASH calls upon local, state, provincial, regional and federal governments, as well as all related organizations, to stand accountable for the development and maintenance of educational opportunities for *all* students that are fully inclusive and ultimately effective; and that the United States government be urged to vigorously enforce, at all levels, legislation *already enacted* [emphasis in original] that assures such accountability, development, and maintenance.

POLICY STATEMENTS OF DISABILITY GROUPS

Disability groups offer a range of perspectives on inclusion. The Learning Disabilities Association 1993 position paper, for example, does not support inclusion for all students. It states,

> The Learning Disabilities Association of America does not support "full inclusion" or any policies that mandate the same placement, instruction, or treatment for *ALL* [emphasis in original] students with learning disabilities. Many students with learning disabilities benefit from being served in the regular classroom. However, the regular education classroom is not the appropriate placement for a number of students with learning disabilities who may need alternative instructional environments, teaching strategies, and/or materials that cannot or will not be provided within the context of a regular classroom placement.

Children and Adults with Attention Deficit Disorders (Ch.A.D.D.) continues to support the continuum of placements. Its 1993 position on inclusion states,

> We believe that the concept of inclusion should reflect society's commitment that every child be educated in the environment that is most appropriate to that child's identified needs. CH.A.D.D. supports inclusion defined as education which provides access to appropriate support and remediation at every level to facilitate each child's ability to participate and achieve. The environment in which these services can best be delivered depends on the needs of the individual student.
>
> Many children with disabilities are educated successfully in regular classrooms with appropriate accommodations and supports. However, others require alternative environments to optimize their achievement. Ch.A.D.D. supports this continuum of services and placements.

The American Speech-Language-Hearing Association (ASHA) *Position Statement: Inclusive Practices for Children and Youth with Communication Disorders* framed its 1996 position with the recognition that

> the provision of speech, language, and hearing services in educational settings is moving toward service-delivery models that integrate intervention with general education programming, often termed inclusion. Inclusion has numerous strengths, including natural opportunities for peer interaction, and available research suggests cautious optimism regarding its effectiveness in promoting communication abilities and skills in related developmental domains. ASHA believes that the shift toward inclusion will not be optimal when implemented in absolute terms. Rather, the unique and specific needs of each child and family must always be considered.

ASHA's policy position identifies their broad goal of inclusion:

> The broad goal of inclusive service delivery must be compatible with continued recognition of the individual's unique needs and concerns. Inclusive practices are recommended as a guide in the development of intervention programming for children and youth with communication disorders.

The Arc (formerly the Association for Retarded Citizens) issued in 1993 a *Report Card to the Nation on Inclusion in Education of Students with Mental Retardation.* The report affirmed the following principles:

- All schools should value all students and include them in all aspects of school life.
- Preparation for life in the community best occurs when all students of different backgrounds and abilities learn and socialize together in classrooms and other school settings where all have a

chance to achieve and receive instruction designed to develop and enhance successful living within the community.

• Each student with a disability belongs in an age-appropriate classroom with peers who are not disabled.

• Each student has the right to receive individualized education which provides choices, meets the student's needs, and offers the necessary support.

The United Cerebral Palsy Associations' "Policy on Full Inclusion of Individuals with Disabilities" (1993) states,

> United Cerebral Palsy Associations, Inc. and its affiliate organizations support the goal of *full* [emphasis in original] inclusion of individuals with disabilities into every aspect of life and area of society, including the home, the school, the workforce and the community regardless of severity of disability, as enumerated in the Americans with Disabilities Act.

The National Association of the Deaf, in its 1995 "Position Statement on Full Inclusion," defines *full inclusion* as "the placement of all children with disabilities in their neighborhood schools, irrespective of their unique abilities and needs." The statement continues,

> The National Association of the Deaf (NAD) does not support full inclusion and is opposed to elimination of, or restrictions on the use of, placement options mandated by the "Full Continuum of Alternative Placements" regulation of IDEA. While the regular classroom in the neighborhood school may be the appropriate placement for some deaf and hard of hearing students, for many it is not. The NAD is committed to preserving and expanding the use of the full continuum of alternative placements to ensure that each deaf or hard of hearing child receives a quality education in an appropriate environment. (cited in Johnson & Cohen, 1994, p. 78)

The president of the National Family Association for Deaf-Blind (NFADB) has written:

> We believe in inclusion because it provides for the child who is deaf-blind the opportunity to be with peers who can become companions and friends. Since the child who is deaf-blind will most probably at adulthood function in a community with seeing and hearing peers and not be segregated from that community, we believe that joining the community early is more beneficial than joining it after the school years. Moreover, we believe that the knowledge and skills gained through education can occur as well in an inclusive setting as in a segregated setting. (cited in Ford & Fredericks, 1993 p. 18)

VIEWS OF GENERAL EDUCATION ORGANIZATIONS

Some general education organizations have adopted policies concerning inclusion. In 1992, the Association for Supervision and

Curriculum Development (ASCD) was one of the first general education organizations to support inclusion. It stated,

> Federal and state funding for special programs (e.g., Chapter 1, special education) is predicated on the identification, assessment, and labeling of children with handicaps or deficits in basic skills. Increasing empirical evidence demonstrates that this labeling stigmatizes children and tends to result in segregated services and lower teacher expectations.

The ASCD proposed that a "non-labeling approach to special program regulations can result in elimination of tracking and segregated services for children with unique needs."

Also in 1992, the National Association of State Boards of Education (NASBE) published *Winners All: A Call for Inclusive Schools.* In it, NASBE recommended that state boards

> 1. create a new belief system and vision for education in their states that include *ALL* [emphasis in original] students; 2. encourage and foster collaborative partnerships and joint training programs between general educators and special educators to encourage a greater capacity of both types of teachers to work with the diverse student population found in fully inclusive schools; and 3. sever the link between funding, placement, and handicapping label. Funding requirements should not drive programming and placement decisions for students. (p. 27)

The National Education Association (NEA), the nation's largest teacher organization, has supported and encouraged "appropriate inclusion." At its 1994 convention, the association adopted the following *NEA Policy on Inclusion*:

> The National Education Association is committed to equal educational opportunity, the highest quality education, and a safe learning environment for all students. The Association supports and encourages *appropriate inclusion. Appropriate inclusion* [emphasis in original] is characterized by practices and programs that provide for the following on a sustained basis:
>
> - A full continuum of placement options and services within each option. Placement and services must be determined for each student by a team that includes all stakeholders and must be specified in the Individualized Education Program.
> - Appropriate professional development, as part of normal work activity, of all educators and support staff associated with such programs. Appropriate training must also be provided for administrators, parents, and other stakeholders.
> - Adequate time, as part of the normal school day, to engage in coordinated and collaborative planning on behalf of all students.
> - Class sizes that are responsive to student needs.
> - Staff and technical assistance that is specifically appropriate to student and teacher needs.

- Inclusion practices and programs that lack these fundamental characteristics are inappropriate and must end.

The American Federation of Teachers (AFT), at its 1994 convention, adopted an inclusion policy that calls for

- Opposing programs that aim to put all disabled students in regular classes without considering their abilities and the benefits to them or other students
- Denouncing practices such as failing to offer services, professional development or paraprofessionals to aid inclusion
- Pressing for full funding of the federal mandate to educate all disabled students
- Granting teachers rights in the special education processes, including the right to appeal student placements
- Negating court decisions that limit discipline of disabled students
- Limiting the number of disabled students in a single classroom
- Helping all students meet high standards, regardless of their placement ("AFT Sets," 1994, p. 6)

AFT president Albert Shanker has used his weekly opinion columns, as well as other articles (Shanker, 1994a, 1994b), to characterize "full inclusion" as requiring all children with disabilities to be included in general education classes, regardless of their ability to function there. In addition to Shanker's writings, the AFT has sponsored a study of inclusion, conducted by Peter D. Hart Research Associates, (1994). The study surveyed some 400 AFT members: 62% were general classroom teachers, 17% were special education teachers, 2% were counselors, and 19% were "other." Their study provides the following data:

- Twenty-one percent of the schools in the country have adopted full inclusion, and the remaining 79% have taken steps to move in this direction.
- A third of the general education teachers who have had special education students in their classroom report that these students require special medical and nursing attention.
- Barely a fifth of the general education teachers have received any training [for inclusion].
- Nearly a quarter of the general education teachers say they do not have access to certified special education instructors and therapists for consultation.
- Fewer than half of the general education teachers report that they have been involved in developing and reviewing the students' IEP [individualized education program].
- A quarter of the teachers report that there are students who have been identified as disabled who should not have been so identified.
- Two-thirds of the teachers say that there are students who have not been identified as disabled who should have been so identified.

- Among the general education teachers who have special education students in their class, there is an even split between those who feel [these students] should be there and those who do not.

Although this AFT study offers interesting data, its major findings seem open to question. No other study with generally comparable data confirms the report that "21% of the schools in the country have adopted full inclusion, and the remaining 79% have taken steps to move in this direction." Indeed, data in other studies suggest that such a report is greatly exaggerated. In addition, the finding that "a third of the general education teachers who have had special education students in their classroom report that these students require special medical and nursing attention" is not supported by national data concerning students with medical needs. Indeed, using the most generous calculation, students with health impairments requiring any medical or nursing attention in school compose far fewer than 10% of those served by IDEA (U.S. Department of Education, 1995).

CONCLUSION

Views about inclusive education vary among special education groups, disability groups, and general education groups. These differences reflect the unique characteristics of the organizations, including their constituencies, historical experiences, and ideology. The organizations that do not support inclusion have gone on record more as opposing inclusion when it is implemented poorly than as opposing the principle itself.

REFERENCES

AFT sets the inclusion stance. (1994, July 25). *Education Daily*, 6.

American Speech-Language-Hearing Association. (1996). *Position statement: Inclusive practices for children and youth with communication disorders*. Rockville, MD: Author.

The Arc. (1993). *Report card to the nation on inclusion in education of students with mental retardation*. Arlington, TX: Author.

The Association for Persons with Severe Handicaps. (1993). *Resolution on inclusive education*. Seattle: Author.

Children and Adults with Attention Deficit Disorder. (1993). *Ch.A.D.D. position on inclusion*. Plantation, FL: Author.

The Council for Exceptional Children. (1993a). *CEC policy on inclusive schools and community settings*. Reston, VA: Author.

The Council for Exceptional Children. (1993b). *DEC position on inclusion*. Reston, VA: Council for Exceptional Children, Division for Early Childhood.

Council of Administrators of Special Education (CASE). (1993). *CASE future agenda for special education: Creating a unified system*. Albuquerque, NM: Author.

Ford, J., & Fredericks, B. (1993). Inclusion for children who are Deaf-Blind. *Network*, *3*(3), 6–9.

Johnson, R.C., & Cohen, O.P. (1994). *Implications and complications for deaf students of the full inclusion movement*. Washington, DC: Gallaudet University.

Learning Disabilities Association of America. (1993). *Full inclusion of all students with learning disabilities in the regular education classroom*. Pittsburgh: Author.

National Association of State Boards of Education (NASBE). (1992). *Winners all: A call for inclusive schools*. Alexandria, VA: Author.

National Education Association. (1994). *NEA policy on inclusion*. Washington, DC: Author.

NCD calls for end of special education as you know it. (1994). *Special Educator*, *10*(1), 5.

Shanker, A. (1994a). Full inclusion is neither free nor appropriate. *Educational Leadership*, *52*(2), 18–21.

Shanker, A. (1994b). Inclusion and ideology. *Exceptional Parent*, *24*(10), 39–40.

Taylor, S. (1988). Caught in the continuum: A critical analysis of the principle of least restrictive environment. *Journal of The Association for Persons with Severe Handicaps*, *13*(1), 41–53.

United Cerebral Policy Associations. (1993). *Policy on full inclusion of individuals with disabilities*. Washington, DC: Author.

U.S. Department of Education. (1995). *Seventeenth annual report to Congress on the implementation of the Individuals with Disabilities Education Act*. Washington, DC: Author.

14

EVALUATION OF
INCLUSIVE EDUCATION

As inclusive education programs have expanded across the United States, both supporters and opponents have sought information concerning inclusion's effectiveness. Increasingly, states, school districts, and educational researchers are evaluating inclusive programs and, along with individuals concerned with educational policy, are asking crucial questions regarding the benefits of inclusion.

This chapter highlights and summarizes research data describing these benefits. It does not focus on consequences for specific groups of students with disabilities, nor is it meant to be exhaustive. The chapter begins with reports on large-scale studies and then examines, in turn, studies concerning academic, social, and behavioral benefits to school-age students with disabilities; the impacts on school-age students without disabilities; and the impacts on preschool children, both with and without disabilities. The chapter concludes with reports from some local school districts, excerpted from the National Center on Educational Restructuring and Inclusion's (NCERI's) *National Study of Inclusive Education* (1994, 1995). That study describes impacts on students both with and without disabilities, family members, and school personnel.

LARGE-SCALE STUDIES

Owing to the limited time period in which inclusive education programs have been implemented, there have been few large-scale evaluations of program and student outcomes. In a report for the

President's Committee on Mental Retardation, Nisbet (1994) stated, "Inclusion research published to date commonly takes the form of ethnographic studies, narratives, case studies, anecdotes, and surveys, although the range is rapidly expanding and new studies are published every month" (p. 152).

Based on a comprehensive survey of the literature, a 1993 report for the Michigan Department of Education stated,

> While there is currently little quantitative data of statistical significance to support full inclusion, there are clear patterns among the research that indicate improved outcomes as a result of integrated placements. These improved outcomes are even more noticeable in the qualitative data that exists in human services research. (*Final Report*, 1993, p. 5)

Findings from three meta-analyses concerning the most effective setting for educating students with disabilities have been summarized by Baker, Wang, and Walberg (1994).

> These meta-analyses generate a common measure, called effect size . . . that compared the effects of inclusive versus noninclusive educational practices for special-needs students. The effect sizes demonstrate a small-to-moderate beneficial effect of inclusive education on the academic and social outcomes of special-needs students . . . which means that special-needs students educated in regular classes do better academically and socially than comparable students in noninclusive settings. (p. 34)

Before turning to studies of outcomes in specific categories, it is appropriate to examine the experiences of two states: Vermont and Pennsylvania. In the mid-1980s, Vermont instituted the "homecoming" project, which brought students from institutional and out-of-district placements to their "home" district. (As noted in Chapter 10, Vermont is the leader among the states in the extent to which students with disabilities have been placed in general education settings.) *Vermont's Act 230* (1993) is a multiyear study of the impact of Act 230 on implementation of inclusion in the state. It reported the following:

- Grades for students served in general education settings were not significantly different than their grades had been when in special education classes.
- General education teachers, special educators, parents, and the students themselves judged special education students to have comparable performance in the general education class settings in all of the categories measured: behavior, social interaction, classroom performance, and overall success. For example, 92% of the general education teachers, 95% of the special educators, 91% of the parents, and 94% of the students responded affirmatively to the question, "Overall, do you feel the student was successful in school?"

In Pennsylvania, the Department of Education initiated a "Quality Education Initiative" (QEI) to assess the outcomes in inclusive settings of using innovative approaches that had been recognized for use in general education. Summarizing the results of 3 years of implementation of the (QEI), Wang (1996) reported the following:

- Regular education students in the inclusive classes showed an above-the-national-norm mean score on standardized tests for all three years of QEI implementation.
- The achievement data indicate that the inclusion of special education students did not negatively affect the achievement of the regular education students.
- The students [without disabilities] in the inclusion classes were found to have outperformed students in comparison classes in both reading and mathematics by the end of the second year of implementation.
- Special education students in the inclusive classes made about a 1-year gain in Normal Curve Equivalent (NCE) scores for all 3 years for sites where 3 years of gain data were available for analysis.
- No noticeable differences were exhibited in the behavior patterns and classroom activities between mainstreamed special education students and their regular education peers. Both groups of students were observed to exhibit a similar pattern of effective classroom behavior.
- The comparatively greater frequency of interaction between teachers and support personnel and mainstreamed special education students was achieved with no loss in positive outcomes for regular education students. (pp. 158–160)

A number of other statewide studies are under way, including those in Massachusetts (Rossman & Anthony, 1992), Michigan (Christmas, 1992), Oregon (Arrick et al., n.d.), Utah (McDonnell, McDonnell, Hardman, & McCune, 1991), and Vermont (Hasazi, Furney, & Johnstone, 1994). Reports from these studies are interspersed throughout the chapter.

ACADEMIC OUTCOMES FOR STUDENTS WITH DISABILITIES

Academic benefits are central to school participation for all students. Studies of academic outcomes for students with disabilities have reported the following:

- When comparing student academic achievement in inclusive versus resource programs, only slight measurable differences were discerned. The inclusive model results, however, were more favorable and more cost effective (Affleck, Madge, Adams, & Lowenbraun, 1988).

- Although students with mild disabilities included full time in a general class progressed more slowly than their peers, the gap was not widening as rapidly as that between students in "pull-out" programs and their typical peers (Deno, Murayama, Espin, & Cohen, 1990).

- Students with severe disabilities have higher levels of "active academic responding" and lower levels of competing behaviors when they are in the general education setting compared with the separate special education setting. The most powerful tool in the general education setting was peer modeling (Keefe & VanEtten, 1994).

- Students with learning disabilities made academic gains as reflected in scores on criterion-referenced tests and report cards (Chase & Pope, 1993).

- Students in inclusive settings had higher-quality individualized education programs (IEPs) and higher levels of engaged time compared with those in separate classes (Hunt, Farron-Davis, Beckstead, Curtis, & Goetz, 1994).

- There were higher levels of engaged time for elementary students with and without disabilities in classrooms in which there were students with significant disabilities (Hollowood, Salisbury, Rainforth, & Palombaro, 1994).

- Students with disabilities learned targeted skills in general education classrooms (Hunt, Staub, Alwell, & Goetz, 1994; Wolery, Werts, Caldwell, & Snyder, 1994).

- Using the Metropolitan Achievement Test to make comparisons between students with learning disabilities in two demographically similar schools, Jenkins, Jewell, O'Connor, Jenkins, and Troutner (1994) found that the students in the school serving these students in the general classroom had significantly higher overall average gains than did those students served in the control school using a pull-out resource room model.

- Students with significant disabilities had greater success in achieving IEP goals than did matched students in traditional programs (Ferguson, 1992).

- Parents of students with moderate to severe disabilities, who had previously been educated in self-contained classrooms reported academic, behavioral, and social outcomes that they felt would not have occurred except in the general education setting in which the children were now being educated (Ryndak, Downing, Jacqueline, & Morrison, 1995).

SOCIAL AND BEHAVIORAL OUTCOMES
FOR STUDENTS WITH DISABILITIES

For all students, in the course of interacting with each other, with their teachers, and with other school staff, school provides a setting for social and behavioral outcomes. Studies of social and behavioral benefits for students with disabilities have found that

- Students with disabilities were as likely to engage in positive social interactions with peers as were students who did not have disabilities (Ray, 1985).
- When compared with studies of outcomes concerning friendships and loneliness among students with learning disabilities in resource room settings, youths in inclusion settings fare at least as well socially (Vaughan, Elbaum, & Schumm, in press).
- General class participation for students with severe disabilities increases the frequency of interactions of these students with peers without disabilities, both in and outside of the classroom (Hunt, Farron-Davis, et al., 1994; Kennedy & Itkonen, 1996).
- Based on a study that compared students with severe disabilities placed in general education and self-contained classrooms, those placed in general education classrooms had higher levels of social contact with students without disabilities, received higher levels of support from others, and gave higher levels of support to others, and had substantially larger friendship networks composed primarily of students without disabilities (Fryxell & Kennedy, 1995).
- Demonstrated gains in social competence were widened for students in inclusive settings compared to those of students in segregated settings (Cole & Meyer, 1991).
- Social acceptance and opportunities for interactions were not associated with the child's level of functioning in integrated settings (Evans, Salisbury, Palombara, Berryman, & Hollowood, 1992).
- General class participation is an important factor in determining the composition and stability of social networks for high school students with disabilities (Kennedy & Itkonen, 1996).
- "Contrary to expectations and findings from other social skill assessment and self-esteem studies reported in the literature, students in mainstreamed settings . . . consistently rated their social competence higher than those in residential placements, achieving significance on the category of self-control. The setting/program variable produced the greatest main effect" (Cartledge, Cochran, & Paul, 1996, p. 33).

- Gains occurred in student self-esteem (Burello & Wright, 1993), acceptance by classmates (Christmas, 1992; Marwell, 1990), social skills (McDonnell et al., 1991), and social competence (Cole & Meyer, 1991; Saint-Laurent & Lessard, 1991).
- Inclusive programs provide positive experiences and generate improved attitudes on the part of the children (Giangreco, Edelman, Cloniger, & Dennis, 1992; Rainforth, 1992; Stainback & Stainback, 1992; York, Vandercook, MacDonald, Heise-Neff, & Caughey, 1992).

OUTCOMES FOR STUDENTS WITHOUT DISABILITIES

Staub and Peck (1994) addressed outcomes for students without disabilities in inclusive classes. They defined *inclusion* as the full-time placement of children with mild, moderate, or severe disabilities in general classrooms. The authors noted that "this definition explicitly assumes that regular class placement must be considered as a relevant option for *all* [emphasis in original] children, regardless of the severity of their disabilities" (p. 36).

In considering outcomes for students without disabilities, Staub and Peck (1994) addressed what they identified as three common fears:

1. *Will inclusion reduce the academic progress of children without disabilities?* Staub and Peck, reporting on studies that have used quasi-experimental designs to compare the progress of students without disabilities in inclusive classrooms with that of matched children in classrooms without students with disabilities, stated, "These studies have consistently found no deceleration of academic progress for nondisabled children in inclusive classrooms" (p. 36). The authors furthermore reported that "surveys conducted with parents and teachers who have been directly involved in inclusive settings generally show that both parties have positive views about inclusive programs and do not report any harm to the developmental progress of nondisabled children" (p. 36).

2. *Will children without disabilities lose teacher time and attention?* Reporting on a study that investigated this issue in depth, Staub and Peck summarized the study findings as follows: "The presence of students with severe disabilities had no effect on levels of allocated or engaged time. Further, time lost to interruptions of instruction was not significantly different in inclusive and noninclusive classrooms" (p. 36). Staub and Peck asserted that "these findings are supported by survey responses

from teachers and parents who have direct experience with inclusive classrooms" (p. 37). Reporting on high school students who had been involved in inclusive classrooms in rural, suburban, and urban areas of Washington State, Staub and Peck stated that "these students did not believe that their participation in inclusive classrooms had caused them to miss out on other valuable educational experiences" (p. 37).

3. *Will students without disabilities learn undesirable behaviors from students with disabilities?* Citing the research on this topic, Staub and Peck reported that the evidence indicates that students without disabilities do not acquire undesirable or maladaptive behavior from peers with disabilities.

In reporting the potential benefits of inclusion for students without disabilities, Staub and Peck (1994) identified five positive outcomes as documented in the research:

1. Reduced fear of human differences accompanied by increased comfort and awareness
2. Growth in social cognition
3. Improvements in self-concept
4. Development of personal principles
5. Warm and caring friendships (pp. 37–39)

A special issue of the *Journal of The Association for Persons with Severe Handicaps* (1994, April) addressed the effects of the inclusion of students with severe disabilities in general education classrooms and schools on their peers who do not have disabilities and the general education community. Authors were invited to use a variety of research methodologies, including quantitative, qualitative, and critical theory approaches (Meyer, 1994, p. 251). Following are some findings of studies featured in the 1994 *Journal*.

• Helmstetter, Peck, and Giangreco (1994) analyzed a statewide survey of high school students and reported that more positive outcomes were associated with more contact and more substantive interaction (e.g., increased responsiveness to the needs of others, valuing relationships with people with disabilities, personal development, increased tolerance of other people, development of personal values, increased appreciation of human diversity, positive changes in social status with peers).

• Kishi and Meyer (1994) reported on a 6-year follow-up of an elementary school program of social interaction with students with severe disabilities. They found significantly more positive attitudes, higher levels of reported social contact at the time of follow-up, and more support for full community participation as a function of the earlier social contact.

- Hunt, Staub, Alwell, and Goetz (1994) studied the achievement of students in cooperative learning groups. They reported that students with severe disabilities both independently demonstrated targeted basic skills and generalized them. Members of the group without disabilities performed as well on targeted academic objectives as members of a control group within the classroom that did not include a student with severe disabilities.

Additional studies on impacts of inclusion on students without disabilities have reported that

- There was no evidence of harmful effects on students who did not have disabilities, and their attitudes, values, and beliefs, as well as those of others in the setting, were favorably affected (Biklen, Corrigan, & Quick, 1989; Haring, Breen, Potts-Conway, Gaylord-Ross, & Gaylord-Ross, 1987; Murray-Seegert, 1989; York et al., 1992).
- Disruptions to classroom learning time were not associated with the presence of students with significant disabilities (Hollowood et al., 1994).
- There was no decline in academic or behavioral performance of classmates without disabilities on standardized tests and report card measures (Sharpe, York, & Knight, 1994).
- Benefits to students with disabilities occurred without curtailing the educational program available to students without disabilities (Co-teaching, 1991).
- Findings of improved outcomes were confirmed by parents who reported their perceptions regarding the effect of general education classroom placement of students with severe disabilities on their children who did not have disabilities (Giangreco et al., 1992).

OUTCOMES FOR PRESCHOOL CHILDREN WITH AND WITHOUT DISABILITIES

The evaluation research base for inclusion in early childhood and preschool programs has a longer history and is more extensive than that for school-age children. Nisbet (1994) stated that "over the past 25 years, there has been an extensive body of research on preschool integration" (p. 153). Citing summaries of this research by Buysse and Bailey (1993) and Peck, Odom, and Bricker (1993), Nisbet offered the following conclusions:

- First, it is clear that integration has positive effects on the social competence and interactions of preschoolers with disabilities. Findings include more time playing with peers, more positive interactions with peers, and more verbalizations with peers.
- Second, integration opportunities also appear to have positive effects on other behavioral outcomes, such as more sophisticated play with toys.
- Third, integrated and segregated settings seem to be equal in terms of measured developmental progress on standardized tests; thus, any argument[s] that segregated settings might provide more specialized and more effective interventions are not valid.
- Fourth, no negative outcomes have been reported for normally developing children. (p. 153)

This summary is echoed by a report of the Early Childhood Research Institute on Inclusion (Odom et al., 1995):

At least four reviews of research occurring over the last 15 years (Buysse & Bailey, 1993; Lamorey & Bricker, 1993; Odom & McEvoy, 1988; Peck & Cooke, 1983) have concluded that children with disabilities in inclusive preschool programs make at least as much progress on standardized assessments of cognitive, language, motor, and social development as do children enrolled in noninclusive special education preschools. (p. 8)

The authors go on to cite randomized studies (Jenkins, Odom, & Speltz, 1989; Jenkins, Speltz, & Odom, 1985) that "found similar progress (i.e., few significant differences) of children with disabilities enrolled in inclusive and noninclusive settings" (p. 9); and a study (Guralnick & Groom, 1987) that found that "children with disabilities engaged in more developmentally advanced forms of play when their play partner was a typically developing child than when the play partner was a child with disabilities" (pp. 9–10).

The American Speech-Language-Hearing Association (ASHA) surveyed the research concerning inclusive service delivery models of speech and language interventions. They cited several studies documenting the effectiveness of various types of inclusionary programs for children and youth with communication disabilities (Cirrin & Penner, 1995; Cole, Mills, Dale, & Jenkins, 1991; Coufal, 1990; Dyer, Williams, & Luce, 1991; Ellis, Schlandecker, & Regimbal, 1995; Farber, Denenberg, Klyman, & Lachman, 1992; Wilcox, Kouri, & Caswell, 1991).

Social relationships have been a key area of attention in early childhood studies, especially in light of findings that children with disabilities spend significantly less time interacting with their peers than do typically developing children. Purposeful efforts are necessary to support the social inclusion of children with and without disabilities; the results of these efforts are reviewed in Odom and

Brown (1993). Summarizing these findings, Odom et al. (1995) stated, "When teachers support social integration through a variety of strategies in the classroom there are positive changes in children's interactions" (pp. 11–12).

Strain (1990) was even more emphatic:

> No study that has assessed social outcomes for children in integrated versus segregated settings has found segregated settings to be superior. This is important because one of the things that parents of young children with handicaps most desire for their youngsters is to develop friendships with their same-age nonhandicapped peers. And if we ask this question, "What development outcomes are most likely to lead to successful post-school adjustment?" social skills is always the answer.
>
> [N]ormally developing children have shown *only* [emphasis in original] positive developmental and attitudinal outcomes from integrated experiences.
>
> There is *no* [emphasis in original] evidence that children with particular handicapping conditions or severe levels of impairment are poor candidates for integrated programs. (pp. 292–294)

Positive parental attitudes are a critical component in early childhood and preschool programs. Citing nine different studies, Odom et al. (1995) stated,

> Research that has focused on parent perspectives regarding inclusion confirms that parents of children both with and without disabilities have largely positive perspectives on inclusion. . . . [T]he most consistently reported benefit that parents anticipate is that children without disabilities will become more sensitive and more accepting of differences. Increased social contact between children with and without disabilities is another benefit which is frequently cited by parents. (pp. 12–13)

Yet another study reported that both parents and teachers of children who were developing in typical fashion perceived important benefits accruing to the children as a result of being involved in integrated placements (Peck, Carlson, & Helmstetter, 1992).

Further documentation of the positive effects of inclusive programs has been provided by Bruder (1993), who pointed out that "the provision of integrated preschool special education has been cited as a quality indicator of service delivery models for this age group (McDonnell & Hardmann, 1988; Strain, 1990)" (p. 38). This point regarding overall program quality has been supported by Strain (1990):

> Programs that are characterized by integrated service delivery tend to be state-of the-art in a variety of other dimensions, including extensive parental involvement; highly-structured scope, sequence, and

method of instruction; and attention to repeated outcome assessments. (p. 294)

SCHOOL DISTRICT EVALUATIONS OF INCLUSION OUTCOMES

Increasingly, school districts with inclusive education programs are conducting evaluation studies. Reports of some of those studies are excerpted here from the NCERI's *National Study of Inclusive Education* (1995). The districts' self-reported information focuses largely on issues of implementing inclusive programs and student outcomes.

At the Fort Bragg Unified School District (California), inclusive education takes place at two elementary schools, the middle school, and the high school. The district reported the following:

> Multiple examples of positive changes in student behavior are evident across the grade levels. Academic changes have been verified by standardized test scores, authentic assessment, and plain old observation. Social changes are evident as well, importantly within the general education population, as well as [among] inclusion students and their families. Simply put, regular education students have become humanized, and special education students have the opportunity to become known as individuals with their own personalities. (p. 43)

At the Napa Valley Unified School District (California), elementary and middle schools are implementing inclusive education programs. The district reported,

> Significant changes, both socially and educationally, have been observed and documented for the fully included students. Changes ranging from increased independence and self-esteem to elevated reading levels have been noted. Many of these outcomes are evaluated through teacher/parent/student observations and interviews as well as standardized testing and authentic assessment. Changes in . . . attitudes and self-esteem have been noted in the students without noticeable disabilities. The Full Inclusion Program was a major reason Carneros Elementary School was named a California Distinguished School in 1993. (p. 53)

At the Brevard County School District (Florida), all of the students with special needs are served in their neighborhood schools. The district reported,

> We have seen a lot of caring and acceptance from the regular education students toward our more challenged students. They are very protective and understanding of them. The special needs students are growing tremendously. There are EMH [emotionally and mentally handicapped] students that are excited by learning. The parents of our Downs students and autistic students report a tremendous growth in vocabulary and communication. Students that came from a

self-contained setting and exhibited a lot of anxiety about the regular classroom appear to be relaxed and comfortable with their new placement. (p. 72)

In the Gwinnett County Public Schools (Georgia), inclusion programs operate at four elementary schools and a middle school. The district reported,

> Student outcomes for students with disabilities have been outstanding. All students are exceeding IEP objectives over progress in self-contained classes; parents report increased generalization of learning at home; school staff consistently reported positive changes in students once they are "included"; students with disabilities resist going back to their self-contained classmates and participating with them in "handicapped only" activities. We have noted that students learn well when taught by regular education staff, special education staff, and peers. (p. 92)

In the Lawrenceburg Community Schools (Indiana), where all students are served in the elementary school, the district stated,

> Changes in students have been two-fold. . . . [N]onhandicapped students . . . have come to be more aware of both the strengths and weaknesses of their handicapped peers in ways that are less prejudicial and hateful. For handicapped youngsters, the main change is connected to their increased level of expectations as to both academics and behavior. We evaluated these outcomes through a climate audit study conducted by an independent group from Indiana University. (p. 113)

The Howard County Public Schools (Maryland) is exploring ways to evaluate outcomes for students with special needs other than the standard classroom grades and achievement toward IEP objectives. The district reported,

> First, we have undertaken a change in the way IEP goals and objectives are written. All special educators have been trained in this new approach, which is more child-centered, measurable and based on demonstrated need, rather than [curriculum oriented]. This, coupled with portfolio assessment, should help establish baseline data from which to measure outcomes. In addition, there will be a move to explore data collection on actual classroom behaviors. . . . This county also is part of a pilot program sponsored by the State of Maryland to assess students who are not part of the statewide assessment program already in place. This form of assessment will involve data collection and behavior demonstration through video. (p. 156)

The Anne Arundel County Public Schools (Maryland) serve some 68,000 students in 113 schools. As part of the state's Systems Change Project, inclusion initiatives are being conducted in several of the district's feeder systems. Cooperative teaching is used extensively. The district reported,

A study comparing the academic performance of ninth-grade students co-taught in general education classrooms with similar classrooms without co-teaching compared performance on the state's ninth-grade minimum competency tests and classrooms grades. [Students in the co-taught classes and the comparison classes had similar academic profiles and backgrounds.] Results found that the co-taught classes, with a general educator and special educator working collaboratively with a heterogeneous group of special and general education students, can produce significantly better results than general education class-rooms in achieving academic requirements for high school gradua-tion. In particular, a significantly greater percent of ninth-grade stu-dents from co-taught classes passed statewide minimum competency tests in three different content areas than students from content classes that did not include special education students and were not co-taught by a general educator and a special educator. The findings suggest that the combined effect of two teachers' capabilities, one strong in content and curriculum knowledge, the other in adaptive teaching strategies and classroom modifications, can in fact enable the general classroom to successfully address the learning needs of a diverse group of students, including mainstream special education students. Moreover, the results suggest that all students within a co-taught class benefit from this service delivery model and that school improvement plans should consider such collaborative models in de-veloping education reform initiatives for all students. (p. 149)

The Springfield Public Schools (Massachusetts) are part of a state initiative on inclusion and restructuring. They reported,

The students have also shown signs of acceptance and elation. School is a place where you are accepted for who you are. You don't need to be fixed or changed before you can be integrated. This phi-losophy has caused students to work hard and take a risk. Stu-dents who would not have associated in the past are finding that they share more likenesses than differences. Students are working collaboratively and liking it. Students are sharing ideas, time, and their classrooms and for the first time are accepting each other as unique individuals complete with faults, but most importantly with strengths. (p. 172)

The Hillsdale Community Schools (Michigan) educate almost all of the district's students, kindergarten through eighth grade, in age-appropriate general education classrooms with support from Chap-ter 1, local gifted and talented, and special education staff. They reported,

Parental involvement has been both positive and supportive. Parents of handicapped students have welcomed the opportunity to see their children educated with their age mates in nonexclusive settings. Par-ents of nonhandicapped [students] were cautious until they saw achievement results that were not depressed and a social milieu that was friendly and relaxed. Students have been our biggest surprise. Conventional wisdom held that children were cruel to one another and the handicapped would face ridicule and scorn. Nothing could be further from the truth. Our experience has been that the children have been kind, supportive, and protective of their handicapped classmates. Often the adults who have been involved have learned kindness and tolerance from observing the children in their care. Of all the surprises we have found with this project, none has been as dramatic as this one. (p. 177)

The Cumberland School Department (Rhode Island) conducts inclusion programs at the five elementary schools and in the middle school. The department reported,

> Many special education students are making "leaps and bounds gains," academically and with fine motor skills. This may be due to specific instruction or [to] modeling others or just due to the amount of stimulation in the room. Other observations include beginning or improved speech and reading. Also, noticeably improved [are] maturity, motivation, independence, confidence, self-esteem, and general happiness with life. Important [strides have occurred in] making . . . friends; [having] a place to belong at the lunch table; the disappearance of problem behavior; and social growth such as [learning] manners, how to behave in a group, and . . . appropriate ways to gain attention and acceptance. [Students with special needs] benefit tremendously from being exposed to normal kids and normal conversations.
>
> [T]he benefits of inclusion have spilled out of school into the personal lives [of students with special needs] where, for the first time, they received phone calls, birthday party invitations, and play invitations to new friends' homes.
>
> It is important not to overlook the enormous benefit to regular education students who are a part of the inclusion experience. Teachers report that students who are in the class with their included peers become kinder and more helpful individuals. Self-centered children are now very sensitive to others' needs. They praise one another's accomplishments and are far less competitive. (p. 289)

The Mansfield Independent School District (Texas) is one of three districts that received a grant in 1992 from the state's Council for Developmental Disabilities to implement inclusive education. In 1994, the state expanded the program evaluation to include a review of student records, parent surveys, general and special education teacher and principal surveys, and classroom observations. Conducted by an outside evaluation consultant, the study reported the following:

> At all grade levels, 94 percent of the students with disabilities were educated on their home campus; of these, 96 percent were on general education classroom rosters; and 54 percent of students with disabilities receive 100 percent of their instruction in general education classes. On a 5-point scale, 76 percent of the general education teachers responded 4.0 or above that students enrolled in subject area classes are engaged in IEP-specified learning activities with class-

room adaptations and supports. In terms of assistance to teachers, at 100 percent of the campuses training was provided in tolerance and respect for differences; at 100 percent of the campuses principals reported that staff development opportunities concerning inclusion were provided to all teaching personnel. Districtwide, 67 percent of the teachers reported that they used peer tutors a minimum of two times a week; 76 percent of the teachers reported that they frequently used peer tutors and incorporated student cooperative learning activities in their classroom; 94 percent reported no negative impact on the academic grades of students without disabilities. In terms of parental attitudes, 92 percent of the parents of general education students reported that they felt their child benefited from more contact with students with disabilities. (Hess, 1994, cited in *National Study,* 1995, p. 332)

Summarizing the evaluation data in a report of the National Association of State Boards of Education, Roach (1995) stated,

Students with disabilities in inclusive settings have been shown to acquire social and communication skills previously undeveloped in segregated placements; they also show increased levels of student interaction, increased interaction with their peers, and positive postschool adjustments. In addition, included students show increased achievement of IEP objectives, as well as higher quality IEPs developed for students in inclusive settings.

As a result of inclusion, parents of students with disabilities also experience a wider circle of friends; they also develop a more positive set of parental expectations for their children.

Benefits for the general student population include acquiring more accepting attitudes about people with disabilities, more positive attitudes about their peers with disabilities, increased tolerance of other people, and a reduced fear of people who are different. In addition, research has shown improvement in the self-concept of the general student population in an inclusive environment and the development of problem-solving skills applied to real life situations.

Inclusive teachers have been shown to have a greater ability to accept and be open to change, an increased level of professional confidence, improved planning skills, and an increased awareness of all students' needs.

Finally, inclusive schools have been found to be more outcome-based and [to] have a more cooperative and collaborative environment, with teachers using active learning procedures for all students. (p. 9)

CONCLUSION

The research and evaluation data on inclusion indicate a strong trend toward improved student outcomes (academically, socially, and behaviorally) for both special education and general education students. A 1993 report on inclusive placements for general and special education students noted the following:

When one contrasts such [positive] indications [regarding inclusion] with the fact that there appears to be little, if any, evidence in research to support superior student outcomes as a result of placement in segregated settings, one must seriously question the efficacy of spending ever-increasing sums of money to maintain dual systems. (*Final Report*, 1993, pp. 5–6)

REFERENCES

Affleck, J.Q., Madge, S., Adams, A., & Lowenbraun, S. (1988). Integrated classroom resource model: Academic viability and effectiveness. *Exceptional Children, 54*(4), 339–348.

Baker, E.T., Wang, M.C., & Walberg, H.J. (1994). The effects of inclusion on learning. *Educational Leadership, 52*(4), 33–35.

Biklen, D., Corrigan, C., & Quick, D. (1989). Beyond obligation: Students' relations with each other in integrated classes. In D.K. Lipsky & A. Gartner (Eds.), *Beyond separate education: Quality education for all* (pp. 207–221). Baltimore: Paul H. Brookes Publishing Co.

Bruder, M.B. (1993). Early childhood community integration: An option for preschool special education. *OSERS News in Print, 5*(3), 38–43.

Burello, L.C., & Wright, P.T. (Eds.). (1993, Winter). Strategies for inclusion of behaviorally challenged students. *Principal Letters, 10*, 1–4.

Buysse, V., & Bailey, D.B. (1993). Behavioral and developmental outcomes in young children with disabilities in integrated and segregated settings: A review of comparative studies. *Journal of Special Education, 26*, 434–461.

Cartledge, G., Cochran, L., & Paul, P. (1996). Social skill self-assessments by adolescents with hearing impairment in residential and public schools. *Remedial and Special Education, 17*(1), 30–36.

Chase, V., & Pope, E. (1993, February 24). *Model for mainstreaming: The synergistic approach.* Paper presented at the Learning Disabilities Association of America Conference, San Francisco.

Christmas, O.L. (1992). *The 1992 Michigan non-mandated aide pilot project.* Lansing: Michigan State Education Department.

Cirrin, F.M., & Penner, S.G. (1995). Classroom-based and consultative service delivery models for language intervention. In M.E. Fey, J. Windsor, & S.F. Warren (Eds.), *Communication and language intervention series: Vol. 1. Language intervention: Preschool through the elementary years* (pp. 333–362). Baltimore: Paul H. Brookes Publishing Co.

Cole, D.A., & Meyer, L.H. (1991). Social integration and severe disabilities: A longitudinal analysis of child outcomes. *Journal of Special Education, 25*(3), 340–351.

Cole, K., Mills, P., Dale, P., & Jenkins, J.R. (1991). Effects of preschool integration for children with disabilities. *Exceptional Children, 58*, 36–45.

Co-teaching: Regular education/special education and co-teaching reference guide. (1991). Lansing: Michigan State Department of Education.

Coufal, K.L. (1990). *Collaborative consultation: An alternative to traditional treatment for children with communicative disorders.* Doctoral dissertation, University of Nebraska, Lincoln, 1989. *Dissertation Abstracts International, 51/02*, 694a.

Deno, S., Murayama, G., Espin, C., & Cohen, C. (1990). Educating students with mild disabilities in general education classrooms: Minnesota alternatives. *Exceptional Children, 5*(2), 150–161.

Dyer, K., Williams, L., & Luce, S. (1991). Training teachers to use naturalistic communication strategies in classrooms for students with autism and other severe handicaps. *Language, Speech, and Hearing Services in Schools, 22,* 313–321.

Ellis, L., Schlandecker, C., & Regimbal, C. (1995). Effectiveness of a collaborative consultation approach to basic concept instruction with kindergarten children. *Language, Speech, and Hearing Services in Schools, 26,* 69–73.

Evans, I.M., Salisbury, C.L., Palombara, M.M., Berryman, J., & Hollowood, T.M. (1992). Peer interactions and social acceptance of elementary age children with severe disabilities in an inclusive school. *Journal of The Association for Persons with Severe Handicaps, 17*(4), 205–212.

Farber, J., Denenberg, M.E., Klyman, S., & Lachman, P. (1992). Language resource room level of service: An urban school district approach to integrative treatment. *Language, Speech, and Hearing Services in School, 23,* 292–299.

Ferguson, D. (1992). *Regular Class Participation System (RCPS): A final report.* Eugene: University of Oregon.

Final report of the Inclusive Education Recommendations Committee: Findings and recommendations. (1993). Lansing: Michigan State Department of Education.

Fryxell, D., & Kennedy, C.H. (1995). Placement along the continuum of services and its impact on students' social relationships. *Journal of The Association for Persons with Severe Handicaps, 20*(4), 259–269.

Giangreco, M.F., Edelman, S., Cloniger, C., & Dennis, R. (1992). My child has a classmate with severe disabilities: What parents of nondisabled children think about full inclusion. *Developmental Disabilities Bulletin, 20*(2), 1–12.

Guralnick, M.J., & Groom, J.M. (1987). The peer relations of mildly delayed and nonhandicapped preschool children in mainstream playgroups. *Child Development, 58,* 156–172.

Haring, T.G., Breen, C., Potts-Conway, V., Gaylord-Ross, M.L., & Gaylord-Ross, R. (1987). Adolescent peer tutoring and special friend experiences. *Journal of The Association for Persons with Severe Handicaps, 12*(4), 280–286.

Hasazi, S., Furney, K.S., & Johnstone, A.P. (1994). *A study of the implementation of Vermont's Act 230.* Unpublished manuscript, University of Vermont, Burlington.

Helmstetter, E., Peck, C.A., & Giangreco, M.F. (1994). Outcomes of interactions with peers with moderate or severe disabilities: A statewide survey of high school students. *Journal of The Association for Persons with Severe Handicaps, 19*(4), 263–276.

Hollowood, T.M., Salisbury, C.L., Rainforth, B., & Palombaro, M.M. (1994). Use of instructional time in classrooms serving students with and without severe disabilities. *Exceptional Children, 61*(3), 242–253.

Hunt, P., Farron-Davis, F., Beckstead, S., Curtis, D., & Goetz, L. (1994). Evaluating the effects of placement of students with severe disabilities in general education versus special class. *Journal of The Association for Persons with Severe Handicaps, 19*(3), 200–214.

Hunt, P., Staub, D., Alwell, M., & Goetz, L. (1994). Achievement by all students within the context of cooperative learning groups. *Journal of The Association for Persons with Severe Handicaps, 19*(4), 290–301.

Jenkins, J.R., Jewell, M., O'Connor, R.E., Jenkins, L.M., Troutner, J. (1994). Accommodations for individual differences within classroom ability groups: An experiment in school restructuring. *Exceptional Children, 60*(4), 344–358.

Jenkins, J.R., Odom, S.L., & Speltz, M.L. (1989). Effects of integration and structured play on the development of handicapped children. *Exceptional Children, 55,* 420–428.

Jenkins, J.R., Speltz, M.L., & Odom, S.L. (1985). Integrating normal and handicapped preschoolers: Effects on child development and social interaction. *Exceptional Children, 52,* 7–17.

Keefe, E., & VanEtten, G. (1994, December 8). *Academic and social outcomes for students with moderate to profound disabilities in integrated settings.* Paper presented at conference of The Association for Persons with Severe Handicaps, Atlanta.

Kennedy, C.H., & Itkonen, T. (1996). Social relationships, influential variables, and change across the life span. In L.K. Koegel, R.L. Koegel, & G. Dunlap (Eds.), *Positive behavioral support: Including people with difficult behavior in the community* (pp. 287–304). Baltimore: Paul H. Brookes Publishing Co.

Kishi, G.S., & Meyer, L.H. (1994). What children report and remember: A six-year follow-up of the effects of social contact between peers with and without severe disabilities. *Journal of The Association for Persons with Severe Handicaps, 19*(4), 277–289.

Lamorey, S., & Bricker, D. (1993). Integrated programs: Effects on young children and their parents. In C.A. Peck, S.L. Odom, & D.D. Bricker (Eds.), *Integrating young children with disabilities into community programs: Ecological perspectives on research and implementation* (pp. 249–270). Baltimore: Paul H. Brookes Publishing Co.

Marwell, B.E. (1990). *Integration of students with mental retardation.* Madison, WI: Madison Public Schools.

McDonnell, A., & Hardmann, M. (1988). A synthesis of "best practice" guidelines for early childhood services. *Journal of the Division for Early Childhood, 12*(4), 328–341.

McDonnell, A., McDonnell, J., Hardmann, M., & McCune, G. (1991). Educating students with severe disabilities in their neighborhood school: The Utah elementary model. *Remedial and Special Education, 12*(6), 34–45.

Meyer, L.H. (1994). Editor's introduction: Understanding the impact of inclusion. *Journal of The Association for Persons with Severe Handicaps, 19*(4), 251–252.

Murray-Seegert, C. (1989). *Nasty girls, thugs, and humans like us: Social relations between severely disabled and nondisabled students in high school.* Baltimore: Paul H. Brookes Publishing Co.

National Study of Inclusive Education. (1995). New York: The City University of New York, National Center on Educational Restructuring and Inclusion.

Nisbet, J. (1994). Educational reform: Summary and recommendations. In *The national reform agenda and people with mental retardation: Putting people first* (pp. 151–165). Washington, DC: President's Committee on Mental Retardation.

Odom, S.L., & Brown, W.H. (1993). Social interaction skills interventions for young children with disabilities in integrated settings. In C.A. Peck, S.L. Odom, & D.D. Bricker (Eds.), *Integrating young children with disabilities into community programs: Ecological perspectives on research and implementation* (pp. 39–64). Baltimore: Paul H. Brookes Publishing Co.

Odom, S.L., & McEvoy, M.A. (1988). Integration of young children with handicaps and normally developing children. In S. Odom & M. Karnes (Eds.), *Early intervention for infants and children with handicaps: An empirical base* (pp. 241–268). Baltimore: Paul H. Brookes Publishing Co.

Odom, S.L., Peck, C.A., Hanson, M., Beckman, P.J., Kaiser, A.P., Lieber, J., Brown, W.H., Horn, E.M., & Schwartz, O.S. (1995). *Inclusion of preschool children with disabilities: An ecological systems perspective.* Unpublished manuscript, Vanderbilt University, Early Childhood Research Institute on Inclusion, Nashville, TN.

Peck, C.A., Carlson, P., & Helmstetter, E. (1992). Integrating non-handicapped preschoolers: Developmental impact on non-handicapped children. *Exceptional Children, 51*(1), 41–48.

Peck, C.A., & Cooke, T.P. (1983). Benefits of mainstreaming at the early childhood level: How much can we expect? In R. Gaylord-Ross (Ed.), *Research issues in special education* (pp. 76–93). San Diego: College Hill Press.

Peck, C.A., Odom, S.L., & Bricker, D.D. (Eds.). (1993). *Integrating young children with disabilities into community programs: Ecological perspectives on research and implementation.* Baltimore: Paul H. Brookes Publishing Co.

Rainforth, B. (1992). *The effects of full inclusion on regular education teachers.* San Francisco: California Research Institute.

Rainforth, B., York, J., & Macdonald, C. (1992). *Collaborative teams for students with severe disabilities: Integrating therapy and educational services.* Baltimore: Paul H. Brookes Publishing Co.

Ray, B.M. (1985). Measuring the social position of the mainstreamed handicapped child. *Exceptional Children, 52*(4), 57–62.

Roach, V. (1995). *Winning ways: Creating inclusive schools, classrooms, and communities.* Alexandria, VA: National Association of State Boards of Education.

Rossman, G.B., & Anthony, P.G. (1992). *Restructuring from within: The Massachusetts experiment with integrating all students in the classroom.* Unpublished manuscript, University of Massachusetts, Amherst.

Ryndak, D.L., Downing, J.E., Jacqueline, L.R., & Morrison, A.P. (1995). Parents' perceptions after inclusion of their child with moderate or severe disabilities in general education settings. *Journal of The Association for Persons with Severe Handicaps, 20*(2), 147–157.

Saint-Laurent, L., & Lessard, J.C. (1991). Comparison of three educational programs for students with moderate metal retardation integrated in regular schools. *Education and Training of the Mentally Retarded, 26*(4), 370–380.

Sharpe, M.N., York, J.L., & Knight, J. (1994). Effects of inclusion on the academic performance of classmates without disabilities. *Remedial and Special Education, 15*(5), 281–287.

Stainback, S., & Stainback, W. (1992). Schools as inclusive communities. In W. Stainback & S. Stainback (Eds.), *Controversial issues confronting special education: Divergent perspectives* (pp. 29–44). Needham, MA: Allyn & Bacon.

Staub, D., & Peck, C.A. (1994). What are the outcomes for nondisabled students? *Educational Leadership, 52*(4), 36–40.

Strain, P.S. (1990). LRE for preschool children with handicaps: What we know, what we should be doing. *Journal of Early Intervention, 14*(4), 291–296.

Vaughan, S., Elbaum, B.E., & Schumm, J.S. (in press). Are students with learning disabilities in inclusion classrooms better liked and less lonely? *Journal of Learning Disabilities.*

Vermont's Act 230: Three years later. A report on the impact of Act 230. (1993). Montpelier: Vermont Department of Education.

Wang, M.C. (1996). Serving students with special needs through inclusive education approaches. In J. Lupart, A. McKeough, & C. Yewchuck (Eds.), *Schools in transition: Rethinking regular and special education* (pp. 143–163). Toronto, Ontario: Thomas Nelson Canada.

Wilcox, M.J., Kouri, T., & Caswell, S. (1991). Early language intervention: A comparison of classroom and individual treatment. *American Journal of Speech-Language Pathology, 1,* 49–62.

Wolery, M., Werts, M.G., Caldwell, N.K., & Snyder. E.D. (1994). Efficacy of constant time delay implemented by peers tutors in general education classrooms. *Journal of Behavioral Education, 4*(4), 415–436.

York, J., Vandercook, T., MacDonald, C., Heise-Neff, C., & Caughey, E. (1992). Feedback about integrating middle-school students with severe disabilities in general education classes. *Exceptional Children, 58*(3), 244–258.

15

AN INCLUSION TALKBACK
CRITICS' CONCERNS AND ADVOCATES' RESPONSES

As the preceding chapters have underscored, inclusive education programs are developing rapidly in school districts across the United States. In 1995, the National Center on Educational Restructuring and Inclusion (NCERI) reported that more than 900 school districts nationwide were implementing such programs (*National Study*, 1995); this represented a threefold increase over the number of programs identified in the previous year's study (*National Study*, 1994). At the same time, criticisms of inclusion continue. In the hope of encouraging a productive dialogue on the issues, these criticisms are presented here, along with responses from advocates of inclusive education.

Critics: Inclusion advocates take a "one size fits all" approach.
Advocates: The law is clear in requiring a program designed to meet the individual needs of each child served. School districts effectively implementing inclusive education provide the individualized approach that the law and good educational practice require through the provision of supplemental aids and support services, designed to enable each child in an inclusive setting to succeed. When inclusive education is successful, it provides a continuum of supports within the general education classroom for all students with disabilities. This last point is supported by a growing body of research that indicates successful inclusive edu-

cation programs and positive outcomes for all students, with and without disabilities.

Critics: Inclusive education may have positive social outcomes for students with disabilities, but it does not have positive outcomes for students without disabilities.

Advocates: The law guarantees all children with disabilities an appropriate education in the least restrictive environment (LRE) and requires that it be in the general education classroom when that is the appropriate setting for a child. The courts have held that although the consequence for other children is not to be ignored, the standard is very high. In none of four "full inclusion" federal circuit court decisions spanning the years 1989–1994 did the courts find harmful effects for the general education students' education. (*Daniel R.R. v. Board of Education,* 1989; *Greer v. Rome City School District*, 1991; *Oberti v. Board of Education*, 1993; *Sacramento City Unified School District v. Rachel H.*, 1994). In *Oberti* (1993), for example, the court described "the reciprocal benefits of inclusion to the non-disabled students in the class" (p. 1217) and found that "the non-disabled children will likewise benefit from inclusion" (pp. 1221–1222). Data documenting positive outcomes for all students are found in a growing body of research and reports from school districts implementing inclusive education programs.

Critics: Special education children need time with specialists, and this service can be provided only out of the general classroom. If a student with special needs is in an inclusive education setting, then he or she will not be able to receive the specialized service out of the classroom.

Advocates: Inclusive education is not a location; it is a model whereby the child with disabilities is a full member of an age-appropriate general education class in the same way that children without disabilities are full members of the class. This does not mean that all services for a child must always take place *in* a general education classroom. For example, the teaching of braille or the use of a white cane are essential prerequisites for a child who is blind to participate fully in the classroom. The Full Inclusion Task Force of the National Federation of the Blind supports the training of children who are blind in the "tools of blindness" by trained specialists, with the general education teacher trained to reinforce these skills. This same principle applies to students with other disabilities. For specific topics, for limited periods of time, the child (indeed, any child in the class) may receive needed specialized instruction outside of that classroom.[1] The key component is that the general education teacher has overall responsibility for all of the children's education and, as appropriate, reinforces that which the specialists provide.

Critics: The large number and disproportionate percentage of minority students being labeled as disabled and placed in special education is not a civil rights matter. The comparison of separate special education with racial segregation is inappropriate because students in separate placements are there voluntarily.

Advocates: Such arguments ignore the dramatic disproportion of students from ethnic groups in special education overall, and particularly in those categories that are most separate, producing a form of double segregation. Based on data from 39 states, African American students are twice as likely as Caucasian students to be in special education; and although one tenth of the Caucasian students have the label "mentally retarded," a quarter of the African American students in special education have this label.

Critics: Teachers are unprepared to teach in an inclusive education classroom.

Advocates: General educators can develop the desired specialized skills to assist students with disabilities placed in their classrooms. It is essential that college teacher training programs become more responsive and prepare future teachers to work with diverse student populations in their classrooms. School districts are responsible for upgrading the skills of teachers and developing programs for all staff, both before inclusive education is initiated and as ongoing professional development. The instructional strategies most often reported by teachers and administrators as important to the success of inclusive education programs are strategies that experienced and qualified teachers use for all children. Among these are cooperative learning, curricular modifications, "hands on" teaching, whole language instruction, use of peers and "buddies," thematic and multidisciplinary curriculum, use of classroom aides, and use of instructional technology. Although teachers report that students with significant acting-out behaviors are their greatest chal-

---

[1]At Baltimore's Eastern Technical High School, for example, the Resource Center serves *all* students "who have special needs, whether they are deemed gifted and talented in English or identified as having a severe discrepancy between their intellectual ability and their achievement in mathematics" (Hardin & McNelis, 1996, p. 41).

lenge, many school districts have initiated successful programs to meet these needs.

Critics: Teachers should be allowed to determine whether they will have children with disabilities in their classroom; they should not be required to do so.

Advocates: It is not acceptable for educators to choose which children they will teach in a classroom. Public school systems cannot allow teachers to deny children with disabilities their rights and, when appropriate, the opportunity to be educated in a general education setting with their peers. It is neither fair nor lawful that, more than 2 decades after the passage of the Education for All Handicapped Children Act of 1975 (PL 94-142), students with disabilities must wait until schools or teachers are ready.

Critics: The federal government, the states, and school districts provide financial and technical support when inclusive education is first initiated; but then those supports erode, leaving the school district and the teacher to address the needs of children without adequate support.

Advocates: The lack of ongoing technical and financial supports for inclusive education is a warranted concern that must be met by continuing involvement from parents, teachers, and organizations. School districts report that to implement inclusive education for successful outcomes for all students, school administrations must take seriously ongoing staff development and the continuation of supports. Inclusion does not mean "dumping" children in a classroom but building an individualized education program [IEP] that will meet the needs of the individual child.

Critics: The entire education system is "broken." By returning special education students to the general classroom, such students will receive less than they did in the separate system.

Advocates: Special education students served in separate programs do not realize significant education outcomes. Longitudinal research indicates that outcomes for students in special education programs are limited in terms of student learning, graduation rates, postsecondary education and training, and community living. A crucial voice among inclusion advocates is that of adults with disabilities. These adults believe that segregated programs did not serve their needs and often made them feel inferior, isolated, and different from their peers. They also report that the segregated programs did not prepare them for living a full and productive life after school.

If general education is "broken," and special education has not served the needs of its students, then restructuring education into a unitary system will best meet the needs of teachers, students, and parents.

Critics: The least restrictive environment (LRE) requirement relates solely to social interaction between students with disabilities and their peers without disabilities, and the law's requirements concerning an "appropriate education" are applicable solely to academic learning.

Advocates: The law, as the courts have interpreted it, states that both the LRE and the "appropriate education" mandates involve the whole child and the full range of schooling's benefits, academic and social. The law does not require the sacrifice of the one for the other. For example, in *Oberti v. Board of Education* (1993), the court addressed the comparison of educational benefits available in a general class and the benefits of a special education class. The Third Circuit opinion, upholding the parents' demand for an inclusive placement, stated, "Many of the special education techniques used in the segregated class could be successfully imported into a regular class. . . . [T]he regular teacher could be trained to apply these techniques" (p. 1222). In *Sacramento City Unified School District v. Rachel H.* (1994), in which, again, the court upheld parents' demand for an inclusive placement over school district opposition, the Ninth Circuit found that the goals and objectives of the student's IEP could be achieved in the general education class, with curricular modifications and supplementary aids and services.

Critics: Inclusion is being advocated only by a few ideologically driven professionals and some emotional parents of students with disabilities.

Advocates: Inclusive education programs are expanding rapidly across the United States, in urban, suburban, and rural districts. Among these districts, students with all categories of disability, at all levels of severity, and at all grade levels are being educated with successful outcomes. Rather than a few emotional parents requesting inclusive education for their children, there is increased support for inclusive opportunities among parents of children with all categories of disabilities, and especially at the preschool level. This movement is demonstrated both by the growing number of court cases relating to efforts at inclusion, as well as by increasing numbers of parent groups that have formed to support inclusion. At nationwide hearings, "a majority of witnesses who testified on the subject of least restrictive environment indicated strong support for integrated placements" (National Council on Disability, 1995). Rather than a few ideologically driven professionals, a growing number of professionals believe that as research continues to document positive outcomes for all students, there will be a growing demand by professionals and parents for inclusive education. In light of the prejudice and harmful discrimination that people with disabilities face in school and community, educating all children in inclusive classrooms is a desirable goal in and of itself.

Critics: School districts are implementing inclusive education as a way to save money.

Advocates: Current state funding formulas encourage the placement of students in more- rather than less-restrictive settings (U.S. Department of Education, 1995). More than half of the states are reviewing their funding of special education, both to redress this problem and to address other special education funding issues. School districts report that to implement inclusive education effectively, the money should follow the children. Furthermore, funds saved from ending the separate systems should be used to support an integrated system, one that benefits all of the children. There is substantial evidence that the dual system wastes resources—in administrative duplication, in ineffective practices, and in subsidies of private school placements. Indeed, it is anticipated that over time school districts will save money and better serve all children, thereby spending public money more prudently and effectively.

Critics: The full inclusion of students with disabilities is a "movement" that is taking hold very quickly and is likely to have a profound and destructive effect on public education.

Advocates: American public education faces many problems, among them the continuing failure of schools to educate a sizable percentage of the nation's children, resulting in loss of support for public education; sharp cuts in education budgets; the increasing impoverishment of large numbers of the nation's families; the endemic violence, spread of drugs, teenage pregnancy, and family dissolution that confront a growing number of children; and continuing racism in schools. The special education system is yet another of the problems. It is not fair, however, to ask students with disabilities to wait until all of the other education problems are solved before they can become part of the struggle to bring change to the education system. Perhaps the core of the problem is not that inclusion has taken hold very quickly but that school restructuring to meet the needs of all students has moved so slowly.

CONCLUSION

Although the majority of reports on inclusive education are positive, critical reports concerning aspects of inclusive education have been presented. (See Fuchs & Fuchs, 1994, 1994–1995a, 1994–1995b; Hocutt, 1996; Kauffman, 1993, 1994; Shanker, 1994.) Such reports must be given serious attention. However, in contrasting such reports with the studies noted in Chapter 14 and the reports from more than a thousand school districts in the *National Study* (1994, 1995), an important factor that emerges concerns the "appropriate implementation" of inclusive education programs. What advocates of inclusion mean by appropriate implementation is the opposite of "dumping." Rather than a "one size fits all" approach, inclusive education programs of necessity address the needs of individual children. Rather than focus solely on issues of placement, advocates of inclusion gain support from the Individuals with Disabilities Education Act (IDEA) of 1990 requirement that students be provided with an education "appropriate" for their needs. In the language of IDEA, "supplementary aids and support services" are provided to meet the needs of students and their teachers and other personnel. The segregated special education programs of a dual system do not—and cannot—provide the "appropriate" education required by the law. As such, when implemented appropriately, inclusive education programs can be and are successful for the full range of students with disabilities and for their peers without disabilities.

REFERENCES

Daniel R.R. v. State Board of Education El Paso Independent School District, 874 F.2d 1036 (5th Cir. 1989).

Fuchs, D., & Fuchs, L.S. (1994). Inclusive schools movement and the radicalization of special education reform. *Exceptional Children, 60*(4), 294–309.

Fuchs, D., & Fuchs, L.S. (1994–1995a). Counterpoint: Special education—Ineffective? Immoral? *Exceptional Children, 61*(1), 303–306.

Fuchs, D., & Fuchs, L.S. (1994–1995b). Sometimes separate is better. *Educational Leadership, 52*(4), 22–26.

Fuchs, L.S., Fuchs, D., Hamlett, C.L., Phillips, N.B., & Karns, K. (1995). General educators' specialized adaption for students with learning disabilities. *Exceptional Children, 61*(5), 444–459.

Greer v. Rome City School District, 950 F.2d 688 (11th Cir. 1991).

Hardin, D.E., & McNelis, S.J. (1996). The Resource Center: Hub of inclusive activities. *Educational Leadership, 52*(4), 41–43.

Hocutt, A.M. (1996). Effectiveness of special education: Is placement the critical factor? *The Future of Children, 6*(1), 77–102.

Individuals with Disabilities Education Act (IDEA) of 1990, PL 101-476, 20 U.S.C. § 1400 *et seq.*

Kauffman, J.M. (1993). How to achieve radical reform of special education. *Exceptional Children, 60*, 6–16.

Kauffman, J.M. (1994). Two perspectives on inclusion: One size does not fit all. *Beyond Behavior, 5*(3), 11–14.

National Council on Disability. (1995). *Improving the implementation of the Individuals with Disabilities Education Act: Making schools work for all of America's children.* Washington, DC: Author.

National Study of Inclusive Education. (1994). New York: The City University of New York, National Center on Educational Restructuring and Inclusion.

National Study of Inclusive Education. (1995). New York: The City University of New York, National Center on Educational Restructuring and Inclusion.

Oberti v. Board of Education, 995 F.2d 1204 (3rd Cir. 1993).

Sacramento City Unified School District v. Rachel H., 14 F.3d 1398 (9th Cir. 1994).

Separate and unequal. (1993, December 13). *U.S. News & World Report,* 46–60.

Shanker, A. (1994). Full inclusion is neither free nor appropriate. *Educational Leadership, 52*(2), 18–21.

U.S. Department of Education. (1995). *Seventeenth annual report to Congress on the implementation of the Individuals with Disabilities Education Act.* Washington, DC: Author

SCHOOL
RESTRUCTURING

Inclusion will succeed to the extent that it links itself with other ongoing restructuring efforts: with the detracking movement, authentic assessment, site-based management, and so on. Restructuring means looking at not just what kind of classrooms we want, but what kind of world we want, and how we prepare children to be members of that broader community.
—*Sapon-Shevin, in O'Neil (1994–1995, p. 11)*

When students with disabilities are included in general education classrooms one by one, their participation is little more than as islands in the mainstream. For inclusion to be successful for all students, teachers, and school districts, its implementation must become systemic. Programs of inclusive education then become both a cause and a consequence of educational restructuring. The drive to upgrade standards and to include *all* students in these reforms has created tension for educators. Educational reform efforts, such as those led by James Comer, Henry Levin, Ted Sizer, and Robert Slavin, suggest, as Ron Edmonds put it in 1979, the possibility of

211

raising the "floor" and thus narrowing the gap for everyone. A point of congruence between school effectiveness efforts and the movement toward inclusion is that both require a new approach, one that puts students at the center of the educational reform, in order to bring about a restructured educational system.

Placing students at the center of educational reform will not solve all of the problems facing U.S. public education. It will not by itself overcome racism, sexism, handicappism, class divisions, or the social consequences of poverty and pervasive violence. Nor is it a substitute for needed funds or for competent and dedicated personnel. Rather, it provides a conceptual framework for the work of educational reform, for establishing schools that serve and succeed for all students, and for a society that includes all as full and contributing members.

The changing educational perspective is summarized by Burello (1995) in three "discourses guiding public education": 1) the best of traditional practice, 2) the reforms of inclusive education, and 3) a restructured education system.

Discourse #1: The Best of Current Practice

Children come to school with varying abilities, motivation, and life experiences. When these internal factors cause them to fail in school, it is the school district's responsibility to provide remedial, compensatory, or special services. Generating resources necessary to support these services requires identifying and labeling students as at-risk, Chapter One, or Special Education students. Specialists have developed tools and strategies to assess and plan for these students, often in separate settings, to meet their extraordinary needs. Specially trained personnel working in specially designed and delivered programs can provide the remedial and compensatory instruction that afford these students equitable educational outcomes.

Discourse #2: The Reforms of Inclusive Education

All students attend the school to which they would normally go if they did not have a disability. Students with disabilities at the school site are distributed in their natural proportions in regular education programs that are age and grade appropriate. No student would be denied placement at the school site on the basis of the severity of [his or her] disability unless [he or she] were a danger to themselves or others. All student are in, and they can only earn their way out. Special education support services are primarily provided within the context of the regular education program in addition to other cooperative and peer support practices. Only in this way can students be assured of an equitable and appropriate education.

Discourse #3: A Restructured Education System

Since the community is where life occurs, education for life after school should begin in the neighborhood school and successively expand to the community at large. It is not necessary to label or separate students in order to provide them with an appropriate education. All students have special needs, although some are more unique than others. The primary needs for all students are to learn to live, work, and participate in community life. These goals can be accomplished by educating all children together. When teachers, with varying expertise, work collaboratively using a variety of strategies and technologies, they can address the needs of all students. Students and other members of the school community benefit when they work together daily to meet those individual and diverse needs. Achieving educational equity and excellence requires unifying all members of the school community around a vision and set of outcomes for all students.

The restructuring of schools to achieve successful outcomes for all children involves embracing the conviction that

- Schooling makes a difference.
- Schools are capable of changing to well educate all students together.
- The capacity of children and teachers to learn is unlimited.

Although these concepts have their bases in the educational research and reform literature, they are belied by the premises and practices of the current dual system of special and general education. This section addresses the lack of overall school restructuring efforts for students with disabilities; describes restructuring efforts that involve students with disabilities; and presents a conceptualization of a unitary rather than a dual school system, one that produces successful outcomes for all students.

REFERENCES

Burello, L. (1995, July 18). *School changes which facilitate inclusion.* Paper presented at the Inclusive School Institute on "Changing Paradigms: Educating Students with Disabilities in Regular Classrooms," Fairfield, NJ.

Edmonds, R. (1979). Some schools work and more can. *Social Policy, 9*(5), 26–31.

O'Neil, J. (1994–1995). An interview with Jim Kauffman and Mara Sapon-Shevin. *Educational Leadership, 52*(4), 7–11.

16

SCHOOL RESTRUCTURING FOR SOME STUDENTS

Since the publication of *A Nation at Risk* (National Commission on Excellence in Education, 1983), various school restructuring efforts have occurred. For the most part, however, the separate system called "special education" has not been involved in these educational restructuring efforts at the local or federal levels.

The absence of fundamental change in special education is evidenced by the following:

- During the 1982–1983 school year, 31% of special education students were served in separate classes or more restrictive settings. A decade later, in the most recent year for which there are national data (1991–1992), 30% of special education students were served in separate classes or more restrictive settings. For students with mental retardation, the percentage served in separate classes or more restrictive settings was 70% in 1982–1983 and 69% in 1991–1992 (U.S. Department of Education, 1985, 1995).
- Every state department of education across the United States and all but a handful of school districts have a separate special education administrative system.
- The federal and state systems of funding special education encourage the separation of special and general education (Parrish, 1993a, 1993b, 1994).
- The 1995 reform of the U.S. Department of Education's monitoring of state implementation of federal programs, integrating the review of several categorical programs into one coordinated effort, failed to include special education.

- Teacher education programs and state teacher certification systems (as well as the new federally supported national "master teacher" certification program) perpetuate separation between general and special educators.

EXCLUSION OF STUDENTS WITH DISABILITIES FROM FEDERAL REFORMS

The most salient aspect in the slow pace of change in special education is the exclusion of students with disabilities from the reform activities. In its 1995 report to the president and Congress, the National Council on Disability stated, "A review of eight major federal initiatives [between 1990 and 1992] involving school-age children and youth shows that six did not include specific provisions for students with disabilities" (p. 9). The exclusion of students with disabilities is evident in such reform activities as the new curricular standards, the national and state assessment programs, and the programs of school choice.

The U.S. Department of Education has funded professional associations to develop national standards in their field. Most of these have not considered issues concerning students with disabilities. A National Center for Educational Outcomes (NCEO) research associate, speaking at the 1994 Council for Exceptional Children (CEC) annual meeting, stated that most of the standards projects will "have to go back and demonstrate how [their] standards include students with disabilities" (cited in "Include Disabled," 1994, p. 3). Speaking at the 1995 annual meeting of the National Association of State Directors of Special Education (NASDSE), Christopher Cross, president of the Council for Basic Education, whose group is advising the national history standards project, said, "We had 200 people from Los Angeles with us for three days. And I did not meet, during that period of time, with one person who represented teachers or the administrative structure in special education" (cited in "Reformer," 1995, p. 5).

Referring to a draft of science standards developed by the National Committee on Science Education Standards, the federally funded NCEO found that the committee had failed to address the needs of students with disabilities. Noting that an earlier draft had referred to "all students in all grades regardless of ability," NCEO director, James Ysseldyke, said, "The science standards people have tried to incorporate language that would refer to and support students with disabilities. But they have backed off from what they have been saying. That's what is disappointing." The NCEO asserted that the standards must acknowledge not only alternative teaching styles, which they do, but also students' different learning styles. "We think teachers using the standards will want to have access to these alternative strategies for the diverse learners who will most likely be in many of their classes," commented Ysseldyke (cited in "Group Says," 1995, pp. 1, 3).

The practice of measuring educational outcomes for students with disabilities is inconsistent among the states. The NCEO reported that in 1993, students with disabilities participated in assessments in only 44 states, with the participation rates ranging from fewer than 10% of students with disabilities in Colorado to more than 90% in Kentucky. A 1994 NCEO study reported that only 19 states could identify the participation rates of students with disabilities in their standardized statewide assessments. Kentucky and Maryland reported 100% participation of students with disabilities in statewide assessments, whereas Louisiana and North Carolina reported the lowest rates (5% and 7%, respectively).

A 1995 study by the Indiana state education department collected data from 37 states. Twenty-seven of the 33 states with standardized tests reported that some students with disabilities did not participate. Whereas in some states this is a result of the students' individualized education program (IEP), in others—Hawaii and Colorado, for example—entire groups of students are excluded (e.g., those in self-contained classes, those attending special education programs more than half of the time, those in line to receive a special diploma). In Texas, 42% of the students with disabilities take the Texas Assessment of Academic Skills, but in reporting results the scores of special education students are excluded ("National Survey," 1995, pp. 1, 3). The U.S. Department of Education believes that states may be deliberately mislabeling some students as having disabilities in order to exclude them from statewide assessments. A survey of 12 New York elementary schools found that those reporting improved scores had identified as having disabilities more than twice the percentage of students as did schools with consistently high achievement ("ED Points," 1995, pp. 1, 3).

The importance of this issue is reflected in a chapter by the NCEO included in the 1994 Report to Congress on the implementation of the Individuals with Disabilities Education Act (IDEA) of 1990 (PL 101-476)[1]:

---

[1]Two NCEO reports provided fuller data on state guidelines concerning, first, including students with disabilities in assessments (Thurlow, Scott, & Ysseldyke, 1995a) and, second, accommodations in assessments for students with disabilities (Thurlow, Scott, & Ysseldyke, 1995b).

- Students with disabilities are disproportionately excluded both from State and national assessments. Even where guidelines about inclusion and exclusion exist, they are inconsistently implemented.
- Accommodations for the special testing needs of students with disabilities are inconsistently applied. Thus, the accommodations or lack of accomodations can further complicate the task of assessing and analyzing results for these students.
- There are variations in how students with disabilities are defined and how their educational results are reported. These variations exist from State to State, between State programs and national data collection programs, among the various types of national programs, and even within national programs sponsored by individual agencies. (1994, pp. 167–168)

The NCEO has estimated that the National Assessment of Educational Progress (NAEP), the nation's education report card, excludes half of the nation's students with disabilities. In May 1995, the NAEP Board of Directors voted not to allow any "nonstandard" administration of the examination. At the August 1995 NAEP board meeting, Sharon Robinson, U.S. Department of Education Assistant Secretary for Research and Improvement, declared that for the NAEP not to support inclusive testing would be to "deny the future" ("NAEP Lukewarm," 1995). Robinson estimated that up to 85% of students with disabilities could take NAEP tests without adaptations or accommodations and pointed to federal law that requires the NAEP to do all that it can to enable as many students with disabilities as possible to participate. Despite this plea, the NAEP board said that it feared that "the price of assessing disabled students would force it to cut the number of nondisabled students it can test in subjects ranging from art to science" ("NAEP Lukewarm," 1995). However, a federal district court in 1972 held that the absence of resources did not allow a school district to deny opportunities to students with disabilities any more than they could deny such opportunities to students without disabilities (Mills v. Board of Education, 1972).

When the U.S. Department of Education provided additional funds, the NAEP agreed for the first time to allow accommodations for special education students, such as extended time, large-print texts, and audio cassettes in some of the 1996 national mathematics and science tests. In addition, the NAEP no longer gives schools broad authority to exclude students from its samples in grades 4, 8, and 12; only those students whose IEPs specifically say that they cannot participate are to be excluded ("NAEP to Test," 1995, p. 1). For any child excluded from participating, the school district must complete a form stating why the student was left out of the test ("Guidelines Expected," 1995).

Ysseldyke has underscored society's collective responsibility to include students with disabilities in assessment programs: "We value only what we measure, and if [students with disabilities] are not in the picture, then people assume that they're not responsible for educating them. Out of sight is out of mind" (cited in "National Survey," 1995, p. 3). But it is not only a matter of fairness. Testing programs that do not include students with disabilities could be challenged under Section 504 of the Rehabilitation Act of 1973 (PL 93-112) and the Americans with Disabilities Act (ADA) of 1990 (PL 101-336). Court decisions must also be taken into account in relation to equitable use of resources. The positive benefits of including students with disabilities in statewide instructional and assessment programs are documented in L. Stufflebeam's finding that as a result of the use of the states' comprehensive and inclusive model (KIRIS), "students with educational disabilities are receiving more attention related to instruction and content" (cited by A. Moll, personal communication, February 22, 1995). Excluding students with disabilities from these assessments carries two pernicious messages: 1) that their education is not a matter of concern and 2) more fundamental, that they cannot achieve. Conversely, including them affirms that their education is the responsibility of the education system, that those who lead the system (e.g., superintendents, principals) will be held accountable for the education of students with disabilities, and that they can be expected to achieve—when provided the appropriate education.

A study of public school choice programs in five cities found that students with disabilities were excluded from them ("Limited Programs," 1995). This occurred despite provisions in IDEA that require school districts to take "reasonable steps" to include children with disabilities in all programs available to peers without disabilities and despite Section 504 of the Rehabilitation Act of 1973, which grants people with disabilities "meaningful access" to any program receiving federal funds (cited in "Study," 1995). An evaluation of magnet schools that report that their students do better than those attending public, private, or parochial high schools makes the limits of such opportunities for students with disabilities all the more consequential (Viadero, 1996).

In light of these instances of excluding students with disabilities from federally supported educational reform activities, the attention to them in the Goals 2000: Educate America Act of 1994 (PL 103-227) is a significant breakthrough. Speaking at the annual meeting of the Council for Exceptional Children, Tom Hehir, director of the Office of Special Education Programs, U.S. Department of

Education, stated, "Goals 2000 says 'all' students and means all" (cited in Sklaroff, 1994, p. 5).

Reviewing the educational reform efforts of both the 1990s and previous periods, Goodman (1995) stated,

> Many school reform proposals and projects, while making technical changes, actually reinforce the underlying values, power relationships, and learning experiences embedded within the conventional ways of educating children.
>
> [T]his manner of school change has insidious implications. The public, which often pays for these reforms, is told that significant changes will be made in the name of this new movement, but because the underlying values, practices, and content of schooling are never substantively addressed, these changes fail to make much difference in the intellectual lives of teachers and their students. (p. 3)

Put another way, too often educational reforms have produced "change without difference" (Roemer, 1991, p. 447). In a critical examination of the reform efforts since the mid-1980s, Astuto (1995) contended that the limited results have been a consequence of a set of assumptions that constrain schools. He presented a set of counter assumptions. These counter assumptions provide the basis for restructured inclusive schools that are producing significant outcomes for all students. The current and counter assumptions are as follows:

Current assumption: The purpose of schooling in a democracy is to allow children to progress on the basis of their own ability and talent, that is, meritocratically.

Counter assumption: The purpose of schooling in a democracy is to extend the benefits of the society to all children by preparing them to gain access to those benefits.

Current assumption: Achievement in school rests predominantly in the hands of the individual student.

Counter assumption: Individual achievement in school is influenced markedly by the adjustment of the school to the student.

Current assumption: Educational achievement is enhanced by competition and comparative assesment of students, schools, and school districts.

Counter assumption: Educational achievement is enhanced by conditions of cooperation that reflect trust, confidence, support, and challenge among and between teachers and learners.

Current assumption: Individuals are motivated to achieve institutional objectives by incentives.

Counter assumption: Individuals are self-motivated to achieve institutional objectives unless blocked by the organizational environment.

CONCLUSION

Despite considerable research indicating the lack of successful outcomes for students in special education and a growing concern voiced by adults with disabilities and others about the social construct of a separate system for some students, a dual system of general and special education continues to operate at the federal, state, and local school district levels. At the federal level, administrative reforms to blend categorical programs exclude special education. At the state level, separate bureaucracies and funding formulas keep the two systems apart. At the local level, although inclusive education activities take place, the dual structure remains. In addition, the broad national reforms ignore or exclude students with disabilities, not only in regard to the various standards projects but also in the national assessment efforts, teacher training and certification, and school choice. This largely is the result not of specific actions but, rather, of a set of pernicious assumptions about schooling, students with disabilities, and educational reform.

Numerous rationales have been developed to explain away the fact that students with disabilities have been ignored in the educational reforms since the mid-1980s. The following rationales and their responses serve as a useful summary of the state of school reform in the 1990s and the as-yet-unfulfilled mandate to include students with disabilities within that reform.

Rationale: The education of students with disabilities does not need reform.

Response: The data presented in Section I of this volume make clear that the separate special education system does not well serve students with disabilities, and fundamental reform is necessary.

Rationale: Because the education of students with disabilities is the province of the separate special education system, whatever reforms are necessary are not part of the broader educational change.

Response: Given that the root issue in the failure of the special education system is its separateness, the reform of special education necessarily requires its integration with broader educational restructuring.

Rationale: General education reforms must take priority; only then will the resources necessary for change in educating students with disabilities become available.

Response: Piecemeal or sequential reforms are strategically flawed, and asking students with disabilities to "wait" is both immoral and illegal. The courts have held that school districts cannot deny opportunities to students with disabilities because of financial limitations while providing them to students without disabilities.

Rationale: The education of students with disabilities is not a matter of general concern.

Response: The continuing failure to well educate students with disabilities, which requires inclusion with their peers without disabilities, is reminiscent of Ron Edmonds's (1979) comment about the nation's failure to well educate poor and minority students, namely that we can do things differently depending "on how we feel about the fact that we haven't done it so far" (p. 29).

REFERENCES

Americans with Disabilities Act (ADA) of 1990, PL 101-336, 42 U.S.C. § 12101 *et seq.*

Astuto, T. (1995). *Roots of reform: Challenging the assumptions that control change in education.* Andover, MA: Network/Regional Lab.

Edmonds, R. (1979). Some schools work and more can. *Social Policy, 9*(5), 26–31.

ED points to study linking special ed, placements. (1995, January 23). *Education Daily,* 1, 3.

Goals 2000: Educate America Act of 1994, PL 103-227, 20 U.S.C. § 5801 *et seq.*

Goodman, J. (1995). Change without difference: School restructuring in historical perspective. *Harvard Educational Review, 65*(1), 1–29.

Group says science standards shun kids with disabilities. (1995, March 8). *Education Daily,* 1, 3.

Guidelines expected soon on including students in NAEP. (1995). *Special Educator, 11*(7), 4.

Include disabled in standards, special ed advocates insist. (1994). *Research Report on Education Research, 26*(9), 3.

Individuals with Disabilities Education Act (IDEA) of 1990, PL 101-476, 20 U.S.C. § 1400 *et seq.*

Limited programs bar choices for disabled students. (1995, January 13). *Education Daily,* 1, 3.

Mills v. Board of Education, 348 F. Supp. 866 (D.D.C. 1972).

NAEP lukewarm about testing disabled students. (1995, August 7). *Education Daily,* 1, 3.

NAEP to test more disabled, Spanish-speaking students. (1995, August 30). *Education Daily,* 1, 3.

National Commission on Excellence in Education. (1983). *A nation at risk: The imperative for educational reform.* Washington, DC: U.S. Government Printing Office.

National Council on Disability. (1995). *Improving the implementation of the Individuals with Disabilities Education Act: Making schools work for all of America's children.* Washington, DC: Author.

National survey shows states exclude disabled from tests. (1995, May 8). *Education Daily,* 1, 3.

Parrish, T.B. (1993a). Federal policy options for funding special education. *CSEF Brief, 1,* 1–4.

Parrish, T.B. (1993b). State funding provisions and least restrictive environment: Implications for federal policy. *CSEF Brief, 2,* 1–4.

Parrish, T.B. (1994, April 28–May 1). *Fiscal issues relating to special education inclusion.* Paper presented at the National Center on Educational Restructuring and Inclusion invitational conference on inclusive education, Racine, WI.

Reformer: Special ed shuns standards debate at its peril. (1995, November 15). *Education Daily,* 5.

Rehabilitation Act of 1973, PL 93-112, 29 U.S.C. § 701 *et seq.*

Roemer, M. (1991). What we talk about when we talk about school reform. *Harvard Educational Review, 61,* 434–448.

Sklaroff, S. (1994, April 20). Goals 2000 seen spurring "inclusion" movement. *Education Daily,* 5.

Study: Laws guarantee school choice for disabled. (1995, January 24). *Education Daily,* 3.

Thurlow, M.L., Scott, D.L., & Ysseldyke, J.E. (1995a). *A compilation of states' guidelines for including students with disabilities in assessments.* Synthesis Report 17. Minneapolis: University of Minnesota, National Center on Educational Outcomes.

Thurlow, M.L., Scott, D.L., & Ysseldyke, J.E. (1995b). *A compilation of states' guidelines for accommodations in assessments for students with disabilities.* Synthesis Report 18. Minneapolis: University of Minnesota, National Center on Educational Outcomes.

U.S. Department of Education. (1985). *Seventh annual report to the Congress on the implementation of the Education of the Handicapped Act.* Washington, DC: Author.

U.S. Department of Education. (1995). *Seventeenth annual report to Congress on the implementation of the Individuals with Disabilities Education Act.* Washington, DC: Author.

Viadero, D. (1996). Students learn more in magnets than other schools, study finds. *Education Week, 15*(24), 6.

17

SCHOOL RESTRUCTURING
FOR *ALL* STUDENTS

Although many states and local school districts have implemented educational reforms during the 1990s, in only a few of these has reform focused on the overall educational system, with explicit inclusion of students with disabilities. In two states, Kansas and Kentucky, reform *has* been targeted on the entire educational system. In other states, inclusion is a component of the state's restructuring efforts. This is the case in Connecticut, Delaware, Florida, Hawaii, Illinois, Indiana, Massachusetts, Michigan, Minnesota, Ohio, Texas, and Vermont.

PATTERNS OF EDUCATIONAL RESTRUCTURING

Whereas some school districts initiate broad school restructuring efforts that include special education and general education students, most do not. According to reports from school districts in the *National Study of Inclusive Education* (1995 [henceforth *National Study*]), there is no set pattern for initiating inclusive education reforms. Reforms in general education programs often lead to reform in special education, thereby resulting in inclusion. Likewise, if inclusion begins as a reform effort in special education, reform in general education philosophy and practice may result. In other words, the two streams become a cause and a consequence of each other, so that as a school improvement plan is developed, inclusive education is, for the most part, an integral part of the plan. And, as districts reshape their Title I programs to be more comprehensive, special education programs are reevaluated for reform. With special education and Title I coexisting in about two thirds of U.S. elementary schools, an opportunity exists for integrating special and general education, although legislative intent, funding mechanisms, and populations are targeted differently. Leadership from district officials, noncategorical special education certification, and staff development and joint planning were found to be common factors in districts that successfully integrated the two programs (Carlson & O'Reilly, 1996).

The use of federal funds for students in need of special services and with disabilities is governed by a complex set of factors. Federal rules governing the expenditure of funds allocated for distribution under the Individuals with Disabilities Education Act (IDEA) of 1990 (PL 101-476) prohibit other than labeled students from gaining more than indirect or "incidental benefit." Proposals made in 1995 by the U.S. Department of Education for the reauthorization of IDEA recommended abolishing the "incidental benefit" rule. The National Governor's Association issued a policy statement seeking authority for states to use up to 10% of their IDEA funds for noncategorical support for students with disabilities ("Governors Seek," 1995, p. 3). The Center for Special Education Finance proposed blending finances for special-needs students. Crafting a middle ground between the (near) absolute separation of funds that has typified the 1980s and 1990s (i.e., prohibiting commingling or anything more than "incidental benefit") and proposals for a single block grant for all students in need of special services or with disabilities *or* incorporation of these students within the schoolwide programs under Title I of the Elementary and Secondary Education Act of 1994, the center recommended setting aside "bridge money" to foster cooperation ("Program Blending," 1995, p. 2; see also Verstegen, 1995).

Verstegen's (1995) report is one of the few analyses that relates financial issues in education to other issues. For example, in addition to recommending financial changes, Verstegen cited other needed changes in special education policies and practices in order to implement "a more unified vision of reform," including incorporation of the activities of the general education teacher in a student's individualized education program (IEP); professional development activities for both general and special education personnel; and changes in preservice education, teacher certification, and the organization of state education agencies.

As states engage in educational restructuring, an increasing number of them report that to have significant outcomes, all students must be a part of the reform efforts. Again, Kansas and Kentucky are two examples of such efforts. In Kansas, three separate reform efforts have been coordinated into a single model development. The individual initiatives were: 1) special education reform; 2) a general education school restructuring; and 3) a combined social, health, and educational service reform agenda (Skrtic & Sailor, 1993). In Kentucky, the Kentucky Education Reform Act (KERA) addresses the needs of all students (*KERA Program Outline*, 1994). This landmark legislation, adopted in 1990, involves changes in school governance, finance, school organization, curricula, and staffing. Key features include multi-age classes at the elementary school level and a Collaborative Teaching Model, which sustains students with a variety of ability levels in a general education setting. Teams of general education teachers and "strategic" teachers (special education, Title I, bilingual, and remedial teachers) work together on a daily basis, planning and implementing programs for all students.

SCHOOL DISTRICT REPORTS ON REFORM

The following are excerpts from school district reports of educational restructuring efforts contained in the *National Study* (1995).

> We have experienced several unexpected outcomes from our restructuring efforts. Teachers who would never have had the opportunity to work together have for the first time crossed educational lines. Bilingual teachers teach with general education teachers. Special education teachers teach with bilingual and regular education teachers. Inclusion has caused educators to cross cultural, educational, and philosophical boundaries. It has produced a model for ongoing professional development. Educators team teaching are learning new techniques from one another on the job. Experimentation is at an all-time high. The need to retool is apparent, and there is a thirst for knowledge not seen in some time. Teachers are reading professional magazines and forming study groups in an effort to better understand the diverse needs of students before them. The inclusion of a multicultural curriculum is another critical aspect of successful inclusive practices. It is an exciting time to be an educator. (p. 172)
>
> *Springfield Public Schools, Massachusetts*

> In the fall of 1990, as a result of school improvement/restructuring, Gier School started an inclusive education program. . . . [S]pecial education support was given in the students' classroom rather than in a pull-out program as was the past practice. Due to the nature of the program, inclusive education has also brought support to nonhandicapped youngsters needing additional assistance. As a result of the school system's restructuring and reform, a belief system was developed in the 1989–90 school year. . . encompass[ing] our school district's

belief in inclusion. All of the beliefs reflect the idea of inclusion. (p. 178)

Hillsdale Community Schools, Michigan

Inclusive education philosophy is deeply embedded in other reform/ restructuring efforts across the district. The district's two newest schools have been architecturally and philosophically designed to accommodate all learners' needs in individual, small group, and large group settings. (p. 187)

Chaska Public Schools,
Independent School District #112, Minnesota

Inclusion has been directly related to restructuring and reforming the school district. At the same time that inclusion began and students were integrated into the [general education] programs, Gifted and Talented, which had previously been a pull out program, was changed over to an enrichment program for all students. (p. 206)

Clinton Township School District, New Jersey

Inclusion is not a disability discussion. What we've done is to restructure service delivery for every child in the building. . . . [I]f you believe that all kids have a right to be here and learn at their own rate, then inclusion is not an issue. (p. 252)

Washington Local School District, Ohio

Inclusion efforts preceded the district's restructuring activities. Inclusion is now considered to be the accepted approach, i.e., the bridge between the old special education structure and the more appropriate arrangement for special needs students. Currently, every school (six elementary, one middle, and one high school) has embraced the inclusion model. (p. 286)

Coventry Public Schools, Rhode Island

Inclusion has had a tremendous impact on curriculum restructuring and instruction for all our diverse learners. Structural arrangements provided through cooperative learning models have been advocated to facilitate academic and social learning. Problem solving has been increasingly stressed to assist students. Teachers are encouraged to assist students in learning how to learn through approaches such as the "Strategies Intervention Model." Emphasis has been shifting from a focus on content toward a focus on learning strategies, such as teaching skills, processes, and practices that allow learners of all ages to sustain and update their acquisition and application of specific knowledge. More emphasis is being placed on teaching the child and not just the text. (p. 318)

Alvarado Independent School District, Texas

There is a plethora of reform/restructuring activities underway in the district. In some schools, the label "inclusion" has become a way of life and is no longer a focus of reform. In other schools, they are just beginning to become aware of the implications of inclusion and they are grappling with issues. . . . Across the district, inclusion is a big part of many schools' "Learning Plan," which is developed yearly. (p. 353)

Federal Way Public Schools, Washington

Inclusion has always remained at the core of restructuring and reform activities in the district. Whenever new teaching strategies are considered, inclusion is the core of the conversation. Questions are posed such as: Will this fit our direction around inclusion? How will this strategy enhance learning for all children? (p. 341)

Franklin Northeast Supervisory Union, Vermont

NONGOVERNMENTAL REFORM EFFORTS

The National Center on Educational Restructuring and Inclusion (NCERI) canvassed the major nongovernmental educational reform efforts to determine the extent to which they included students with disabilities. Highlights of these reports are presented in the paragraphs following:

Coalition of Essential Schools
Thank you for your request for information on inclusion in Coalition schools. Unfortunately, my response is an "everything and nothing" response. While we do not have specific data regarding students with disabilities here in our Providence office, the notions that "teaching and learning should be personalized," and [that] "the school goals should apply to all students" are two of the Nine Common Principles that undergird our work. Therefore, I suspect that you might find some innovative ideas regarding inclusion in some of our member schools. (C. Holden, personal communication, 1995)

Development Studies Center
I should mention that while inclusiveness and responsiveness to diversity are fundamental principles underlying our work [in 24 schools around the country], it is only recently that we have begun to explicitly consider how our programs do (or do not) meet the needs of students with disabilities, and we have not developed any specific programs for disabled students. (V. Battistich, personal communication, 1995)

EQUITY 2000
Because EQUITY 2000 [established by the College Board in 1990 and currently underway in 14 school districts serving nearly 500,000 students in six urban sites] reaches all students, it does include students with disabilities—particularly those who have been "tracked" or "grouped" into lower-level courses that do not lead to a college-prep path of study. As you know, students are often placed in dead-end, watered-down courses because counselors or teachers make assumptions [about] those students' academic abilities simply because of their race, ethnicity, gender, or because they may

have a disability. EQUITY 2000 changes that by emphasizing that all students should be on a high-level academic path that can open the door to college.

[A]lthough EQUITY 2000 is not focused exclusively on students with disabilities, it has a significant impact on the academic opportunities and achievements of those students [because] it seeks to raise standards and achievement of all students. (V. Jones, personal communication, 1995)

Foxfire

We have networks of teachers around the country who incorporate the Foxfire approach to education in their everyday classes—all grade levels and almost all subject areas. We have a few special education teachers who use the approach. (K. Cannon, personal communication, 1995)

National Center for Effective Schools

In response to the NCERI's query, the National Center for Effective Schools (NCES), at the School of Education, University of Wisconsin, offered some general information on the work of the NCES but referred further inquiry to the university's Department of Rehabilitation Psychology and Special Education, whose work "more directly relates to . . . programs for students with disabilities and inclusive education." (B.T. Madison, personal communication, 1995)

New Standards

New Standards is very committed to including all students in our assessments. This commitment is a matter of record. [For example, New Standards' Broad Principles state that] "schools will be free to use very different methods to help students achieve the new standards, and our assessments will provide students with many ways to demonstrate their competence, enabling them to take advantage of their particular backgrounds and experiences. We will work to keep our assessments free of any cultural, gender or racial bias and make them accessible to students whose native language is not English." [New Standards' instructions for teachers state that] "if you have mainstreamed students in your classroom, you may use any sort of assistance (reading items aloud, etc.) which you normally use according to the student's IEP." (P. Daro, personal communication, 1995)

Paideia

Philosophically, Alfred Adler's original work (upon which Paideia is based) is in full agreement with inclusion as a general practice, and we here at the [National Paideia] Center suggest it to those principals in Paideia schools where it isn't currently practiced. Whether by accident or design, well over half of the schools we work with in ongoing programs practice inclusion for most or all of the populations that might otherwise have been segregated.

Here's where the picture gets a little less clear, however. Far too few of those schools have made coherent effort to support their inclusion programs with "supplementing aids and supports, staff development," etc. If my informal survey reveals one key problem, it's the lack of consistent support for the program as it's being implemented. (T. Roberts, personal communication, 1995)

Re:Learning

Enclosed are some materials which will give you an overall sense of the E[ducation] C[ommission of the] S[tates] Re:Learning initiative. You will not find details about the inclusion of disabled students in these materials. [NCERI is referred to the Coalition of Essential Schools for information.] (J. Bray, personal communication, 1995)

Success for All

[The Success for All] approach to students at risk has three interrelated thrusts. First, our most important goal with respect to special education is to keep kids at risk of identification for learning disabilities out of the [special education] system by providing them with excellent instruction, one-to-one tutoring, family support services, or other adaptations to make sure that all are succeeding in reading in the early grades. Second, if students do end up with IEPs for learning disabilities or mild mental retardation despite our best efforts, we try to see that the students are treated the same way as everyone else. That is, they are in heterogeneous homerooms all day except for reading, when they are regrouped like everyone else.

[T]he third thrust has to do with students with more severe learning deficits. We provide inclusion of all children, but are inconsistently successful at this. One of our Roots and Wings schools, Green Holly in Lexington Park, MD, is outstanding at this. (R.E. Slavin, personal communication, 1995; see also Chapter 26)

CONCLUSION

For the most part, inclusive education activities are initiated at the local school district level rather than through state-level or federal restructuring efforts. In too many school districts, inclusive education remains an isolated activity. Increasingly, however, the placing of special education students into general education classrooms with the necessary supports and aids (i.e., inclusive education) precipitates broader school reform or school restructuring efforts that include both special and general education students. Basically, they become the cause and the consequence of each other.

In 1996, 21 years after passage of the Education for All Handicapped Children Act of 1975 (PL 94-142), inclusive education is poised to "take off." In 1979, Ron Edmonds, a scholar of school effectiveness, stated that "we know how to develop effective schools, but we have yet to develop effective districts." NCERI's 1995 *National Study of Inclusive Education* has documented that this is true of inclusive education. Inclusion in the mid-1990s is at the same point that quality education of African American students was in the late 1970s. For inclusive education to become part of the fabric of U.S. education, the following are essential:

- In the renewal of IDEA, Congress must reaffirm the rights of all students with disabilities to a free appropriate public education, to due process rights (along with their parents), and to a bias-free evaluation.
- The right of students with disabilities to an appropriate education must be a parent's prerogative, just as it is for children without disabilities. The child's education must not be conditioned on undergoing an evaluation that cedes decision making to the professionals.
- Inclusive education must become fully infused in the work of educational reform. This includes all federally supported reform efforts (e.g., the Goals 2000: Educate America Act 1994, the curricular development and standards-setting projects, the teacher-training and certification reforms), the state reform efforts, and the large-scale independent reform efforts.
- Restructured schools must become ones in which diversity in student population and learning modalities is valued and in which outcomes for all students are given the highest priority.
- Careful attention must be given to ensure that recognition of the capacities and strengths of students with disabilities is not lost in "sympathy" and "understanding."
- Major changes must be undertaken in teacher education programs, as well as in the certification and licensure of teachers, to prepare all school personnel to work in inclusive settings.
- Federal and state funding practices must be reformed to support inclusive education.
- The voice and experience of teachers, in general education as well as in special education, must be utilized to benefit all students.
- The voice and experience of people with disabilities must be brought into the schools as expertise to benefit all students.
- Parental involvement in the schools must transcend the limitations of a due process focus and become a true partnership among equals.

REFERENCES

Carlson, E., & O'Reilly, F.E. (1996). Integrating Title I and special education service delivery. *Remedial and Special Education*, *17*(1), 21–29.

Edmonds, R. (1979). Some schools work and more can. *Social Policy*, *9*(5), 26–31.

Education for All Handicapped Children Act of 1975, PL 94-142, 20 U.S.C. § 1400 *et seq.*

Elementary and Secondary Education Act of 1994, PL 103-382, 20 U.S.C. § 6301 *et seq.*

Goals 2000: Educate America Act of 1994, PL 103-227, 20 U.S.C. § 5801 *et seq.*

Governors seek authority to merge IDEA, other money. (1995, August 3). *Education Daily,* 3–4.

Individuals with Disabilities Education Act (IDEA) of 1990, PL 101-476, 20 U.S.C. § 1400 *et seq.*

KERA program outline: Inclusion of students with disabilities in general education settings. (1994). Frankfort: Kentucky Department of Education.

National Study of Inclusive Education. (1995). New York: The City University of New York, National Center on Educational Restructuring and Inclusion.

Program blending could ease special needs fragmentation. (1995, July 31). *Education Daily,* 1–2.

Skrtic, T.M., & Sailor, W. (1993). *Barriers and bridges to inclusive education: An analysis of Louisiana special education policy.* Lawrence: Kansas University Affiliated Program.

Verstegen, D.A. (1995). *Fiscal provisions of the Individuals with Disabilities Education Act: Historical overview.* Palo Alto, CA: Center for Special Education Finance.

18

THE THIRD WAVE
OF SCHOOL REFORM

The first wave of reforms following the publication of *A Nation at Risk* (National Commission on Educational Excellence, 1983) focused on external factors: higher standards (e.g., strengthened graduation requirements, competency statements, no pass/no play, attendance rules), new—and often mandated—curricula, strengthened teacher certification requirements, and a substantial increase in funding. The second wave of reforms, which is ongoing, focuses on the roles of adults (e.g., teacher empowerment, school-based management, parental choice, voucher schemes, charter schools, private-sector contract management of public schools). It has shifted the locus of attention if not from state capitals at least to local schools and from mandated and short-term activities to collaborative, cooperative, and protracted efforts. This chapter calls for a third wave of school reform, one that ushers in a restructured and inclusive education system that serves well all students in a unitary fashion.

The reforms of the first two waves, although not inconsiderable, have left the basic educational system intact. The third wave requires a paradigmatic shift in education, one that rejects a dual and separate general and special education system in favor of a single unitary system that educates *all* students successfully *and* together. Such a system will be characterized by the following:

- A strength-based design
- Active learning
- Moving from student to life-long learner
- Striving for success from the start

- Parents and community as partners
- New roles for school adults
- Viewing differences as strengths

STRENGTH-BASED DESIGN

Students do their best when they feel respected. Respect for students is expressed at the school level when staff know students as individuals and value their involvement. The anonymity of large schools is one characteristic that must be changed. Walberg and Walberg (1994) have documented the negative consequences in terms of achievement of large schools and large school districts.

> During the past half century, three pronounced trends in state policy have occurred: Districts and schools have dramatically risen in enrollments; states have steadily raised their share of revenues for public schools; and local shares have declined. Yet organizational theory and evidence suggest that these trends should make public education less efficient. This hypothesis is tested in 38 states that voluntarily cooperated in administering the National Assessment of Educational Progress mathematics examination to random within-state samples of eighth-grade students. Both correlations and regressions (controlling for per-student expenditures and student demographics) show that achievement is inversely related to both size indices and state funding share. (p. 26)

Beyond issues of size, the school day must be organized so that each child is known as an individual to one or more adults in the school. A 1995 report on restructuring of high schools, titled *Breaking Ranks*, from the National Association of Secondary School Principals, has recommended a number of steps in this direction. The report's author, Gene Maeroff, has stated:

> As a first step toward banishing anonymity and apathy, the high school must reduce scale and personalize the experiences of students. [Students] must gain a sense of identification and connectedness. Teachers should spend time with fewer students so that they can build relationships with them. . . . [E]ach student in the restructured high school [should] have a "personal adult advocate," a person in the school who meets individually with the youngster on a regular basis and serves as a liaison between the student and others in and out of the school. (Maeroff, 1996, p. 60)

As a further step toward individualization, *Breaking Ranks* calls for a "personal learning plan" for each student. Noting that this is similar to the individualized education program (IEP) required for students identified as having disabilities, Maeroff (1996) stated, "No longer will a young person have to wear a label to get personal attention" (p. 60).

Challenging the conventional wisdom that schools did not make a difference for low-income and minority students, Ron Edmonds, in the early 1980s, identified schools in which such students were successful. These schools were characterized by the following five factors, which came to be labeled as the "correlates of school effectiveness" and can also be considered key features of a strength-based model for inclusion:

- Teacher behaviors that convey the expectation that all students are expected to obtain at least minimum mastery
- The principal's leadership and attention to the quality of instruction
- A pervasive and broadly understood instructional focus
- An orderly, safe climate conducive to teaching and learning
- The use of measures of pupil achievement as the basis for program evaluation (Edmonds, 1982)

New research on the nature of intelligence and learning has consequences for pedagogy and for a strength-based model. The work of Gardner (1983) on multiple intelligences is especially pertinent. Rather than the traditional one-dimensional formulation of intelligence, Gardner has identified seven intelligences: linguistic, musical, logical-mathematical, spacial, bodily kinesthetic, interpersonal, and intrapersonal. Goldman and Gardner (1989) have stated,

> Multiple intelligences theory, with its focus on the development and nurturing of each individual's different proclivities, dictates the need for a more diverse and individual-centered curriculum. . . . [W]hether the emphasis falls on a common curriculum, or on specialized options, there is every reason to tailor the mode of instruction as much as possible to the inclinations, working styles, and profiles of intelligence of each individual student. (p. 133)[1]

The nature of human temperament is, obviously, pertinent to student learning. Psychologists, for example, have identified four aspects of basic human temperament: novelty seeking, avoidance of harm, reward dependence, and persistence (Angler, 1996). As with Gardner's "multiple intelligences," in any individual there is a "jagged profile" across these dimensions. The tailoring to the "inclinations" of the individual student that Goldman and Gardner invoke in light of multiple intelligences theory applies as well to ideas concerning human temperament within a strength-based model.

---

[1]See also Chapter 25 by Goldman and Gardner.

ACTIVE LEARNING

The traditional concept of schooling, which has not changed significantly in spite of several reform movements, places the student in a passive role as the recipient of instruction. Basically, the student is the vessel into which the school pours knowledge. In a restructured school, the student is at the center as an active, engaged worker (Lipsky, 1992).[2]

The learning process becomes less one of memorizing answers and more one of discovery and higher-level thinking. It is, for example, the *doing* of science, the *seeing* of mathematics as a tool, the *understanding* of reading as a way for each learner to construct knowledge and to gain pleasure. Engaging students in their own learning then becomes the basis for new instructional strategies and curriculum efforts. Cooperative learning, peer tutoring, use of manipulatives, and community-based learning are a few examples of instructional strategies that engage all students and promote collaboration among all students in active roles. The use of performance as a demonstration of knowledge learned promotes active learning.

The concept of active learning undergirds, for example, the whole language approach to reading. Demonstrating the symbiotic interrelationship among curriculum reform, changes in the society, and the roles of students, Adams and Bruck (1995) have written,

> The whole language movement can be seen as but one reflection of a broader movement—a movement that extends across the curriculum, that grows from profound reconception of the goals of education, and that is fueled by concern over productivity and competitiveness in the information age. The purpose of education can no longer be to help students acquire any simple and listable set of facts and skills. It must instead be to help them acquire knowledge and understanding in the deepest and most useful senses of those words. What our students need most is to develop the thoughtfulness to discern when and what they do not understand, along with the confidence and capabilities to go out and learn it on their own. (p. 18)

MOVING FROM STUDENT TO ADULT

Students cannot learn all that they need to know while in school to become contributing adult members of society. In part, this is a result of both the growing body of knowledge and the shortening

---

[2]For an earlier formulation of the "consumer as producer" concept (i.e., the student—the "consumer" of educational services—is at the same time the "producer" of the learning), see Gartner and Riessman (1974).

half-life of knowledge. What students need are greater skills in the "ways" and "hows" of learning. Learning is not an activity of one place, the school building. Integrating independent learning activities outside of the classroom, as well as offering community service opportunities, provides a broader forum for learning. Community-referenced curricula, traditionally limited to students labeled as severely impaired, is a positive approach for all students. Learning how to learn (e.g., the "strategic learning approach" [Schumaker & Deshler, 1994–1995]), as well as teaching students to use the full range of resources available to gain access to information (e.g., computer technology), are further aspects of learning that go beyond the schoolhouse, ways that will prepare students to continue to learn as adults.

ACHIEVING SUCCESS FROM THE START

When a student has failed to learn something identified by the school as important, the system is likely to respond that the child and/or parent are at fault. Often, this is viewed from a sociological and psychological framework, if not in terms of the more pernicious genetic explanation. The division between general and special education is an example of placing blame on the child rather than demanding responsibility from the system. Recognizing student failure as a failure of the school to meet the student's needs is an essential first element of developing a restructured school. As industry has long recognized, it is considerably more expensive to fix something done wrong than to make sure you do it right the first time. A parable makes the point:

> Once upon a time, there was a town whose playground was at the edge of the cliff. Every so often a child would fall off the cliff. Finally, the town council decided that something should be done about the serious injuries to children. After much discussion, however, the council was deadlocked. Some council members wanted to put a fence at the top of the cliff, but others wanted to put an ambulance at the bottom. (Slavin, 1996, p. 4)

Recognizing that students fare better when they succeed the first time, Slavin (1996) has called for "*neverstreaming*: implementing prevention and early intervention programs powerful enough to ensure that virtually every child is successful in the first place" (p. 5). Slavin cited a number of programs that have this effect: Success for All (Slavin, Madden, Karweit, Dolan, & Wasik, 1992, 1996; see also Chapter 26); Reading Recovery (Lyons, 1989; Pinnell, Lyons, DeFord, Bryk, & Seltzer, 1994); Prevention of Learning Disabilities

(Silver & Hagin, 1990); early childhood interventions such as the Carolina Abecarian Project (Campbell & Ramey, 1994); and family support and integrated services such as the Comer Project (Comer, 1988) and Schools of the 21st Century (Zigler, Finn-Stevenson, & Linkins, 1992). Slavin (1996) has asserted,

> If we know how to ensure that virtually every child will become a skillful, strategic, and enthusiastic reader, then it is criminal to let children fall behind and only then provide assistance. Neverstreaming, not mainstreaming or special education, should be the goal for all children who are at risk. (p. 7)

PARENTS AND COMMUNITY AS PARTNERS

The community owns the schools; however, creating a school environment that encourages collaboration with parents and community members is a complex task. Often, parents and community members in a school district do not feel involved or welcomed by the school administration and staff. Increasingly, some school districts are attempting to change this by developing programs to bring the various stakeholders together.

A 1995 report of the American Association of School Administrators cited factors that keep parents from being involved: school practices that do not accommodate the growing diversity of families, time and child care constraints, parents' negative prior experiences with schools, and lack of support for cultural diversity (Decker, Gregg, & Decker, 1995). Part of showing respect for students means making it clear to students that their parents are held in esteem by the school. Developing student education in partnership with parents, reporting regularly to parents in a jargon-free manner, developing opportunities for family learning activities (e.g., "family science," "family math"), using the expertise of *all* parents, and creating opportunities for students to learn in the community are all worthy initiatives that have been inaugurated in some schools and deserve to be expanded.

Too often, schools view parents and other family members as "para-educators," who can reinforce the curriculum, rather than as independent adults with unique strengths. The school–family relationship is not one of junior and senior partners, nor even one of "equals." Parents' concerns are specific to their child(ren), their knowledge of the child(ren) is comprehensive, and their involvement is lifelong. School personnel, conversely, are concerned with all children, their knowledge of the children is school specific, and their involvement is time delimited. The goal must be to combine and blend these differing strengths, not to homogenize them.

NEW ROLES FOR SCHOOL ADULTS

In a restructured school, the roles of teachers and other school officials have shifted from those typical in isolated settings to those appropriate for a collaborative model. In the traditional model, teachers worked as isolated individuals. In a restructured school environment, students are seen as "workers" in the production of their own learning. As a consequence of this change, teachers assume the role of coaches and facilitators of students in their work. They work in more collaborative roles with colleagues and as managers of other adults in the classroom (e.g., paraprofessionals, school aides) and in the community. Gardner has proposed the role of "school–community broker" for this purpose (Goldman & Gardner, 1989, p. 134).

A further consequence of these reconceptualizations is a shift in the role of school and district administrator to that of a facilitator and coordinator who is closer to the point of service delivery. Two principles that are pertinent to education restructuring are that, first, decision making, including resource allocation, should be made at the level closest to the substantive work; and, second, those involved in the core work should be included in the decision-making process.

VIEWING DIFFERENCES AS STRENGTHS

Sacks (1995) blended Gardner's concepts concerning multiple intelligences with the unique characteristics of people with disabilities. He described the views of a biologist, Temple Grandin, who has autism:

> She thinks that there has been too much emphasis on the negative aspects of autism and insufficient attention, or respect, paid to the positive ones. She believes that, if some parts of the brain are faulty or defective, others are very highly developed—spectacularly so in those who have savant syndromes, but to some degree, in different ways, in all individuals with autism.
> [M]oved by her own perception of what she possesses so abundantly and lacks so conspicuously, Temple inclines to a modular view of the brain, the sense that it has a multiplicity of separate, autonomous powers or "intelligences"—much as the psychologist Howard Gardner proposes in his book *Frames of Mind*. He feels that while the visual and musical and logical intelligences, for instance, may be highly developed in autism, the "personal intelligences," as he calls them—the ability to perceive one's own and others' state of mind—lag grossly behind. (p. 290)

The balance of loss and enhancement among other groups of people with disabilities has been described by Sacks (1995):

It has been well established that in congenitally deaf people (especially if they are native signers) some of the auditory parts of the brain are reallocated for visual use. It has also been well established that in blind people who read braille the reading finger has an exceptionally large representation in the tactile parts of the cerebral cortex. . . . [I]t seems likely that such . . . differentiation of cerebral development would follow the early loss of a sense and the compensatory enhancement of other senses. (p. 140)

The concept of enhancement is of particular importance to education. According to A.R. Luria,

A handicapped child represents a qualitatively different, unique type of development. . . . If a blind or deaf child achieves the same level of development as a normal child, then the child with a defect achieves this *in another way, by another course, by other means* [emphasis in original]; and, for the pedagogue, it is particularly important to know the uniqueness of the course along which he must lead the child. This uniqueness transforms the minus of the handicap into the plus of compensation. (Luria, cited in Sacks, 1995, p. xvii)

CONGRUENCE OF INCLUSION AND SCHOOL RESTRUCTURING

In the mid-1990s, issues of school reform and inclusive education have been addressed in a number of noteworthy studies and reports. Segments of several of these reports are reproduced in this section, both as a way to emphasize key topics in the school reform debate and as a means of highlighting the distinctions between traditional and inclusive school systems.

A 1994 report prepared for the Broward County (Florida) School Board identified major classroom issues in restructuring and inclusion, shown in Table 18.1. Burello (1995) contrasted issues of the "current system" with "a better system," shown in Table 18.2.

The "Restructuring and Inclusion Project," conducted by the Institute on Disability at the University of New Hampshire, has helped oversee a project to merge school restructuring and inclusion (cited in Jorgensen & Fried, 1994). To facilitate this integration, the project's Education and Excellence Committee identified 1) principles of school restructuring, 2) principles of inclusive education, and 3) selected principles that reflect effective inclusive education for all students. These are reproduced here as follows:

1. Principles of School Restructuring
   A. Students must master a number of essential skills and be competent in certain areas of knowledge.

Table 18.1. How does inclusion "fit" with school reform?

Traditional model	Restructured model	Inclusive model
Each teacher operates in isolation from other teachers	Teams of teachers jointly plan for a group of students	Special education teacher is a part of the teaching team
Emphasis on students' working on their own to solve problems	Emphasis on cooperative learning and collaboration to solve problems	Emphasis on natural support systems; collaboration among teachers and students
Determining eligibility for special programs so students can be removed from the general classroom	Determining eligibility for special funding but not providing services within the general classroom	Determining eligibility for special funding but providing services within the general classroom
Focus on time and accumulation of credits	Focus on outcomes	Focus on outcomes
Focus on isolated development	Focus on application of skills in a real-world context	Focus on skill application in real-world context
All students on the same page on the same day	Students work at their own rates in their own styles	Students work on meaningful goals while engaged in activities with their peers
Adults taking required courses to update certification	Continuous learning/community of approach	ESE [exceptional and special education] and general teachers learning from each other on a continuous basis

  B. Teaching style and time allotted to achieve mastery will be
     individualized.
  C. The governing metaphor of the school should be "student as
     worker."
  D. Staff should be generalists first and specialists second.
  E. Graduation from high school should not be an expectation of
     students who merely spend time in school, but should be
     awarded based on achievement of rigorous performance-based
     learning outcomes.

 2. Principles of Inclusive Education
  A. Teachers should use methods and materials that are effective
     for heterogeneous groups of learners.
  B. Students with disabilities should be assigned to classrooms
     and schools using the same decision guidelines applied to typi-

Table 18.2. Issues contrasting the "current system" with a "better system"

Issue	Current system	A better system
Students	Divides students into "regular" and "special"	Acknowledges a continuum of competence
Diagnosis	Lots of time/effort to determine category/label	Identifies needs in relationship to curriculum and learning goals
Instruction	Presumes "special" strategies; emphasizes individualization for "special" students	Effective instruction for all students; individualization important for all
Services	Special services in separate places	Special support in regular places
Professional relationships	Establishes barriers	Promotes collaboration
Outcomes	Academic achievement is the only valued outcome	Lifestyle, job, home, friends, and choice

cal students. There should be no more students with disabilities assigned to a classroom or school than would naturally occur, given the laws of chance.
C. All students can learn.
D. Students with disabilities are valued members of society and their school communities.
E. All students benefit from learning together with students who are different from themselves—including diversity of race, culture, sex, talents, temperament, and experience.

3. Selected Principles that Reflect Effective Inclusive Education for All Students
A. Principles related to how people work and learn together:
1. All students are valued members of society and of their school communities. "All students" means "every single student."
2. All students benefit from learning together with others who represent a spectrum of diversity, including race, culture, gender, age, talents, temperament, and experience.
B. Principles related to how schools are organized and the roles people play:
1. Class sizes are small enough so that teachers can personalize instruction.
2. Schools help students think clearly, develop their intellectual and creative potential, and learn to use their minds well.

      3. Schools respect each student's gifts and talents by recognizing and honoring demonstrations of effort and achievement.
- C. Principles related to assessment, curriculum, teaching, performance, and achievement by students:
  1. All students can learn and are provided with the necessary supports to do so.
  2. Students work to master a common set of districtwide, performance-based learning objectives in essential skills and areas of knowledge that have been delineated by the faculty, with parent and community input, as related to students' success in life. These performance objectives are reflected in the ways that schools are organized, time and staff are utilized, and student mastery is assessed.
  3. Teachers understand the diversity in students' styles of learning and apply that understanding in the classroom. They personalize instruction and the conditions under which students work to achieve mastery so that students' unique talents and abilities are developed and appreciated.

CONCLUSION

The needed third wave of school reform integrates central features of school restructuring with inclusive education. Riding the crest of this wave are student outcomes, which serve as the primary impetus for and represent the promise of meaningful system reform. Throughout the reform effort, it is important to remember that goals of excellence and equity are not antagonistic. Rather, both are essential, and each is necessary for the achievement of the other.

REFERENCES

Adams, M.J., & Bruck, M. (1995). Resolving the "great debate." *American Educator, 19*(2), 10–20.

Angler, N. (1996, January 2). Variant gene tied to a love of new thrills. *New York Times*, A1, B11.

Breaking ranks: Changing an American institution. (1996). Reston, VA: National Association of Secondary School Principals.

Burello, L. (1995, July 18). *School changes which facilitate public education.* Paper presented at "Inclusive School Institute—Changing Paradigms: Educating Students with Disabilities in Regular Classrooms," Fairfield, NJ.

Campbell, F.A., & Ramey, C.T. (1994). Effects of early intervention on intellectual and academic achievement: A follow-up study of children from low-income families. *Child Development, 65,* 409–426.

Comer, J. (1988). Educating poor minority children. *Scientific American, 259,* 42–48.

Decker, L.E., Gregg, G.A., & Decker, V.A. (1995). *Getting parents involved in their children's education.* Arlington, VA: American Association of School Administrators.

Edmonds, R. (1982). Programs of school improvement: An overview. *Educational Leadership, 40*(3), 4–11.

Engel, D.M. (1993). Origin myths: Narratives of authority, resistance, disability, and law. *Law & Society Review, 27*(4), 785–826.

Gardner, H. (1983). *Frames of mind: The theory of multiple intelligences.* New York: Basic Books.

Gartner, A., & Lipsky, D.K. (1990). Students as instructional agents. In W. Stainback & S. Stainback (Eds.), *Support networks for inclusive schooling: Interdependent, integrated education* (pp. 81–94). Baltimore: Paul H. Brookes Publishing Co.

Gartner, A., & Riessman, F. (1974). *The service society and the consumer vanguard.* New York: Harper & Row.

Goldman, J., & Gardner, H. (1989). Multiple paths to educational effectiveness. In D.K. Lipsky & A. Gartner (Eds.), *Beyond separate education: Quality education for all* (pp. 121–139). Baltimore: Paul H. Brookes Publishing Co.

Jorgenson, C.M., & Fried, R.L. (1994, Spring). Merging school restructuring and inclusive education: An essential partnership to achieve equity and excellence. *Equity and Excellence, 2,* 10–16.

Lipsky, D.K. (1992). We need a third wave of educational reform. *Social Policy, 22*(3), 43–45.

Lyons, C.A. (1989). Reading Recovery: A preventative for mislabeling young "at-risk" learners. *Urban Education, 24,* 125–139.

Maeroff, G.I. (1996). Apathy and anonymity: Combatting the twin scourges of modern post-adolescence. *Education Week, 15*(24), 60, 46.

National Commission on Educational Excellence. (1983). *A nation at risk.* Washington, DC: U.S. Government Printing Office.

Pinnell, G.S., Lyons, C.A., DeFord, D.E., Bryk, A.S., & Seltzer, M. (1994). Comparing instructional models for the literacy education of high-risk first graders. *Reading Research Quarterly, 29,* 9–40.

Sacks, O. (1995). *An anthropologist on Mars.* New York: Alfred A. Knopf.

Schumaker, J.B., & Deshler, D.D. (1994–1995). Secondary classes can be inclusive, too. *Educational Leadership, 52*(4), 50–51.

Silver, A.A., & Hagin, R.A. (1990). *Disorder of learning in childhood.* New York: John Wiley & Sons.

Slavin, R.E. (1996). Neverstreaming: Preventing learning disabilities. *Educational Leadership, 53*(5), 4–7.

Slavin, R.E., Madden, N.A., Karweit, N.L., Dolan, L., & Wasik, B.A. (1992). *Success for All: A relentless approach to prevention and early intervention in elementary schools.* Arlington, VA: Educational Research Service.

Slavin, R.E., Madden, N.A., Karweit, N.L., Dolan, L., & Wasik, B.A. (1996). *Every child, every school: Success for All.* Newbury Park, CA: Corwin.

Walberg, H.J., & Walberg, H.J., III. (1994). Losing local control. *Educational Researcher, 23*(5), 19–26.

Zigler, E.F., Finn-Stevenson, M., & Linkins, K.W. (1992). Meeting the needs of children and families of the 21st century. *Yale Law and Policy Review, 10*(1), 69–81.

IV

THE REFORM OF EDUCATION AND THE REMAKING OF AMERICAN SOCIETY

The issue of [educational] integration . . . provides an opportunity for raising serious questions about the kind of society we desire and the nature and functions of schooling.
—Barton and Landsman (1993, p. 41)

As Barton and Landsman (1993) have underscored, the issues of inclusive education go to the very nature of society: Who is to be included and who is not? In the course of U.S. history, participation in the electorate and in the life of society has been limited by race, gender, religion, class, and cognitive capability. Participation in the public schools has followed the same pattern.

In both the electoral and the educational systems, formal exclusions from participation have been progressively removed. The first step was by legislatively and/or judicially removing the exclusion. The second step was by legally mandating the right to "inclusion." The third step was by developing policies and practices that guide inclusion and participation. For the most part, all adult U.S. citizens are eligible to vote, and all children can be enrolled in the public schools. Over time, the electoral and the educational systems have abolished exclusion as a matter of law and have affirmed the right of "inclusion." What neither system has settled is the nature, implications, and consequence of that participation, for both the individuals and the institutions. For example, in the 1990s, 130 years after the Civil War, the U.S. Supreme Court continues to wrestle in "redistricting" cases with ways to ensure fair and equal representation for descendants of former slaves. In the educational system, the treatment of students who are "different"—be it in race, ethnicity, language, national origin, or physical or mental condition—presents continuing issues of contention. The interrelationships between the educational system and the broader polity are the subject of this section's Chapter 19.

REFERENCE

Barton, L., & Landsman, M. (1993). The politics of integration: Observations on the Warnock Report. In R. Slee (Ed.), *Is there a desk with my name on it? The politics of integration* (pp. 41–49). London: Falmer Press.

19

EDUCATION AND
THE FUTURE SOCIETY

The system of public education is an instrument of the society, designed to socialize and prepare the young for their role(s) as adults. At the same time, it is both a reflection of society's priorities and values and a battleground of competing visions. The dual system of general and special education and the discourse about who is to be educated and how illustrate both this reflection and the shape of the battles in the public education system. This chapter examines the relationships between the educational system and the broader society and the role(s) of people with disabilities in both.

EDUCATION IN POSTINDUSTRIAL SOCIETY

When the work of a society is manual, rote, and routine, its school system values those who can best be prepared for such work. When the nature of the work changes, then those who can best be prepared for the new work are more valued. Indeed, the structure and shape of the school system become isomorphic with that work. Changes in society—in the nature of work and in the composition of the work force—are both a cause and a consequence of new designs for education and schooling. At the same time, the conceptualization of disability—as a deficit or a difference, for example—is affected by society's work and then becomes a factor in educating those it decides to label as "disabled."

During the second half of the 19th century in the United States the dominant activity of the nation's work force shifted from agriculture to manufacturing: "In 1900 more than a third of all workers were in farming; by midcentury only about 10 percent were so employed, and by the 1980s fewer than four in one hundred were" (Lavin & Hyllegard, 1996, p. 5). This shift had consequences for the shape and character of the emerging public education system.

> The drive to test, categorize and select children for differential treatment in educational institutions has a history which is inextricably linked with the provision of state funded education in Western democracies. Mass schooling often paralleled a need made apparent by industrial capitalism for a more docile and morally correct workforce. When education was made available to all children, schools became arenas of competition for life chances. (Meadmore, 1993, p. 27)

The treatment of students with disabilities followed a similar pathway. According to Skrtic (1991), "The segregated special education classroom emerged in conjunction with compulsory school attendance to preserve the legitimacy of the prevailing organizational paradigm by symbolizing compliance with the public demand for universal public education" (p. 170).

The decades following World War II saw a shift from manufacturing to service work. The United States in the 1990s is still in the throes of changing from an industrial to a postindustrial society. The largest portion of the work force is employed in the services and governmental sectors. Lavin and Hyllegard (1996) have described this major transformation:

> Shrinkage in the agricultural and blue-collar sectors of the labor force has been offset by explosive growth in the share of jobs in the white-collar sector: between 1900 and the 1980s, clerical and sales jobs more than tripled, while the share of the top tier of the white-collar category—professional, technical, and managerial workers—expanded from about 10 percent to almost 30 percent of the work force. (p. 5)

The effects of these changes are not uniform across society. Some of the work force are engaged in intellectually stimulating work, whereas others have been relegated to low-level service work, increasingly divorced from the mainstream of the work force.

Just as the regimen of the production line influenced the shape of public education in the industrial era, the nature of postindustrial society and its work have consequences for the educational system of the 21st century. Such work is collaborative, calling more for skills in solving problems than existing knowledge and requiring flexibility more than routine. Characterizing the new workplace is both growing diversity among the work force (e.g., the increases in women, in minority group members, in people with disabilities) and an increasing focus on cooperation and teamwork among the workers. In this new climate, educational equity would be viewed, according to Skrtic (1991), as

> a precondition for excellence in the post-industrial era, for collaboration means learning collaboratively with and from persons with varying interests, abilities, skills, and cultural perspectives, and taking responsibility for learning means taking responsibility for one's own learning and that of others. Ability grouping and tracking have no place in such a system. (p. 181)

For a large portion of the growing population, however, future work opportunities are not promising. Unfortunately, the educational system is not changing rapidly enough to address the problem. In particular, "special education is implicated in this problem because, as a form of tracking, it is uniquely placed within public education to serve the necessary sorting function" (Skrtic, 1996, p. 106).

Table 19.1 shows Keating's (1996) summary of the characteristics of education in the industrial and information ages. Focusing on the changes needed in education to prepare for the work of a postindustrial society is not sufficient. Schooling in a democracy must be more than mere preparation for a fixed or forecasted future. As Goodman (1995) has argued, schooling must play a role in shaping that future, a future that is only in part economic.

HOW SOCIETY TREATS DIFFERENCE

A critical challenge in the future will be how society conceptualizes and, in turn, treats difference. Will society continue to view differ-

Table 19.1. Characteristics of education in the industrial and information ages

Characteristics	Industrial age	Information age
Pedagogy	Knowledge transmission	Knowledge building
Prime mode of learning	Individual	Collaborative
Educational goals	Conceptual grasp for the few; basic skills for the many	Conceptual grasp and intentional knowledge building for all
Nature of diversity	Inherent, categorical	Transactional, historical
Dealing with diversity	Selection of elites, basics for broad population	Developmental model of lifelong learning for broad population
Anticipated workplaces	Factory, vertical bureaucracies	Collaborative learning organizations

Adapted from Keating (1996).

ence as a deficit or abnormality, or will society see difference as an aspect of the human condition? The former set of attitudes and consequent behaviors provide the basis for separate and segregated systems—whether in schools, for people with disabilities, or in society, for people of differing language, beliefs, or backgrounds.

Negative conceptualizations of difference are endemic in school practice. This is seen most clearly in procedures for "certifying" students as "disabled" and in need of special education services. Such procedures were established by federal mandates to challenge the exclusion of "different" people from schools and other public programs. A litany of "due process" requirements provide a facade of fairness; however, they perpetuate the stigma of difference. "Impartiality is the guise that partiality takes to seal bias against exposure" (Minow, 1990, p. 376).

Disability rights theoreticians challenge the traditional paradigm of disability, rejecting the individual deficit model. Hahn (1994) has pointed out that, as with other disadvantaged groups (e.g., women, African Americans, Latinos, Native Americans, Asian Americans, gays and lesbians, older adults), people with disabilities are striving to translate previously devalued personal characteristics into a positive sense of self-identity. Hahn wrote, "A consciousness that disability simply signifies another human difference instead of functional restrictions might form the basis [for] an increased appreciation of diversity and heterogeneity in everyday life" (p. 18). This view understands and thus treats difference as "normal," as a characteristic of the human condition.

The "dilemma of difference," as Minow (1990) called it, will recur for members of disadvantaged groups when

> programs . . . presume the status quo to be natural, good, or immutable, where the status quo assigns the label of difference and its burdens to some and refuses to make room for a range of human conditions. Reframing social experience to transcend the difference dilemma means challenging the presumption that either one is the same or one is different, either one is normal or one is not. (p. 95)

In Canada, Section 15 of the Charter of Rights and Freedoms, adopted in 1982, attempts to provide an effective balance between equality and attention to "difference." Although it is difficult to judge the charter's success, it does provide essential recognition that in the face of difference in condition, historic or contemporary, equality is not achieved by identical treatment. It states,

1. Every individual is equal before and under the law and has the right to the equal protection and equal benefit of the law without discrimination and, in particular, without discrimination based

on race, national or ethnic origin, colour, religion, sex, age, or mental or physical disability.

2. Subsection (1) does not preclude any law, program, or activity that has as its object the amelioration of conditions of disadvantaged individuals or groups including those that are disadvantaged because of race, national or ethnic origin, colour, religion, sex, age, or mental or physical disability.

Addressing the balance of equity in the contest of disability, Funk (1987), a founder of the Disability Rights Education and Defense Fund (DREDF), wrote,

The concepts of equal opportunity and integration must be based on the reality of the differing needs and potential of people who are disabled. Thus equal opportunity must be defined as providing each individual with the chance to achieve, to develop [his or her] abilities and potential to the fullest. (p. 24)

This formulation presents an advancement over the current, overriding equation of "difference" with deviance. Used as a basis for public policy, it would counter the argument that we spend "too much" on services for certain population groups, whether in the schools or in social welfare programs. This formulation, however, retains the belief that the "difference" resides in the individual, a belief with pernicious consequences.

The assumptions about difference [are] deeply entrenched in our social institutions, and in the legal rules that govern them. One assumption treats difference as inherent in the "different" person rather than a function of comparisons; another assumption establishes as the norm for comparison the experience of only some people, such as English-speaking students, or white men, or able-bodied persons; a third assumption imagines an "objective" observer who can see without a perspective, uninfluenced by situation or experience. Differences perceived by judges, employers, and school administrators seem natural and inevitable. (Minow, 1990, p. 375)

A "social relations" approach both transcends the individualistic formulation and provides an alternative to traditional legal treatments of difference. This approach moves the focus from the individual to the social construction of differences. This new approach

has its roots in a dramatic shift of attention during the twentieth century—across the sciences, social sciences, and humanities—toward relationships rather than to the discrete items under observation. For many, this shift has brought a new focus on relationships between people within which individuals develop a sense of autonomy and identity. For others, the shift turns to the relationship between the knower and the known. . . . Another topic of attention is the relationship between the parts and the wholes, and still another is the mutual dependence of theory and context. From work in relativity theory and the indeterminacy principle in physics to deconstructive strategies in literary interpretation, these relational concerns are occupying scholars in challenges to the assumptions of their fields. (Minow, 1990, pp. 379–380)

SCHOOL REFORM THAT HONORS DIFFERENCE

Incorporating a respect for differences into educational restructuring does not mean "fixing" special education or increasing "mainstreaming" or partial integration opportunities for students in self-contained special education programs. Rather, as emphasized throughout this volume, it requires a paradigmatic shift and is a challenge to the very nature of the dual system. To have positive outcomes for all students, education must become inclusive and unitary. Such a belief is reflected in an education system that

> become[s] inclusive of all of the needs, interests and experiences of the diverse range of students which it is supposed to be serving. Such an education, in its inclusivity, would be a richer, more diverse and more stimulating education, and a more appropriate preparation for post-school life in an egalitarian community not only for those students who are disadvantaged by the current arrangements, but indeed for all students. (Ramsay, 1993, pp. viii–ix)

Drawing upon Maslow's hierarchy of needs, the argument for inclusive education can be seen in the context of the human need for belonging. As Kunc (1992) has stated,

> The fundamental principle of inclusive education is the valuing of diversity within the human community. Every person has a contribution to offer to the world. Yet, in our society we have drawn narrow parameters around what is valued and how one makes a contribution.
>
> [W]hen inclusive education is fully embraced, we abandon the idea that children have to become "normal" in order to contribute to the world. Instead, we search for and nourish the gifts that are inherent in all people. We begin to look beyond typical ways of becoming valued members of the community, and in doing so, begin to realize the achievable goal of providing all children with an authentic sense of belonging.
>
> As a collective commitment to educate *all* [emphasis in original] children takes hold and "typical" students realize that "those kids" do belong in their schools and classes, typical students will benefit by learning that their own membership in the class and the society is something that has to do with human rights rather than academic or physical ability. In this way, it is conceivable that the students of inclusive schools will be liberated from the tyranny of earning the right to belong. It is ironic that the students who were believed to have the least worth and value may be the only ones who can guide us off the path of social destruction. (p. 38)

A restructured educational system thus prepares us for a new society while modeling the characteristics of that future.

This inclusive perspective has applications both for school change and for society at large. The work of the President's Committee on Mental Retardation embodies such a comprehensive approach. As expressed in the subtitle of its 1994 report, "The National Reform Agenda and People with Mental Retardation: Putting People First," the committee views people with disabilities as valued members of society. The committee's report emphasizes the importance of including people with mental retardation not only in education but in all activities: employment, housing and community living, social services, health care, and welfare reform. One can envision societal changes that benefit all members of the community. For example,

- Employment that emphasizes teamwork and necessary supports for workers to increase their work productivity and job satisfaction
- Housing arrangements that are integrated across lines of race, economic condition, age, and health status
- Social services that are general rather than parochial
- Health care that is comprehensive and affordable and that focuses on wellness
- Welfare reform that balances individual with social responsibility, that builds structures that encourage growth and future development, and that recognizes the reciprocal relationships between employment and family

The shift of focus from the individual to the social context can be seen in reviewing the options considered in providing services for Amy Rowley (*Board of Education v. Rowley*, 1982), a student who is deaf. The school system "assumed that the problem was Amy's: because she was different from other students, the solution must focus on her" (Minow, 1990, p. 82). Implicit here was a conceptualization of teaching and learning that posited a one-to-one relationship between teacher and student: The teacher teaches and the student learns. Instead, however, one can conceptualize the class as a learning community and Amy as a collaborative "worker" with her classmates. This shifts the focus from Amy, and the problem—and the remedy—thus involves *all* of the students.

> After all, if Amy cannot communicate with her classmates, they cannot communicate with her, and all lose the benefit of exchange. Moreover, conducting the class in both spoken and sign language would engage all the students in the difficult and instructive experience of

> communicating across traditional lines of difference. All the students could learn to struggle with problems of translation and learn to empathize by experiencing first hand discomfort with an unfamiliar mode of expression. It would be educational for all of them to discover that all languages are arrangements of signs and to use group action to improve the situation of an individual. (Minow, 1990, p. 84)

Recognizing the social nature of the problem and "involving classmates in the solution affords a different stance toward the dilemma of difference: it no longer makes the trait of hearing impairment signify stigma or isolation but responds to that trait as an issue for the entire community" (Minow, 1990, p. 84). The consequence not only involves the person with disabilities but also has consequences for the learning and perspectives of students without disabilities.

> When students in the majority avoid the experience of not being understood, or not understanding what others say, they fail to learn about the limits of their own knowledge. They miss a chance to discover the importance of learning another language. By their very comfort in the situation, they neglect the perspective of any student they consider different from themselves. (p. 29)

Benefits to students without disabilities in inclusive classes have been identified by Staub and Peck (1994). These include reduced fear of human differences accompanied by increased comfort and awareness, growth in social cognition, improvements in self-concept, development of personal principles, and warm and caring friendships.

The process of program implementation for inclusion can counter the negative view of difference. "How schools see integration is critical: Is integration understood as an outsider coming in, or as creating a school culture so that it accepts all comers?" (Biklen, cited in Slee, 1993, p. 3). Biklen's use of the word *integration,* with its connotation of race relations and its broader sense of social relationships, is significant. It reminds us that real integration can be achieved not by "allowing" people from "minority" groups into the existing society but by transforming the society. This formulation moves the discussion from one of recognizing differences to that of distributing power. "Forging ways out of the difference dilemma requires remaking institutions so that they do not establish one norm that places the burden of difference on those who diverge from it" (Minow, 1990, p. 94). In this connection, Minow has furthermore asserted that

> integration . . . offers no solution unless the majority itself changes by sharing power, accepting members of the minority as equal participants and resisting the temptation to attribute as personal inadequacies the legacy of disadvantage experienced by the group. Neither separation nor

integration can eradicate the meaning of difference in a minority group that does not fit the world designed for the majority. (1990, p. 25)

Linking inclusion with the need to examine issues of "majority" versus "minority" provides the opportunity for a change in power and status relationships. Inclusive education goes beyond a "readiness" model, which requires that students with disabilities "prove" their readiness to be in an inclusive setting, and views the general education setting as the norm, both as a moral standard and as a pedagogical requirement. Inclusive education goes beyond programs of "mainstreaming," which posit two separate systems—general and special education—to embrace a restructured school system, one that is unitary and that can provide success for all children.

The issues do not confront the United States alone. *The Salamanca Statement and Framework for Action on Special Needs Education* (1994), adopted by representatives of 92 governments and 25 international organizations, addresses the topic of broader societal goals for all children. It states, in part, the following:

We believe and proclaim that:

- Every child has a fundamental right to education, and must be given the opportunity to achieve and maintain an acceptable level of learning.
- Every child has unique characteristics, interests, abilities, and learning needs.
- Educational systems should be designed and educational programmes implemented to take into account the wide diversity of these characteristics and needs.
- Those with special education needs must have access to regular schools which accommodate them within a child-centered pedagogy capable of meeting these needs. (pp. viii–ix)

The *Salamanca Statement* (1994) then turns from goals to educational practice:

Experience in many countries demonstrates that the integration of children and youth with special educational needs is best achieved within inclusive schools that serve all children within a community. It is within this context that those with special educational needs can achieve the fullest educational progress and social integration. (p. 11)

The *Statement* asserts that, as the result of a restructured education systems,

Regular schools with this inclusive orientation are the most effective means of combating discriminatory attitudes, creating welcoming communities, building an inclusive society and achieving education for all; moreover they provide an effective education to the majority of children and improve the efficiency and ultimately the cost-effectiveness of the entire educational system. (p. ix)

"Inclusive schooling," contends the *Statement,* "provides the most effective means for building solidarity between children with special needs and their peers" (p. 12). Significantly, the *Statement* (1994) places educational policy in a broader framework:

> The trend in social policy during the past two decades has been to promote integration and participation and to combat exclusion. Inclusion and participation are essential to human dignity and to the enjoyment and exercise of human rights. Within the field of education, this is reflected in the development of strategies that seek to bring about a genuine equalization of opportunity. (p. 11)

The *Salamanca Statement* (1994) offers a critically needed vision, it establishes a standard, and it provides a yardstick for measuring progress. Of particular significance is the *Statement's* explicit support of inclusive education and its linking of that initiative to matters of broader societal benefit.

CONCLUSION

The enduring question in U.S. history has been the balance between the *pluribus* and the *unum,* the many and the one. As Martin Luther King, Jr., said in a sermon at Ebenezer Baptist Church in 1967, we are each a part of a "network of inescapable mutuality," stitched together "into a single garment of destiny" (cited in Cloud, 1995, p. 23). Describing what he called "secular humanism," Gates (1994) has stated that "[secular humanism] asks what we have in common with others, while acknowledging the diversity among ourselves" (p. A23). Ralph Ellison's formulation regarding black identity offers insights in regard to this volume's concerns. According to Bernstein (1995), Ellison "insist[ed] throughout his life that black identity was inseparable from American identity, and that indeed there is literally nothing in the American identity that does not partake of its quotient of blackness."

The debate about inclusive education is both a battleground for and a reflection of the "dilemma of difference." Inclusive education in restructured schools not only provides benefits for all students but also serves as an exemplar for an inclusive society, one that is diverse and democratic. As alienation threatens community, inclusive education is the seedbed in which we learn to nurture and live in a democratic society.

REFERENCES

Bernstein, R. (1995, December 20). Black identity, racism and a lifetime of reflection. *New York Times*, A20.

Board of Education v. Rowley, 102 S. Ct. 3034 (1982).

Cloud S., Jr. (1995, January 16). New national mood divides Americans. *Daily News*, 23.

Funk, R. (1987). Disability rights: From caste to class in the context of civil rights. In A. Gartner & T. Joe (Eds.), *Images of the disabled: Disabling images* (pp. 7–30). New York: Praeger.

Gates, H.J., Jr. (1994, March 27). A liberalism of heart and spine. *New York Times*, A23.

Goodman, J. (1995). Change without difference: School restructuring in historical perspective. *Harvard Educational Review, 65*(1), 1–29.

Hahn, H. (1994, April 28–May 1). *New trends in disability studies: Implications for educational policy.* Paper presented at the National Center on Educational Restructuring and Inclusion invitational conference on inclusive education, Racine, WI.

Keating, D.P. (1996). The transformation of schooling: Dealing with developmental diversity. In J. Lupart, A. McKeough, & C. Yewchuck (Eds.), *Schools in transition: Rethinking regular and special education* (pp. 119–141). Toronto, Ontario: Thomas Nelson Canada.

Kunc, N. (1992). The need to belong: Rediscovering Maslow's hierarchy of needs. In R.A. Villa, J.S. Thousand, W. Stainback, & S. Stainback (Eds.), *Restructuring for caring and effective education: An administrative guide to creating heterogeneous schools* (pp. 25–39). Baltimore: Paul H. Brookes Publishing Co.

Lavin, D.E., & Hyllegard, D. (1996). *Changing the odds: Open admissions and the life chances of the disadvantaged.* New Haven, CT: Yale University Press.

Meadmore, D. (1993). Divide and rule. In R. Slee (Ed.), *Is there a desk with my name on it? The politics of integration* (pp. 27–38). London: Falmer Press.

Minow, M. (1990). *Making all the difference: Inclusion, exclusion, and American law.* Ithaca, NY: Cornell University Press.

President's Committee on Mental Retardation. (1994). *The national reform agenda and people with mental retardation: Putting people first.* Washington, DC: Author.

Ramsey, E. (1993). Foreword. In R. Slee (Ed.), *Is there a desk with my name on it? The politics of integration* (pp. viii–ix). London: Falmer Press.

The Salamanca statement and framework for action on special needs education. World conference on special needs education: Access and equality. (1994). New York: UNESCO.

Skrtic, T.M. (1991). The special education paradox: Equity as the way to excellence. *Harvard Educational Review, 61*(2), 148–207.

Skrtic, T.M. (1996). School organization, inclusive education, and democracy. In J. Lupart, A. McKeough, & C. Yewchuck (Eds.), *Schools in transition: Rethinking regular and special education* (pp. 81–118). Toronto, Ontario: Thomas Nelson Canada.

Slee, R. (Ed.). (1993). *Is there a desk with my name on it? The politics of integration.* London: Falmer Press.

Staub, D., & Peck, C.A. (1994). What are the outcomes for nondisabled students? *Educational Leadership, 52*(4), 36–40.

V

AMPLIFICATION OF
INCLUSION ISSUES

What is most important—and what is conspicuously absent from
[current educational reform] literature—is the recognition that
school restructuring efforts [must] be built upon an open dis-
course regarding the type of culture we wish to build and the
relationship between schooling and this future society.
                                        —Goodman (1995, p. 7)

In this section, a number of authors amplify material and issues
addressed in previous chapters. In Chapter 20, Thomas K. Gilhool
describes the findings of the landmark 1971 *PARC* (*Pennsylvania*
Association for Retarded Children v. Commonwealth of Pennsylva-
nia) case and the conditions facing parents of children with disabilities prior to passage of the Education for All Handicapped Children Act of 1975 (PL 94-142). In Chapter 21, Thomas B. Parrish
presents details concerning special education finance and inclusive
education. In Chapter 22, Diane Lipton analyzes the four circuit
court "full inclusion" cases that occurred between 1989 and 1994.
In Chapter 23, Harlan Hahn examines inclusive education from a
disability rights perspective. In Chapter 24, Harvey Pressman and
Sarah Blackstone provide a rich array of material demonstrating

the use of technology in implementing inclusive education. In Chapter 25, Jenifer Goldman and Howard Gardner explore the meaning of Gardner's multiple intelligences concept for the education of students with disabilities in inclusive settings. Finally, Chapters 26 and 27, by Robert E. Slavin and Henry M. Levin, respectively, provide case studies of major educational restructuring efforts that serve all children together, including those with disabilities.

20

THE EVENTS, FORCES, AND ISSUES THAT TRIGGERED ENACTMENT OF THE EDUCATION FOR ALL HANDICAPPED CHILDREN ACT OF 1975

THOMAS K. GILHOOL

MAY 9, 1995

Chairman Frist, Chairman Cunningham, Members of the Senate Subcommittee on Disability Policy and the House Subcommittee on Early Childhood, Youth and Families. I am honored and delighted to be here this morning at the opening of your hearings on the re-authorization of the landmark legislation originally enacted as the Education for All Handicapped Children Act of 1975. I thank you for your thoughtfulness in seeking a historical overview of the roots and sources of that Act.

The subject matter of the 1975 Act and its faithful successor Acts— the effective education of *all* handicapped—reaches to nearly every family in the United States, for there is hardly an extended family in the country which has not been touched by presence in the family of a

This chapter presents the testimony of Thomas K. Gilhool, counsel for Plaintiffs in *Pennsylvania Association for Retarded Children (PARC) v. Commonwealth of Pennsylvania* (1971) before the Joint Subcommittee Hearings on the Events, Forces, and Issues that Triggered Enactment of the Education for All Handicapped Children Act of 1975.

child who has a significant disability. Reauthorization of the Act will require you again to recognize the national interest in extending a decent equality to these children and to protect persons vulnerable to recurrent historic prejudices, as Madison in Federalist No. 51 wrote that the Congress of this large republic was designed to do.

I had the privilege during 1969 to 1972 to represent the Pennsylvania Association for Retarded Children in *Pennsylvania Association for Retarded Children v. Commonwealth of Pennsylvania*, the first "right to education" case. With my colleagues at the Public Interest Law Center of Philadelphia, I have in most of the years since—except for a leave of absence during 1987–1989 to serve as secretary of education of the Commonwealth of Pennsylvania and to teach 8th grade during the 89–90 school year at Roberts Vaux Middle School in inner-city Philadelphia—continued to represent the Pennsylvania Association, renamed in the mid-70s the Pennsylvania Association for Retarded *Citizens*, and at one time or another most of its counterpart associations in the several states and the National Association, as well as, as they thrived following the *PARC* case and the Congress's mid-1970s enactments, many of the organizations of adult disabled people themselves in a great range of undertakings in which they sought full and equal citizenship.

I am here to tell you briefly about

1. What the states were doing and not doing in the immediate years before, which led to the *PARC* litigation and to the 1975 Act
2. What made my clients go to court and especially the legacy of stereotype and exclusion which they, the *PARC* Court and the Congress acted to overcome
3. The crucial substantive requirements of the *PARC* case and the Act and their important effects
4. Still more briefly, a word or two of the resonance of all of this now[1]

WHAT THE STATES WERE DOING

In the decades up to 1975, in every state in the Union, all parents of severely disabled children and most parents of "moderately" or "mildly" disabled children could expect to, and did, experience one or more of the following from schools charged with universal education:

---

[1]L. Lippman & I. Ignacy Goldberg, *Right to Education: Anatomy of the Pennsylvania Case* (New York: Teachers College Press, 1993), more fully tell the tale of the run-up to the case; *Robert L. Burgdorf*, in *The Legal Rights of Handicapped Persons: Cases, Materials, and Text* (Baltimore: Paul H. Brookes Publishing Co., 1980, pp. 75, 90–315) tells more fully of its aftermath.

- A phone call from their school, at any time, saying "your retarded child is *uneducable and untrainable.* Come pick him up and take him out of school."
- "Your retarded child is *disrupting* the class. Come take him out of school."
- "Your child can no longer profit from education. Take him away."
- Or, from the beginning, a school letter saying: "Your five- (or six-, or seven-) year-old does not have a mental age of five. He may not attend our school."

Such schools as took or kept, for any time, retarded children often put them in classes in the basement, frequently next to the boiler room, sometimes in the boiler room.

This behavior of schools and this experience of children, their parents and families arose from the laws of Pennsylvania which were at issue in the [PARC] case and which, like the laws of *all* of the states, provided and had for a long time provided for

- "Temporary or permanent exclusion from the public schools of children who are found to be uneducable and untrainable in the public schools. . . . When a child is thus certified the public schools shall be relieved of the delegation of providing education or training for such child. The Department of Public Welfare shall thereupon arrange for the care, training and supervision of such child in a manner not inconsistent with the laws governing mentally defective individuals."[2]

---

[2]The last two sentences of this § 13–1375 of the Pennsylvania School Code repeated an ancient injunction:

> For the welfare of his Ideal Commonwealth, Plato suggested a law which should provide "That the wives of our guardians are to be common, and their children are to be common, and no parent is to know his own child, nor any child his parent. . . . That the proper officers will take the offspring of the good parents to the pen or fold, and there they will deposit them with certain nurses [for education]; but the offspring of the inferior, or of the better when they chance to be deformed, will be put away in some mysterious, unknown place, as they should be."

But as to that, Justice McReynolds in *Meyer v. Nebraska,* 262 U.S. 390, 402 (1923), had written for the United States Supreme Court:

> Although such measures have been deliberately approved by men of great genius, their ideas touching the relation between individual and State were wholly different form those upon which our institutions rest; and it hardly will be affirmed that any legislature could impose such restrictions upon the people of a State without doing violence to both letter and spirit of the Constitution.

- "A board of school directors may refuse to accept or retain beginners who have not attained a mental age of five years."
- "Exceptions for compulsory attendance: Any child who . . . has been found to be unable to profit from further school attendance and who has been reported to the board of school directors and excused."

These were the state statutes that the Pennsylvania Association and thirteen retarded children by their families, and for the class of all such Pennsylvania children, sued to enjoin as unconstitutional under the Fourteenth Amendment. They sought, in January 1971, instead to open Pennsylvania's schools and to require under the Equal Protection Clause that the public schools provide each of their children "a free public program of education and training appropriate to his capacities." Thirteen school districts were defendants representing the defendant class of all 501 Pennsylvania school districts, as was the commonwealth, its secretary of education, and a deputy secretary of public welfare.

The widespread and systematic school exclusion was the immediate experience to which the *PARC* case was directed. But the way in which parents came to bring the case, and the reasons why, are deeper still and illumine why that experience was what it was and why the court's decision in the *PARC* case had the resonance it has had.

THE ORIGINS OF THE FAMILIES' EXPERIENCE
AND THE ROOTS OF PARC'S DECISION TO SUE

In 1968, the Pennsylvania Association for Retarded Children, which like its counterparts across the country had been founded just after World War II by young parents, many of whom were veterans, had completed the last of its many investigations of the Pennhurst State School and Hospital, Pennsylvania's flagship public retardation institution.

In that same year, Earl Butterfield of the University of Kansas, commissioned by John Kennedy's then-new President's Committee on Mental Retardation, completed his data-based study (expenditures, demographics, staffing, etc.) of public retardation institutions throughout the United States. Published in *P.C.M.R., Changing Patterns in Residential Services for the Mentally Retarded* (1969) ranked Illinois, Connecticut, Michigan, and Pennsylvania *highest* in effort among the states to provide decent institutional care. Butterfield concluded: If it were shown that these states—

Pennsylvania, Michigan, Connecticut, Illinois—provide inadequate care in their institutions, then there truly would be reason to seek completely different treatment alternatives for this nation's mentally retarded people.

The Pennsylvania Association's 1968 investigation of the Pennhurst institution showed its conditions and "care" there to be grotesque and life there for retarded people to be nasty, brutish, and short.[3]

That investigative report launched in the Association a 12-month-long, plenary, and agonizing reconsideration of its objectives. From those deliberations the Association concluded that it would work to close large public residential institutions for the retarded, to end them, and to seek instead for their children whatever arrangements and services which might be necessary to undergird a decent life and citizenship in the community.

Borrowing from the civil rights movement of African Americans, the Pennsylvania Association resolved, among other efforts, to use the courts to secure law-based change. They considered several approaches and chose to lay an Equal Protection claim for access to the schools and an integrated, effective education therein. Their claim built upon *Brown v. Board of Education,* where, in 1954, the United States Supreme Court had unanimously declared: "Education . . . where the state has undertaken to provide it [to any], is a right which must be made available to all on equal terms."

Indeed, John W. Davis had predicted in the opening sentence of his argument to the Court for the defendant State of South Carolina that if the black children should succeed in *Brown,* the benefits for the schools could no longer be denied on the ground of gender or "on the ground of mental capacity."

For the Pennsylvania Association, to open the schools *would be* to end these grotesque institutions and to advance a decent and productive citizenship for their retarded children: Butterfield had reported 79% of the more than 200,000 retarded people in the institutions in 1968 had been sent there when they were school-age children. In this, the Pennsylvania Association has been proved correct. In 1970 alone, more than 15,000 children of school age had been sent to

---

[3]Within a decade a federal district court in Pennsylvania had so found as to Pennhurst itself, *Halderman v. Pennhurst,* 446 F. Supp. 1295 (E.D. Pa. 1977), etc. Within 10 months thereafter, a federal district court had so found as to Michigan's newest institution, *Michigan Association for Retarded Citizens v. Smith,* Civ. Action. No. 78-70384 (E.D. Mich. 1978). In Connecticut, the same as to its largest institution, *Connecticut A.R.C. v. Mansfield,* (Civ. Action No. 78-653 D. Conn. 1980).

institutions; by 1982, four years after the effective date of PL 94-142, fewer than 1,200 were. Since then, the number approaches—and by the turn into the new century should achieve—zero.

How ever had it come to be that disabled children were sent off to such places? These awful institutions had been created, and the exclusionary practices of the public schools which accompanied them had been established, by force of state law in every state in the first two decades of this century.

These were extraordinary changes from preceding patterns of American life, and they affected people with retardation in similar terms in every state. What brought them?

> Previously in the 19th century men like [Samuel Gridley] Howe believed that "after a few years of instruction the idiot would return to his home or parish." This was why Howe did not want his school to become custodial.
>
> The times, however had changed. As [Walter] Fernald [in 1903] stated: "The good Doctor [Howe] wrote before the tide of immigration had set so strongly to our shores. . . . What is to be done with the feeble-minded progeny of the foreign hordes that have settled and are settling among us?[4]

The new immigration, the largest in our history until recent years, was from Southern and Eastern Europe. The United States Public Health Service commissioned H.H. Goddard, author of the scurrilous but best-selling *Kallikak Family* (1912), to administer the new Binet IQ test to those arriving in steerage at Ellis Island. "Giving the immigrant the benefit of every doubt," they found that 79% of the Italians were feeble-minded, 80% of the Hungarians, 83% of the Jews, and 87% of the Russians.[5]

These decades were "a time when xenophobia had become almost a national disease," "when negroes and immigrants were being lumped together as inassimilable aliens."[6] From this hysteria, Jim Crow, state-imposed segregation by race, was established by law in the southern states[7] and public institutions for the "life-long segregation" of "the feeble-minded, idiotic, epileptic and etc." and the concomitant exclusion of "defective" children were everywhere established.

---

[4]P. Tyor, *Segregation or Surgery: The Mentally Retarded in America* (1972).

[5]*N.Y. Times*, "Alien Defectives," January 13, 1913, p. 10; H.H. Goddard, "Mental Testing and the Immigrants," *J. Delinquency* 2 (1917): 249, 252.

[6]K.M. Stampp, "The Tragic Legend of Reconstruction," Introduction to *Era of Reconstruction* (1965), 19–20.

[7]C.V. Woodward, *The Strange Career of Jim Crow*, rev. ed. (1974).

The Pennsylvania statute creating the Pennhurst institution was express: "Be it enacted, etc., that the Eastern Pennsylvania State Institution for the Feeble-Minded and Epileptic shall be devoted to the segregation of epileptic, idiotic, imbecile or feeble-minded persons." The pamphlet that drove it, *The Menace of the Feeble-minded in Pennsylvania* (1913), expressly sought: "A Comprehensive plan for the lifelong segregation of these unfortunates . . . on state lands of no great value, far from dangerous contact with communities or transportation."

The pamphlets and the enactments everywhere were of the same cut: *The Menace of the Feebleminded in Connecticut* (1915); *The Burden of Feeble-Mindedness* (Massachusetts, 1912); *The Feeble-Minded, Or, The Hub to Our Wheel of Vice* (Ohio, 1913); cf. *The Negro: A Menace to American Civilization* (South Carolina, 1907).

The view of retarded and otherwise disabled persons as dangerous was actively inculcated.[8] It was explicitly recognized that affirmative steps would be necessary to segregate those "whose parents are averse to such actions" (California State Board of Charities and Corrections, *Biennial Report* 30 [1916]), including "detaining [them] against the desire of the parent (*Biennial Report of the Bd. of Comm'rs of State Institutions to the Governor and Legislature of the State of Nebraska* 9 [1915]).

The states by statute ordered physicians, teachers and social workers to report all persons "believed to be feeble-minded" (*South Dakota, Oregon*); made it "one of the special duties of any health officer and nurse to institute proceedings to secure the proper segregation of feeble-minded persons" (*Kentucky, Tennessee*); encouraged health, welfare and social workers to be "constantly on the lookout" (*Kansas*) and authorized a wide variety of public and private persons (*California*: "any peace officer"; *North Carolina*: "ministers, teachers, or physicians;" *Oklahoma*: "trustees of any township"; *Vermont*: "the selectman of any town"; Wyoming: "the county prosecutor") or sometimes simply "any reputable citizen" (*Delaware, Illinois, Louisiana, Tennessee, West Virginia*) to institutionalize a person if a parent or relative "either neglected or refused to do so"

---

[8]The secretary of the National Conference on Charities and Corrections and chair of its Committee on Colonies for the Segregation of Defectives, urging a campaign to persuade the public of the dangerousness of the idiotic and feeble-minded, explained that "the average citizen is afraid of the insane. A few among them are so dangerous that the whole class is feared. . . . The dangers of the idiotic are less obvious." National Conference on Charities and Corrections, *Proceedings* 30 (1903): 248–249.

(*Mississippi, Tennessee, West Virginia, Alabama, Oklahoma*). One state (*Washington*) simply made it a criminal offense, punishable by a $200 fine, for parents refusing to perform their "duty" to segregate in the state institution their "feebleminded" son or daughter.[9]

It is little wonder that upon the enactment of PL 94-142 in 1975, the late Nicholas Hobbs, then provost of Vanderbilt University, celebrated the Act's restoration of parental authority over the rearing of their children and its requirement that states and school boards give primacy of place to parents to direct the education of their children. He called the Act "the most conservative piece of social legislation adopted by the Congress in 50 years."

It is this history of state-imposed exclusion and segregation noted briefly by the *PARC* court (343 F. Supp. at 294–295), but fully before the Congress in three years of extensive hearings from 1972 to 1975, which the Congress acted to reverse in the Education for All Handicapped Children Act. In so acting the Congress invoked, as seldom it does, its powers under the Fourteenth Amendment to enforce the Equal Protection Clause.

THE CRUCIAL REQUIREMENTS
OF THE *PARC* DECREE AND PL 94-142

On several counts Nicholas Hobbs's estimation of PL 94-142 is surely correct:

1. *Parental Direction of Their Child's Education*   The Act restored parents and families to primacy of place in the design and direction of their child's public education. It does so by requiring that parents be included in the formulation of their child's individualized educational program (IEP) and in its periodic revision and by guaranteeing parental recourse to hearing and to the federal courts to enforce the education of their child. It is this assurance of parental direction of their child's education that Seymour Sarason, in *Why Current School Reform Will Almost Surely Fail* (1993), has identified as one of only two significant structural improvements in public education in the second half of the 20th century.

2. *The Integration Imperative*   The Act reverses the patterns of separation and isolation imposed upon disabled children at the

---

[9]The era's statutes and legislative materials, from all of the states, are collected in an Appendix to the Brief of the National Association for Retarded Citizens in *City of Cleburne v. Cleburne Living Center*, 473 U.S. 432 (1985).

turn of the century. The integration imperative of the Act prohibits "removal of a handicapped child from the regular education environment unless that child cannot, with the assistance
of supplementary aids and services, be satisfactorily educated
in the regular school environment." In this, the Act reflects the
provision of the *PARC* decree (Paragraph 7), that "placement in
a regular public school class is preferable to placement in a special public school class."

3. *The Requirement that Schools Know and "Adopt" "Effective,"
   "Promising" Practices*   In three provisions, the Act prohibits
   play-school. Instead, it requires the formulation and delivery to
   each child of an effective education: One, the Act requires states
   and districts to see to it that all teachers, both "regular" and
   "special," are fully informed of and continuously trained in
   "promising practices" in the education of children. Second, the
   Act requires every district as well as the states to "*adopt* promising practices." Third, the Act's requirement of "a free appropriate public education" has been held by the United States
   Supreme Court to mean an education "reasonably calculated to
   enable the child to achieve [real] educational benefits" (*Board
   of Education v. Rowley*, 458 U.S., 178 [1982]).

   These provisions reflect and improve upon the *PARC* decree's
   requirement that "every child . . . be provided . . . a free, public
   program of education and training appropriate to his capacities," *actually* be provided (¶ 43), and that the Commonwealth
   design, plan and deliver "the range of programs of education,"
   "arrangements for their financing" and "the recruitment, hiring and training" "necessary to the effectuation" of that requirement (¶ 50).

4. *Effective Early Education*   The *PARC* decree (¶ 44) in a provision not matched by the Act until 1986, required that "wherever [Pennsylvania schools] provide a pre-school program . . .
   for children less than six, every retarded child of the same age
   shall be provided . . . a pre-school program . . . appropriate to
   his capacities."

5. *All, Every One: A Zero-Reject School System*   Undergirding all
   of these is the central and pervasive requirement of the *PARC*
   decree and the Act: that all handicapped children shall be educated, every one. None may be excluded.

   William Ohrtman, Pennsylvania's Director of the Bureau for
the Education of Exceptional Students at the time of the *PARC* decree, borrowed from the common commercial Quality Assurance

language of the day and declared "the decree requires a *zero-reject* school system for children with disabilities." This requirement *does* place pressure on school districts, teachers, principals, and teacher training institutions to know and actually to practice the state of the art in the effective education of disabled children. But that is exactly what the *PARC* decree and the Act intended.

THE RESONANCE OF *PARC* AND THE 1975 ACT, IN 1995

In adopting as the law of the entire land the constitutional principles articulated in the *PARC* case, the Education for All Handicapped Children Act of 1975 did nothing less than extend equal citizenship to all disabled children and their families and prefigure the extension of equal citizenship to all adults with disabilities as well.

"The principle of equal citizenship," a distinguished constitutional scholar had occasion to write shortly after the 1975 enactment,

> presumptively insists that the organized society treat each individual as a person, one who is worthy of respect, one who "belongs." Stated negatively, the principle presumptively forbids the organized society to treat an individual either as a member of an inferior or dependent caste or as a non-participant.[10]

You will be asked, in the name of overblown fears not unlike those which propelled the original exclusion of children with disabilities and their segregation, to draw exceptions to the rigorous and universal application of the principles of equal citizenship expressed in the original Act. There are still some school boards who would rather exclude disabled children. And there will always be some teachers whose first and even second inclination may be not to be bothered. But the point of the Act is to call school boards to their public responsibilities, to call teachers to be their best professional selves, and to require school districts and state education authorities actually to supply the professional support and the conditions of practice that will enable them to do so.

Skelly Wright, in *Hobson v. Hansen,* wrote that a primary function of the Fourteenth Amendment, in which this great Act is rooted, is to purge "the arbitrary quality of thoughtlessness" from all important relationships between a state and its citizens. Thaddeus Stevens, Pennsylvania's greatest public person, in 1835 the father

---

[10]Karst, K. (1977). "The Supreme Court, 1976 Term—Forward: Equal Citizenship Under the Fourteenth Amendment," *Harv. L. Rev. 91*(1), 6.

of Pennsylvania's public schools, from 1859 leader of the Radical Republicans in the Congress, and the primary progenitor of the Fourteenth Amendment would, I believe, agree.

I thank you for the thoughtful beginnings of your deliberations on reauthorization of this most thoughtful Act.

21

Fiscal Issues Relating to Special Education Inclusion

Thomas B. Parrish

This chapter has been broadened somewhat beyond a strict definition of *inclusion* to consider the relationship between a range of program reforms and financing provisions. However, the major reform issues discussed here still pertain to the provision of services for special education students in less restrictive settings and to greater integration between special education and all other educational programs. This chapter focuses on questions such as how fiscal incentives to serve students with special education needs in more restrictive settings can be removed and how limited educational resources can be used more efficiently by providing better coordination and articulation across educational programs. It will be argued that maintaining fiscal and program barriers between regular and categorical program offerings is a form of program segregation that leads to restrictiveness in the provision of educational services.

The chapter is divided into discussions of state and then federal special education and finance reform issues. State issues are discussed first because states have the primary responsibility for the provision of special educational services and supply, by far, the most financial support for these programs.[1] Although it was the

This chapter was originally presented at the National Center on Educational Restructuring and Inclusion invitational conference on inclusive education, Racine, Wisconsin, April 28–May 1, 1994.

[1]For the last year in which these data were available, fiscal year 1987–1988, the state share was 56%, the local share 36%, and the federal share 8% (*Fourteenth Annual Report to Congress to Assure the Free and Appropriate Public Education of All Children with Disabilities* [1993, Table AH1, P.A 208–210]. [Washington, DC: U.S. Department of Education])

federal Education for All Handicapped Children Act (EAHCA), passed in 1975 that ensured a free and appropriate public education for all students with disabilities, only about 8% of special education funding now comes from federal sources. This is despite an authorization and what many considered to be a promise of federal support of up to 40% of the excess costs of special education services at the time of the passage of EAHCA.

Since the passage of EAHCA, special education costs and enrollments have grown considerably. The number of students receiving special education services nationally has grown from 8.2% of public school enrollments in FY 1977 to approximately 11% in FY 1994. More than $19 billion in local, state, and federal funds were spent for special education and related services in 1987–1988, the latest year for which such data are available. Of this amount, states and localities provided over 91%, with a federal share of approximately 8%. Although special education costs have represented a growing share of overall elementary and secondary school spending over the past 2 decades, federal aid per eligible student has held steady. This continuing growth in the number of students identified for special education services and the corresponding increases in cost have resulted in an unprecedented degree of public scrutiny over the past few years.[2] In addition to these issues are growing concerns over the fiscal incentives for more restrictive, high-cost placements that are contained in some state special education funding formulas, as well as the lack of flexibility in the use of these funds. Policy makers are increasingly realizing that fiscal provisions may provide major stumbling blocks to reform at the local level.

This chapter outlines some of the major issues regarding special education finance and program reform at the state and federal levels. Each of the states and the federal government has a different set of policies and procedures for determining allocations of special education aid to local school districts. A great deal has been written and numerous typologies developed to try to categorize these alternative funding mechanisms. Although these alternative approaches are discussed and some policy recommendations put forth, this chapter does not endorse a single funding approach. Each of these alternatives was designed to achieve different policy objectives, and it is only through the greater definition of these policy

---

[2]Examples of this interest include major articles regarding special education programs and costs in *U.S. News & World Report* (December 13, 1993) and *The New York Times* (April 6, 7, and 8, 1994).

and program objectives by the federal government and each of the individual states that choices among competing financing provisions can be made. However, there are a set of general principles that underlie this [chapter]. These are that there are no *incentive-free* financing systems, that financing policy will have a *strong influence* on local program provision, and, consequently, that in developing fiscal policy it is essential to develop provisions that will *support, or at least not obstruct*, program goals.

DEFINING PROGRAM REFORM

The major purpose of this chapter is to discuss the relationship between special education finance policies and the provision of services for special education students in less restrictive placements. These policies will generally include the removal of fiscal *dis*incentives or the incorporation of fiscal incentives for moving students from private to public schools, from specialized to neighborhood schools, and toward greater integration with regular education students throughout the school day.

In addition, however, this discussion of special education reform will also include issues related to greater flexibility in the use of local resources, the development of unified systems of service provision within schools, and the creation of intervention systems for all students. These concepts are added to this discussion with the idea that one way to avoid restrictiveness in the placement of students is to avoid identifying them as special education in the first place when alternative types of interventions are sufficient to meet their needs. These types of program reform mechanisms are driven by the idea that the very designation of special education may be restrictive regardless of where or how services are provided. When students get into special education they tend not to get out. Therefore, this program designation may restrict the breadth of their schooling experience and, indeed, opportunities throughout their lifetime. Of course, we also know that for many students the designation of special education, with its accompanying guarantees and procedural rights, *is* needed to ensure that appropriate services *are* provided that will open opportunities in school and throughout life that otherwise might be closed. Thus, it is not argued that special education be eradicated but that it also should not be the only financial option for students in need of remedial or accommodative services.

Another reason for opening the discussion of program reform to include the concept of providing a seamless set of services to meet the needs of all students, whether they have regular, special, bilingual, or compensatory education requirements, is the idea that the barriers built around these programs lead to the separation of the associated programs and services. These walls lead to the inefficient use of resources through the required maintenance of multiple administrative units, accounting structures, and facilities; and to inefficiencies in the provision of services for students with multiple special needs. For example, it would seem that separate programming for the student with regular education, special education, and limited English service needs would likely be an instructional disaster. It is argued that the separation of these programs within schools also leads to the provision of separated, and therefore restrictive, services. This opens the discussion of program reform and the consideration of accompanying fiscal provisions to the consideration of schooling systems in a more holistic manner.

WHAT DOES FINANCE HAVE TO DO WITH IT?

The concept that appropriate instructional programs and related services cannot be provided without adequate financial support has long been recognized. A newer concept, but one that is becoming widely recognized, is that *the policies that underlie educational financing mechanisms may be as important in affecting program provision as the amounts allocated.* Even the simplest funding systems contain incentives and disincentives that directly influence the orientation, quantities, and types of service to be provided at the local level.

An unprecedented amount of special education finance reform activity is occurring in the states at present. Interviews with representatives of all 50 states revealed that the major factor driving these fiscal reforms is state funding systems containing *disincentives* for the kinds of program practices that the states are now attempting to foster. States are increasingly realizing that program policies and guidelines, training, and support will have little impact on program provision while appreciable *fiscal disincentives* to these changes remain in place. In an era of increasing fiscal constraint, local decision makers are hard pressed to pursue reform initiatives that will reduce the financial support they receive from state and federal sources. In these instances, the policy messages from the state and federal governments are clearly mixed. Local districts are asked to do one thing but receive financial encouragement to do just the opposite.

It also seems clear that changes in fiscal policy alone will be insufficient to result in program change. States reporting the most success in coordinating program and fiscal reform emphasize the need for financial incentives, or at least the removal of disincentives, as well as the provision of a comprehensive system of inservice, training, and ongoing support for the desired changes.

SPECIAL EDUCATION FINANCE REFORM IN THE STATES

As shown in the last column of Table 21.1, over half of the states are currently actively pursuing special education finance reform. To fully appreciate this level of change requires an understanding of how painful this type of activity can be to state policy makers. Education is the largest single budget item in most states, and changes in the amount of state aid received by local districts inevitably create dissension. Given the very strong advocacy groups associated with special education, special education funding issues can be among the most contentious that state policy makers have to confront. The fact that over half of the states are now actively engaged in changing their special education funding formulas provides strong evidence that a very powerful set of social conditions and reform issues is driving these changes.

What Conditions Drive Reform?

Telephone interviews with state directors of special education or their representatives in all 50 states indicated that fiscal incentives for more restrictive placements were among the major factors driving reform. This was not an issue in all states. For example, some states have formulas, like the federal formula under IDEA, that do not provide fiscal incentives for higher-cost placements. Other issues driving reform were rising costs and enrollments and lack of flexibility in the local use of special education funds.

In the states where fiscal incentives for restrictiveness were a major issue, two major, and often separate, elements of the funding provisions were driving these concerns. These two elements are, first, aid differentials within the public system that relate to the type of placement and, second, differentials between the amounts of state aid received for private versus public special education placements.

Restrictiveness from Public Aid Differentials   Table 21.1 divides the states into four basic types of funding systems. The states with public funding differentials favoring more restrictive placements tend to be those with resource-based systems or pupil-weighting systems that vary based on the primary setting in which students receive services. Both of these types of funding systems tend to fea-

Table 21.1. Special education finance reform in the United States.

State	Current funding formula	Basis of allocation	State special ed. $ for target population only	Implemented reform within last 5 years	Considering major reform
Alabama	Pupil weights	Placement & condition		✓	✓
Alaska	Pupil weights	Type of placement			✓
Arizona	Pupil weights	Disabling condition			
Arkansas	Pupil weights	Type of placement		✓	✓
California	Resource-based	Classroom unit			✓
Colorado	% Reimbursement	Allowable costs	✓		✓
Connecticut	% Reimbursement	Actual expenditures		✓	✓
Delaware	Resource-based	Classroom unit			✓
Florida	Pupil weights	Disabling condition		✓	✓
Georgia	Pupil weights	Disabling condition	For 90% of funds	✓	
Hawaii	Pupil weights	Placement & condition	✓		
Idaho	% Reimbursement	Actual expenditures	✓		✓
Illinois	Resource-based	Special education staff/enroll.	✓		✓
Indiana	Pupil weights	Disabling condition		✓	✓
Iowa	Pupil weights	Type of placement			✓
Kansas	Resource-based	No. of sp. ed. staff	✓		✓
Kentucky	Pupil weights	Disabling condition	✓		✓
Louisiana	% Reimbursement	Actual expenditures		✓	
Maine	% Reimbursement	Allowable costs	✓		
Maryland	Flat grant	Special education enroll.			
Massachusetts	Flat grant	Total district enroll.			
Michigan	% Reimbursement	Allowable costs	✓		✓
Minnesota	% Reimbursement	Actual expenditures		✓	
Mississippi	Resource-based	No. of sp. ed. staff			✓
Missouri	Resource-based	No. of sp. ed. staff			✓

State	Funding mechanism	Funding basis			
Montana[a]	% Reimbursement	Allowable costs	✓	✓	✓
Nebraska	% Reimbursement	Allowable costs	✓		
Nevada	Flat grant	Classroom unit			
New Hampshire	Pupil weights	Type of placement			✓
New Jersey	Pupil weights	Placement & condition		✓	✓
New Mexico	Pupil weights	Type of placement			✓
New York	Pupil weights	Type of placement			✓
North Carolina	Flat grant	Special ed. enroll.	✓		✓
North Dakota	% Reimbursement	Actual expenditures	✓		
Ohio	Resource-based	Classroom unit			✓
Oklahoma	Pupil weights	Disabling condition			✓
Oregon	Pupil weights	Special ed. enroll.	✓		✓
Pennsylvania	Flat grant	Total district enroll.		✓	
Rhode Island	% Reimbursement	Actual expenditures	✓	✓	
South Carolina	Pupil weights	Disabling condition			✓
South Dakota	% Reimbursement	Allowable costs			✓
Tennessee	Resource-based	Classroom unit		✓	
Texas	Pupil weights	Type of placement		✓	✓
Utah	Pupil weights	Type of placement		✓	✓
Vermont[b]	Flat grant	Total district enroll.		✓	
Virginia	Resource-based	Classroom unit	✓	✓	✓
Washington	Resource-based	Classroom unit			✓
West Virginia	Flat grant	Special ed. enroll.		✓	
Wisconsin	% Reimbursement	Allowable costs	✓	✓	
Wyoming	% Reimbursement	Actual expenditures	✓	✓	

Pupil weights = two or more categories of student-based funding for special programs, expressed as a multiple of regular education aid. Resource-based = funding based on allocation of specific education resources [e.g., teachers or classroom units]. Classroom units are derived from prescribed staff–student ratios by disabling condition or type of placement. % Reimbursement = funding based on a percentage of allowable or actual expenditures. Flat grant = a fixed funding amount per student or per unit.

[a] Montana passed reforms scheduled for implementation in the 1994/1995 school year.

[b] Vermont's special education funding formula also contains a substantial % Reimbursement component.

ture an array of alternative types of primary service configurations, with state aid varying by type of placement. The concept underlying this type of system is that the amount of aid a district receives for a student with special needs should be directly related to the cost of providing services.

While the concept of a cost-based system clearly provides a strong rationale for determining state aid differentials, with the recent heightened focus on issues relating to inclusion, these types of systems are now sometimes seen as being overly restrictive. High cost placements, which receive greater allocations of aid under these types of systems, tend to be the more restrictive placements. While this need not necessarily be the case, it is difficult to know how to categorize a "fully included" child under such a system. For example, although a relatively large weight could be created for the special education placement category "regular education classroom," it would be difficult to determine a single, appropriate weighting amount. The degree of support, and therefore the costs, needed to substantially reduce the restrictiveness of a placement for an individual student will vary considerably by student. While it may be possible to derive an appropriate set of weights associated with an array of alternative inclusive placements (e.g., regular class placement with varying levels of support), states with these types of systems tend to be looking for alternative types of funding mechanisms.

An example of how this type of problem is described in the popular press comes from a feature article in *U.S. News & World Report*: "Texas pays local school districts ten times more for teaching special education students in separate classrooms. The result? Only five percent of special education students in Texas are taught in regular classrooms" (December 13, 1993, p. 47).

Incentives for Private Placements A second problem cited by states regarding funding incentives for restrictive placements deals with separate special education funding mechanisms for public and private special education schools. This problem seems to be especially acute in states with strong private schooling traditions. The question does not seem to be whether private schooling should be part of the array of placement options available within the state. Rather, these concerns focus on fiscal incentives favoring the use of private as opposed to public settings for high-cost, low-incidence students.

A quote describing this private schooling phenomenon also comes from *U.S. News & World Report*: "Cities like New Haven (Connecticut) actually save money when they send students to out-of-district schools, even though these schools can cost the state more than $100,000 per student, because the state picks up the bulk of the cost" (December 13, 1993, p. 50).

Issues relating to fiscal incentives in favor of private placements seem especially difficult for states to resolve. For example, although Massachusetts recently made major changes in its public special education funding system, incentives for public schools to use private placements were retained. Massachusetts has a strong private schooling tradition with a very vocal set of constituents. Similar concerns have been raised in New York, where a proposal to remove incentives to use private placements has been met with considerable resistance. Use of private placements varies considerably across the states. While states like New York and New Jersey show 7% and 5.75% of their special education students in private placements, respectively, Wisconsin shows less than .05% and Utah 0%.[3]

Lack of Flexibility at Local Level A lack of flexibility at the local level is also driving state fiscal reform. The concept of local flexibility seems to include a number of issues. An important concern in a number of states is a lack of fiscal mechanisms to support more inclusive services, thereby greatly restricting local flexibility in the design of appropriate services. A second concern relates to the inability to use special education funds or to the availability of other funds to support instructional interventions outside of special education. The major concern seems to be that when special education is the only available source of funding for remedial services, there will be constant pressure on special education enrollments and costs.

For example, some states do not require that special education funds be spent on special education services. The fourth column in Table 21.1 shows the states without this type of requirement. This type of flexibility can, of course, have a broad range of applications. It may mean that special education funding is completely rolled into the general state aid allocation and can be used for any purpose. In other states, these alternative uses may be limited to prereferral or other types of remedial or intervention services.

Intensive System for All Students In states such as Vermont and Pennsylvania, specific systems of prereferral interventions have been established and implemented in schools throughout the state. Pennsylvania has developed the concept of Instructional Support Teams (ISTs), which has been described as the linchpin of their

---

[3]*Fifteenth Annual Report to Congress on the Implementation of The Individuals with Disabilities Education Act* (1993) (Washington, DC: U.S. Department of Education), p. A-53.

financial reform package. Although Pennsylvania requires that special education funds be spent on special education services, for auditing purposes IST services are included in these costs. This program provided for a phase-in of ISTs in all of the schools of the state over a 5-year period. During the phase-in, participating schools were to receive grants of $30,000 per year to hire an IST teacher. This teacher is responsible for leading the IST process at the school and for providing any interim interventions that the team may recommend.

The IST team comprises the referring teacher, the IST teacher, and the school principal. This proposal also called for the state to provide an intensive year of training for all school staff during the first year of implementation, followed by a year of follow-up training. Coupled with a state aid system that contains no fiscal incentives for high-cost placements or for identifying a greater number of special education students, this system is designed to provide local districts with the resources and discretion they need to provide a broad array of educational services to students with varying educational needs. It was anticipated that the availability of IST services and the fact that state special education aid is not tied to the number of students identified would cause the state's special education counts to drop. Thus, after 2 years it was expected that local districts would be able to support the cost of IST teachers through savings from this reduction of direct special education services. The extent to which the state has been able to fully follow this phase-in schedule and the success of this implementation effort are unknown.

Attempts to incorporate alternative intervention systems in states where special education aid is directly tied to the number of students identified may face even more formidable implementation hurdles. As special education counts drop in these types of systems, local districts may stand to lose considerable state special education aid. In Oregon, for example, the funding system is based on a single weight that is applied to all special education students up to a cap of 11%. Because there is no requirement that these funds be spent on special education services, districts have discretion to set up alternative intervention systems such as ISTs. However, as special education counts drop in these districts, state aid is lost. As a result, phone interviews with local special education directors in Oregon revealed that those who had previously incorporated IST-type systems in an attempt to drop their overall special education counts were now under pressure to get their special education counts back up to the funding ceiling of 11%.

Flexibility in Reallocating Transportation Costs Another important issue relating to local flexibility in the use of funds as districts try to incorporate more inclusive practices relates to separate, categorical funding for transportation services. As districts attempt to move students with disabilities back to their neighborhood schools, they face considerable start-up costs in relation to making the school fully accessible and in purchasing multiple sets of specialized equipment for separate neighborhood schools rather than just a single set of equipment in a specialized school. These costs may be largely offset through savings in transportation costs. However, in state funding systems where transportation is categorically funded, dollars saved through reduced transportation services cannot be recouped for use in other ways (e.g., to support the start-up costs of inclusion). At both the state and district levels there are important issues relating to the need to have special education funds follow students as they move to less restrictive placements.[4]

Better Program Coordination A final issue relating to the need for increased flexibility in the use of funds at the local level is the perceived barriers to providing better articulated and coordinated sets of services across categorical program areas. Far too often in schools with high levels of special needs, regular, special, compensatory and limited English proficient (LEP) programs exist in virtual isolation from one another. Major concerns focus on inefficiencies that result from the need for multiple administrative and accountability structures, alternative forms of eligibility determination that tend to be cumbersome and costly, and the inevitable segregation that results from separated services.

The lack of integrated, well-articulated services can be especially disastrous for students with multiple needs. At the extreme, imagine the school day for a regular education student who is LEP, receives compensatory instruction, and is receiving a special education–related service in a school in which all of these special programs are run separately from one another. Whether the separation of these services is really due to a lack of flexibility in state and federal funding and monitoring provisions or whether the separation of these services is embedded in local tradition or actually has a basis in state and federal law requires further investigation.

---

[4]This phenomenon is described in "Resource Implications of Inclusion: Impressions of Special Education Administrators at Selected Sites" (1994, February) (Palo Alto, CA: Center for Special Education Finance).

Alternative Criteria for Design of
State Special Education Funding Formulas

Given these concerns about state funding formulas and the fact that some are known to contain incentives for more restrictive services, what criteria should be used to evaluate state special education funding systems? Table 21.2 lists a set of criteria, or standards, that have traditionally been used in considering alternative ways of allocating special education aid to local jurisdictions.

Through invited presentations, the author has had the opportunity to present these alternative criteria to statewide policy audiences in a number of states that are actively considering special education finance reform. In each case there has been general agreement that each criterion is a desirable attribute to try to incorporate in a reformed state special education funding system. The problem, however, is that while these criteria are not exactly mutually exclusive, a major focus on one criterion may come at the expense of the others.

For example, depending on how equity is defined, a highly equitable system might be one that is tightly linked to variations in local costs of providing special education services. Districts that spend more on special education services because their resource costs are higher, they serve more students, or they serve students with more severe needs would receive more state aid in recognition of these cost differentials. However, such a system may have a fairly substantial reporting burden, may lack flexibility, and may not be placement neutral. Conversely, a system in which special education funds are allocated only on the basis of total district enrollment (e.g., as in Pennsylvania and Massachusetts) will be identification and placement neutral but may be perceived as inequitable because it fails to link aid allocations to local variations in pupil needs. A system that is fully adequate and predictable may have problems related to cost control, and so on.

Thus, in attempting to develop an ideal set of special education funding provisions for a given state or for the federal government, it is essential that policy makers choose among the criteria they wish to foster. This concept is also directly tied to the idea that no system, no matter how simple, will be incentive free.

For example, it is said that the federal funding system is placement neutral because the amount of funding allocated is the same, regardless of how students are served. Although many will believe this to be a desirable attribute, this type of system does contain a fiscal incentive. As the funding level will be the same regardless of

Table 21.2. Criteria for evaluating special education funding formulas

Understandable

- The system is understandable by all concerned parties (legislators, legislative staff, state department personnel, local administrators, and advocates).
- The concepts underlying the formula and the procedures to implement it are straightforward and "avoid unnecessary complexity."

Equitable

- Student equity: Dollars distributed to ensure comparable program quality regardless of district assignment.
- Wealth equity: Inverse relationship between state dollars distributed and local wealth.
- District-to-district fairness: All districts receive comparable resources for comparable students.

Adequate

- Funding is sufficient for all districts to provide appropriate programs for special education students.

Predictable

- LEAs know allocation in time to plan for local services.
- System produces predictable demands for state funding.
- SEA and LEAs can count on stable funding across years.

Flexible

- Local agencies are given latitude to deal with unique local conditions in an appropriate and cost-effective manner.
- Changes that affect programs and costs can be incorporated into the funding system with minimum disruption.
- Local agencies given maximum latitude in use of resources in exchange for outcome accountability.

Identification Neutral

- The number of students identified as special education is not the only, or primary, basis for determining the amount of special education funding to be received.
- Students do not have to be labeled "special education" (or any other label) in order to receive services.

Reasonable Reporting Burden

- Costs to maintain funding system are minimized at both local and state levels.
- Data requirements, record keeping, and reporting are kept at a reasonable level.

Fiscal Accountability

- Cost accounting ensures that special education funds are spent for special education programs and services.

(continued)

Table 21.2. *(continued)*

* Procedures are included to contain excessive or inappropriate special education costs.

Cost-Based
* Funding received by districts for the provision of special education programs is linked to the costs they face in providing these programs.

Placement Neutral
* District funding for special education is not based on type of educational placement.
* District funding for special education is not based on handicapping label.

Cost Control
* Observed patterns of growth in special education costs statewide are stabilized over time.
* Observed patterns of growth in special education identification rates statewide are stabilized over time.

Outcome Accountability
* State monitoring of local agencies is based on various measures of student outcome.
* Districts showing positive results for students are given maximum program and fiscal latitude to continue producing them.

Connected to Regular Education Funding
* Separation of funding will be likely to lead to separation of services.
* Special education funding should be tied conceptually, or directly, to the regular education finance system.

Adapted from Hartman (1992) and Parrish (1993).

the level of service provided, the fiscal incentive is to provide *less* service at a *lower* cost. While this will not always be the result, there is strong evidence through testimony and research that program provision may be strongly influenced by funding policy.[5] Similarly, in "identification neutral" systems, such as Massachusetts and Pennsylvania, which do not contain an incentive to identify students, the fiscal incentive is *not* to label students *special education*. While this may be the policy objective in some states, it is essential

---

[5]This relationship has been widely acknowledged by state and local providers in seminars on this subject provided by the author. This phenomenon was also demonstrated by J. Dempsey, D. Fuchs, and L.S. Fuchs, in " 'Flat' versus 'weighted' reimbursement formulas: A longitudinal analysis of state-wide special education funding practices" (1993) (*Exceptional Children*, 59(5), 433–443). It's also quite logical to expect local program managers to make program decisions at the margin that follow available funding sources.

to realize the incentive and disincentive structures incorporated in alternative funding systems. *As funding provisions will drive program policy, policy makers must identify the program policies they wish to follow and adopt a funding system that will foster, or at least not inhibit, them.*

State Fiscal Policies that Foster Inclusion

As federal law requires that the least restrictive placement be provided to children with special education needs, this is clearly one criterion that all special education funding formulas should attempt to foster.[6] How might this best be achieved?

First, fiscal incentives for more restrictive placements must clearly be removed. Theoretically this could be achieved under any type of special education funding system. Even systems that are driven by type of student placement could conceivably develop a weighting structure that would foster inclusion through the creation of higher weights for an array of higher- and lower-cost regular education placements. However, thus far, the states attempting to foster inclusion have shown a greater inclination to move toward funding systems that do not differentiate funding based on student placement.

Second, states must make decisions about the extent to which they wish to encourage private special education placements. Some states may decide that private, as opposed to public, placements are more restrictive under any circumstance and may wish to create fiscal disincentives for their use. Other states may decide that private placements are an integral component of the continuum of available placements for their special education students and that these types of placements should not be discouraged. Regardless, it is difficult to understand why any state would wish to create fiscal incentives *favoring* private placements (i.e., why private placements should be encouraged over comparable public placements). In some states, however, this is clearly what is happening. Although comparable public services may not be currently available in these states, in some cases this is simply because districts have never been allowed the option of taking the state aid they are allotted in support of private tuition to develop comparable public services.

---

[6]Section 300.550 of Title 34, *Code of Federal Regulations*, stipulates that "Special classes, separate schooling or other removal of handicapped children from the regular educational environment occur only when the nature or severity of the handicap is such that education in regular classes with the use of supplementary aids and services cannot be achieved satisfactorily."

Third, the private schooling issue is one example of the importance of developing funding systems in which dollars follow the child as he or she moves to less restrictive placements. Another example is the need for savings in transportation costs to follow special education students to their neighborhood schools to offset other types of costs associated with this type of move. This is an issue for states as they try to foster inclusionary practices and for districts as they try to implement them. Districts may have internal resource allocation mechanisms in place that support places rather than students. As students move from specialized to neighborhood schools, districts will also need to rethink their internal resource allocation systems.

Fourth, states reporting the most success in fostering inclusion cite the need to fund inclusion training in addition to reforming their state funding system. As the fiscal disincentives to inclusion are removed, districts must be provided training and assistance in overcoming the many practical difficulties associated with these types of changes.

Fifth, states should fund and encourage statewide intervention systems for all students. Students who are identified as special education because this is the only way to provide them with remedial services have had their service options restricted. As the full spirit of inclusion would seem to include retaining students in regular education who do not require the additional protections and legal guarantees associated with special education, state funding systems that actively support alternative interventions for all students will foster inclusionary practices.

FEDERAL SPECIAL EDUCATION FINANCE REFORM

It is not possible for a jurisdiction to consider the merits of alternative types of fiscal policy apart from identifying the specific types of program reforms it wishes to foster and prioritizing among the types of competing funding criteria. Thus, in considering alternative federal funding options, it is important to ask, *What is the federal position on special education program reform?* Federal law clearly calls for the provision of special education services in the least restrictive environment. In accordance, federal special education funding policy does not create incentives for more restrictive placements. Under IDEA, the same federal allocation is granted to all states based on the number of special education students identified in the state up to a limit of 12%. The level of funding received is not dependent on the label placed on the student, the level of services they receive, or the setting in which they are served.

However, federal funding policy has been criticized on the basis of some of the other funding criteria. For example, the IDEA funding mechanism does contain an incentive for identifying special education students up to a cap of 12%. It does not foster flexibility in use of funds, as IDEA funds cannot be spent on alternative intervention services. Federal funding provisions also do not appear to foster unified services across categorical programs. Some state policy makers believe that these federal policies are serious limitations that work to stifle reform at the state and local levels.

IDEA Funding Has Incentive to Identify Students

Perhaps the predominant set of arguments in this regard relates to federal incentives to identify special education students up to the federal funding cap of 12%. States such as Vermont and Pennsylvania, which have adopted funding systems that have specifically been designed not to reward further special education identification, find that they are losing federal special education support as their numbers of identified students drop. These reductions have been accomplished through interventions such as providing special education services in regular education classrooms, allocating resources for prereferral services, and severing the tie between state special education funding and the number of students identified for special education services.

These states feel that this reduction in the count of special education students is a change for the better. They argue that they are often serving a broader range of students with special learning needs and in a less restrictive and more appropriate manner. They contend that assessments are expensive and serve little educational purpose; that once students enter special education, they never get out; that the system itself can be debilitating for students by casting a stigma on them and by limiting and shaping their educational options; and that many students can better and more efficiently be served outside the formal special education system. Policy makers involved in funding reform in these states often express great concern that current federal policies run counter to their efforts.

Proponents of these reforms argue that IDEA funding should also be based on this type of total enrollment-based system. Such a system would contain no incentives to identify more special education students or to serve special education students in certain types of placements. What are some of the arguments in favor and against changing the basis of allocation for IDEA funds to an enrollment base?

Arguments in Favor of Enrollment-Based Allocation System for IDEA Funds

The change in federal policy being proposed is essentially a return to the way funds were previously distributed under the EHA, which based allocations to states on the number of all children (i.e., the population of all students ages 3–21). What are the arguments supporting this type of change in federal policy?

Working outside special education is more cost effective. Special education is costly. An initial assessment has been estimated to cost $1,206 per student (Moore, Strang, Schwartz, & Braddock, 1988). For those students receiving special education transportation services, the average cost was shown to be $1,583 per year. Two separate studies (Moore et al., 1988; Shields et al., 1989) showed that only about 62% of the special education dollar at the local level went to direct special education instructional services. For students with mild disabilities in resource room programs, an average of 22% of all funds for special education services was spent on assessment and 15% on special education program administration (Shields et al., 1989). Concerns about the cost effectiveness of assessment practices are raised by the number of studies finding that the tests and methods used to classify students as learning disabled do not provide information that resource specialists or regular teachers report to be of use in developing instructional programs for these students (Lovitt, 1967; Shepard & Smith, 1981; Ysseldyke, Algozzine, Shinn, & McGue, 1982).

Some students will be better served outside special education. In addition to cost savings, there are other important reasons to try to serve students outside special education when possible. Regardless of the label assigned to the student, special education programs, by their very nature, tend to isolate students and to lead to more restrictive services. Affiliation with special education tends to have a negative connotation for students that stays with them throughout their schooling and perhaps throughout their lives. Once students are identified as special education, they tend to stay in the program. The program does not seem oriented to short-term interventions that return students to regular education status in a relatively brief period of time. The special education bureaucracy seems to hinder school-level flexibility and discretion.

Overidentification is now the major issue. In 1975, when federal special education funding shifted from a population-based system to a special education pupil count system, it was estimated that large segments of the special education population were being underserved. Many states are now reporting that *over*identification rather than *under*identification is their major concern.[7]

Procedural safeguards will remain in place. Movement to a population-based, rather than an identified student-based, funding system would not jeopardize any of the procedural safeguards under current law. While the number of students with mild disabling conditions (e.g., students with learning disabilities) would be expected to diminish under such a system, the more clearly identifiable students, for whom IDEA was primarily intended, should be largely unaffected by such a change.

Arguments Against Enrollment-Based Allocation System for IDEA Funds

Some special education advocates, and others, argue against such a change in federal policy. Some of the positions they express are as follows:

The system would not be fair to states and districts with higher incidence rates. A population-based funding system assumes comparable incidence rates of special education students across states and districts. States and LEAs with greater numbers of special education students would tend to lose federal support under a population-based funding system. Districts might have higher percentages of special education students because of differences in the characteristics of the students they enroll and because they have been especially proactive in identifying the needs of and setting up programs for special-needs students. A population-based funding system would financially penalize those very districts that have been most responsive to the state and federal call to fully identify and serve special education students.

Procedural safeguards cannot be maintained if students are not identified. The foundation for the whole system of procedural safeguards that has been established for special education students is identification and assessment. Students cannot be protected under the law unless they are singled out and identified.

A retreat from the traditional federal role of fostering and promoting special education services would occur. The traditional federal role in special education has been one of leadership for and

---

[7]This contention is supported by an overall 29.9% increase in the number of children served in Part B and Chapter 1 Handicapped programs since the inception of Part B in 1976 through the 1990–1991 school year. The 1990–1991 school year showed an increase of 2.8%, which was the largest increase in a decade.

protection of students with special needs. A return to a population-based funding system would send a message to states and communities that the federal government is backing away from this position.

Fiscal accountability would be jeopardized. Because funds cannot be tracked to students who are not identified, a population-based funding system reduces assurances of fiscal accountability at a time when such controls are seen as increasingly important by taxpayers.

Current levels of special education funding would be threatened. Traditional levels of support for special education services would be likely to diminish when they no longer can be attributed to specific special education students with legal entitlements. Overall funding for special education services could erode over time.

Many of the arguments in favor of and opposed to this type of change in federal policy are compelling. In light of the seriousness of these concerns, in this era of escalating educational needs and dwindling public resources, a global change in this direction may be premature. In addition, if the federal government were to adopt an enrollment-based funding system in its entirety, the redistribution effects across states could be considerable. Table 21.3 shows one estimate of the potential fiscal impact on states.

On the other hand, it seems counter to the federal interest to stifle well-thought-out state-level reforms designed to increase the efficiency of services to students with special needs. A more tentative federal approach might be to "hold harmless" selected states making specific reform efforts. On a trial basis, states might be sheltered from reductions in federal support under IDEA as they allow their special education enrollments to drop. Such a system could require federal approval of a well-defined state plan to serve a broader base of students with special learning needs, both inside and outside the context of traditional special education. Such a program could be closely monitored to assess the impact on students still identified as special education, as well as on all other students with special learning needs requirements.

What Other Federal Fiscal Policies Might Directly Support Special Education Program Reform?

Beyond the types of "hold harmless" provisions, federal funding policy could foster inclusionary practices by granting supplements to states with more inclusive services and perhaps through carrying out fiscal sanctions against states with less inclusive services. There has been some discussion at the federal level as to whether federal aid under IDEA should be withheld from states with funding systems that contain disincentives for inclusion. However, because these funding systems can be very complex, it is sometimes difficult to determine if this type of disincentive actually exists. In addition, it is not always easy to know how to implement an alternative system that would not have other types of negative effects. Rather than trying to get into the tricky business of assessing the incentives and disincentives inherent in funding systems, why not simply judge states on the basis of results (i.e., the degree to which inclusionary practices are actually being implemented throughout the state)?

Beyond this, the fact that over one half of the states are currently in the process of reforming their special education finance formulas provides clear evidence of an unusual opportunity for the federal government to influence the direction of these reforms. Many of these states report that they are trying to move to state funding systems that will foster more inclusion. They also report that they are experiencing difficulty in developing a clear set of preferred alternatives. Financial support and technical assistance for states attempting to make these types of changes could provide considerable leverage in moving states closer to federal policy objectives in the provision of inclusionary practices. Such an approach is also likely to be much more effective in the long run than the imposition of sanctions. Because it has also been reported that the removal of fiscal disincentives to inclusion is not enough, federal support for the provision of training for inclusionary practices would also foster this policy objective.

CONCLUSION

It is clear that the successful implementation of such program reforms as more inclusionary practices will not occur in the face of fiscal disincentives. In addition, however, changes in fiscal policy alone will not suffice. This type of reform vision must be accompanied by a specific set of defined goals as well as needed technical assistance and training.

Inclusion can conceivably be fostered within the context of any type of funding system. Making sure that this actually occurs, however, requires a more careful definition of exactly what practices are to be fostered under the concept of inclusion. Is the policy goal to increase the numbers and types of services to be provided to students outside of the context of special education or simply to reduce restrictive placements for special education students? Beyond this, is there a related policy goal to break down barriers in categorical

Table 21.3. Estimated redistribution effects under a population-based system

State	Actual Part B grant 1992–93 ($)	Resident population Ages 3–21, 1992	Population-based Part B grant 1992–93 ($)	Gain or loss from a population-based system ($)	Percentage gain or loss
Alabama	40,121,862	1,155,768	32,195,398	(7,926,464)	−19.8
Alaska	5,148,324	184,188	5,130,793	(17,531)	−0.3
Arizona	24,285,654	1,065,950	29,693,403	5,407,749	22.3
Arkansas	18,751,830	670,305	18,672,204	(79,626)	−0.4
California	200,622,009	8,404,782	234,125,970	33,503,961	16.7
Colorado	22,708,014	942,826	26,263,626	3,555,612	15.7
Connecticut	25,387,257	794,300	22,126,244	(3,261,013)	−12.8
Delaware	4,737,016	178,772	4,979,923	242,907	5.1
District of Columbia	1,137,654	125,646	3,500,030	2,362,376	207.7
Florida	99,773,518	3,194,673	88,991,709	(10,781,809)	−10.8
Georgia	43,099,754	1,896,573	52,831,471	9,731,717	22.6
Hawaii	5,415,839	302,533	8,427,444	3,011,605	55.6
Idaho	8,873,864	340,956	9,497,766	623,902	7.0
Illinois	82,748,038	3,140,735	87,489,197	4,741,159	5.7
Indiana	45,450,032	1,565,409	43,606,473	(1,843,559)	−4.1
Iowa	24,586,762	779,259	21,707,258	(2,879,504)	−11.7
Kansas	18,187,305	708,859	19,746,176	1,558,871	8.6
Kentucky	32,350,420	1,042,458	29,039,003	(3,311,417)	−10.2
Louisiana	30,494,614	1,299,403	36,196,535	5,701,921	18.7
Maine	11,023,403	327,976	9,136,192	(1,887,211)	−17.1
Maryland	36,079,237	1,248,747	34,785,447	(1,293,790)	−3.6
Massachusetts	55,977,325	1,453,544	40,490,330	(15,486,995)	−27.7
Michigan	64,287,893	2,629,520	73,248,648	8,960,755	13.9

Minnesota	32,950,587	1,247,292	34,744,917	1,794,330	5.4
Mississippi	24,737,520	804,162	22,400,963	(2,336,557)	-9.4
Missouri	41,904,337	1,414,507	39,402,905	(2,501,432)	-6.0
Montana	7,197,085	237,166	6,606,563	(590,522)	-8.2
Nebraska	14,406,869	460,216	12,819,906	(1,586,963)	-11.0
Nevada	8,175,786	336,618	9,376,926	1,201,140	14.7
New Hampshire	7,896,801	292,214	8,139,995	243,194	3.1
New Jersey	73,054,014	1,914,046	53,318,203	(19,735,811)	-27.0
New Mexico	15,529,365	480,608	13,387,952	(2,141,413)	-13.8
New York	125,568,396	4,574,769	127,436,051	1,867,655	1.5
North Carolina	51,397,213	1,789,361	49,844,943	(1,552,270)	-3.0
North Dakota	4,869,339	183,594	5,114,246	244,907	5.0
Ohio	82,817,272	2,982,279	83,075,202	257,930	0.3
Oklahoma	27,533,519	910,566	25,364,982	(2,168,537)	-7.9
Oregon	19,295,872	796,281	22,181,427	2,885,555	15.0
Pennsylvania	78,161,371	3,018,856	84,094,101	5,932,730	7.6
Rhode Island	8,431,830	248,603	6,925,155	(1,506,675)	-17.9
South Carolina	32,227,929	1,013,215	28,224,402	(4,003,527)	-12.4
South Dakota	5,989,377	212,441	5,917,816	(71,561)	-1.2
Tennessee	44,210,780	1,335,112	37,191,255	(7,019,525)	-15.9
Texas	144,662,710	5,237,382	145,893,985	1,231,275	0.9
Utah	19,384,361	675,822	18,825,888	(558,473)	-2.9
Vermont	4,141,765	154,802	4,312,208	170,443	4.1
Virginia	48,688,884	1,658,593	46,202,233	(2,486,651)	-5.1
Washington	35,424,175	1,393,266	38,811,209	3,387,034	9.6
West Virginia	17,508,072	487,541	13,581,079	(3,926,993)	-22.4
Wisconsin	35,942,408	1,396,590	38,903,804	2,961,396	8.2
Wyoming	4,689,084	145,920	4,064,789	(624,295)	-13.3
TOTALS	1,918,044,345	68,855,004	1,918,044,345		

program provision at the school level? These policy objectives differ and will require somewhat different fiscal remedies. In shaping appropriate fiscal policy, it is important to identify the related program reform objectives as precisely as possible. Given the strong link between fiscal and program policy, program objectives should be well considered and carefully defined prior to any serious consideration of the related fiscal policy alternatives.

REFERENCES

Hartman, W. (1992). State funding models for special education. *Remedial and Special Education, 13*(6), 47–57.

Lovitt, T.C. (1967, December). Assessment of children with learning disabilities. *Exceptional Children*, 233–239.

Moore, M.T., Strang, E.W., Schwartz, M., & Braddock, M. (1988). *Patterns in special education service delivery and cost.* Washington, DC: Decision Resources Corporation.

Parrish, T. (1993). *Policy objectives for special education and funding formulas.* Palo Alto, CA: Center for Special Education Finance.

Shepard, L., & Smith, M.L. (1981). *Evaluation of the identification of perceptual-communicative disorders in Colorado.* Boulder: University of Colorado.

Shields, P.M., et al. (1989). *Alternative programs and strategies for serving students with learning disabilities and other learning problems. Final report.* Menlo Park, CA: SRI International.

Ysseldyke, J., Algozzine, B., Shinn, M., & McGue, M. (1982). Similarities and differences between low achievers and students classified learning disabled. *Journal of Special Education, 16*(1), 73–85.

22

THE "FULL INCLUSION" COURT CASES: 1989–1994

DIANE LIPTON

The principle of placing children with disabilities in the "least restrictive environment" is revolutionary when contrasted with the long-standing practice of institutionalizing and segregating children with disabilities from children without disabilities in our public schools. Recognizing that the educational system is the socializing institution for all children, Congress embraced this "least restrictive environment" principle and targeted the integration of disabled children into the public schools as a critical step to achieving full social, economic, and political participation.

Although the federal special education law mandating that children with disabilities be educated in the "least restrictive environment" (LRE) and with their non-disabled peers to the maximum extent appropriate has been in effect since 1975, implementation of this mandate is highly inconsistent, at best.

In the first decade of the law's implementation, several lawsuits were brought in the federal courts by parents to obtain integrated placements for disabled children, particularly for children with significant physical and/or cognitive disabilities. Some of these first cases involved efforts to move disabled children from segregated "handicapped only" schools to special education classes on regular public school campuses. Once on regular school campuses, even if placed in self-contained special education classes, disabled students would at least be in closer physical proximity to non-disabled stu-

---

This chapter is from Lipton, D. (1994). The "full inclusion" court cases: 1989–1994. *NCERI Bulletin, 1*(2), 1–8; reprinted by permission.

dents and opportunities for integration could occur. The integration sought after usually involved opportunities for disabled children to participate in non-academic or non-core activities and classes such as lunch, recess, art and music.

These "first generation" LRE court cases had mixed and inconsistent results, with some courts finding that widespread placement in segregated "handicapped only" schools satisfied legal requirements and others finding that such segregation was often unnecessary and in violation of the strong preference for integration and mainstreaming embodied in the mandates of the federal law. Still other cases involved students with physical disabilities, such as cerebral palsy or deafness, in which federal courts concluded that the physical accommodations and methodologies related to these accommodations took precedence over "the least restrictive environment" issues.

By contrast, in an important case of this period, and a precursor of the more recent "inclusion" cases, in *Roncker v. Walters*, 700 F.2d 1058 (6th Cir. 1983), the Sixth Circuit upheld the right of a boy with mental retardation to remain in a special day class in a regular public school instead of being removed to the school district's proposed placement in a segregated "handicapped only" school. The court in *Roncker* articulated a standard underscoring the law's presumption in favor of regular education placement. In ordering placement in the more integrated regular public school, the court stated,

> Where the segregated facility is considered superior, the court should determine whether the services which make that placement superior could be feasibly provided in a non-segregated setting. If they can, the placement in the segregated school would be inappropriate under the Act. (700 F.2d at 1063)

Despite this very favorable ruling for integration in *Roncker*, the law's integration mandate was not strongly supported by the federal courts in the 1980s. Nevertheless, many parents, advocates, educators and academicians continued to push for full implementation of the LRE requirements using various non-litigation strategies.

In addition to advocacy, research on the integration of students with severe disabilities proliferated during the 1980s in many special education departments and institutes in universities around the country. The overwhelming data from this research supported and crystallized the benefits of integration for disabled and nondisabled children as well. These benefits cut across all educational domains—social, language, academic, and psychological areas. The research data also demonstrated that progress in these areas positively correlates with the amount of integration. The more disabled children participate in classroom activities with non-disabled peers with appropriate support services, the better they do. During these years, there was also a proliferation of strategies and technologies developed by teachers and researchers on modifying and adapting curricula to meet diverse student needs in the general education classroom and on promoting interactions between disabled and non-disabled children.

The 1980s also marked crucial advances establishing the civil rights of persons with disabilities, culminating in 1990 with passage of the federal Americans with Disabilities Act. Many states throughout the 1980s had also adopted state laws guaranteeing various civil rights for persons with disabilities. Disabled people and their families became increasingly visible and vocal as a political and economic force. The strength of the civil rights movement and its legislative victories had its effect on the education of children with disabilities. Parents were increasingly demanding that their children with disabilities come out of isolation and segregated environments and go to school with children without disabilities as a matter of civil rights. The education research–driven support for integration worked in concert with this values-driven civil rights approach to bring about pockets of increased integration within every state and even within school districts that otherwise had many students still segregated in special schools.

Evolving from a growing body of research, experience with integration, a shift in public policy, and consciousness about disability and civil rights, a second generation of integration issues has emerged in the 1990s. Parents, especially parents of younger children, are seeking much greater levels of integration than special education classes, even those in regular public schools, can provide. Supported by data demonstrating the questionable effectiveness of "pull-out" programs and separate classes, the current trend for the organization and delivery of services for students with significant or "severe" disabilities is toward full mainstreaming or "full inclusion" models. As used here, the term "full inclusion" means full-time membership and participation in the regular education classroom for students with disabilities with appropriate modification of the regular education curriculum and the provision of special education supplemental services.

The trend toward full inclusion, however, is far from universally accepted. The great majority of school districts, many still operating segregated schools or locating special education classes in separate "portables" placed on the "back 40" of regular school campuses are highly resistant to even the idea of full inclusion. Students from racial and ethnic minority groups are still disproportionately placed in segregated facilities.

Again in the 1990s parents are using the legal process to challenge the status quo through litigation. These cases are shaping new contours of the integration imperative. Against the backdrop of a raised political and social consciousness of disability issues as civil rights issues and with nearly two decades of experience with the law's implementation, the courts have been faced with a new series of LRE cases—the "full inclusion" cases of the 1990s. In these cases, the federal appellate courts have been called upon to interpret the law's mainstreaming provision and to establish standards for determining when regular education class placement is appropriate for a particular child.

The "full inclusion" cases, starting with *Daniel R.R. v. State Board of Education El Paso Independent School District*, 874 F.2d 1036 (5th Cir. 1989), involve the issue of mainstreaming children with mental retardation into regular education classes full time with special education support services. To date, the four federal appellate courts to directly address this issue have all upheld the right of children with significant cognitive disabilities to attend regular education classes full time when the educational (academic and nonacademic) benefits for the individual disabled child call for such placement. These decisions mark a dramatic shift in public policy and judicial interpretation of the law and the weight to be given congressional preference for educating children with disabilities in regular public school classes.

What is frequently misunderstood about the "full inclusion" cases, however, is the fact that they do not call for full-time mainstreaming for all children with disabilities. The courts acknowledge diverse student educational needs, that under the law a continuum of alternative placements must be available to meet these needs and that placement decisions must be based on individualized determinations. The courts also recognize some limitations to the integration mandate itself. Consideration of the effect on other students in the regular class and the costs of integrating students with severe disabilities into the regular education class are relevant issues in applying the legal preference for integration to a particular child.

The following discussion describes the "full inclusion" decisions in the federal courts of appeal and the legal standards that have evolved from these cases for determining when full-time placement in a regular class with supplementary aids and services is appropriate for an individual child. The U.S. Supreme Court may have occasion to review these full inclusion cases sometime in the near future. But for the present, the courts have opened the doors to the regular education classroom for many more children with disabilities.

THE LEGAL ANALYSIS

The Individuals with Disabilities Education Act (IDEA) (as did the Education of All Handicapped Children Act) specifically requires that

> to the maximum extent appropriate, handicapped children including children in public or private institutions or other care facilities are educated with children who are not handicapped, and that special classes, separate schooling, or other removal of handicapped children from the regular educational environment occurs only when the nature or severity of the handicap is such that education in regular classes with the use of supplementary aids and services cannot be achieved satisfactorily. (20 U.S.C. § 1412[5][B]; see also 34 C.F.R. § 300.550[b])

Under this provision, it is clear that a school district has the statutory obligation to affirmatively demonstrate that a particular special education student cannot be satisfactorily educated in a regular education class, with supplementary aids and services.

Congress's strong preference for integrated placements as set forth in Section 1412(5)(B) is at the core of the law. Senator Stafford, the ranking minority member of the Subcommittee on the Handicapped, which had primary jurisdiction of the bill, expressed the importance of integration to reverse a long history of prejudices toward persons with disabilities.

> I think that today Congress makes a very important statement. It makes a necessary statement of principle about how we intend our handicapped children to be treated in the educational process. . . . This statement that we make will help because it is designed to bring our children together, those with and without handicaps to try to undo the prejudice in education. (121 *Cong. Rec.* 20,432 [1975])

The importance of the integration principle to all children, disabled and non-disabled, was reiterated throughout the legislative process. Integration in school was seen as key to the ultimate goal of integration in society. Senator Stafford emphasized the importance of integration in the effort to remove attitudinal barriers.

> If we allow and, indeed, encourage handicapped children and non-handicapped children to be educated together as early as possible,

their attitudes toward each other in later life will not be such obstacles to overcome. A child who goes to school every day with another child who is confined to a wheelchair will understand far better in later life the limitation and abilities of such an individual when he or she is asked to work with, or is in a position to hire, such an individual. (121 *Cong. Rec.* 10,960 [1975])

To guard against the devastating effect of negative predictions and placements based on stereotypes and misconceptions, Congress ensured that the act contained strong procedural safeguards.

Congress recognized that the comprehensive procedures set out in the law are necessary to guard against unnecessarily segregated placements. Congressman Miller, the ranking member of the House Committee on Select Education, specifically referred to the "safeguards against the unnecessary placing of handicapped children in segregated classes" (121 *Cong. Rec.* H 7764 [1975]). He stressed that the "burden of proof in terms of the effectiveness of a program ought to rest with the administrator or teacher who seeks for one reason or another to remove a child from a normal classroom" (Id.). Senator Williams, the principal author of the bill, restated that the procedures were intended to "ensure that handicapped children are educated with children who are not handicapped" (121 *Cong. Rec.* 20,432 [1975]).

The substantive standards established in Section 1412(5)(B) allow the removal of the child from the regular education class only when the school district can prove that the child cannot be satisfactorily educated with supplementary aids and services.

Since 1989 in *Daniel R.R. v. State Board of Education* (874 F.2d 1036 [5th Cir. 1989]), the federal courts have developed a standard for determining when placement full time in a regular education class with supplementary aids and services is appropriate and when removal to a special education class is educationally justified.

In *Daniel R.R.*, the first of these cases, the Fifth Circuit was called upon to apply the "strong preference in favor of mainstreaming" contained in Section 1412(5)(B) to a case involving the education of a child with mental retardation in a regular education class. This decision contains an excellent framework for analyzing the application of Section 1412(5)(B), which has been adopted with some modification by other appellate courts.

The Circuit Court stated in *Daniel R.R.* that the first step is to "examine whether the state has taken steps to accommodate the handicapped child in regular education" (874 F.2d at 1048):

The Act requires states to provide supplementary aids and services and to modify the regular education program when they mainstream handicapped children. If the state has made no effort to take such accommodating steps, our inquiry ends, for the state is in violation of the Act's express mandate to supplement and modify regular education. If the state is providing supplementary aids and services and is modifying its regular education program, we must examine whether its efforts are sufficient. The Act does not permit states to make mere token gestures to accommodate handicapped students; its requirement for modifying and supplementing regular education is broad. (Id. [emphasis added])

The Fifth Circuit, in *Daniel R.R.*, set forth two limits to the accommodation requirements: 1) the regular education teacher is not required to devote all or most of his or her time to the disabled child, and 2) the regular education program need not be modified beyond recognition (824 F.2d at 1049).

The next step set forth by the Court is to examine whether the child will benefit from regular education. The Circuit Court underscored the importance of not placing too much emphasis on academic achievement.

We reiterate, however, that academic achievement is not the only purpose of mainstreaming. Integrating a handicapped child into a non-handicapped environment may be beneficial in and of itself. Thus, our inquiry must extend beyond the educational [academic] benefits that the child may receive in regular education.

We also must examine the child's overall educational experience in the mainstreamed environment, balancing the benefits of regular and special education for each individual child. For example, a child may be able to absorb only a minimal amount of the regular education program, but may benefit enormously from the language models that his non-handicapped peers provide for him. In such a case, the benefit that the child receives from mainstreaming may tip the balance in favor of mainstreaming, even if the child cannot flourish academically. (Id. at 1049)

In recognizing the purposes and benefits of mainstreaming, the Fifth Circuit underscored a critical principle. The benefit test is not whether the disabled student can perform at the same level or pace as her non-disabled classmates. As the Fifth Circuit clearly articulated in *Daniel R.R.*:

We recognize that some handicapped children may not be able to master as much of the regular education curriculum as their non-handicapped classmates. This does not mean, however, that those handicapped children are not receiving any benefit from regular education. Nor does it mean that they are not receiving all of the benefit that their handicapping condition will permit. If the child's individual needs make mainstreaming appropriate, we cannot deny the child access to regular education simply because his education achievement lags behind that of his classmates. (*Daniel R.R.*, at 1047)

Finally, the Fifth Circuit states that the Court may examine the effect of the disabled child's presence on other children. Again, the standards are narrowly defined. If the child is "so disruptive" that the education of other students is "significantly impaired," placement in the regular education environment would not be appropriate (874 F.2d at 1049, citing 34 C.F.R. § 300.552 [Comment]). In addition, regular education placement may not be appropriate if the disabled child requires "so much of the instructor's attention that the instructor will have to ignore the other student's needs in order to tend to the handicapped child" (Id.). However, the court also stated that a teacher's assistant or aide must be considered to lessen the burden on the teacher.

Following the *Daniel R.R.* decision, the Eleventh Circuit issued a decision unequivocally supporting placement in regular classes if appropriate for children with mental retardation.

In *Greer v. Rome City School District* (950 F.2d 688 [11th Cir. 1991]), the Court considered whether the school district was obligated under Section 1412(B)(5) to place a child with Down syndrome who "functioned like a moderately mentally handicapped child . . . with significant deficits in language and articulation skills" (p. 5) in a "regular class with non-handicapped students at her neighborhood school" (Id. at 691). The facts of *Greer* are almost identical to those of the *Holland* case discussed below. The court described the facts as follows:

> The school district presented Christy's parents with a proposed IEP for Christy, which had been drawn up by school officials prior to this meeting. School officials explained to Christy's parents that she required more attention than other children in the regular kindergarten class, that she was not keeping up with the kindergarten curriculum, and that she required repeated rehearsal and practice of basic skills in an individualized setting. The school psychologist expressed his belief that, although Christy may make some progress in a regular kindergarten class, she would make more progress in a special education class. In support of his belief, the psychologist explained that special education teachers were specifically trained to work with children like Christy, but he did not give any concrete examples of other children like Christy who had progressed in special education. (Id.)

The special education administrator testified at the administrative hearing that Christy could not make progress in the regular class but could make progress in a self-contained segregated class (Id. at 692).

At trial the administrator attempted to defend her position by stating that "it was very clear that Christy's cognitive functioning level . . . is a severe impairment" (Id. at 693). This statement reflects a bias and predetermination that because of a "severe impairment" regular class placement is automatically discounted.

As in all of the full inclusion cases, the parties presented conflicting expert testimony reflecting differing educational philosophies and biases. In *Greer*, as in *Holland*, however, the Court concluded that the evidence clearly established that Christy made academic progress in the regular kindergarten (Id. at 693).

The Eleventh Circuit adopted the *Daniel R.R.* court's two-part test to determine compliance with Section 1412(5)(B):

> First we ask whether education in the regular classroom with the use of supplemental aids and services can be achieved satisfactorily. See Section 1412(5)(B). If it cannot and the school intends to provide special education or to remove the child from regular education, we ask, second, whether the school has mainstreamed the child to the maximum extent appropriate. (Id. at 696)

The Eleventh Circuit held that the case before it turned on the first prong of the two-part test and stated,

> To resolve this issue we must examine whether the school district has taken steps to accommodate the handicapped child in the regular classroom. The regulations promulgated pursuant to the Act require school districts to provide a "continuum of alternative placements . . . to meet the need of handicapped children." The continuum required must "make provision for supplementary services (such as resource room or itinerant instruction) to be provided in conjunction with regular class placement." The Act itself mandates that a handicapped child be educated in the regular classroom unless such education cannot be achieved satisfactorily with the use of supplemental aids and services. Thus, before the school district may conclude that a handicapped child should be educated outside the regular classroom, it must consider whether supplemental aids and services would permit satisfactory education in the regular classroom. The school district must consider the whole range of supplemental aids and services, including resource rooms and itinerant instruction, for which it is obligated under the Act and the regulations promulgated there under to make provision. (Id.)

The Court discussed several factors to be considered in deciding whether education in regular education can be achieved satisfactorily:

> First, the school district may compare the educational benefits that the handicapped child will receive in a regular classroom, supplemented by appropriate aids and services, with the benefits that the handicapped child will receive in a self-contained special education environment. We caution, however, that "academic achievement is not the only purpose of mainstreaming. Integrating a handicapped

child into a non-handicapped environment may be beneficial in and of itself" (quoting *Daniel R.R.*). Accordingly, a determination by the school district that a handicapped child will make academic progress more quickly in a self-contained special education environment may not justify educating the child in that environment if the child would receive considerable non-academic benefit, such as language and role modeling, from association with his or her non-handicapped peers.

Second, the school district may consider what effect the presence of the handicapped child in a regular classroom would have on the education of other children in that classroom. . . . A handicapped child who merely requires more teacher attention than most other children is not likely to be so disruptive as to significantly impair the education of other children. In weighing this factor, the school district must keep in mind its obligation to consider supplemental aids and services that could accommodate a handicapped child's need for additional attention.

Third, the school district may consider the cost of the supplemental aids and services that will be necessary to achieve a satisfactory education for the handicapped child in a regular classroom. (Id. at 697)

The Court further explained that even if the cost of "appropriate supplemental aids and services would be incrementally more expensive than educating the child in a self-contained special education classroom," a school district may have to place the child in a regular education class (Id. at 697). However, the Court noted a limitation to the costs a school district must incur; if the cost of educating a disabled child in a regular classroom "is so great that it would significantly impact upon the education of other children in the district, then education in a regular classroom is not appropriate." (Id.)

In applying the facts to the law in *Greer,* the Court stated that

first, school officials failed to consider the full range of supplemental aids and services, including resource rooms and itinerant instruction, that could be provided to assist Christy in the regular classroom. . . . School officials determined that Christy's "severe impairment" justified placement in a self-contained special education classroom without considering whether Christy could be accommodated with appropriate supplemental aids and services in a regular classroom. (Id. at 698)

In *Greer*, the Court found that the school district violated the integration requirements of Section 1412(5)(B) and the regulations that interpret that section by failing to consider the full range of supplemental aids and services that could assist Christy in the regular classroom and the benefits of regular education placement, by failing to modify the curriculum to accommodate Christy and by predetermining the placement without following the proper IEP procedures (Id).

Following *Greer*, the next court to address the specific issue of "full inclusion" of a child with developmental disabilities was the Third Circuit in *Oberti v. Board of Education* (995 F.2d 1204 [3d Cir. 1993]).

In *Oberti* the Third Circuit also affirmed a lower court decision that the school district failed to consider the appropriate factors in removing Rafael, an 8-year-old boy with Down syndrome, from the regular classroom and placing him in a segregated special education class. The school district maintained that Rafael could not remain in a regular classroom because of his behavior problems. Even after any behavior difficulties abated in the following years the school still did not take any steps to mainstream Rafael (Id. at 1208–1209).

In addition to identifying the factors relevant to determining the appropriateness of regular class placement, the Third Circuit emphasized that where the law's mainstreaming requirement is specifically at issue, the burden of proving compliance with this requirement is squarely on the school district. The Court explained:

> The Act's strong preference in favor of mainstreaming, 20 U.S.C. 1412(5)(B), would be turned on its head if parents had to prove that their child was worthy of being included, rather than the school district having to justify a decision to exclude the child from the regular classroom. (Id. at 1219)

The Court outlined the factors that should be considered in determining whether a child can be satisfactorily educated in a regular classroom: 1) whether the school district has made reasonable efforts to accommodate the child in a regular classroom with supplementary aids and services; 2) a comparison of the educational benefits available in a regular class and the benefits of a special education class; and 3) the possible negative effects of inclusion on other students.

In examining the facts of this case, the Circuit Court found that the school's efforts to accommodate Rafael in the regular class were insufficient:

> The School District made only negligible efforts to include Rafael in a regular classroom. Specifically, the court found that during the 1989–90 school year, the only period during which the School District mainstreamed Rafael in a regular classroom, the School District placed Rafael in the developmental kindergarten class "without a curriculum plan, without a behavior management plan, and without providing adequate special education support to the teacher" (*Oberti II*. 801 F. Supp. at 1402; see also Id. at 1396, 1398). Further, the court found that the School District has since refused to include Rafael in a regular classroom largely based on the behavioral problems experienced by Rafael in the kindergarten class during the 1989–90 school year

(Id. at 1396, 1403). For the 1990–91 year, the court found that Rafael was placed in a segregated class with "no meaningful mainstreaming opportunities" (Id. at 1397), and that "the School District's consideration of less restrictive alternatives for the 1990–91 school year was perfunctory (Id. at 1396; Id. at 1220–21).

The Third Circuit placed heavy emphasis on the use of supplementary aids and services as a means of accommodating a disabled child. The use of these services in the regular classrooms, the Court explained, is the key to resolving any tension between the law's presumption in favor of regular placement and providing an individualized program tailored to the specific needs of each disabled child (Id. at 1214).

As to the second factor, the educational benefits, the Third Circuit found that "many of the special education techniques used in the segregated [special education] class could be successfully imported into a regular classroom and that the regular teacher could be trained to apply these techniques" (Id. at 1222). The Court took particular note of the "unique benefits the child may obtain from integration in a regular classroom, which cannot be achieved in a segregated environment, i.e. the development of social and communication skills from interaction with non-disabled peers" (Id. at 1216). The Court also noted "the reciprocal benefits of inclusion to the non-disabled students in the class" (Id. at 1217) and "found that the non-disabled children will likewise benefit from inclusion of Rafael in a regular classroom" (Id. at 1221–1222). On reviewing the evidence presented by the respective experts, the Third Circuit concluded that a comparison of the educational benefits for Rafael of regular versus special education placement did not support a segregated placement or comply with the law (Id. at 1222).

As for the need to modify the curriculum, the Court stated:

> We agree with the district court's legal conclusion that, although including Rafael in a regular classroom would require the School District to modify the curriculum, the need for such modification is "not a legitimate basis upon which to justify excluding a child" from the regular classroom unless the education of other students is significantly impaired (citing *Oberti II*, 801 F. Supp. at 1403). (Id.)

Thus, the Court in *Oberti* agreed with the Court in *Greer*, that the modification of the curriculum is significant only with respect to its effect on other students. The degree of curriculum modification needed for a particular disabled child is not determinative in and of itself.

Finally, the Third Circuit in *Oberti* addressed the third factor, the potentially "disruptive effect" of Rafael in the regular class, by noting that Rafael's behavior problems several years earlier were "exacerbated and remained uncontained due to the inadequate level of services" when Rafael was in the regular kindergarten (Id. at 1222–1223). With appropriate services there was no reason to believe any behavior problems could not be addressed in the regular class if these problems were still present (Id.). The Court concluded that "consideration of the possible negative effects of Rafael in the regular classroom did not support the School District's decision to exclude him from the regular classroom" (Id. at 1223).

In the fourth and most recent of the federal appellate court decisions, *Sacramento City Unified School District v. Rachel Holland* (No. 92-15608 [9th Cir. 1994]), the Ninth Circuit affirmed and adopted the district court's analysis and adhered closely to the standards set forth by the circuit courts in *Daniel R.R.*, *Greer*, and *Oberti* to analyze the application of Section 1412(5)(B) to this case. This case involved the issue of whether Rachel Holland, now an 11-year-old girl who is "moderately mentally retarded," could be educated satisfactorily full time in a regular class with supplementary aids and services.

As the Ninth Circuit explained, the following factors were applied in determining if Rachel could be satisfactorily educated in the regular class with supplementary aids and services: 1) the educational or academic benefits for the child in the regular class as compared to the benefits of a special education classroom; 2) the non-academic benefits of integration with non-disabled children; 3) the effect of the presence of the handicapped child on the teacher and other children in the regular classroom; and 4) the costs of supplementary aids and services. (*Holland*, No. 92-15608 at 628).

Similar to the court in *Oberti*, the district court in *Holland* did not treat the extent of curriculum modification as a separate and distinct factor. Instead the court explained that this factor is relevant only with respect to the other factors, including the degree of burden on the regular education teacher and the child's "sense of belonging" in the classroom (*Board of Education, Sacramento City Unified School District v. Holland*, 786 F. Supp. 875, 880 [E.D. Cal. 1192]). This analysis is also consistent with the *Daniel R.R.* decision. In *Daniel R.R.*, the Fifth Circuit stated that curriculum modification was relevant with respect to the amount of teacher time the disabled child required and to establishing whether the child received any benefit (*Daniel R.R.*, 874 F.2d at 1048–1049). The district court in *Holland*, however, did consider the extent to which Rachel's needs coincided with the needs of her classmates. The court concluded, based on the testimony of Rachel's second-grade teacher, Ms. Crone, that Rachel is a full member of the second-grade class. She participates in all activities. For the class as a whole, Crone's major areas of emphasis are socialization, behavior and communication. These are the same areas of emphasis in Rachel's IEP. (Id. at 881)

In applying these factors, the district court closely examined the evidence and the extensive record in *Holland*. Further description of how the district court applied the facts of this case to the legal standard is, therefore, particularly instructive. With respect to the first factor, the comparative educational benefits of regular and special education classes, the district court recognized that the goals and objectives of Rachel's IEP can be achieved in the regular class, with curriculum modification and supplementary aids and services. The court found credible the testimony that Rachel made "significant academic progress" in the regular education class at the Shalom School, that she is learning language and modeling other skills from her non-disabled peers, and that "her motivation to learn stems from the regular class placement." Because of the conflict among the experts, the trial court found the testimony of Rachel's second grade teacher, Ms. Crone, "all the more important" (Id. at 881), citing her testimony describing Rachel's academic progress on her IEP goals, reciting both English and Hebrew alphabets, her expanded communication and language abilities and sentence length.

The court also relied on evidence that Rachel derived significant nonacademic benefits from regular class placement, particularly in her social and communication skills, that Rachel had developed greater self-confidence and independence, is excited and enthusiastic about school, and "relishes the new friendships she has developed at the Shalom School" (Id. at 882). The court acknowledged Ms. Crone's characterization of Rachel as being a "typical second grader" in many respects, a full member of her second-grade class, an eager participant and motivated learner (Id.).

In addition to finding the benefits of regular class placement for Rachel, the court found that the school district failed to meet the burden of showing that the special education class was at least equal or superior to the regular education class in providing academic benefit (Id. at 880). The court also found "no empirical evidence" to support the district's assertion that Rachel's goals and objectives could best be met in a special education setting (Id. at 881–882). Her school district special education teacher reported a very slow rate of learning, little progress, little interaction with peers, and testified that she derived little benefit from being "shuttled" into a regular kindergarten class for brief visits (Id. at

882). What the District's case did demonstrate most strikingly was their bias (the school district's and their assessment team's bias) against mainstreaming anyone with Rachel's IQ (Id. at 881). Mr. Froshnider, an expert witness for the school district who assessed Rachel, admitted that "we have never recommended one hundred percent inclusion" (R.T. 55:18–26, 101:2–5, 179: 13–16).

In the district court, Judge Levi noted the sharply different points of view of the experts for the school district and the parents. He attributed the contrary assessments of Rachel to "conflicting educational philosophies":

> The Diagnostic Center witnesses [school district's assessors] do not believe that a child with Rachel's IQ can be effectively educated in a regular classroom. They believe that Rachel's education at this point should focus on functional skills, such as handling money, doing laundry, and using public transportation. Conversely, the *Holland* experts believe that all handicapped children, even children with much greater handicaps than Rachel, are best educated in regular classrooms. They believe that it is a mistake to limit Rachel's learning opportunities to functional skills. . . .
>
> [B]ecause of the radically different points of view from which they start, their observations on Rachel's academic progress are by no means objective. Nonetheless, the court finds more credible the *Holland* witnesses' testimony concerning Rachel's academic progress. First, these witnesses have more background in evaluating handicapped children placed in regular classrooms, and they had greater opportunity to observe Rachel over an extended period of time in normal circumstances. Moreover, it appears that for much of the formalized testing by the Diagnostic Center, Rachel was uncomfortable and unhappy. Finally, [to] the extent that the *Holland* witnesses have a preference for mainstreaming, it is a preference shared by Congress and embodied in the IDEA. (*Holland*, 786 F. Supp. at 881)

Finally, the district court addressed two concerns related to Rachel's effect on others in the class (Id. at 883). First, based on testimony from her classroom teachers, the Court found that Rachel clearly does not present a disruption or distraction for other students (Id.). With respect to the second consideration (whether Rachel's presence in the classroom is unduly burdensome on the teacher and takes up too much of the teacher's time), the Court relied on a variety of evidence. Her second-grade teacher, for example, testified that Rachel presents no such burden (Id.).

In the face of the consistent testimony from three regular education teachers who actually had Rachel in their classes, the school district tried to rely on the testimony of a district first-grade teacher, Sharon Helmar, at the administrative hearing, who speculated that Rachel would be a burden to her. This teacher never had Rachel in her class and, in fact, did not know Rachel at all. The school district also cited the teacher's testimony stating, "Ms. Helmar also made it clear that in order to pass her second grade class, the students must be able to pass a reading requirement, which Rachel could not do" (*Holland*, No. 92-15608, Appellant's Brief at 22). This exemplified the District's misunderstanding. As the appellate courts in the "inclusion" cases have stated unequivocally, the law does not require disabled children to be performing at grade level in order to participate in regular classes. (See *Daniel R.R.* supra at 1047–48, *Greer* supra at 697.)

Given the weight of the testimony, the district court found that based on the relevant facts, Rachel had been receiving at least, a "satisfactory education" in regular class.

On the factor of the cost of mainstreaming, the Ninth Circuit in *Holland* affirmed the district court's findings that the school district failed to present any persuasive or credible evidence that educating Rachel in a regular classroom with appropriate services would be significantly more expensive than educating Rachel in the district's proposed setting or that the costs of regular class placement would adversely affect the education of other children in the school district (*Holland*, No. 92-15608 at 630–631).

CONCLUSION

The IDEA explicitly provides that children with disabilities be educated in regular education classes unless "education in regular classes with the use of supplementary aids and services cannot be achieved satisfactorily" (20 U.S.C. § 1412[5][B]). The determination of whether a child has been mainstreamed to the maximum extent appropriate requires a fact-specific individualized inquiry and the application of the facts to the legal standards articulated by the appellate courts. In order for these legal standards to make a real difference in the lives of children with disabilities, educators must continue to develop and implement educational methodologies and reforms that ensure that all children can receive a meaningful education in the regular education classroom.

23

NEW TRENDS IN DISABILITY STUDIES
IMPLICATIONS FOR EDUCATIONAL POLICY

HARLAN HAHN

In the final quarter of the 20th century, the adoption of PL 94-142, Section 504 of the Rehabilitation Act, and the Americans with Disabilities Act has signaled profound changes in disability policy. These developments have been promoted both by the growth of the disability rights movement and by an emerging transition from a "functional limitations" paradigm, which concentrates on the effects of impairments, to a "minority group" model that opens numerous opportunities for research on social and political discrimination. Although much of the new legislation was based on the "minority group" perspective, many analyses of educational and other issues have continued to reflect vestiges of the earlier emphasis on "functional limitations."

Perhaps the clearest example of the contrast between these two paradigms is revealed by changing definitions of disability. Whereas the prior model was founded on medical concepts (which stress physiological limits) or economic orientations (which focus on vocational restrictions), the foundation of the "minority group" approach is a sociopolitical definition. According to this view, disability is a consequence of the interaction between individuals and the environment. Thus, disability is no longer a personal defect or deficiency;

This chapter is from Hahn, H. (1995). New trends in disability studies: Implications for educational policy. *NCERI Bulletin,* 2(1), 1–6; reprinted by permission.

instead, it is primarily the product of a disabling environment. As a result, education in a segregated or discriminatory environment is almost certain to have an adverse impact on disabled students, regardless of the rationale that attempts to justify it. In addition, researchers are beginning to develop a multidisciplinary field of "disability studies," based on the experience of disabled persons, that might contribute a significant dimension to teaching about diversity. The implications of these trends not only seem to indicate a clear analogy between disability and race, ethnicity, or gender, but they also highlight epistemological issues that may affect a wide range of educational policies.

Nonetheless, the gradual decline of the functional limitations paradigm has also been marked by a form of resistance that has tended to marginalize disabled children and adults. In education, for example, desegregation has been translated euphemistically as "mainstreaming," standards of equality have been redefined as the "least restrictive environment," and remedies have emphasized legal protection and professional intervention instead of empowerment. (As a term that implies integration, "inclusion" can be interpreted from a disability rights perspective as virtually equivalent to desegregation.) While some concepts may reflect basic misunderstandings about the nature and meaning of disability, many also appear to indicate a tendency by educators to regard the rights of disabled persons as "special" rather than as fundamental guarantees available to every citizen.

The purpose of this chapter is to explore the educational implications of the "minority group" model for the study of disability. The first section examines the effects of medical, economic, and sociopolitical definitions on educational policies and practices. The second portion investigates the impact of the educational environment on disabled students. Proposals for changing schools, especially to promote equality and to end discrimination on the basis of disability, are presented in conclusion. The presentation, therefore, is designed to provide both an analysis of emerging issues in disability research and a vision of the future.

EDUCATIONAL IMPLICATIONS OF DISABILITY DEFINITIONS

The Medical Approach

Perhaps the most popular understanding of disability is based on a medical definition. This orientation probably emerged during the

Enlightenment from the philosophy of liberal individualism that replaced the religious interpretation of disability as either a curse of the devil or a legitimate object of charity. From a medical vantage point, the problems of a disability arise almost exclusively from pathological impairments, or a physical or mental inability to perform so-called normal tasks. But hardly anyone is capable of performing all of life's activities at a "normal" level, a fact that gives credence to the familiar adage that "everyone is handicapped," at least in some respect. Moreover, medical standards or measurements of "normal" functioning—or of corporeal perfection—are never specified precisely. And, by the time most disabled students enter the schoolroom, they usually have completed an extensive program of treatment or rehabilitation designed to restore their functional capacities to the maximum extent possible.

From the perspective of many disabled individuals, their principal difficulties do not result from physical or mental limitations or from functional concerns. On the contrary, their major problems reflect the discrimination that emerges from efforts to cope with an environment generally designed by and for the nondisabled. Consequently, a growing number of disabled people perceive disability as another manifestation of human differences rather than as a lack of functional capabilities. In their view, the principles of the *Brown* decision can be applied to disabled students without significant modification. Separate educational facilities are inherently unequal. And, if the separation of African American and white students—as well as women and men—can have a debilitating impact on the academic attainments of the former groups, the segregation of disabled and nondisabled young people seems virtually certain to have similar effects.

From this viewpoint, the failure of medical research to provide a satisfactory explanation or remedy for the major difficulties confronting disabled children and adults probably can be attributed to three factors. The first is the inapplicability of the "medical model," derived from experience with acute illnesses, to chronic or permanent bodily conditions. Especially irrelevant is Parson's structural-functional definition of the "sick role" as an exemption from ordinary social responsibilities provided that "patients" submit to professional supervision and devote all of their energies to the eventual goal of full recovery. But disabled people are neither "sick" nor can they be relegated to little more than an unending role as "patients." And, of course, in most cases, the complete restoration of all physical and mental capabilities is not a feasible objective.

Second are the constraints of a clinical orientation that usually confine the search for causes and solutions to problems concerning disability to an area demarcated by the outer boundaries of the human body. Educators and other professionals interested in disability often encounter an apparently inescapable dilemma: They can force the individual to adapt to the present environment, or they can adapt the environment to the person. But, since complete recovery seems precluded by the concept of permanent or chronic conditions, attention must eventually shift to the latter endeavor.

Finally, disabled children and adults are plagued by the issue of biological inferiority. Whereas other groups have generally succeeded in disproving this explanation of social inequality based on gender, race or ethnicity, and sexual orientation, this interpretation is still commonly associated with the disadvantaged status of people with disabilities. The logical implications of the argument, however, would seem to require policy makers to establish a specific level of physical and mental competence, or mastery of the existing environment, as a prerequisite for exercising the rights of citizenship, including the right to "a free, appropriate education." While some American eugenicists obviously would have favored such criteria earlier in the 20th century, this possibility has been seemingly foreclosed by the *PARC* and *Mills* decisions. Mastery of an unaccommodating and inhospitable environment is not an acceptable requirement for participation in a democratic society.

The Economic Orientation

The perspective most widely adopted in public policy reflects an economic understanding that tends to equate disability with unemployability. Although disabled children and adults may have played a productive role in many households prior to the separation of home and work, this definition seemed to derive in part from their historical status as beggars and recipients of private charity. The concept of the "sick role" also supported the creation of social-welfare policies granting benefits to disabled persons deemed incapable of securing employment; and, somewhat inconsistently, vocational rehabilitation programs provide some of them with training, often for entry-level jobs that offer few opportunities for promotion.

Both the meager benefits and the confusion fostered by economic approaches to disability have seemed to reinforce Marxist claims that disabled workers are part of an "industrial reserve army" relieving capitalist economies from excessive demands for employment. In fact, during World War II, disabled people joined housewives, racial or ethnic minorities, and aging workers as replacements in the labor force for nondisabled males serving in the armed forces; and they were excluded from employment again by discriminatory medical exams when veterans returned from military combat. Other investigations have indicated that the increased payment of disability benefits may reflect the failure of many workers to adjust to the transition from an industrial to a service economy. And physical appearance has seemed to become an increasingly significant criteria for employment. One analysis even has indicated that policy makers may be relatively satisfied as long as excess political rewards and advantages "do not flow to groups that are perceived as blatantly dissimilar." As a result, economic and political elites expect schools to furnish them with a constant supply of relatively young, attractive, nondisabled workers (especially white males) with middle-class values; and a disproportionate share of government funding is devoted to educating individuals who possess these traits. By contrast, of course, fewer resources are allocated to schools and programs that attempt to teach comparatively unattractive, working-class, aging, or disabled students as well as women and racial or ethnic minorities.

These patterns are not likely to persist indefinitely, however. With the adoption of measures prohibiting employment discrimination and requiring employers to provide "reasonable accommodations" for disabled workers under the Americans with Disabilities Act, as an example, teachers face the challenge of preparing students with disabilities for skilled managerial and professional rather than entry-level positions. Employers are also likely to confront growing litigation to narrow the definition of "bona fide occupational qualifications," which often contain unspoken assumptions that have a discriminatory impact on job applicants with disabilities. And mounting controversies about employer preferences regarding physical appearance may emerge as cultural issues become increasingly salient in a hegemonic post-industrial economy.

The Sociopolitical Definition

The foundation of the "minority group" model is a sociopolitical definition of disability that focuses on the external environment instead of personal traits. This shift enabled researchers to recognize that disabled people have many of the same characteristics as other minorities. Not only are they plagued by extraordinarily high rates of poverty, welfare dependency, and unemployment, but they also confront obstacles in housing, transportation, social communication, and public accommodations that are equivalent to traditional barriers separating whites and African Americans. And, of course, many disabled women and men have been educated in a school system that is fundamentally segregated.

From a sociopolitical perspective, the basic source of this inequality can be traced to public attitudes. Although relatively little attention has been devoted to the comparison, for example, Richardson's research on pictures of children revealed that preferences for a nondisabled playmate seemed to develop at an earlier age and to be more prevalent than the choice of white dolls in Clark's famous experiment. Perhaps the principal missing element in the former studies, which appeared to disclose a deep-seated rejection of youngsters with various types of disabilities by nondisabled adults, as well as children, is any discussion of self-hatred. But most disabled persons have probably been too heavily burdened by stigmatizing attitudes for researchers to give serious consideration to this issue. In fact, psychological adjustment has been the major palliative traditionally proposed by social scientists for dealing with both functional difficulties and the stigma of a visible or labeled disability.

Perhaps the principal reason for the relative neglect of attitudes in disability research can be ascribed to a pervasive sense of paternalism that may have been bequeathed by the legacy of benevolent charity. But disabled children and adults are seldom unaware of the negative feelings faintly concealed beneath the surface of social interactions that frequently are exposed by a tendency to shun or avoid them. The failure of nondisabled professionals to focus on this phenomenon may represent a forum of denial created in part by guilt. And, of course, institutional practices that reinforce this pattern of avoidance by segregating disabled and nondisabled students in the schools only tend to exacerbate the effects of stigma.

Although psychoanalytic concepts concerning the symbolism of bodily injury can also be adduced to interpret unconscious aversion to people with disabilities, probably the most readily available explanation for unfavorable attitudes toward disability can be traced to "stranger anxiety," or the tendency of infants to display discomfort in the presence of anyone who appears alien or unfamiliar. Although this process might contribute to a definition of the self by permitting children to distinguish between what is "like me" and "not like me," it also seems to underscore the point that disparaging views of disability often are based on reactions to visible human differences rather than on perceptions of functional loss. In addition, such responses may be subtly reinforced by media images of an idealized physical appearance or attractiveness that viewers are encouraged to emulate.

In fact, it has been proposed that attitudinal discrimination against disabled persons can be traced either to "existential" anxiety, the fear of progressive debility and death, or to "aesthetic" anxiety, a repugnant feeling about physical features that are culturally defined as undesirable or unappealing. While "existential anxiety" has been related to the "functional limitations" paradigm, "aesthetic anxiety" has been linked with the "minority group" model. The association between aesthetic displeasure and bodily deviance or strangeness seems to underscore the importance of desegregation or inclusion in the education of nondisabled as well as disabled students. All children must learn that human beings come in different "packaging" and that everybody is entitled to dignity and respect, regardless of physical appearance. Students with visible disabilities can play a crucial role in teaching their nondisabled counterparts this valuable lesson. Furthermore, the dangers of paternalism indicate that efforts to protect disabled children from the unfavorable responses of their classmates are inadvisable. The insults of the playground can be cruel, but learning to cope with offensive comments there probably represents indispensable preparation in acquiring the social skills they may need in later years.

Changing Educational Environments

The implications of the sociopolitical definition clearly indicate a need to alter the educational environment rather than to pursue continuous efforts to modify the functional characteristics of disabled students. Since separation on the basis of disability is apt to leave an enduring imprint on the hearts and minds of disabled young people, desegregation or inclusion is a fundamental component of this process. In addition, other changes might be appropriately guided by the principle of Equal Environmental Adaptations, which is designed to provide commensurate advantages for disabled and nondisabled persons. (This concept has also been proposed as a standard for interpreting the "reasonable accommodations" clause of the Americans with Disabilities Act.) Perhaps the clearest example of this criterion is symbolized by the presence of chairs in most classrooms. Chairs are an accommodation to the needs of nondisabled students; but they are of no value to many disabled persons, such as myself, who are considerate enough to bring our own chairs. Without chairs, nondisabled students would undoubtedly become fatigued from standing or sitting on the floor, they would probably be discouraged from attending classes, and their performance on tests and other evaluations might be adversely affected. Since the sociopolitical perspective treats disability as a generic concept rather than as a product of specific diagnostic or other classifications, commensurate benefits for disabled students must extend beyond providing accessible restrooms, widening the aisles between library stacks, and installing ramps or elevators for wheelchair users; they should also include a broad range of accommodations to various types of disabilities. Chairs are a major item in many school budgets, but Equal Environmental Adaptations cannot be measured by economic considerations alone. Perhaps most important, they signify only one facet of the "taken-for-granted" environment that confers many significant advantages on the nondisabled and corresponding disadvantages on disabled students. Increased acceptance of the sociopolitical definition of *disability* is likely to yield numerous other examples of similar disparities in educational settings.

Persons with sensory disabilities have been especially disadvantaged by the intrinsic inequality of educational environments. Many books are unavailable in braille or on tape for students with vision impairments, and schools may not provide readers. Perhaps the most common form of discrimination in classroom instruction, however, results from an exclusive reliance on verbal communication. As a result, the education of students with hearing impairments usually has occurred in residential institutions that offered a basis for organized cohesion; and deaf persons have made more progress in forming a distinctive culture than any other group of people with disabilities. At least part of the solution in each case seems to require increased experimentation with written and audiovisual as well as multiple modes of communication.

The most significant—and the most expensive—component of the educational environment, however, consists of personnel. While there is a danger that teachers may be unduly influenced by first impressions of the appearance of students that are perpetuated through subsequent grades, no definitive method or formula for the effective teaching of students with disabilities has been discovered. In fact, these issues raise even broader questions about what the schools should teach, at what pace, and for what purpose. Obviously the debate about these matters cannot be resolved here. But the mere fact that the controversies persist can be interpreted as indicating that the line between mental and physical disabilities may not be as clear as it is commonly drawn. They often overlap; but, especially in the absence of a precise statement of priorities such as the relative importance of academic materials and social skills, the conclusion that some disabled children are incapable of attaining significant educational objectives would seem to be unwarranted or at least premature. Much of the information that students are presently expected to learn in the schools also reflects the demands of an environment designed for the nondisabled that can, of course, be modified or altered. By contrast, the eventual goal of the disability rights movement is an environment adapted to the needs of everyone, including children who bear the label of severe mental retardation; men and women at the peak of their physical and intellectual prowess; and aging persons with chronic, progressive, or terminal health problems.

Another critical key to the puzzle is indicated by a major conclusion of one of the first examinations of disability to adopt the "minority group" model. This study of disabled children, which was appropriately titled "The Unexpected Minority," discovered that youngsters with major physical and other disabilities frequently acquire skills at a rate that defies the expectations of developmental psychologists. While some of them have difficulty with problems that nondisabled children ordinarily resolve at a relatively early age, they often display talents that their nondisabled peers do not gain until a later stage of development. Perhaps part of the reason for these variations can be ascribed to discrepancies between the experience of disabled and nondisabled children. The finding also indicates the pitfalls of attempting to establish "normal" standards of personal abilities, but it presents a serious challenge to school curricula that are usually based on modal patterns. Further research on the development of disabled children could yield significant improvements in planning educational programs.

Perhaps the most crucial challenge facing teachers, however, emerges from the task of relating to the everyday experience of disabled individuals. Most educational theories have been formulated with little, if any, regard for disability; and most teachers are not disabled themselves. As a result, disabled students and their teachers may stare at each other daily in the classroom across a vast chasm produced by divergent understandings and lifestyles. Given the prevalence of paternalistic attitudes, teachers may sympathize rather than empathize with their disabled pupils; or they may have trouble in coping with barely conscious feelings of avoidance and aversion. Perhaps an increased appreciation of the strengths instead of the presumed deficiencies of disabled students might improve the attitudes of teachers whose negative perceptions of inclusion often seem to be based on the belief that they will be overburdened by an excessive need for attention and assistance.

The issues created by the gap between disabled students and nondisabled teachers also involve complex epistemological questions implicit in the controversy within higher education over plans to promote the study of cultural diversity. Part of this debate, of course, revolves about the contention that conventional canons of academic knowledge tend to silence the voice of the Other, or groups that have traditionally been marginalized or excluded from the mainstream of society. Among researchers interested in disability studies, questions about whether or not a "disability culture" can be identified are still controversial. Perhaps a major part of the difficulty is that, unlike most other minorities, disabled people do not have a sense of generational continuity that would otherwise permit the legacy of their accumulated experiences to be transmitted over time. Nor have universities generally regarded the subject as a legitimate area of scholarly inquiry. As a result, disabled people have no history, no prominent role models, and little awareness of the advantages as well as the disadvantages of their distinctive perspective. Thus, parents, teachers, and other professionals have been deprived of a critical source of information and insights. Yet, inspired in part by the disability rights movement, growing numbers of disabled people have begun to share common experiences and viewpoints. Increased investigations of these experiences could add a valuable dimension to the curriculum at all levels.

Does this mean that IQ and other tests might be culturally biased on the basis of disability? Although hardly any attempts have been made to conduct item-by-item analyses, the answer seems to be a tentative yes. Most instruments are designed to measure existing competence rather than individual potential. Since almost all women and men with disabilities have been molded and taught in a disabling environment, these assessments can scarcely be expected to provide an accurate indication of their actual capabilities. In order to remove these disadvantages, educational programs for disabled students must be evaluated by an appropriate standard of equality.

Toward Equality in Education

From the opening line of the Declaration of Independence to the historic words of the Supreme Court in the *Brown* decision, equality has been a central value in the American political tradition. Yet, there are significant variations in standards that have been proposed to measure this concept. From a sociopolitical perspective, some of these definitions can be appropriately applied to the circumstances of disabled students, while other meanings seem either undesirable or not politically feasible.

Perhaps one of the most traditional, and least stringent, conventional interpretations of this standard is the concept of equality before the law. Although this definition is supposed to yield fairness or impartiality, the mantle of objectivity that surrounds judicial rulings—and educational tests—based on this concept of equality often seems to conceal the interests both of the persons implementing this principle and of the groups to which it is applied. As a result, for example, many feminists, who became frustrated by patriarchal values that permeate the law, have abandoned the quest for this form of equality; and they have urged judges and law makers to make decisions based on an explicit consciousness of the disadvantaged status of women. The same point is applicable to people with disabilities. Since their principal problems stem from discriminatory attitudes at a conscious or an unconscious level, many of them do not expect nondisabled policy makers to approach educational issues in a neutral or impartial manner. Particularly troubling to some is the negative phrasing of the concept of "the least restrictive environment," which was derived from court cases about incarceration rather than about discrimination based on race, ethnicity, or gender.

Another relatively conservative view that has been widely accepted in American law is the notion of equality of opportunity. According to this perspective, the basic conditions of equality in "the race of life" are satisfied as long as all of the contestants are lined up evenly at the starting line. In an analogy that is especially compatible with the American economic system, the outcome of this competition is supposedly determined by the principles of meritocracy that have seemingly been reflected in educational policy by a questionable belief in innate intelligence. But this metaphor ignores the context or the environment in which the competition is conducted. If the lane of the race track assigned to disabled contestants is filled with obstacles, for example, the competition can hardly be considered fair. And, for most disabled children and adults, the obstacles presented by architectural inaccessibility, communication barriers, the effects of stigmatizing attitudes, and the demands of a discriminatory environment often appear to be almost insurmountable. The solution, of course, is to "clear the track" by changing the environment instead of the person.

A related concept, which has often been implicitly invoked in discussions of discrimination based on race or ethnicity, is represented by what might be called a converging equality. From this perspective, many political leaders believe that they have fulfilled their responsibilities so long as the social and economic conditions of minorities indicate improvements or gradual progress toward a deferred dream of genuine parity. In education, this interpretation of equality appears to be represented by compensatory or remedial programs designed to reduce the gap between disadvantaged groups and segments of the population that are privileged by the circumstances of their birth or by their capacity to adapt or assimilate to the cultural demands of society. But this viewpoint leaves inequalities created by the institutional arrangement of power between dominant and subordinate groups fundamentally undisturbed. The discrepancy between this view and a stricter standard of equality signifies a major conflict between white liberals and many African Americans. And the hope for convergence has seldom been realized. Empirical indicators reveal that, while the status of racial or ethnic minorities and women has improved somewhat in recent decades, these gains have commonly been overshadowed by even greater gains in the position of white or Anglo males. The traditional faith in education as a route to upward mobility is revealed by the fact that the major possible exception to this generalization may be reflected by patterns of college enrollment among these minorities and women. Despite the provisions of PL 94-142, Section 504 of the Rehabilitation Act, and the Americans with Disabilities Act, available evidence indicates that similar trends among disabled students appear to be slight or nonexistent.

Perhaps the most appropriate standard for assessing an educational milieu fitted to the interests and needs of students with disabilities is equality of results. Assuming the possibility of defining the skills and knowledge that any person might need to survive or to flourish in a suitable environment beyond the classroom, education would continue until each student meets the required criteria. Teaching would be conducted at least in part through individual tutorials adapted to the pace at which youngsters with different developmental patterns learn. This procedure would eliminate the need for tests that attempt to assess aptitude or potential; instead, attention would focus on the creation of standardized evaluations of demonstrated performance and on the identification of necessary or essential requirements for participation in a democratic society. This approach is based on the radical assumption that all human beings have equal dignity and worth. In many respects, an even more desirable proposal is embodied in the idea of equal shares, which could be pursued by mobilizing educational and other resources to combat poverty and to ensure that everybody can secure an acceptable measure of personal or material success. Implementation of the concepts of equal resources or shares, however, would probably necessitate a substantial redistribution of financial revenue from those occupations that obtain fiscal benefits primarily from the private sector of the economy to other groups, such as children, who receive such rewards in large measure from public programs. As a result, both concepts are likely to arouse intense political resistance among adults who believe that they are entitled to enjoy their status as the beneficiaries of social and economic privileges without paying for them.

As America approaches the close of the 20th century, therefore, the most immediate issue on the agenda of educational programs for students with disabilities appears to revolve about acceptance of the principle of Equality of Environment Adaptations. The objective of this concept, which reflects only a slight extension of the conservative criterion of equal opportunities, is simply to establish parity, or commensurate benefits, for disabled and nondisabled school children. Although the costs of such a policy cannot be calculated yet because little systematic attention has been devoted to "taken-for-granted" advantages conferred on the nondisabled, further research is likely to uncover many additional examples of this form of inequality. In the long run, equal results may be even less expensive than equal opportunities. At a minimum, however, disabled students should not be forced to bear the stigma of a segregated school system; and mastery of the existing environment should not be considered a necessary prerequisite to exercising the rights of citizenship.

Like many other disadvantaged groups, such as women, African Americans, Latinos, Native Americans, gays and lesbians, and aging individuals, people with disabilities are striving to translate previously devalued personal characteristics into a positive sense of political identity. Part of this development has prompted a realization that, in the aftermath of a disabling incident, people generally tend to view their surroundings differently and that a "differenced" perspective can be a source of creativity that may eventually promote empowerment. Many young people with disabilities have displayed capacities to respond successfully to unusually difficult challenges that are similar to the traits educators have increasingly identified as the hallmark of students who are perceived as especially talented or gifted. People with disabilities also may acquire unusual adaptation skills as a result of their continuous efforts to cope with an inhospitable environment. Inspired by such observations and by the impetus of the disability rights movement, therefore, researchers have begun to advocate the reorganization of administrative units in universities to form a multidisciplinary curriculum in disability studies that would offer essential training not only for teachers but also for other professionals who provide services to disabled persons, including social work, gerontology, architecture, occupational therapy, nursing, medicine, and rehabilitation counseling. This approach would be based primarily on the compiled experiences of disabled people themselves rather than on theories derived from other disciplines.

Perhaps most important, a consciousness that disability simply signifies another human difference instead of functional restrictions might form the basis for a future countercultural movement to promote an increased appreciation of diversity and heterogeneity in everyday life. In a culture that seems to revere youth, heterosexuality, a powerful masculinity, whiteness, physical attractiveness, and body perfectibility, this objective may represent one of the most important missions that society can pursue.

REFERENCES

Americans with Disabilities Act (ADA) of 1990, PL 101-336, 42 U.S.C. § 12101 *et seq.*

Brown v. Board of Education, 347 U.S. 483 (1954).

Education for All Handicapped Children Act of 1975, PL 94-142, 20 U.S.C. § 1400 *et seq.*

Mills v. Board of Education, 348 F. Supp. 866 (D.C. 1972).

Pennsylvania Association for Retarded Citizens (PARC) v. Commonwealth of Pennsylvania, 334 F. Supp. 1257 (E.D. Pa. 1971).

Rehabilitation Act of 1973, PL 93-112, 29 U.S.C. § 701 *et seq.*

24

Technology and Inclusion
Are We Asking the Wrong Questions?

HARVEY PRESSMAN AND SARAH BLACKSTONE

To many people, the title of this chapter may sound a little weird. One school superintendent we tried it out on responded, "Are we asking the wrong questions about technology and inclusion? Geez, I didn't know we were supposed to be asking *any* questions about the connection between those two things. I wasn't even aware there *was* a connection." Another administrator (an elementary school principal) looked at the title, threw up her hands, and exclaimed, "To be perfectly honest, I really have no idea what questions to ask about the uses of any of the technology in my building."

We don't find these reactions surprising, but we do think it's time for educational decision makers to take a closer look at how technology is being used to facilitate, support, and/or strengthen the implementation of inclusive education in regular classrooms and how it might be used a lot more effectively toward that end. Unfortunately, it is also still necessary to ask whether and how technology may be being used to subvert or undermine the inclusion process.

Have we been asking the wrong questions about technology and inclusion? If a question leads to answers that increase segregation or that decrease children's access to the tools needed to learn alongside their peers, it is probably the wrong question. To us, examples of the wrong questions are

1. How can we give children with disabilities in our school more equal access to our computer laboratories?
2. When is it appropriate to bring children with disabilities back

329

to the resource room for a technology "hit," so they can go back to regular education for other stuff?
3. How can we use new technologies to adapt standardized tests so we can assess individuals with disabilities?
4. During what activities should the individual who uses a speech output communication device be allowed to use it?
5. How can we set up a computer workstation in the back of the classroom for a student with severe motor impairment who needs it to write, speak, do math, and so on?
6. How much one-on-one practice with a computer (or assistive device) do students need before they are ready to go into a regular education classroom?

Many of these questions are based on erroneous assumptions about "readiness." They imply that technology is an end in itself, rather than a tool that can enhance learning and participation within the regular classroom. Other questionable assumptions reflected by these questions are that 1) drill and practice with a computer reflects "best practice" or is even a particularly effective way of mastering skills, 2) standardized tests should be used in non-standardized ways with the kinds of students who weren't originally included in the standardization sample, 3) computer labs are an effective place to put computers to facilitate the learning that takes place in a school, or 4) educational tools (computers and assistive technology) that allow a child to communicate and participate in classroom activities alongside peers and to access the curriculum more successfully should not *always* be available to students who need them.

In short, the idea of segregating students with disabilities to provide them with technology time as a way of preparing them for inclusion is an old, outmoded, and discredited idea about readiness now reappearing, all dressed up in new technology duds. Even in the new clothes, it is a clear indicator that the "emperor" (or whoever the decision maker might be) doesn't have a strong sense of how to use technology as a tool that facilitates inclusion and enables students with disabilities to receive an appropriate education.

Over the past 6 years, we have worked in over 10 different communities around the country as advisers to public school programs that seek to use technology to promote inclusion. We have collaborated with colleagues, compared information with people who come to hear our conference presentations, and explored what others are doing in this field. Our experiences have led us to conclude that a very different set of questions needs to be asked about the role of technology in inclusion. These new questions should be the ones that guide decisions made by school district leaders with regard to the deployment of technology for the purpose of inclusion. We believe, for example, that we should be long past debating such issues as 1) whether technology is a significantly effective tool in promoting fuller inclusion, or 2) whether the use of technology for this purpose is sufficiently cost-effective to be used in an extensive way as a part of a child's educational plan to ensure participation in a least restrictive environment, or even 3) whether a district has the right or option to deny access to the technology necessary to the full inclusion of an individual child. We have enough data to know that the answer to the first two questions is yes, and the answer to the third question is no (cf. Wall & Siegel, 1994).

Trying to make inclusion work without technology is like trying to win a fight with one hand tied behind your back. The core issue now is *how* to use technology to promote as full and successful an inclusive situation as possible.

DIVERGENCE BETWEEN POLICY AND PRACTICE

Policy and practice diverge dramatically in the application of technology for students with special needs. Current laws and regulations support inclusion and mandate consideration of technology for students with IEPs [individualized education programs], including computers and other assistive devices (communication aids, electric wheelchairs, assistive listening devices, and so on). In practice, however, technology more often has become yet another reason to remove children with disabilities from the regular classroom, rather than a useful tool for integrating them.

One reason offered is that it is easier and more "beneficial" to provide technology services to students with special needs in segregated settings. After all, special needs personnel may already know more about technology than our classroom teachers (or "it is their job to 'bite the bullet' and learn about technology"). Also, parents may believe their children are likely to get better technology services outside the regular classroom and therefore become more willing to sanction the "pull-out" models of service delivery, despite the demonstrated efficacy of collaborative models in which teachers and support service professionals work together in today's classroom.

Mandates from the 1990 amendments to the Individuals with Disabilities Education Act (IDEA) (PL 101-476), as well as the early childhood legislation (PL 99-457) and the Americans with Disabilities Act (ADA) (PL 101-336), combine to make it clear that school systems are required to have an individual technology plan in place as a part of each student's IEP, unless the system can demonstrate that they have considered and rejected technology alternatives for good reasons. By extension, given what we now know about the value of technology in promoting IEP goals that relate to inclusion (access to the curriculum, peer-to-peer communication, ways to assess progress), the individual's technology plan should necessarily specify how technology will be used for the purpose of inclusion. As parents discover their legal rights, school systems will very likely be increasingly forced into unnecessary and potentially expensive mediation hearings unless their leaders are smart enough to incorporate inclusion as part of the individual's technology plan as a matter of course.

For many children with severe disabilities, a technology plan needs to be in place even before the child enters kindergarten, at age 3 or earlier. Depriving children of tools they need to have prior to entering school in order to be able to function more successfully in an inclusive situation upon entry into kindergarten may turn out to be one of the most penny wise and pound foolish things that schools do.

Children with severe communication impairments who require augmentative and alternative communication (AAC), for example, need to have access to technology (e.g., communication devices, wheelchairs, seating systems, computer software) well in advance of entering kindergarten. Exposure to the necessary technology *before* they enter school may determine how successfully children learn to read, write, and participate in other curricular activities; how well they can be included; and whether they will require far more expensive private school placements. In the short term, inclusion, even with the expenditures needed for technology, can be more cost-effective than paying for special segregated, private schools and classrooms requiring transportation, tuition, etc. Looking ahead, individuals who participate with their peers in regular classrooms, even those with severe disabilities, are far more likely to become independent, tax-paying adults.

TECHNOLOGY TOOLS AS
DIVERSITY ACCOMMODATION TOOLS

With the increasing diversity of American classrooms, which more than ever before are shared by children with varying physical abilities, learning needs, and cultural backgrounds, schools need to understand technology tools as diversity accommodation tools. Many children with special needs learn differently. Some simply learn more slowly. Most, however, require specific accommodations and supports to access the curriculum. It is also true that so-called "normal" children also have diverse learning styles. Children who speak English as a second language, those who come from challenging social situations, and those disadvantaged by poverty can benefit greatly from schools that know how to accommodate learning style differences within each classroom. Far too many children are probably kept out of full participation in the curriculum because of the inability of staff to respond to diverse learning style differences (cf. Pressman & Dublin, 1995).

Computers are powerful tools that can provide multisensory information in ways that captivate and motivate children involved in the learning process. Computers (and computer-based devices) also can provide alternative ways to access text, write, speak, see, listen, calculate, move, and experience the world. Many classroom teachers are not yet fully prepared to provide technology scaffolds to children with diverse learning styles and/or to those with disabilities who may have very specific needs. The excuses for not doing so are becoming less and less credible.

USING TECHNOLOGY TO FACILITATE INCLUSION: USEFUL MODELS

The programs described below illustrate our belief that technology is a necessary (though obviously not a sufficient) component of successful inclusion and that both technology and inclusion benefit all the children in a classroom. Staff who have been involved in these programs and projects share the opinion that inclusionary practices in our schools may be critical not only to compliance with the law but, more importantly, to the achievement of meaningful educational outcomes for students who are disabled, disadvantaged, and, too often, disenfranchised. (Unfortunately, far too few classroom teachers yet have sufficient access to the kinds of user-friendly computers and multimedia software and reference materials that make it easier to accommodate learning style differences in all children.) The successes and the failures of these programs can provide important lessons to policy makers who are interested in utilizing technology to promote inclusive education.

CompuCID

CompuCID (the *Compu*ter *C*lassroom *I*ntegration *D*emonstration) was a 3-year demonstration project operated on federal demonstration funds by the Foundation for Technology Access from 1989 to 1992. It focused on the use of computers as tools to promote the integration of students with special needs into regular classrooms in six school systems across the country. The program was designed to help school staff who work with students with disabilities, the students themselves, and their parents learn about the many ways that computers can help children and youth who are mainstreamed to more fully participate in regular classroom learning activities. A "technology team" consisting of 1) a practicing local educator with extensive experience using computer technology and 2) a person with a disability or the parent of a person with a disability who also had an extensive background in the use of computers, worked in each participating school with three demonstration classroom teachers. The teachers were selected for their commitment to integration, their initial flexibility and enthusiasm for incorporating the use of in-classroom computers into their regular curriculum and daily routine, and their potential as future agents of change within their schools.

The project sought to demonstrate how computers and cooperative learning can enhance the integration of differently abled students into public school classrooms and also to demonstrate that technology and a philosophy that "all children should be together" could create a quality education for children. In the demonstration schools, computers (which had previously been banished to segregated spaces) were integrated into the regular classroom. Children with special needs returned from their unnatural state of exile to the regular classroom. And the demonstration classroom teachers learned how to use computers to integrate regular curriculum goals and increase participation in classroom activities for every student.

In this context, students with special needs weren't just being "mainstreamed" (i.e., being allowed to occupy the same space as their non-disabled peers). Rather, teachers in the demonstration classrooms learned how to use computers to help make "full inclusion" a reality. They learned how to

• Incorporate students with different ability levels in the same lesson, to the benefit of both
• Put students into small cooperative group learning experiences with their non-disabled peers
• Help students with special needs use the computer to access the regular curriculum from which they had previously been excluded

Perhaps the two most innovative outcomes of the CompuCID project were the use of cooperative learning techniques using the computer for *the specific purpose* of integrating students with special needs with their peers; and the mastery by a group of typical teachers of specific software and its use in promoting cooperative learning activities across a wide range of age groups, disability categories, and ability levels (Grady & Timms, 1991; FTA, 1993; Male, 1993).

CAST

At the Harvard-Kent School in Charlestown, Massachusetts (and in four other schools around Boston), the Center for Applied Special Technology (CAST) is demonstrating a way to deal with the increasing diversity of the American classroom. CAST bases its efforts on the belief that true inclusion is difficult to achieve because "it requires a curriculum, not simply a classroom that is accessible."

A working model of inclusive classrooms can be found in CAST's Equal Access project, where it has developed and tested models for supporting inclusion with technology. CAST believes that the fixed print of traditional textbooks, for example, is as equally serious an impediment to the integrated learning of many students as staircases are to the student in a wheelchair. Printed text presents information in the same way for everyone, yet students' varied learning styles call for alternative formats, and their learning difficulties require individualized help and support. A bright student with dyslexia may be able to understand the concepts in her history, science, or literature class; but she may have difficulty decoding text. This will limit her ability to learn those concepts from printed textbooks. A student with a visual impairment who cannot read a standard print size is also excluded from learning information presented in traditional textbooks.

The idea of providing equal access to the existing classroom curriculum through technology is a powerful one. Computer technology offers a means for presenting curricula in multiple, barrier-free formats and puts appropriate, individualized tools within the grasp of students with widely varied abilities, disabilities, and learning styles. A student with a disability can work effectively in the mainstream because technology can capitalize on strengths and offer alternative access and instructional methods to accommodate differences.

CAST is spearheading the development of software that exemplifies how to incorporate access and instructional features. One outstanding example is the *Wiggleworks* curriculum that CAST has developed for Scholastic. This early reading (K–2) curriculum not only takes full advantage of a multimedia format to promote student motivation and success in early reading but also builds in alternative access routes for children with disabilities and makes it easy for individuals to work together cooperatively. It keeps track of who worked with whom and makes it easy for children without disabilities to turn off the many special features built in to give kids with disabilities easier access to the curriculum (e.g., enlarged type, word-by-word sound). CAST is also working on a beta version of a "Captions Courageous"/captioning program that has applications for children that go well beyond its stated purpose of being a tool for those who are hearing impaired or deaf (CAST, 1994).

Teacher-Led Computer Demonstration

The Teacher-Led Computer Demonstration (TLC) project, which operated at the Hardy School in Arlington, Massachusetts, from 1992 to 1995, was funded by the U.S. Department of Education. The TLC project sought to learn more about how to get every classroom teacher in the school to start down the path of classroom computer integration. The project's goals focused on 1) promoting achievement gains in core skill areas, 2) enhancing students' ability to think for themselves, 3) helping teachers learn how to combine the use of cooperative learning techniques with computer technology, 4) helping underachieving students learn to work as tutors in cross-age "computer-tutoring" situations, and 5) involving the families of the school's underachieving students in their computer learning activities.

A full-time technology integration coordinator, or "lead teacher," drawn from the regular faculty, helped other faculty members learn how to incorporate the use of computers in their classroom teaching, aiming especially at more successful learning for their underachieving students. Each year, a different classroom teacher took over this role. In order to be able to fulfill the "lead teacher's" extra responsibilities outside the classroom (e.g., in-service training, technology troubleshooting, teaching demonstration lessons around the building, administering the project), the teacher got a full-time teaching assistant for the classroom. Each year, one third of the teaching force joined the project, so that, by the third and last year of the demonstration, TLC was helping *all* the classroom teachers at the Hardy learn strategies that incorporate the integrated, in-classroom use of computers in ways that can raise academic achievement of underachieving students.

The project also reached out to parents by helping them learn how to use computers at home to improve skills and encourage enjoyment of learning. Students designated as "Technokids" (about half of whom had IEPs) got to take the school's computers home every weekend and over vacations; and their family members and friends were encouraged to engage in home computer activities with them.

Some of the elements of the project that may make it especially relevant to schools trying to use technology to promote the inclusion of students with disabilities include

1. TLC chose kids with learning difficulties (about 40% had IEPs), anointed them "Technokids," and then helped to "jump start" them in a new, more confident alternative direction, through a series of carefully selected technology interventions: early success experiences, cross-age computer tutoring, home computer activities, cooperative learning roles. For example, the involvement of underachievers in cross-age tutoring and home computer use strengthened their self-image as competent thinkers and problem solvers.

2. The project used software and instructional strategies that deliberately avoided remedial approaches, basic skill drills, "integrated learning" systems (often a synonym for electronic workbooks), and the like with the highest-risk underachievers in the school. Instead, interactive, problem-solving programs are used with cooperative learning, whole-language, and process writing strategies.

3. The project deliberately defined the use of the classroom computer as a tool for *diversity accommodation*, helping teachers understand that the computer can provide a richer variety of teaching strategies and accommodate more widely divergent learning styles, levels of learning, and special learning needs within a single classroom.

To deal head on with the difficult "underground" issues of teacher resistance and reluctance to using technology as a regular tool of classroom instruction, the TLC project required a principal willing to make a commitment to the participation of her entire classroom teaching staff. While giving teachers up to 3 years to get "on board," the 1/3, 2/3, 3/3 sequencing of classroom teacher involvement allowed the most reluctant teachers to wait the longest while their colleagues were building up a groundswell of parental and student enthusiasm and support for in-classroom integration of technology tools.

TLC utilized the "family connection" to reinforce its impact in a way that many educators might see as difficult or even impossible but that turned out to be quite easy and trouble-free. By sending easy-to-use Macintosh computers home with Technokids on a regular basis (thus extending student "time on task" to time at home), by providing basic training to parents in computer learning alongside their children, and by training a cadre of parent volunteer trainers to work with other parents, the project sent a series of clear and important messages to these families: *We trust you. We think you can play an important partnership role with us in supporting your children's learning. Your children may learn in non-traditional ways, but they can be successful and enthusiastic learners. We need your help* (Pressman, 1994).

Berkeley Unified School District

In the late 1980s, the Berkeley (CA) Unified School District (BUSD), a district with an over 65% minority population, made a commitment to inclusive education and to ensuring that children with the most severe disabilities would have access to the technology and support they needed to participate actively in regular education classrooms. Believing children with severe communication impairments to be at particularly high risk, the director of special education developed an augmentative communication team. At the same time, the district became committed to inclusive education. Students being served include children with cerebral palsy, dual sensory impairment, autism, Down syndrome, mental retardation, and other developmental and acquired disabilities.

Each student's augmentative communication team (ACT) comprises parents, special and regular education professionals, and a variety of consultants who meet on a bimonthly basis to address the complicated, ever-changing needs of these students. All but a few of these children are fully included in regular education classrooms with same-age peers. Because of their multiple and severe disabilities, significant adaptations have had to be made for these students to participate in class activities alongside their peers. Few, for example, are at the same cognitive level as their classmates. Nevertheless, parents, teachers, and support service staff agree that all students benefit from inclusion and that without technology it wouldn't be possible.

At meetings, teams reach consensus by developing Action Plans and Participation Plans for staff to follow. Without these plans, support staff and families found IEPs difficult to implement or felt the IEP's implementation was sporadic. Key components of each student's program are technology, the curriculum, and the inclusion specialist. Regular education teachers need team support but demand that it be coordinated and consistent with their curriculum and daily classroom activities.

A variety of outcome measures assessed parent and professional satisfaction with the program, student academic and social outcomes, and cost factors. Satisfaction with the program has remained generally high. All team members (i.e., families members, occupational therapists, speech-language pathologists, physical therapists, special education teachers, inclusion specialists) rated the Action Planning process and level of support provided high. Regular education teachers expressed conflicts about taking time out of their classroom to attend meetings. Some meet with inclusion specialists before and after team meetings at times more convenient for them.

Student outcomes vary from year to year, often reflecting how well a team is functioning. Positive outcomes often are dramatic because academic skills are acquired; friendships with peers formed; and behaviors improve across school, home, and community settings. Early in the program, the district compared the cost of technology and consultations with the projected costs of sending students outside the district for services. Results showed that within a year, it was more cost-effective for students to remain in the district with support than it was for the district to pay the tuition, transportation, and in some cases, lawyer fees that are involved in an outside placement.

Technology in the Classroom: Applications and Strategies for Education of Children with Severe Disabilities

The American Speech-Language-Hearing Association (ASHA) conducted a 3-year project called Technology in the Classroom. Funded by the U.S. Department of Education, the project's goals were to develop materials to help professionals and families meet the needs of 2- to 7-year-old children who could benefit from using assistive technology and computers in the home, school, and community. Project staff worked with local and national sites in developing a series of products to address communication (expressive and receptive), education, positioning, and mobility. Products include

1. Four modules designed to be used by parents, teachers, and support service providers in small groups or individually. Based on distance learning theory, the modules were field-tested both locally and nationally. Modules are entitled: Education; Communication; Hearing and Listening; Positioning and Mobility.
2. A videotape, *Technology in the Classroom*, designed to introduce the modules and provide examples of the use of technology

in inclusionary settings. Samples of best practices were solicited from programs throughout the United States and Europe.

NEW QUESTIONS

The above-cited projects or programs help raise a whole new set of questions that need to be considered. Below we raise and comment on a few of these questions.

1. **Question**: *How can we make sure we are using technology in ways that truly give children equal access to the classroom curriculum?*

   Comments: Software (e.g., Wiggleworks), instructional strategies (cooperative learning, peer tutoring), and training (school-based technology plan, distance learning materials, peer coaching) allow professionals and families to develop needed competencies in the areas of technology and inclusion. Tom Snyder Productions, one of the better software publishers, makes an important, indirect contribution by creating materials with "built-in" cooperative learning features, thus making them usable with individuals of varying ability and skill levels. The CAST Equal Access project is a good example of how to provide greater access to the classroom curriculum. The TLC home learning strategy also helps increase access by giving students who need it the chance to take home technology materials that are integrated into the curriculum. The Berkeley program employs team processes that enable multiply handicapped children with severe communication impairments to be included in regular education classrooms, as described in ASHA's Communication Module.

2. **Question:** *How can we make sure that we are fully exploiting the uses of technology as a diversity accommodation tool, whereby the teacher is providing not just equal physical access to the curriculum but acknowledging the different learning styles of students?*

   Comments: A recent series of eight books by Harvey Pressman and Peter Dublin under the series title *Integrating Computers in Your Classroom* (HarperCollins, 1994) emphasizes the uses of classroom technology as a diversity accommodation tool, explains the concept in detail, and provides many examples of classroom activities designed to facilitate the inclusion of students with disabilities via technology, cooperative learning, etc. Pressman and Dublin are also the authors of a 1995 Harcourt Brace Jovanovich publication called *Accommodating Learning Styles in Elementary Class-*

rooms, which incorporates technology as one important element in a broader strategy that seeks to take different student learning styles into account and includes scores of classroom activities that seek to illustrate the strategy. Probably the best example of the implementation of these principles in a public school is at the TLC project cited above (Pressman, 1994).

3. **Question:** *What can we do to help support the process whereby nondisabled peers of included students become familiar with their technology and become natural classroom technology "aides," thus enabling the adults to recede further in the background during the child's interaction with her peers?*

Comments: Can technology support the practice of classmates helping classmates? Many people who specialize in inclusive education have remarked on the value of peer supports. Teachers report benefits for all children when either same-age or older students assume responsibility for helping a child learn using technology. In Berkeley, teachers give responsibility to classmates on a rotating basis (i.e., a "peer buddy" for a day or week). The "buddy" becomes a supporter and sets the child up at the computer, helps at recess, accompanies the child to the library, and so on. In this way, other kids, in a sense, become *human access tools.* Even first-graders can participate. Children start with adult support (e.g., a child's instructional assistant), which is gradually faded. In the BUSD [Berkeley Unified School District], kids have become "veterans" at peer support over the years, as they accompany kids with disabilities up the grades. A host of new materials that help all children learn more about disabilities and differences (e.g., Smith, *Different Is Not Bad; Different Is the World*) are also available to help those children who wish to learn more about peers with disabilities. (We have included a sampling of materials regarding peer support in the references.)

A child's classroom buddy may become a "ticket" to outside social events. As Anastasia Somoza explained when she was 9 years old:

> I like being in a regular class because I now have lots of friends. At my old school, my friends lived too far away. We could not go to their house because we do not have a car. All the kids at my old school were disabled and it was hard for their parents to bring them to my house.
>
> My best friend at school is called Natalie. She is not disabled. She helps me with lots of things. I am the only one in my class who cannot walk but that's okay. My friends push me around." (in Somoza, 1993)

4. **Question:** *Do the children with disabilities always have to be on the receiving end of peer support?*

Comments: There is also another side of this coin: the use of technology to facilitate peer tutoring in which students with disabilities do the tutoring. As Gartner and Lipsky were among the first to point out, "Programs in which students with handicaps serve as tutors for other students with handicaps and for those without . . . serve to integrate students with handicaps, to promote respect for their capacity, and to enable them to learn by teaching" (1987: 389). The TLC project was one of the first to demonstrate how the introduction of technology into this "reverse" tutoring process can potentiate the process in several important ways. The technology, for example, supports the tutoring, checks the correctness of answers, and helps supplement missing knowledge and factual information while giving the tutor opportunities to remaster some of the material while learning by teaching.

5. **Question:** *How should plans for using technology with children with special needs relate / mesh with the overall plans for technology use in the classroom and the school?*

Comments: In most cases, there is a crying need for serious and systematic technology and inclusion planning at the school level. This is partly because the so-called 5-year plans that school systems spend so much agonizing time developing often ignore this issue of technology and inclusion completely and/or provide limited guidance for school-by-school planning.

The school plan should include consideration of all students in the school, including "special day class" students. Pat Shubert, an educational technology specialist in an urban school district that has made a major commitment to support inclusion with technology (Norfolk, VA), believes it imperative that determination of appropriate inclusive technologies be a team decision and that the first instinct should always be to use technology to accommodate or modify the regular curriculum (Wall & Siegel, 1994).

Exploiting the technology that special-needs students already bring with them to the classroom (*and that school systems may already have paid for*) for broader classroom purposes should prove appealing to school committee members and others concerned with the burgeoning costs of these resources. Often the most sophisticated technology in the classroom is the technology that "belongs" to the student with a severe disability, and rarely do staff members understand how to put it to broader use within the classroom.

Jackie Brand, executive director of the Foundation for Technology Access, points out another reason why the technology plans in each child's IEP should not be "segregated" from the overall technology plan: "Assistive technology," she maintains, "should be part of the whole technology plan for the school. Only when the principal sees himself or herself responsible for the education of all kids will kids with disabilities get an equal education."

Another money saver may be piggybacking purchase of schoolwide software license fees on top of individual costs for the user with special needs, so that the school realizes some economies of scale. There is also an economics issue with respect to inventory. If nobody knows what materials anybody else has or how they may be relevant to the curriculum, it is almost guaranteed that available technology will not be fully utilized. Such technology purchase practices seem penny wise and pound foolish.

What, then, are the important components of a technology plan that incorporates inclusion as an important goal? 1) a plan that focuses on how to successfully integrate the use of technology into the curriculum in a way that gives equal access to students with disabilities, 2) a plan that identifies existing resources and visualizes a broadened use of these resources, 3) a plan that includes a periodic "outing" process for technology currently "in the closet."

6. **Question:** *What kind of joint technology/inclusion professional development experiences are an absolute necessity for classroom educators and their special education collaborators?*

Comments: Advocates of inclusive education have long acknowledged the need for "co-training" for the regular and special educators who work together in a single classroom (Prelock, Miller, & Reed, 1995, provide a recent example of a model for collaborative training of a classroom teacher/speech-language pathologist team in a "language in the classroom" program). When technology enters the picture, however, there are very few successful models of technology co-training for them to draw on. The projects described above have pioneered in developing such ideas. Examples include

- CompuCID utilized an outstanding expert who has written extensively on ways to combine technology and cooperative learning (Male, 1993) as part of an ongoing staff development program that included regular classroom educators, special educators, and CompuCID staff.
- In the TLC project, monthly technology staff development sessions brought classroom teachers and special-needs personnel together in their own cooperative learning activities to cover a wide range of classroom-related topics (e.g., "Using Multi-Media to Accommodate Learning Style Differences in Large Groups").

- The Berkeley, California, initiative uses regular meetings of team members to develop classroom action plans. These meetings include a great deal of mutual learning about technology and inclusion for educators, administrators, families, and supportive service personnel who attend, as well as targeting planning for each individual.

7. **Question:** *How can the technopeasants, technoskeptics, and technophobes who make up the vast majority of classroom teachers be nudged over the line so that they begin to conceptualize technology as an instructional tool?*

Comments: For years, Larry Cuban has pointed out that classroom teachers are (and always have been) the "gatekeepers" who decide which technologies make it into the classroom and which don't (cf. Cuban, *Electronic Learning*, May/June 1995). Clearly, technology cannot be used successfully to promote inclusive education unless and until enough classroom teachers are prepared to integrate currently available technology tools into their classroom teaching routines. The people responsible for the CompuCID project found that out the hard way when their strategies for spreading the many successful practices developed in the demonstration classes they had established as "beachheads" confronted teacher resistance, not so much to using technology as a tool for promoting inclusive education, but, more basically, simply using it as a significant classroom learning tool. The TLC project at the Hardy school attempted to learn from these mistakes by developing a more careful and comprehensive strategy. This included spreading classroom technology integration incrementally over the course of 3 years, paying more attention to "marketing" the value of technology to the typical classroom teacher, and simply not legitimizing the individual teacher's choice to avoid using technology tools capable of helping them succeed with children whom they were failing to help.

Our experience suggests that the key here may be a "carrot and stick" approach that recognizes two concurrent realities:

1. Classroom teachers need (and deserve) more resource support, more help, and more training before we can expect them to seriously pursue the use of classroom technology as an inherent component of how they teach all students and how they include students with disabilities.
2. Educational leaders need to push classroom teachers much harder until they start using the newly available technology tools in significant ways within their classrooms.

Some of the "carrots" seem like "no brainers," but that doesn't necessarily mean they happen in practice very often. They include 1) school systems should buy the easiest possible hardware for new users (i.e., most teachers); 2) schools should help teachers find the easiest and biggest "bang for the buck" software to get started on, so that teachers see some quick returns on their learning investments; 3) schools should provide classroom teachers with some real practical, hands-on, curriculum-based training experiences as their initial introduction to computer use. These experiences should focus on how to integrate technology into significant classroom activities and learning experiences, not the less important things (e.g., mastering some complicated multi-tool program) that so often come up in "introductory" staff development programs.

Some of the "sticks" seem equally obvious: 1) superintendents have to say to principals: "Welcome to the 21st century. I expect your school to be using technology in all your classrooms before the curtain rings down on the 20th"; 2) principals need to act like the instructional leaders they are supposed to be, and say to their teachers: "People, we no longer have a choice about this. The parents in our district wouldn't send their kids to a dentist who hadn't mastered the new technologies developed over the past decade. They wouldn't bring their car to a mechanic who hadn't boned up on how to deal with all the computer technology now built into their vehicles. And they shouldn't have to send their children to classrooms where teachers haven't learned to use these incredible new tools that have already demonstrated their capacity to help motivate children to learn, to accelerate learning in many important skill areas, and to enable you to respond to individual learning style differences in some major new ways. Our responsibility to our community depends on it."

In short, informed leadership is what is most needed. What happens today in most classrooms reflects a leaderless reality. It is simply not realistic to expect most teachers to have the vision to integrate technology into their classroom curriculum on their own. There will always be technopeasants, technoskeptics, and technophobes in our classrooms, at least until the schools of education start doing a lot more to take seriously their responsibilities to prepare the next generation of teachers to be able to integrate technology into the teaching/learning process.

Somebody has to say, "This simply won't do." Higher expectations need to be expressed up and down the line. Principals need to be able to say to the resistant teacher: "I'm not happy. Your ability to use technology well influences your ability to accommodate the

diversity in your classroom, to carry out inclusive education successfully, and to get your students ready for life on the 'outside.'
You need to learn about technology. I've made an effort to provide
the right resources and the right training, etc. You haven't taken
sufficient advantage. I'm responsible to these kids and their parents. Get with the program, or seek other employment opportunities."

8.   **Question:**   *How can teachers begin to see computers and their
many permutations and applications (reference sources, e-mail, math
simulations, word processing, recreational options, creativity cata-
pults, collaboration trainers) as essential tools for all students, particularly those with special needs?*

Comments: Our experience suggests that many classroom
teachers, even when they use technology in their classrooms, see it
as only relevant to one or two particular subjects or tasks, rather
than as a collection of across-the-board tools that can be useful in a
wide variety of ways. There are a variety of "stereotyped" uses of
computers. Each is a little different, but they all function as working
stereotypes for their particular school or system. In some elementary schools, for example, computers get used in the classroom when
children are doing creative writing but are far less often used to
help children develop reading skills. Or a math teacher in a junior
high school may use classroom technology for skill review but never
as a display or demonstration device before the whole class.

It is only when teachers broaden their comprehension of the
wide variety of uses of computer technology that we can expect them
to value the technology sufficiently as a way of accommodating the
diversity of learning styles with which they have to cope, or as a
way of achieving their own key classroom goals. When that happens, the use of technology becomes a higher personal priority for
them. A good example is the use of multimedia encyclopedias on
CD-ROM. In the TLC project, several teachers significantly increased their use of classroom computers when these talking encyclopedias became available, whereas in the past they had kept the
computer in the corner like some misbehaving child.

9.   **Question:**   *How can you tell whether technology investments
made in support of inclusive education are paying off?*

Comments: Most schools have little or no idea of the returns
they get on any of their technology investments and, in truth, have
probably purchased the technology they own without much reference to specific outcomes. But there are ways to measure meaning-

ful outcomes that relate to the value of technology in the inclusion process, as well as to the included child. Some of these that have been tested in the projects described above include

- The TLC project monitored changes in student self-perceived learning competence over time, using Susan Harter's Perceived Competence Scale for Children (Harter, 1982).
- The CompuCID project developed satisfaction questionnaires (in Spanish and English) for both parents of children involved in the project and school staff (reproduced in CompuCID manual, 1993).
- The TLC project used consultants from Project Zero at Harvard to help train classroom teachers in observing and recording specific student behaviors around the computer, which can be incorporated in the student's individual portfolio assessment.
- CAST has built into the *Wiggleworks* materials a record-keeping system designed to facilitate portfolio tracking of students' writings, individually and collaboratively.

One of the things policy makers might want to do to make life a little more pleasant might be to disabuse themselves of the notion that they can scientifically isolate the impact of technology effects from the overall impact of the inclusion program. We suggest you be satisfied with signs that the inclusion program is having anticipated outcomes if you can see the following:

1. Parent opinion/satisfaction with the accomplishment of IEP goals (academic progress, inclusive education, use of technology). Parents are not only major stakeholders in the inclusive education process, they are also one of the groups that can create the most trouble if they are unhappy. So an adaptation of the parent survey used in CompuCID might be a very good idea. (*Note*: It is also a good idea to hold focus groups with parents in your district before developing any adapted measurement tools.)
2. Use student measures of achievement and social competence (e.g., the *Wiggleworks* materials that provide portfolio content, the Harter Perceived Competence Scale).
3. Economics. Compare the costs and returns on other investments made in the past (e.g., out-of-district placements) to the costs of returns of an inclusive education technology program.

CONCLUSION

School districts throughout the United States face difficult times. Laws and regulations mandate the use of funds to meet the diverse and increasing needs of the student population. Parents and policy makers are becoming more and more dissatisfied with educational outcomes of our schools. Local decision makers can no longer afford to delegate decisions regarding the deployment of technology in their schools without asking some tough questions because it is the decision makers who are at risk of having the egg on their face. This article advocates that school superintendents and other top administrators step forward and take the lead and figure out a way to enter the 20th century before the calendar says it's time to leave it.

Taking the lead may in many cases involve first figuring out a way to stop *spinning your wheels*. Lots of activities around technology and special needs may already be in motion, but these activities may not make sense economically or educationally. Of equal importance is finding a way to avoid *reinventing any wheels*. A few useful models for implementing technology in the service of inclusive education have already been tried and can and should be drawn on. *Reinventing broken wheels*, which happens when school systems use models for technology applications that have already been tried and found wanting in other areas, is perhaps the greatest danger of all.

Asking more of the right questions can lead to finding better answers. Continuing to ask the wrong questions will not. Those leaders who realize that computers and assistive technologies are critical educational tools of the 1990s and who remain committed to inclusive education as the norm rather than the exception will have no choice but to insist that teachers and support personnel use the tools that can best accommodate children's various educational needs and learning styles. We believe that districts with leaders committed to these practices are far more likely to demonstrate positive student outcomes and will also spend less time and money on conflict and mediations.

How to proceed? Here are some concrete suggestions:

1. Get some outside help at the outset. Too many "inside" technology "experts" in school systems understand the machinery and connections part of their jobs a lot better than they understand curriculum and access issues. You'll save yourself a lot of time, money, and headaches.

2. Depend on consultants who are committed to giving away knowledge and will teach district personnel how to do what they do. (CAST is a good example.)

3. Ask parents and teachers to participate in focus groups to develop desired outcomes.

4. Explore ways for regular and special education programs to share costs. For example, special education may purchase software as part of a student's IEP. Regular education may kick in additional monies to buy a site license so children in other classrooms can use the software.

5. Treat technology as any other educational tool. Let students take home assistive technology and computers at night, over weekends, and during holidays and summer vacation.

6. Do everything you can to make the curriculum accessible to all students, but . . . take one step at a time.

REFERENCES

Books, Videos, etc.

AASA, ed. *Learning Styles: Putting Research and Common Sense into Practice.* Arlington, VA: American Association of School Administrators, 1991.

American Speech-Language-Hearing Association (ASHA). *Assistive Technology: We Can Do It!* Videotape segment from Project Technology in the Classroom: Applications and Strategies for the Education of Children with Severe Disabilities. Washington, DC: ASHA, 1992.

Anderson, Mary. *Partnerships: Developing Teamwork at the Computer.* Majo Press, 1988.

Artzt, Alice, and Claire Newman. *How to Use Cooperative Learning in the Mathematics Class.* Washington, DC: NCTM, 1990.

Bellanca, James, and Robin Fogarty, *Blueprint for Thinking in the Cooperative Classroom.* Palatine, IL: Skylight Publishing, 1990.

Blackstone, Sarah W. *Technology in the Classroom: Communication Module. Applications and Strategies for the Education of Children with Severe Disabilities.* Washington, DC: ASHA, 1992.

Brancombe, N. Amanda, Dixie Goswami, and Jeffrey Schwartz, eds. *Students Teaching, Teachers Learning.* Boynton/Cook, 1992.

Calculator, Steve, and Cheryl Jorgensen. *Including Students with Severe Disabilities in Schools: Fostering Communication, Interaction, and Participation.* San Diego: Singular Publishing, 1994. (Includes sections on the role of communication in fostering inclusion and on strategies for including students with severe disabilities in regular class lessons.)

Campbell, B., L. Campbell, and D. Dickenson. *Teaching and Learning Multiple Intelligences.* Seattle: New Horizons for Learning, 1992.

Cassatt-James, E. Lucinda. *Technology in the Classroom: Education Module Applications and Strategies for the Education of Children with Severe Disabilities.* Washington, DC: ASHA, 1992.

CAST, Inc. *Communications Technology for Everyone: Implications for the Classroom and Beyond,* 1994. (An accessible, interactive, multimedia CD-ROM version of the report of a conference held at Northwestern University, available from the Annenberg Washington Program, 1445 Pennsylvania Ave., Washington, DC 20004.)

Center for Applied Special Technology (CAST). *Interfaces* (Quarterly Newsletter) (39 Cross St. Peabody, MA 01960).

Cuban, Larry. *Teachers and Machines: The Classroom Use of Technology Since 1920.* Teachers College Press, 1986.

Dover, Wendy. *The Inclusion Facilitator.* Manhattan, Kansas: Master Teacher, 1994. (A very practical manual including a long section on Collaborative Teaching and Instructional Co-Planning Documents.)

Ellis, Susan, and Susan Leyland. *Cooperative Learning: Getting Started.* New York: Scholastic, 1990.

Foster, E.S. *Tutoring: Learning by Helping.* Minneapolis: Educational Media Corp., 1983.

FTA. *CompuCID Manual.* San Rafael, CA: Foundation for Technology Access, 1993. (Available from FTA, 2173 East Francisco Boulevard, Suite L, San Rafael, CA 94901, 415-455-4575.)

Gardner, Howard. *Frames of Mind: The Theory of Multiple Intelligences.* New York: Basic Books, 1983.

Gardner, Howard. *The Unschooled Mind: How Children Think and How Schools Should Teach.* New York: Basic Books, 1991.

Gardner, Howard. *Multiple Intelligences: The Theory in Practice.* New York: Basic Books, 1993.

Kagan, S. *Cooperative Learning Resources for Teachers.* San Juan Capistrano, CA: Resources for Teachers, 1990.

Keim, Nancy, and Cindy Tolliver. *Tutoring and Mentoring: Starting a Peer Helping Program in Your Elementary School.* San Jose, CA: Resource Publications, 1993.

Lazear, David. *Seven Ways of Knowing: Teaching for Multiple Intelligences,* 2nd ed. Palatine, IL: Skylight Publishing Co., 1991.

Male, Mary. *Technology for Inclusion: Meeting the Special Needs of All Students.* Needham, MA: Allyn and Bacon, 1993.

Marks, T. *Creativity Inside Out: Multiple Intelligences Across the Curriculum.* Reading, MA: Addison Wesley Publishing Company, 1995.

Master Teacher, Inc. *Inclusion Video Series.* Includes "De-Mything Inclusion," "Strategies for Making Curriculum Modifications," and "Strategies for Co-Planning and Co-Teaching." Manhattan, Kansas: Master Teacher, 1994–1995.

Means, Barbara, ed. *Technology and Education Reform: The Reality Behind the Promise.* San Francisco: Jossey-Bass, 1994.

Pressman, Harvey, and Peter Dublin. *Integrating Computers in Your Classroom.* New York: HarperCollins, 1994. (Includes three books on secondary education, four on elementary education, and one on early childhood, including many classroom activities with suggestions for integrating alternative learners.)

Pressman, Harvey, and Peter Dublin. *Accommodating Learning Styles in Elementary Classrooms.* San Diego: Harcourt Brace Jovanovich, 1995. (Incorporates technology as one important element in a broader strategy that seeks to take different student learning styles into account, and includes scores of classroom activities that seek to illustrate the strategy.)

Raskin, R., and C. Ellison. *Parents, Kids, and Computers.* New York: Random House Electronic Publishing, 1992.

Reiff, Judith C. *Learning Styles: What Research Says to the Teacher Series*. Washington, DC: National Education Association, 1992.

Russell, Susan Jo, et al. *Beyond Drill and Practice: Expanding the Computer Mainstream*. Reston, VA: CEC, 1989.

Slavin, Robert. *Cooperative Learning*. New York: Longman, 1983.

Smith, Sally L. *Different Is Not Bad; Different Is the World*. Longmont, CO: Sopris West (1140 Boston Ave., Longmont, CO 80501).

Stainback, Susan, and William Stainback, eds. *Curriculum Considerations in Inclusive Classrooms: Facilitating Learning for All Students*. Baltimore: Paul H. Brookes Publishing Company, 1992.

Stainback, Susan, and William Stainback. "Using Peers in the Education of Students with Severe Handicaps." In Susan Stainback and William Stainback, eds., *Integration of Students with Severe Handicaps into Regular Schools*. Baltimore: Paul H. Brookes Publishing Company, 1985, 87–97.

Vail, Priscilla. *Learning Styles: Food for Thought and 130 Practical Tips for Teachers K–4*. Rosemont, NJ: Modern Learning Press, 1992.

VanDover, Teresa. *A Principal's Guide to Creating a Building Climate for Inclusion*. Manhattan, Kansas: Master Teacher, Inc., 1995. (Includes plans for three parent sessions; 20 staff development sessions with such titles as "The Difference Between Mainstreaming and Inclusion," "What Does the Law Say About Inclusion?" "Are You Legally Responsible for IEP Goals?" "What Do Kids Really Want To Know About Other Kids?" and "Merging Regular Education with Special Education Services.")

Willing, Katherine, and Suzanne Girard, eds. *Learning Together: Computer-Integrated Classroom*. Markham, Ont., Canada: Pembroke Publishers, 1990.

Articles

Ascher, C. "Improving the School-Home Connection for Poor and Minority Students." *The Urban Review* 20 (1985): 109–123.

Blackstone, Sarah W. "Early Communication Training Approaches," *Augmentative Communication News*, 1(1), 3–5. 1990.

Bowers, C.A. "Childhood and the Cultural Amplification Characteristics of Computers: Some Critical Concerns." *Holistic Education Review* 62 (Summer 1993): 35–44.

Carbo, Marie, and Helene Hodges. "Learning Style Strategies Can Help Students at Risk." *Teaching Exceptional Children* 20, no. 4 (Summer) (1988): 55–58.

Carlson, H.L., and D.R. Falk. "Effective Use of Interactive Videodisk Instruction in Understanding and Implementing Cooperative Group Learning with Elementary Pupils in Social Studies." *Theory and Research in Social Education* 17, no. 3 (1989): 241–258.

Cartwright, Sally. "Cooperative Learning Can Occur in Any Kind of Program." *Young Children* (Jan. 1993): 12–14.

Clements, Douglas, Bonnie K. Nastasi, and Sudha Swaminathan. "Young Children and Computers: Crossroads and Directions from Research." *Young Children* (Jan. 1993): 56–64.

Comer, James, "Educating Poor Minority Children." *Scientific American* 259, no. 5 (1988): 42–48.

Cuban, Larry. "Computers Meet Classroom: Who Wins?" *Education Digest* 59, no. 7 (March 1994): 185–201.

Fegella, Kathy, and Janet Horowitz. "Different Child, Different Style." *Instructor* 100, no. 2 (Sept. 1990): 49–54.

Gardner, Howard, and J. Viens. "Multiple Intelligences and Styles: Partners in Effective Education." *The Clearinghouse Bulletin* 4 (2): 4–5.

Gartner, Alan, and Dorothy Lipsky. "Beyond Special Education: Towards a Quality System for All Students." *Harvard Education Review*, 57, no. 4 (Nov. 1987), 389.

Grady, Ann, and Judy Timms. "Computers in the Classroom: A Winning Combination." *OT Week* (September 12, 1991): 6 12–13. (On the CompuCID project.)

Harter, Susan. "The Perceived Competence Scale for Children." *Child Development*, 53 (1982): 87–97.

Holubec, Edythe Johnson. "How Do You Get There from Here? Getting Started with Cooperative Learning." *Contemporary Education* 63, no. 3 (Spring 1992): 181–184.

Klavas, Angela. "Resources for Teachers and Trainers Getting Started with Learning Styles." *Journal of Reading, Writing & Learning Disabilities* 6, no. 3 (July–Sept. 1990): 369–77.

Leland, Christine, and Ruth Fitzpatrick. "Cross-Age Interaction Builds Reading/Writing Enthusiasm." *The Reading Teacher*, 47 (Dec. 1993/Jan. 1994): 292–301.

Loper, Sue. "Learning Styles and Student Diversity." *Educational Leadership* 46, no. 5 (March 1989): 53.

Penn, Patricia, and Robert D. Childers. "Parents as First Teachers: The Family Connections Model." In Rebecca Crawford Burns, ed., *Parents and Schools: From Visitors to Partners*. Washington, DC: NEA Professional Library, 1993, chap. 4.

Prelock, Patricia, Barbara Miller, and Nancy Reed. "Collaborative Partnerships in a Language in the Classroom Program," *Language, Speech, and Hearing Services in Schools* (July 1995): 286–292.

Pressman, Harvey. "Technology in the Classroom: What's it For?" *Teaching Thinking and Problem Solving* (November 1994): 11–13. (On the TLC project.)

Rowley, Roxanne. "Here Come the Big Kids: Cross-Age Tutoring in the Early Childhood Classroom." *Young Children*, 63 (July 1993).

Saks, Judith Brody. "Meeting Students' Special Needs." *The Electronic School*, September 1993, 16–19.

Smith, Linda, and Joseph S. Renzulli. "Learning Style Preferences: A Practical Approach for Classroom Teachers." *Theory-in-Practice* 23, no. 1 (Winter 1984): 44–50.

Snyder, Vicki. "What We Know About Learning Styles from Research in Special Education." *Educational Leadership* 48 (Oct. 1990): 53.

Somoza, Anastasia. "A Child's Perspective." *Exceptional Parent* (September 1993), 17.

Wall, Thomas, and Jessica Siegel. "All Included: Inclusion of Special Education Children in Regular Classrooms Cannot Happen without Technology." *Electronic Learning* (March 1994): 24–34.

25

MULTIPLE PATHS TO
EDUCATIONAL EFFECTIVENESS

JENIFER GOLDMAN AND HOWARD GARDNER

Jamie, a shy but cheerful child, is playing alone in the reading corner of his kindergarten classroom, where he is engrossed in one of his many favorite books. As he leafs through its pages, Jamie softly chants songs in which he invents elaborate stories of his own about the different pictures he encounters in the book. The rich language that Jamie spontaneously produces to himself and to others during free play in the classroom is not to be found at storytelling time, however; instead, he quietly watches as other children offer their ideas. And, later, during the structured reading and writing time consisting of repetition drills and letter copying, the child who earlier in the day was so intently examining a book is easily distracted and becomes quickly frustrated.

As the year progresses, Jamie's reading and speech appear to his teacher to lag increasingly behind the other children in his class. Consequently, she decides to refer Jamie to the school psychologist for psychoeducational assessment. He is given the Wechsler Intelligence Scale for Children–Revised (WISC–R), a standardized test typically used by school personnel for the identification and place-

This chapter was supported by generous grants from the W.T. Grant Foundation, the James S. McDonnell Foundation, Spencer Foundation, The Rockefeller Foundation, and The Bernard Van Leer Foundation. We thank the editors for their comments on an earlier draft.

This chapter is from Goldman, J., & Gardner, H. (1989). Multiple paths to educational effectiveness. In D.K. Lipsky & A. Gartner (Eds.), *Beyond separate education: Quality education for all* (pp. 121–139). Baltimore: Paul H. Brookes Publishing Co.; reprinted by permission.

ment of children with learning problems. The examiner is a stranger to Jamie, the testing takes place in a room in which Jamie has never been before, and it focuses primarily on his verbal and logical skills. During the 1- to 2-hour test, Jamie is asked such questions as: "Why do we wear shoes?" and "In what way are a pencil and crayon alike?" He is asked to define words like *ball*, *summer*, and *book*. Additionally, he is asked to complete a series of mazes, to solve arithmetic problems, and to copy different geometric and block designs.

Afterward, the examiner analyzes Jamie's answers and determines a number that quantifies his "intelligence." It is safe to say that this resulting intelligence quotient, based on verbal and logical skills, does not adequately represent Jamie's full range of abilities. The rich vocabulary and complexity of sentence structure that Jamie demonstrates through his chosen form of expression, singing, seldom surface during the more formal activities in the familiar classroom. It is not surprising, then, that Jamie's performance on this standardized test, administered by a stranger and without any reference to music or musical ability, is far below the norm.

In the ensuing conference, the examiner explains to Jamie's parents that their son produced a subnormal score on the test, and that it would be wise to conduct further tests to determine his eligibility for special education services. Several standardized tests later, it is concluded that Jamie is "learning disabled." A course of education is prescribed for the child who is now classified as "mildly handicapped"; Jamie will go to special and separate rooms to learn with other "special needs children." Tragically, the only thing special about the education Jamie will probably receive is that it will revolve around especially small expectations that perpetuate minimal academic achievement (Granger & Granger, 1986). If Jamie is lucky, he will pass through the educational system with moderate success. But if Jamie is like many of the 4.37 million children enrolled in special education classes in the United States, he may find himself locked into a cycle of learning failure that will affect the course of his educational career, his resulting self-concept, and ultimately, his future as a productive member of society (Armstrong, 1987; Coles, 1988; Gartner & Lipsky, 1987).

THE INADEQUACY OF CURRENT CLASSIFICATION SYSTEMS

The circumstances that lead children like Jamie to be classified as "learning disabled" are not readily justified. Rather than accurately describing his profile of skills and deficits, they may well reflect serious conceptual and practical problems with the current system of classifying children. The problems begin with the classification "learning disabled," an ill-defined and poorly conceptualized term that is used to characterize a vast number of children who are unsuccessful in school. One interpretation of "learning disabled" is that children's learning difficulties find their source somewhere as yet undetermined in the brain. The term also connotes psychological or social causes, such as emotional disturbance or ill-treatment at home, that might explain why a child is experiencing academic problems. Although there do exist children with neurological problems, as well as children who experience learning difficulties for psychological reasons, the fact that *millions* of school children are classified as having "minimal neurological dysfunction" calls the classification into question (Armstrong, 1987; Coles, 1988; Ysseldyke & Algozzine, 1983; Ysseldyke, Algozzine, Richey, & Graden, 1982; Ysseldyke, Thurlow, et al., 1983).

The inadequacies of current classification practices, however, go beyond the conceptual problem of defining "learning disabled." Experts indicate that the instruments used to classify children are often inappropriate and, even worse, are of questionable reliability and validity (Salvia & Ysseldyke, 1987; Sattler, 1988; Ysseldyke, Algozzine, Regan, & Potter, 1980). Moreover, studies have shown that those who administer the tests and make placement decisions are often not knowledgeable enough to interpret the results appropriately (Davis & Shepard, 1983; Gartner & Lipsky, 1987; Ysseldyke & Algozzine, 1983; Ysseldyke, Algozzine, & Epps, 1983; Ysseldyke, Thurlow, et al., 1983).

In the present authors' view, the inadequacy and misapplication of assessment may reflect another order of difficulty as well. We question the theoretical basis on which the learning disabled literature and its classification system are founded. All too often the assumption is made that there is a certain form of ability, or intelligence, on which all children can be readily compared, and that children can be reliably rank ordered in terms of intellectual power. In the following pages we explore an alternative view of intelligence and assessment, one that challenges the idea that a child's intellectual capacities can be captured in a single intelligence quotient, and one that seeks to view productively the difference in children's abilities and proclivities.

THE THEORY OF MULTIPLE INTELLIGENCES

Traditionally, intelligence has been conceptualized as a single overall construct that encompasses all cognitive processes of significance, one that changes very little with age and experience, and that can be adequately summarized as a single metric unit. The notion of the mind as a quantifiable faculty has spawned the vast collection of intelligence tests and short-answer instruments that are designed to be administered and scored within a brief time. These instruments yield cognitive behavioral profiles; however, the information they elicit is largely dependent on the restrictions of the particular tests. For example, standardized tests typically involve responding to rapid-fire questioning asked in a setting remote from familiar and comfortable surroundings. Such testing conditions tend to highlight areas of weakness rather than locate areas of strength.

Perhaps most strikingly, intelligence tests also primarily highlight only two kinds of tasks: those requiring linguistic skill and those requiring skill in logical problem solving. An individual who has relatively developed linguistic and logical capacities should succeed on these tasks; an individual with significant limitations in one or both of these areas will perform poorly. This emphasis on logical and verbal abilities has traditionally characterized the Western view of cognition and intelligence, and is a bias commonly associated with both psychological and educational settings.

Many educators and scientists, along with much of the lay public, still subscribe to this view of intelligence. Even so, the articles of faith upon which it was founded have undergone searching critiques in recent years. Part of the critique has simply involved a recognition that particular mental processes, like learning and memory, are far more complicated and multifaceted than had generally been held. Another critique has proposed that the mind is itself composed of different modules or "intelligences," each of which operates according to its own principles. As a frequent corollary, it is held that power in one intellectual domain holds little if any predictive value for power in other intellectual domains—thus the notion of a unidimensional intelligence makes dubious scientific sense. Continuing in this vein, Howard Gardner, the second author of this chapter, has presented a theory of multiple intelligences known as MI-theory (1983) that contests the existence of a single intelligence or of general intellectual operations. Instead of accepting the notion of intelligence as a single entity, no matter how simple or complicated, Gardner posits the existence of several separate families of abilities. According to the theory, intelligence is not adequately captured by the ability to answer items on standardized tests. Instead, the scientific investigation and the educational evaluation must move beyond the stereotypical pupil abilities that happen to be valued in the West to encompass a broader range of abilities.

A NEW DEFINITION OF INTELLIGENCE

Gardner redefines intelligence as the ability to solve a problem or to fashion a product in a way that is considered useful in one or more cultural settings. Armed with this definition, Gardner sets up a number of criteria for what counts as a human intelligence. The evidence on which he draws comes from numerous disparate sources: knowledge about the breakdown of cognitive capacities under different forms of brain damage, for example, and the existence of isolated capacities in "special" populations, such as prodigies, idiot-savants, and autistic children. He also draws on the scattered evidence obtained from studies of cognition in different cultures, of cognition in diverse species, from psychometric correlations, and from studies of training and generalization of skills (Gardner, 1987b).

Weaving together these many lines of evidence, Gardner arrived at seven candidate intelligences: linguistic, musical, logical-mathematical, spatial, bodily-kinesthetic, interpersonal, and intrapersonal. It is important to stress that these seven intelligences should not be interpreted as the only acceptable candidates. Most, if not all, of the intelligences harbor several separate skills, and careful analysis can be readily conducted in order to identify a yet richer spectrum of intellectual facilities. The nomination of these seven different intelligences is most crucially intended to support the notion of a plurality of intelligence, rather than to insist on the absolute priority of the particular intelligences cited thus far (Gardner, 1987b).

Let us briefly summarize each of the seven intelligences. The first entry, linguistic intelligence, is a mainstay of traditional psychological analyses. The linguistic intelligence is exemplified, for example, in the poet, orator, or lawyer. One of the most heavily studied intelligences, the linguistic faculty can be broken into subcomponents, including syntactic, semantic, or pragmatic aspects, and certain kinds of more specific skills, such as written expression, oral expression, and verbal memory.

A second intelligence, logical-mathematical, is the intelligence that Jean Piaget probed in great detail (Piaget, 1983). As with language, an inventory of subskills can be delineated for logical-mathematical intelligence. The archetype of the problem-solving faculty, this intelligence is exemplified, for example, in the scientist or mathematician.

These two companion intelligences, language and logical-mathematical reasoning, are awarded the highest value in the school and form the basis for standardized assessment. Hence, it is predominantly lack of skill in one of these intelligences that contributes to a child's difficulties in school and increases the probability that the child will be classified as "learning disabled." The utility of these intelligences outside of school, however, is much less certain.

The next entry, spatial intelligence, entails the capacity to represent and manipulate spatial configurations. Spatial problem solving is required, for example, in navigation. Other kinds of spatial problem solving are brought to bear in playing chess or in visualizing an object seen from a different angle. Visual artists also employ this intelligence in the use of space. Thus, a wide range of vocational and avocational roles, including geographers, surveyors, architects, sculptors, painters, and engineers all possess considerable spatial intelligence. Though little valued in the current educational system, spatial intelligence can be an important constituent of success in many cultural pursuits.

Fourth on the list is musical intelligence, which involves the ability to think in musical terms, to be able to hear themes, to understand how they are transformed, to be able to follow those themes in the course of a musical work and, in the best cases, to be able to produce music. Musical intelligence is exemplified by the composer, performer, or other individual with a keen musical ear and music analytic abilities. A fifth intelligence, termed bodily-kinesthetic, refers to the ability to use all or part of one's body to perform tasks, fashion products, or solve problems. Actors, mimes, dancers, athletes, surgeons, and mechanics are distinguished by considerable bodily-kinesthetic intelligence. Except in certain special situations, the musical and bodily-kinesthetic intelligences are not valued educationally. Subsequently, many children who are musically or bodily inclined are more likely to experience learning problems because they are not exposed to the kinds of knowledge that they are fully capable of learning.

Finally, we speak of two other intelligences. Interpersonal intelligence involves the ability to understand other individuals, to develop viable models of how they function and how they are motivated, and to act productively on the basis of that knowledge. In more developed forms, this intelligence permits a skilled adult to read the intentions and desires of others, even when these have been hidden. This skill appears in a highly sophisticated form in religious or political leaders, teachers, therapists, and parents. Most of us experience interpersonal intelligence as a tacit knowledge that carries us successfully through life and its social interactions. For those children who are not skilled in this intelligence and who have difficulty engaging in successful peer relationships, school may be an unhappy burden that their schoolwork might reflect (Gardner, 1987c).

The companion social intelligence, intrapersonal, involves knowledge of the internal aspects of a person: access to one's own range of emotions, the capacity to effect discriminations among these emotions and eventually to label them, and the ability to draw upon them as a means of understanding and guiding one's own behavior. It is difficult to pinpoint an individual or a vocational role that exemplifies this form of intelligence, but it may be useful to think of a psychologically oriented novelist, or an individual whose degree of self-insight has been notably enhanced by psychotherapy. The autistic child is the prototypical example of an individual with impaired intrapersonal intelligence; indeed, the child may not even be able to refer to him- or herself. At the same time, such children often exhibit remarkable abilities in the musical, computational, and/or spatial realms.

All normal members of our species have the potential to develop each of these intelligences to some degree. Theoretically, it is possible that an individual could excel in all intelligences or could perform at the same level in all intelligences; however, such outcomes are empirically rare. In most cases, individuals exhibit a fairly jagged profile of intelligences, revealing relative strengths in some areas and comparative weakness in others. The differences in individual levels of achievement hinge upon the notion that each intelligence proceeds along its own developmental trajectory; hence, the intelligences are manifested in different ways at different developmental levels. Each of the multiple parts of the mind, then, is organized in terms of its individual content rather than reflecting across-the-board laws of development.

Operating within the separate developmental trajectories of each intelligence are one or more "core" operations that are relatively autonomous from the "core" operations in other intelligences. Syntactic and phonological analyses are core operations in the linguistic sphere. Similarly, sensitivity to numbers and causality are "core operations" in the logical-mathematical sphere, and appreciation of pitch and rhythm occupy "core roles" in music. Given the independence of core operations, strength in a particular intelligence does not necessarily predict strength or weakness in another intelligence. By the same token, it is difficult to strengthen a given intelligence by exploiting the core operations of another intelligence.

Thus, individuals differ in the extent to which they are "at risk" or "at promise" in each intelligence. Given an equal number of exposures to a material or exercise, children who advance very rapidly through a set of developmental milestones are considered "at promise," while those who remain at or near the novice status are considered "at risk." In the absence of special aids, those "at risk" in an intelligence will be most likely to fail tasks involving that intelligence. Conversely, those "at promise" will be most likely to succeed. Intensive intervention at an early age may bring a larger number of children to an "at promise" level in an intelligence in which they may initially appear "at risk" (Walters & Gardner, 1985).

MI-BASED ASSESSMENT

Our perspective of multiple intelligences, while viewed initially as a contribution to psychological theory, has come increasingly to be considered with reference to educational formats. In particular, we have focused on ways in which to assess the range of intelligences in school children, and particularly among children on the threshold of formal school. Following is a description of the authors' general philosophy of assessment. This is followed by a detailed description of a particular program, Project Spectrum, on which we have been working for a number of years. Abandoning the IQ test, with its nearly exclusive emphasis on linguistic and logical-mathematical skills, we have moved to implement assessment that captures the expanse of human potential in all intelligences and that identifies each child's unique intellectual propensities. Rejecting the stylized circumstances that surround most standardized measures, the authors utilized a more naturalistic and unobtrusive means of assessment which takes place *within* the classroom. Rather than reducing a child's cognitive capacities to a number, or a set of reading or math indices, we hold that the most valuable depiction of a child's intelligences is conveyed in the rich format of a narrative profile (Malkus, Feldman, & Gardner, 1987).

We envision such a profile as a portrait of distinctive intellectual patterns that focuses on areas of strength and delineates areas where a child is less proficient. Instead of simply "photographing" a child at the moment of testing, our portrait strives to present a holistic and more balanced view, which covers the gamut of each child's intellectual potential. In addition, the profile serves as a guide to the kinds of activities that serve to nurture and support each child's particular abilities. Thus, instead of simply serving to rank and pigeonhole students, this type of assessment could help determine an optimal educational regime.

An important characteristic of this approach is that is does not look at all abilities through the window of logic or language. Rather, it assesses a capacity directly, in terms of its own constituent skills. Thus musical abilities are assessed by having children sing or play tone bells; social abilities are assessed by observing the particular social skills of children during situations that arise naturally in the class. In other words, the assessing of intelligences must include the individual's ability to solve problems or create products using the materials that typify the intellectual realm in question.

An equally important dimension of this assessment approach is the determination of which intelligence is favored when an individual has a choice. One technique for pinpointing this activity is to expose the individual to a sufficiently complex situation that can stimulate several intelligences. Alternatively, one may provide a set of materials drawn from different intelligences and determine toward which one an individual gravitates and how deeply he or she explores it.

As an example, consider what happens when a child sees a complex film in which several intelligences figure prominently: music, people interacting, a maze to be solved, or a particular bodily skill that is exhibited. Subsequent debriefing with the child should reveal the features to which the child paid attention; these should be related to the profile of intelligences in that child. Or, consider a situation in which children are presented with several different kinds of equipment and games. Similar measures of the regions in which children spend time, and the kinds of activities they engage in, should yield insights into the individual child's profile of intelligence.

Another essential criterion of our assessment is that the process of evaluation should be integrally linked to ongoing classroom activities, as children demonstrate their strengths and weaknesses over the course of every school day. We believe that furnishing the classroom with engaging materials and activities that span the many realms of intelligence will maximize the chance of eliciting children's abilities. The materials should be open-ended in design so that children have the opportunity to express themselves in their preferred form of expression. Moreover, the activities and materials should possess challenges that are meaningful for the child and to which the child will wish to return again and again. In other words, we seek to make assessment as enjoyable for the child as it is informative for the adult.

It should be clear, at this point, that the assessment we support is as much a part of curriculum as a self-standing means of evaluation. By linking assessment closely to the regular events of the school year, it may be possible to dissolve the traditionally observed boundary between learning and assessment. Children can be offered games and exercises that expand their horizons, hold their interest, and provide instruction over the course of time. With occasional scaffolding on the part of the teacher, the children may learn from these activities in expected as well as unanticipated ways. And while the child is learning, we (as researchers, evaluators, and teachers) are given an opportunity to look, in an unobtrusive way, at the ways in which the child approaches his or her work and, in the process, assess his or her potential. This integration of assessment into the curriculum serves both to expand and individualize the curriculum, thereby creating an environment that welcomes children who may have special needs.

PROJECT SPECTRUM: APPLICATIONS OF THE THEORY

With both eyes fixed on the above criteria, the authors have developed an assessment technique for use in a preschool environment. Project Spectrum, a joint research project at Harvard and Tufts Universities, features a number of ecologically valid monitoring procedures; these procedures allow us to identify young children's preferences for, and competence in, activities in the several cognitive domains delineated by MI-theory. To date, Project Spectrum has developed 15 specifically targeted exercises that provide rough measures of skill levels in approximately 2 dozen intellectual realms, ranging from music and narrative to social-analytic skills.

Every child in the class is given the opportunity to engage in all the Spectrum activities but is not forced to participate if he or she is reluctant or uncomfortable. In the Spectrum program, the participation of as many children as possible is encouraged by offering the activities within the context of the classroom and having them administered by a familiar adult. Each child's performance on the structured activities and interaction with our materials is recorded in detail during or immediately after the activity, using observation and score sheets that describe the skills involved in negotiating the tasks. In addition, incidental information about each child's activities in the daily classroom is regularly recorded throughout the school year. This assessment procedure secures a considerable amount of information on the intellectual propensities and styles of each child enrolled in a "Spectrum Classroom."

At the end of the school year, all recorded information is culled into a Spectrum Report, an essay of two or three pages that serves as a portrait of the child's distinctive intellectual patterns. The report focuses on areas of strength but also indicates areas where the child could benefit from extra support. A crucial part of the Spectrum Report is a list of suggested activities that can be carried out by the child at home, in school, or elsewhere in the community. The report, then, serves not only as a descriptive form of assessment but also as a guide to the kinds of activities in which a child with this "spectrum of abilities" might profitably be engaged.

In order to indicate how the Spectrum program's assessment techniques differ from traditional standardized tests, it is helpful to describe one of the activities in some detail. In the area of language skills, Spectrum offers the children the opportunity to create a story of their own with the aid of a "storyboard"; the board is replete with interesting and ambiguous figures and props. The cast of characters include such *personae* as a king, a queen, a turtle, and a dragon; the props range from a treasure box filled with colorful "jewels" to caves, arches, and other transformable abodes with which the children can arrange their own scenery.

These materials may inspire children to deliver cohesive narratives and can afford the teacher a detailed view of the kinds of linguistic skills on which children rely when asked to invent a story. For research purposes, each child's story is tape-recorded and then analyzed on dimensions such as thematic coherence, inclusion of temporal connectives, use of dialogue and narrative voices, sentence structure, and level of vocabulary. At the end of the year, the child's performance on this linguistic measure, on other related Spectrum activities, and on any incidental observations is qualitatively discussed in the Spectrum Report. For those children who create a distinctive story, a segment from their story is included in the report. In our experience, parents and teachers appreciated and were sometimes suprised by the length and scope of their children's stories. Parents of a child with a linguistic flair also appreciated particular suggestions about games, activities, and community resources that might prove of special interest to their child.

For all activities, assessment takes place chiefly within the classroom, with the teacher observing and noting particular levels of skill that the children demonstrate on the different tasks. The assessments inform the teacher about children's particular skills in the multiple domains of knowledge; in addition, they may reveal children's interests in materials that they may not have been exposed to otherwise. For example, another Spectrum activity involves the disassembly and reassembly of a simple but real tool: a food grinder. This task elicits skills not readily tapped in the typical preschool classroom: fine motor control, analysis of the detailed structure of an object, and capacity to plan a lengthy sequence of activi-

ties in order to reach a novel goal. In addition, it affords the opportunity for children to reveal their mechanical skills. While some
children are easily frustrated by the task, or do not become engaged
at all in the activity, others demonstrate keen interest and/or skill
in the dismantling and reassembly of this real-world object.

At best, the Spectrum assessment technique plays an integral
part in the classroom, serving as both a measurement instrument
and a source of learning and enjoyment for the children. Spectrum's
philosophy is one of dynamic interaction between assessment and
learning, with emphasis both on learning about children and on
helping to teach them on the basis of that knowledge. We would
like to think that it differs from the typical standardized forms of
assessment, which are designed specifically not to teach and are
often distinctly unenjoyable. The results, at least so far, have been
promising. It is in part on the basis of our experience with Project
Spectrum, and in reaction to the present tendency to classify inor-
dinate numbers of children as "learning disabled," that we are motivated to speculate on the impact that MI-based assessment could
make on special education.

IMPLICATIONS OF MI-BASED
ASSESSMENT FOR SPECIAL EDUCATION

The theory of multiple intelligences and its conceptualization of
assessment has a number of significant implications for special education and its current classification system. First, MI-theory challenges the current definition of "learning disabled" as one based on
impairment etiology in combination with the concept of a unitary
intelligence. To talk about a child as "learning disabled" assumes
there are problems across-the-board and ignores a child's potential
skill in intelligences other than language and logic. In contrast,
multiple intelligence theory questions whether strengths or weaknesses can be seen as occurring across-the-board.

In addition, the theory reduces the impact of mild to severe neurological dysfunction on a child's educational regimen by focusing
on those areas where the child *is* functioning. Furthermore, it suggests that strength in one area can sometimes compensate for or
even be used to teach effectively in an area of apparent weakness.
Thus, a child with difficulties in logical-mathematical reasoning may
be able to master certain mathematical concepts and problems by
exploiting his or her spatial or linguistic skills. Indeed, intelligences
can be used either as the content of an instruction (one teaches the
area of language) or as a means of communicating content (one uses

language to teach mathematics). As an illustration of the way in which the intelligences can be mobilized, let us return to the case of Jamie described at the beginning of the chapter.

Had Jamie been evaluated using the kind of assessment that we propound, his prognosis may well have been different. An example of this may be seen in his natural proclivity for singing, which he demonstrates repeatedly during free play, but seldom in the presence of a group. This incidental information was overlooked by his teacher and disregarded by the tests that deemed Jamie "learning disabled." A more naturalistic and curriculum-oriented assessment that works within the context of the classroom would, for example, take into account the length of time Jamie remained engrossed in the book that particular day and the way he focused on its story through song. Regular observations would record areas in which he spent the most time and indicated the most interest, and would also include remarks on differences in his approach to the various activities in the classroom. A more structured assessment could be conducted to determine the scope of Jamie's musical ability, perhaps by having him play with tone bells or learn musically complex songs.

With this kind of information, Jamie's musical intelligence would not be overlooked. On the contrary, Jamie would be identified as possibly having musical potential; his teacher could provide him with materials and activities to nurture his musical ability and could perhaps suggest to his parents that he take music lessons. To put it directly: seen through the lens of impairment etiology, Jamie was a child intellectually "at risk"; viewed through the prism of multiple intelligences theory, Jamie is now "at promise" in one of the "spectrums" of intelligences.

From the kind of information amassed through naturalistic, MI-based assessment, a different picture of Jamie can emerge—one that portrays a serious and intent child, who is able to focus for lengths of time on things that he finds interesting, and who is especially oriented to singing. His intense interest in looking at the book would indicate that Jamie may be longing to read, but for some reason is unable to do so. With an understanding that this child is potentially interested in learning how to read, has the capacity to focus and become engaged in a task, and is perhaps skilled in a domain of intelligence other than verbal ability, some rays of hope emerge. This is probably not a child who is "learning disabled." Instead, this is perhaps a child who, like many others, has abilities and propensities that are neither elicited nor nurtured by standard curricula and tests.

Based on Jamie's musical orientation, an alternative route could be devised to meet educational goals and serve as a remedy for difficulties. By focusing on Jamie's exploration of vocabulary and language skills through singing, it may be possible to engage enough of his interest and utilize his naturally occurring talent to foster the development of reading skills. For example, Jamie's musical ability might be used to smooth the way into reading, perhaps by learning to read lyrics and stories to songs. Or his musical ability could be used in the service of mathematical learning, by building lessons around rhythmic or metrical analyses or intuitions.

Clearly, the traditional and typically exclusive focus on linguistic and logical skills by formal schooling and assessment seriously shortchanges those children, like Jamie, whose skills lie primarily in other intelligences. Assessment emphasis needs to be spread across the many domains of knowledge so that children are no longer evaluated strictly on the basis of standards that are culturally biased and reflect a narrow view of schooling.

Accommodating modes of instruction to the specific intelligences, however, is not in itself enough. Teachers need to be sensitive to the manner in which each individual intelligence develops and to the kinds of interventions that are likely to be productive in light of that particular development. In other words, the role of instruction must relate to changes across the development of the intelligences. Thus, a knowledge of the normal developmental trajectory of language is extremely important: This knowledge will suggest when it is appropriate (or inappropriate) to begin formal instruction in reading, writing, public speaking, or foreign languages. The typical curriculum in formal schooling, which approaches intelligence as a unitary entity with a universal developmental pattern, shortchanges the education of the intelligences developing within their uniquely prescribed trajectories.

A SPECIAL EDUCATION FOR ALL

Multiple intelligences theory, with its focus on the development and nurturing of each individual's different proclivities, dictates the need for a more diverse and individual-centered curriculum. From the earliest years, students should have available to them the means to explore and be identified as skilled in areas other than those traditionally located in the pedagogical canon. While there would still be some subjects studied by all youngsters, subject matter and teaching approaches would be keyed to the inclinations of particular students. To be sure, students ought to take some core subjects, even as they ought to be offered electives. But whether the emphasis falls on a common curriculum, or on specialized options, there is every reason to tailor the mode of instruction as much as possible to the inclinations, working styles, and profiles of intelligence of each individual student.

The need to identify individual abilities as fully as possible, early in a child's academic career, calls for a new system of assessment and evaluation. In lieu of standardized tests, the type of innovative assessment developed by Project Spectrum would be used to tap the capabilities of younger children. For older youngsters, assessment and evaluation would involve student, teacher, and "outside expert" review of projects and other activities in which students had been involved for sustained periods of time. Desirable school outcomes would be expanded to encompass a range of vocational and avocational roles, with achievement in standard academic areas as one of a number of goals. The school should be a place where students can follow their own intellectual interests, while mastering the materials that will enable them to become productive members of society (Gardner, 1987a).

Providing students with a wider range of materials with which to work and explore their individual skills does not, however, necessitate the development of ability in *every one* of those areas. Quite to the contrary, it has become increasingly clear that individuals cannot hope to be expert in all areas of human knowledge. Even within specific disciplines, such as physics, economics, or the law, no single person can hope to master all the subspecialties of the field.

Just as we have come to acknowledge the impossibility of a universal education, we are now becoming familiar with the notion that individuals do not necessarily master subject matter in the same way. It is not only the individuals with frank learning impairments, such as mild or severe neurological dysfunction, who require special forms of instruction and individually designed strategies; each of us has idiosyncratic learning styles and strengths and can benefit from instructional approaches that speak to our particular configuration of intellectual skills and interests.

The imperative for some form of specialized education for *all* children, not just those with evident learning difficulties, and the desirability of teaching that takes into account an individual's cognitive profile, calls for a radically different approach to education. It no longer makes sense for everyone to learn the same materials in the same way; it is this outmoded approach that explains why so many children were once termed "ineducable" and are now labeled the essentially equivalent "learning *dis*-abled."

It is important to help teachers and those children with manifest special needs, as well as those children whose particular needs are less discernible, to discover the particular curricula and the particular educational approaches that are best suited to each individual. It is equally imperative that individual skills be nurtured outside the school—at home and in the community—as well as within the school program. To help carry out the mission of servicing students' intelligences both in school and extracurricularly, we call for the creation of two new roles: the *student–curriculum broker* and the *school–community broker*.

While not necessarily an expert in particular curricula, the student–curriculum broker would be familiar with the range of curricula appropriate at a particular age and with the ensemble of teaching approaches that might prove effective for a given curricula with selected children. Aided by technological resources, ranging from computerized files of activities to instructional programs especially crafted for certain kinds of learners, the broker attempts to devise a curriculum (or, more precisely, a set of curricular options) that can be considered by the child, his parents, and/or his teachers. The broker would work together with teachers and with an assessment specialist to ascertain whether the plans that have been devised are effective and, if not, would consult on the optimal means for refashioning the plan.

Although the student–curriculum broker would be needed most upon the commencement of formal schooling, the role can be briefly illustrated in terms of the framework that we are using with younger children in Project Spectrum. The broker begins with knowledge of an individual child's intellectual proclivities and styles, as measured by the techniques utilized in Project Spectrum. The broker next considers the range of knowledge areas or domains that are suitable for students of this particular age. The broker would take into account areas previously studied by the child, his or her own preferences, and the expertise of teachers and others in the community. Having collated all of this information, the broker then lays out several suggested lines of study and activities, and reviews them with all of the interested parties designated above.

It should be stressed that the student–curriculum broker's role extends well beyond the recommendation of particular courses or programs. Even when students are taking exactly the same courses as their peers, there is no need for these courses to be presented in the same way. Individual children, and especially those with special problems or unusual abilities, often are particularly able to tackle a subject matter in one way (say, through language), while exhibiting marked difficulties when the curriculum is presented in another way (say, through logical or spatial meanings). The broker should recommend teachers, curricula guides, and ancillary hardware and software materials that would facilitate the student's mastery of a "uniform" curriculum.

The school–community broker carries out an analogous set of matching operations, but does so within the wider community. Whereas the student–curriculum broker works chiefly within the confines of the school, the school–community broker is concerned with those opportunities that are unavailable in the school, but that may be found at home or in the wider community. The school–community broker has available considerable information about mentorships, apprenticeships, organizations, clubs, and other institutions that can provide opportunities for students who exhibit particular cognitive interests, strengths, and styles. It is the broker's job to help students make the appropriate connections with such institutions and to make sure that the connections are in fact working effectively. While the broker owes allegiance to all students in the school, his or her chief services would be provided to those students who exhibit unusual cognitive profiles, or who indicate special needs and/or special skills that the school could not readily handle.

The success of the specialists and brokers would depend in part upon the extent to which their roles can be systematized and rationalized. If every student turns out to be utterly different from the other, the brokers' tasks would be overwhelming. It is therefore more important to ascertain whether there may be families of suggestions or coordinated lines of growth that are applicable to groups of individuals within a community. By encouraging the intelligences within the school environment *and* in the extracurricular community, the wide range of different needs presented by any student population would be better addressed.

THE ROLE OF THE TEACHER IN AN INDIVIDUALIZED SCHOOL

The teacher's primary role has been to introduce students to the intellectual domains that are valued by society: basic skills such as reading and writing in the elementary grades, traditional subject matters like history and biology at the secondary level, and academic subspecialties at the college level. In our view, some of the newly defined educational functions would be taken over by other kinds of specialists, such as the assessors of intelligences and the curriculum and community-brokers introduced above. This division of labor would free the teacher to do what he or she ought to be doing: presenting the accumulated knowledge and skills of the past in appropriate ways to students so that they are given the best possible opportunities for learning (Gardner, 1987a).

Should our general approach to schooling be adopted, we anticipate the following kinds of changes in the teacher role. First of all, demonstrated expertise in the domain would become the primary criterion for entrance and advancement in the field of teaching (Shulman, 1986). Second, teachers would develop expertise in various approaches to the subject matter. Either they would specialize in an approach deemed appropriate to certain kinds of students, such as students with special needs (e.g., dyslexic or dyscalculic children), or they would develop an arsenal of techniques, which could then be deployed appropriately for students who exhibit distinctive strengths and weaknesses. Thus, knowledge of "pedagogical styles" would be wedded to expertise in "domain knowledge."

Our vision also includes a new form of "master teacher" who would work regularly with the other kinds of specialists. The master teacher would have five major assignments:

1. To serve as a role model for new teachers, exhibiting at least some of the alternative ways in which subject matters can be presented to students with different "intelligence" profiles
2. To monitor novice teachers with particular attention to their approaches to subject matter and their teaching techniques
3. To keep abreast of new findings of the area of teaching and to disseminate them to other members of the school community, ranging from principals to apprentices
4. To collaborate with the curriculum, community, and assessment specialists in designing programs of study for individual students and in making sure that the appropriate teachers and sites are available for each student
5. To intervene when the program is not successful and to suggest alternative regimens for the student

Clearly, the roles of teacher and master teacher would be extremely important in this new scheme. Teachers would have the primary responsibility for disseminating knowledge and would be judged by their effectiveness in this central task. Master teachers would be the school generalists, having as their assignment the orchestration of the activities of curricular, community, assessment, and domain specialists, and ensuring that the methods being used are current and effective. Anyone capable of carrying out these functions would have to be a highly trained and skilled professional.

If a school along these lines is to be effective, it is important that all members of the teaching staff, as well as the various specialized brokers, have the mechanisms whereby they can communicate on a regular basis and can register their opinions and impressions, both with each other and with master teachers. This means that periods for conversation and reflection must be built into the regular school schedule; it also indicates the need for efficient communication mechanisms, such as computer networks, whereby teachers can readily share their findings and impressions with their colleagues. Optimally, such opportunities for exchange would lead teachers to develop common ways to think about learning problems and produce suggestions for how best to tap the skills of those children who are not academically successful. Over time, teachers would internalize the ways in which their colleagues think about students and be able to anticipate the kinds of steps their colleagues are likely to take when confronted with particular challenges or opportunities. The time and energy required for such exchange, as well as a convenient means for preserving and obtaining the information accumulated through such discourse, are essential.

If teachers are to be trained to review students' options using evaluative information from assessment in context, schools that operate on such a system need to be established and monitored carefully to make sure that they are fulfilling their tasks. They should then be made available as sites for those who wish to implement a similar approach. On an apprenticeship basis, teachers could enter the school to observe and participate. We are currently involved in one such pioneering effort, a "Key School" in Indianapolis, where a serious attempt is being made to nourish all of the intelligences and to coordinate the diverse forms of information being gathered about all the students (Olson, 1988).

If widely adopted, such an approach to teaching would radically change the appearance of special educator programs. Rather than special education connoting the need for an intervention to help a victim, it would instead be embraced in a positive sense. Indeed, fashioning the curriculum so that it is centered on each individual student, and altering current teacher-training standards so that individual gifts and styles are featured, would make special education the norm rather than the exception. According to such a curriculum, it would be *expected* that "special" services would be needed for every child. Indeed, every child has his or her own particular style of learning. Such individuality is too often overlooked and can suffer under the burden of a uniform curriculum. It is our philosophy that every child is entitled to and can benefit from a more personalized form of schooling.

The benefits gained by children currently depicted as having "special needs" are manifold. No longer would they need to be classified as very different from their peers and segregated into separate classes, for everyone in the school would be accommodated by the curriculum. The vicious circle of labeling, and fulfillment of the label, could perhaps be broken; there might no longer be a need for classifications such as "learning disabled." Rather than being separated from their peers, children could flourish in a community of special education. Further, children with special needs would be exposed to the kind of curriculum that they are largely being denied under the current special education system, and to a richer and more stimulating curriculum that encompasses multiple areas of knowledge.

CONCLUDING NOTE

A narrow view of intelligence has cast a long shadow over school during the past century. As long as it was assumed that individuals could be arrayed in terms of a single intellectual metric, it followed that the majority of students would consider themselves to be of modest intellectual endowment, and that those with the poorest performance on "approved measures" would be stigmatized.

Building upon recent work in cognitive, developmental, and neurosciences, we have put forth a view of the mind as a far more capacious instrument, exhibiting a number of relatively distinct talents. In this view, most children are intelligent in at least some respects, and nearly all can develop a set of potentials that will be socially useful and personally satisfying. Applied to an educational setting, this perspective proves to be an optimistic one: It should be possible to devise methods that reveal intellectual strengths at an early age as well as techniques that can exploit those strengths in the service of wider and deeper learning.

We have no illusions that it will be easy to set up schools that are built around the idea of individual strengths, curricula, and growth patterns. Schools forged in this image should be possible, however. The failure of our society thus far to guide schools in this direction reflects less a lack of resources than a failure of will. Still, unless we are willing to push for educational programs that are committed to developing each individual potential to the fullest extent, we are destined to have a society in which many problems will lie unsolved, and many lives will be incompletely realized.

REFERENCES

Armstrong, T. (1987). *In their own way*. Los Angeles: Jeremy P. Tarcher.

Coles, G. (1988). *The learning mystique*. New York: Pantheon Books.

Davis, W.A., & Shepard, L.A. (1983). Specialists' use of test and clinical judgment in the diagnosis of learning disabilities. *Learning Disabled Quarterly, 19,* 128–138.

Gardner, H. (1983). *Frames of mind: The theory of multiple intelligences*. New York: Basic Books.

Gardner, H. (1987a). *Balancing specialized and comprehensive knowledge: The growing educational challenge*. Paper presented at the Breckenridge Forum, San Antonio, TX.

Gardner, H. (1987b). The assessment of intelligences: A neuropsychological perspective. In M. Meier, A. Benton, & L. Diller (Eds.), *Neuropsychological rehabilitation* (pp. 59–70). London: Churchill Publishers.

Gardner, H. (1987c). The theory of multiple intelligences: Educational implications. In *Language and the world of work in the 21st century*. Boston, MA: Bureau of Transitional Bilingual Education.

Gartner, A., & Lipsky, D.K. (1987). Beyond special education: Toward a quality system for all students. *Harvard Educational Review, 57*(4), 367–395.

Granger, B., & Granger, L. (1986). *The magic feather: The truth about special education*. New York: E.P. Dutton.

Malkus, U., Feldman, D., & Gardner, H. (1987). Dimensions of mind in early childhood. In A.D. Pellegrini (Ed.), *The psychological basis of early education* (pp. 23–38). Chichester, England: John Wiley & Sons.

Olson, L. (1988). Children flourish here: Eight teachers and a theory changed a school world. *Education Week, 7*(1), 18–19.

Piaget, J. (1983). Piaget's theory. In P. Mussen (Ed.), *Handbook of child psychology*. New York: John Wiley & Sons.

Salvia, J., & Ysseldyke, J.E. (1987). *Assessment in special and remedial education*. Boston: Houghton Mifflin.

Sattler, J. (1988). *Assessment of children's intelligence and special abilities*. San Diego, CA: Author.

Shulman, L. (1986). Those who understand: Knowledge growth in teaching. Presidential Address at 1985 Annual Meeting of the American Educational Research Association. *Educational Researcher, 15*(3), 4–14.

Walters, J., & Gardner, H. (1985). The development and education of intelligences. In F. Link (Ed.), *Essays on the intellect* (pp. 1–21). Washington, DC: Curriculum Development Associates.

Ysseldyke, J., & Algozzine, B. (1983). LD or not LD: That's not the question! *Journal of Learning Disabilities, 16,* 29–31.

Ysseldyke, J., Algozzine, B., & Epps, S. (1983). A logical and empirical analysis of current practice in classifying students as handicapped. *Exceptional children, 50,* 160–166.

Ysseldyke, J., Algozzine, B., Regan, R., & Potter, M. (1980). Technical adequacy of tests used by professionals in simulated decision-making. *Psychology in the Schools, 17*, 202–209.

Ysseldyke, J., Algozzine, B., Richey, L., & Graden, J. (1982). Declaring students eligible for LD services. Why bother with the data? *Learning Disabilities Quarterly, 5*, 37–44.

Ysseldyke, J., Thurlow, M., Graden, J., Wesson, C., Algozzine, B., & Deno, S. (1983). Generalizations from five years of research on assessment and decision-making. *Exceptional Education Quarterly, 4*, 75–93.

26

INCLUDING INCLUSION
IN SCHOOL REFORM
SUCCESS FOR ALL AND ROOTS AND WINGS

ROBERT E. SLAVIN

This is a remarkable time in the history of American education. From the White House to the schoolhouse, there is agreement that fundamental reform is needed in our schools. At the policy level, important changes are under way in the establishment of state and national standards, new assessments, and greater flexibility in use of categorical funds. In particular, the reauthorization of Chapter 1 will create great potential for changes in schools serving many disadvantaged children.

At the same time as the potential for change is being opened up at the state and federal levels, this potential is starting to be realized at the school and classroom levels. Changes in curriculum and instruction, including a greater emphasis on cooperative learning, project-based learning, and discovery, are under way. In addition, several comprehensive school reform programs have been developed and widely disseminated, in particular Sizer's (1984) Coalition of Essential Schools, Comer's (1988) School Development Program, Levin's (1987) Accelerated Schools model, and our own Success for All program (Slavin, Madden, et al., 1994). These models differ considerably from each other, but all involve large networks of schools

This chapter was written under funding from the Office of Educational Research and Improvement (OERI), U.S. Department of Education (No. OERI-R-117-R90002). However, any opinions expressed are those of the author and do not represent OERI positions or policies.

attempting thoroughgoing, comprehensive changes in all aspects of school organization and instruction.

For students with special needs, another major reform is under way. This is the move toward inclusion of all students, regardless of disabilities, in regular classrooms in their own neighborhoods (see Gartner & Lipsky, 1987). The inclusion movement goes beyond earlier attempts to mainstream students with special needs, which typically focused on students with mild academic handicaps (such as learning disabilities). Inclusion is intended to provide the supports necessary to integrate all students in regular classes, even those who would not have been included in most mainstreaming plans.

Even though the inclusion movement and the general school reform movement are taking place at the same time, they have largely proceeded on separate tracks. In fact, most of the school reform programs now being widely implemented have only a tangential focus on special education issues, if any at all.

Two reform programs that have had a focus on students with special needs are Success for All and its offspring, Roots and Wings. These programs begin with the idea that all children must be successful from the beginning of their school careers and that classroom instruction in any school must be flexible enough to meet the needs of all students in the regular classroom, regardless of what those needs might be. For students who are at risk for academic difficulties, Success for All and Roots and Wings focus on a policy of "neverstreaming," keeping students out of the special education process by providing them with early and intensive assistance to keep them from falling behind, especially in reading. In particular, firstgraders who are at risk for reading difficulties are given one-to-one tutoring from certified teachers, family support services, or other needed interventions to keep them from failing in this critical skill. Students with more severe academic needs are included in classrooms with appropriate assistance whenever this can be arranged.

The remainder of this chapter describes the Success for All and Roots and Wings programs and their approaches to inclusion of students with special needs.

SUCCESS FOR ALL

The Success for All program began in Baltimore in 1986. It was designed in a collaboration between our group at Johns Hopkins and the Baltimore City Public Schools and piloted in one school in the 1987–1988 school year. Since then Success for All has expanded within Baltimore and is currently being implemented in a total of more than 120 schools in 45 school districts in 20 states from coast to coast.

Basic Principles

Our basic approach to designing a program to ensure success for all children begins with two essential principles: *Prevention and immediate, intensive intervention.*[1] That is, learning problems must first be prevented by providing children with the best available classroom programs and by engaging their parents in support of their school success. When learning problems do appear, corrective interventions must be immediate, intensive, and minimally disruptive to students' progress in the regular program. That is, students receive help early on, when their problems are small. This help is intensive and effective enough to catch students up with their classmates so that they can profit from their regular classroom instruction. Instead of letting students fall further and further behind until they need special or remedial education or are retained in grade, students in Success for All are given whatever help they need to keep up in the basic skills. Typically, Success for All does not require significant additional expenditure but rather shifts existing Chapter 1, special education, and other dollars from remediation to prevention and early intervention. The elements of Success for All are described below (see Slavin et al., 1992, for more detail).

Elements of Success for All

Reading Tutors   One of the most important elements of the Success for All model is the use of tutors to support students' success in reading. One-to-one tutoring is the most effective form of instruction known (see Wasik & Slavin, 1993). The tutors are certified teachers with experience teaching Chapter 1, special education, and/or primary reading. Tutors work one-on-one with students who are having difficulties keeping up with their reading groups. Students are taken from their homeroom classes by the tutors for 20-minute sessions during times other than reading or math periods. In general, tutors support students' success in the regular reading curriculum rather than teaching different objectives. For example, if the regular reading teacher is working on stories with long vowels or is teaching comprehension monitoring strategies, so does the tutor. However, tutors seek to identify learning deficits and use different strategies to teach the same skills.

---

[1]This section is adapted from Slavin et al. (1992) and Slavin et al. (1994).

During daily 90-minute reading periods, tutors serve as additional reading teachers to reduce class size for reading. Information on students' specific deficits and needs passes between reading teachers and tutors on brief forms, and reading teachers and tutors are given regular times to meet to coordinate their approaches with individual children.

Initial decisions about reading group placement and need for tutoring are made based on informal reading inventories given to each child by the tutors. After this, reading group placements and tutoring assignments are made based on 8-week assessments, which include teacher judgments as well as more formal assessments. First graders receive first priority for tutoring, on the assumption that the primary function of the tutors is to help all students be successful in reading the first time, before they become remedial readers. First graders at risk for special education and those who already have individualized education programs (IEPs) indicating reading difficulties receive top priority for tutoring. Often, one or more tutors are special education teachers who work with the lowest-achieving students whether or not they have IEPs.

Reading Program   Students in grades 1–3 are regrouped for reading. That is, students are assigned to heterogeneous, age-grouped classes with class sizes of about 25 most of the day, but during a regular 90-minute reading period they are regrouped according to reading performance levels into reading classes of 15 students all at the same level. For example, a 2-1 (second grade, first semester) reading class might contain first-, second-, and third-grade students all reading at the same level.

Regrouping allows teachers to teach the whole reading class without having to break the class into reading groups. This greatly reduces the time needed for seatwork and increases direct instruction time. We do not expect reduction in class size to increase reading achievement by itself (see Slavin, 1994), but it does ensure that every reading class will be at only one reading level, eliminating workbooks, dittos, or other follow-up activities that are needed in classes with multiple reading groups. The regrouping is a form of the Joplin Plan, which has been found to increase reading achievement in the elementary grades (Slavin, 1987). Regrouping in reading allows schools to keep very diverse students within a heterogeneous class most of the schoolday while meeting students' needs in reading in smaller and more developmentally appropriate settings.

The reading program itself has been designed to take full advantage of having 90 minutes of direct instruction. The reading program emphasizes development of basic language skills and sound and letter recognition skills in kindergarten and uses an approach based on sound blending and phonics starting in first grade (although kindergarten students who show readiness are accelerated into the first-grade program if the school chooses). Students in pre-K, kindergarten, and first grade experience Peabody Language Development Kits to help them build language concepts essential to later reading success. The K–1 reading program uses a series of "shared stories," in which part of the story is written in small type and read by the teachers, while part is written in large type and read by the students. The student portion uses a phonetically controlled vocabulary. The program emphasizes oral reading to partners as well as to the teacher, instruction in story structure and specific comprehension skills, and integration of reading and writing. When they reach the primer reading level, students use a form of Cooperative Integrated Reading and Composition (CIRC) with novels or basals. CIRC uses cooperative learning activities built around story structure, prediction, summarization, vocabulary building, decoding practice, writing, and direct instruction in reading comprehension skills. Research on CIRC has found it to significantly increase students' reading comprehension and language skills (Stevens, Madden, Slavin, & Farnish, 1987).

Eight-Week Reading Assessments Every 8 weeks, reading teachers assess students progress through the reading program. The results of the assessments are used to determine who is to receive tutoring, to suggest other adaptations in students' programs, and to identify students who need other types of assistance, such as family interventions or vision/hearing screening. Eight-week assessment data are also used to follow the progress of students who are at risk for special education placement so that timely and effective interventions can be used to keep them in the regular program.

Preschool and Kindergarten Most Success for All schools provide a half-day preschool and/or a full-day kindergarten for all eligible students. The preschool and kindergarten provide a balanced and developmentally appropriate learning experience for young children. The curriculum emphasizes the development and use of language. It provides a balance of academic readiness and nonacademic music, art, and movement activities. Readiness activities include use of integrated thematic units, Peabody Language Development Kits, and a program called Story Telling and Retelling (STaR) in which students retell stories read by the teachers.

Family Support Team A family support team consisting of any social workers, parent liaisons, counselors, and others who work in the school provides parenting education and works to involve parents in support of their children's success in school. Also, family support staff are called on to provide assistance when there are indications that students are not working up to their full potential because of problems at home. For example, families of students who are not receiving adequate sleep or nutrition need glasses, are not attending school regularly, or are exhibiting serious behavior problems receive family support assistance. Links with appropriate community service agencies are made to provide as much focused service as possible for parents and children. The family support team is often involved in finding ways to meet student needs without assigning them to special education.

Program Facilitator A program facilitator works at the school full time to oversee (with the principal) the operation of the Success for All model. The facilitator helps plan the Success for All program, helps the principal with scheduling, and visits classes and tutoring sessions frequently to help teachers and tutors with individual problems. The program facilitator may work with individual children having particular difficulties to find successful strategies for teaching them and then return the children to the tutors or teachers. He or she helps teachers and tutors deal with any behavior problems or other special problems and coordinates the activities of the family support team with those of the instructional staff.

Teachers and Teacher Training The teachers and tutors are regular teachers. They receive detailed teacher's manuals supplemented by 2 days of in-service at the beginning of the school year and several in-service sessions throughout the year on such topics as classroom management, instructional pace, and implementation of the curriculum.

Special Education Every effort is made to deal with students' learning problems within the context of the regular classroom, as supplemented by tutors. In general, students assigned to special education services in previous years are fully integrated in regular classes (with tutoring or other support if needed). Ideally, no new assignments to resource services are made for reading problems, on the assumption that tutoring services available to all students will be more appropriate. In some schools students with more serious disabilities are maintained in the regular classroom with the assistance of aides or special education teachers to help them during academic periods.

Advisory Committee An advisory committee composed of the building principal, facilitator, teachers, and parent representatives meets regularly to review the progress of the program and to identify and solve any problems that arise.

Research on Success for All

Research on Success for All has emphasized rigorous evaluation of the program in comparison to matched local control schools, with a particular focus on individually administered tests of reading as an outcome variable. Due to funding limitations, not all Success for All schools are being assessed in this way, but we currently have high-quality assessment data from 15 schools in seven districts in seven states. Three of the districts were evaluated by Johns Hopkins staff and four (using identical measures and procedures) by an independent evaluation group at Memphis State University (see Slavin et al., 1994).

A common evaluation design, with variations due to local circumstances, has been used in all Success for All evaluations. Every Success for All school involved in a formal evaluation is matched with a control school that is similar in poverty level (percentage of students qualifying for free lunch), historical achievement level, ethnicity, and other factors. Children in the Success for All schools are then matched on district-administered standardized test scores given in kindergarten or (starting in 1991 in several districts) on Peabody Picture Vocabulary Test (PPVT) scores given by the project in the fall of kindergarten or first grade.

Slavin and Madden (1993) introduced a method for combining the outcomes of experimental–control comparisons over many replications and over time. This technique, called a multi-site replicated experiment, considers each successive cohort and each pair of schools (experimental and control) a replication. For example, across the 15 Success for All schools we have studied, 37 cohorts of first graders have experienced the program and have been assessed on individually administered reading measures. Twenty-one second-grade cohorts and 13 third-grade cohorts have been in the program since first grade. This pooling procedure, a minor variation on meta-analysis commonly used in medical research, allows us to build up an adequate sample over time to do school-level analyses of program effects.

Figure 26.1 shows the mean grade equivalents and effect sizes for all 15 Success for All schools in comparison to their control schools. For students in general, effect sizes averaged more than half a standard deviation each year, meaning that the average Success for All child is performing better than 70% of control students. Analyses at the school level indicate that the effect sizes are significantly different from zero at all three grade levels ($p < .001$). Because standard deviations increase each year in school, a constant

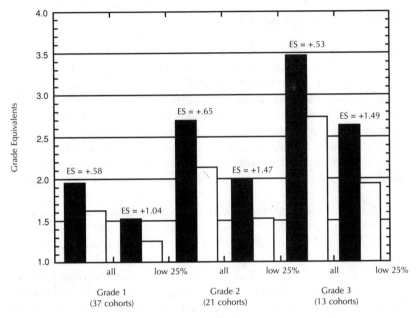

Figure 26.1. Cumulative mean reading grade equivalents and effect sizes (ES) in Success for All schools, 1988–1993. (■ = SFA, □ = Control.) (*Note:* Includes all students in Success for All or control schools since first grade [N = 15 school pairs]. Schools are in Baltimore, Philadelphia, Charleston [SC], Memphis, Ft. Wayne [IN], Caldwell [ID], and Montgomery [AL].)

effect size implies a growing difference in absolute or grade-equivalent terms; Success for All students exceed matched control students by about 3 months in first grade, by almost 7 months by third grade, and by a full year in fifth grade (see Slavin, Madden, Dolan, & Wasik, 1993).

Effects for students in the lowest 25% of their cohorts are consistently larger than for students in general, averaging an effect size of +1.04 in the first grade, +1.47 in second grade, and +1.49 in third grade. By the end of third grade, these most at-risk students are performing better than 93% of matched control students. These effect sizes are significantly different from zero ($p < .001$ in grades 1 and 2, $p < .004$ in grade 3). Larger effect sizes for low achievers than for students in general have been found in almost every evaluation of Success for All. It is primarily due to the tutoring, family support, and other services principally given to the lowest-achieving, most at-risk students. A major goal for Success for All is to build a floor under the achievement of all students, and the large gains made by the lowest achievers is evidence that this is occurring. Further, Baltimore data indicate substantial reductions in the numbers of students assigned to special education and retained in grade (Slavin et al., 1992).

In addition to outcomes across all schools and districts, studies of Success for All have shown strongly positive effects for first graders identified as having learning disabilities (Ross et al., 1994) and for students in a Spanish bilingual version of the program (Slavin & Madden, 1994).

ROOTS AND WINGS

At Lexington Park Elementary School, in a small town in Southern Maryland, 10-year-old Jamal rises to speak. "The chair recognizes the delegate from Ridge School," says the chairwoman, a student from the local high school.

"I'd like to speak in favor of House Bill R130," he begins. "This bill would tell farmers they couldn't use fertilizer on land that is within 20 yards of the watershed. Fertilizer goes into the bay and causes pollution and kills fish. Farmers can still grow a lot of crops even if they don't plant close to water, and we will all have a better life if we can stop pollution in the bay. I yield to questions."

A hand goes up. The chairwoman recognizes a delegate from Carver School.

"How does fertilizer harm the bay?" she asks.

Jamal explains how the fertilizer provides nutrition to algae in the bay, which deprives the larger creatures of oxygen. When he finishes, a delegate from Green Holly School is recognized.

"I'm a farmer," says 11-year-old Maria. "I can hardly pay all my bills as it is, and I've got three kids to feed. I'll go broke if I can't fertilize my whole field!"

The debate on the bill goes on for more than an hour. Students delegates who are playing the role of watermen speak about how their way of life is disappearing because of declining catches due to pollution. Business owners talk about how pollution ruins the local economy. Finally, the committee amends the bill to prohibit farmers from planting near waterways unless they are poor. The bill passes and later on is voted on by the whole House of Delegates.

Lexington Park and three other schools in St. Mary's County, Maryland, are piloting a school restructuring program called Roots and Wings. Roots and Wings is one of nine "break the mold" school designs being funded by the New American Schools Development Corporation (NASDC) to create the schools of the 21st century.

As with Success for All, Roots and Wings is designed to ensure that *every* child, regardless of family background or disability, achieves world-class standards in reading, writing/language arts, mathematics, science, history, and geography. The school, parents, community agencies, and others work in a coordinated, comprehensive, and relentless way from the birth of the child onward to see that children receive whatever they need to become competent, confident, and caring learners. Success for All provides the "roots" of Roots and Wings: the guarantee that every child will make it successfully through the elementary grades, no matter what this takes.

It is essential to ensure that every child can read, compose, and understand math, science, history, and geography; yet this is not enough for children today. Children need to be able to creatively and flexibly solve problems, understand their own learning processes, and connect knowledge from different disciplines. To build these higher-order skills, Roots and Wings provides daily opportunities for students to work collaboratively to solve simulated and real-life problems using the skills and information they are learning in class. This is the "wings" of Roots and Wings: engaging students in activities that enable them to *apply* everything they learn so that they can learn the usefulness and interconnectedness of all knowledge.

Elements of Roots and Wings

World Lab   The debate in the "House of Delegates" illustrates one of the most important and innovative elements of the "wings" of Roots and Wings. This is an integrated approach to science, social studies, and writing called WorldLab. In WorldLab, students take on roles as people in history, in other countries, or in various occupations. The students in the "House of Delegates" have been studying the Chesapeake Bay, focusing on sources of pollution, watersheds, tides, the rain cycle, and the life cycle of aquatic plants and animals. They have also been learning about government, economics, geography, and politics. Their work on these topics is done in preparation for a model state legislature, in which students debate many bills relating to cleaning up the bay. In other WorldLab units, students take on roles as inventors, as delegates to the Constitutional Convention, as advisors to the Pharaohs of Ancient Egypt, as explorers in the 15th century, and so on. In these simulations, students work in small, cooperative groups to investigate topics of science and social studies. They read books and articles about their topics; write newspapers, broadsides, letters, and proposals; use mathematics skills to solve problems relating to their topics; and use fine arts, music, and computer, video, and other technology to prepare multimedia reports. Students ultimately learn all the usual content of elementary science and social studies (plus much more), but they do so as active participants in the scientific discoveries, historical events, and other systems they are studying. Students with special needs participate fully in all of these activities.

Early Learning Programs Part of the "roots" of Roots and Wings is ensuring that all students arrive in first grade with good language and prereading skills, self-esteem, health, and other prerequisites for success. Roots and Wings provides family literacy programs and other preventive services to children ages birth to 3 in at-risk families. In preschool and kindergarten it provides research-based curricula focusing on integrated themes, storytelling and re-telling, many opportunities for oral expression, and cooperative learning activities.

Literacy Integrated reading/writing programs are used in grades 1–5. The first-grade program, Reading Roots, is an adaptation of the Success for All beginning reading program. It integrates phonics and meaning-centered reading to ensure reading success for every child. Reading Wings, starting in the second grade, uses cooperative learning groups in which students read to each other; work together to find the main elements of stories and to help each other learn reading comprehension strategies; and plan, draft, revise, edit, and publish compositions.

Tutoring First graders who are struggling with the beginning reading are given one-to-one tutoring by certified teachers (paid by Chapter 1 or special education). The idea is to give students starting to fall behind in this critical area the most intensive and effective intervention known to bring them up to expectations quickly.

Mathematics MathWings engages students with the powerful ideas of mathematics in an approach keyed to NCTM standards that balances problem-solving, skills, and concept development. Students work in cooperative groups to discover and apply mathematical concepts, making extensive use of manipulatives, calculators, computers, and other resources to solve complex problems.

Family Support and Integrated Services A family support team at each Roots and Wings school works to increase parent participation in the school; to implement programs to improve student attendance, behavior, and adjustment; and to coordinate health, mental health, and social services for families. Health suites in each school help ensure that children and families receive the care they need. The family support teams also help manage an extensive partnership in which volunteers from the local Navy base and area businesses work in the schools as tutors, mentors, activity leaders, and in other roles.

Extended Day An after-school program is offered to all children. During this time, students have opportunities to give or receive cross-age or adult tutoring; to receive any special education or Chapter 1 services needed; or to participate in a variety of arts, music, and other programs.

Neverstreaming As in Success for All, the primary approach to Chapter 1 and special education in Roots and Wings is called "neverstreaming": providing prevention and early intervention that are effective enough to keep most students from needing long-term remedial or special education services. Children who are at risk receive tutoring, family support services, adjustments in the regular classroom, and other services intended to help them succeed in the mainstream.

Special Education and Inclusion Nearly all students with special needs are fully integrated in regular classroom activities, with help from special education aides, teachers, and technology as necessary. One of the pilot schools contains a regional center for children with severe disabilities. Most elementary-age children from this center are involved in all elements of the Roots and Wings curriculum with appropriate assistance.

CONCLUSION

Success for All and Roots and Wings provide two related models of how comprehensive school reform can incorporate a focus on the inclusion of all learners and on prevention of the learning failures that cause so many children to fall behind and ultimately become eligible for special education. Neither program has been able to integrate every child with serious disabilities in the regular classroom, but both are moving toward that goal, trying to find a way to accomplish full inclusion while meeting the academic and social needs of all students.

REFERENCES

Comer, J. (1988). Educating poor minority children. *Scientific American, 259*, 42–48.

Gartner, A., & Lipsky, D.K. (1987). Beyond special education: Toward a quality system for all students. *Harvard Educational Review, 57*, 367–395.

Levin, H.M. (1987). Accelerated schools for disadvantaged students. *Educational Leadership, 44*(6), 19–21.

Madden, N.A., Slavin, R.E., Karweit, N.L., Dolan, L.J., & Wasik, B.A. (1993). Success for All: Longitudinal effects of a restructuring program for inner-city elementary schools. *American Educational Research Journal, 30,* 123–148.

Ross, S.M., Smith, L.J., Casey, J., & Slavin, R.E. (1994, April). *Increasing the academic success of disadvantaged children: An examination of alternative early childhood intervention programs.* Paper presented at the annual meeting of the American Educational Research Association, New Orleans.

Sizer, T. (1984). *Horace's compromise: The dilemma of the American high school.* Boston: Houghton Mifflin.

Slavin, R.E. (1987). Ability grouping and student achievement in elementary schools: A best-evidence synthesis. *Review of Educational Research, 57,* 347–350.

Slavin, R.E. (1994). School and classroom organization in beginning reading: Class size, aides, and instructional grouping. In R.E. Slavin, N.L. Karweit, B.A. Wasik, & N.A. Madden (Eds.), *Preventing early school failure: Research on effective strategies.* Boston: Allyn & Bacon.

Slavin, R.E., Karweit, N.L., & Wasik, B.A. (1992/1993). Preventing early school failure: What works? *Educational Leadership, 50*(4), 10–18.

Slavin, R.E., Karweit, N.L., & Wasik, B.A. (1994). *Preventing early school failure: Research on effective strategies.* Boston: Allyn & Bacon.

Slavin, R.E., & Madden, N.A. (1993, April). *Multi-site replicated experiments: An application to Success for All.* Paper presented at the annual meeting of the American Educational Research Association, Atlanta.

Slavin, R.E., & Madden, N.A. (1994, April). *Lee Conmigo: Effects of Success for All in bilingual first grades.* Paper presented at the annual meeting of the American Educational Research Association, New Orleans.

Slavin, R.E., Madden, N.A., Dolan, L., & Wasik, B.A. (1993). *Success for All in the Baltimore City public schools: Year 6 report.* Baltimore: Johns Hopkins University, Center for Research on Effective Schooling for Disadvantaged Students.

Slavin, R.E., Madden, N.A., Dolan, L., Wasik, B.A., Ross, S., & Smith, L. (1994). "Whenever and wherever we choose . . ." The replication of Success for All. *Phi Delta Kappan, 75,* 639– 647.

Slavin, R.E., Madden, N.A., Karweit, N.L., Dolan, L., & Wasik, B.A. (1992). *Success for All: A relentless approach to prevention and early intervention in elementary schools.* Arlington, VA: Educational Research Service.

Slavin, R.E., & Yampolsky, R. (1991). *Effects of Success for All on students with limited English proficiency: A three-year evaluation.* Baltimore: Johns Hopkins University, Center for Research on Effective Schooling for Disadvantaged Students.

Stevens, R.J., Madden, N.A., Slavin, R.E., & Farnish, A.M. (1987). Cooperative Integrated Reading and Composition: Two field experiments. *Reading Research Quarterly, 22,* 433–454.

Wasik, B.A., & Slavin, R.E. (1993). Preventing early reading failure with one-to-one tutoring: A review of five programs. *Reading Research Quarterly.*

27

DOING WHAT COMES NATURALLY

FULL INCLUSION IN ACCELERATED SCHOOLS

HENRY M. LEVIN

A major debate is raging across the United States on the degree to which all children should be given a common set of opportunities within the nation's schools. This controversy swirls around such practices as tracking by ability group, pulling students from classrooms for special services such as remediation or special education, and the separation of special education students into their own classrooms or schools. The purpose of this chapter is to provide some thoughts on the issue of inclusion for a particular movement of schools, Accelerated Schools. In the context of this chapter, the term *inclusion* refers to the philosophy and practice of providing a common experience for all children in a common setting. Obviously, the real world will be characterized by degrees of inclusion, so the options go beyond "full inclusion" or "full exclusion" of particular types of students in all situations. An attempt will be made to show that even with nuances of practice, a single philosophy embracing inclusion and access must be central to all school activities if it is to take equity and inclusion as the bedrock to which it is anchored.

The specific purpose of this chapter is to present the connection between the Accelerated Schools process and full inclusion of all students in the mainstream of school instructional activities and

This chapter was originally presented at the National Center on Educational Restructuring and Inclusion invitational conference on inclusive education, Racine, Wisconsin, April 28–May 1, 1994.

experiences. The overriding theme will be that "inclusion" should not be viewed as an add-on to a conventional school. It must be viewed as intrinsic to the mission, philosophy, values, practices, and activities of the school. That is, the Accelerated School is a place where full inclusion of all students into the lifestream of the school is foundational in every respect. In contrast, a conventional school with tracking of students by ability grouping and special needs might be coerced to create heterogeneous grouping and inclusion of all students in "regular" classrooms, but the compliance response is likely to be mechanical and to pay obeisance only to the letter of the obligations. Historical analysis has shown that educational impacts are determined largely by the substance of the response rather than procedural compliance (Cuban, 1984). For this reason, I believe that full inclusion must be embedded deeply in the very foundation of the school, in its mission, its belief system, and its daily activities, rather than an appendage that is added on to a conventional school.

In what follows, I will provide a picture of how inclusion is not only compatible with but absolutely integral to the Accelerated Schools process, doing what comes naturally. The remainder of this chapter is divided into three parts. First, I present a brief picture of the Accelerated Schools Project. Second, I show why full inclusion is integral to Accelerated Schools. Finally, I present some examples of how schools provide such inclusion.

ACCELERATED SCHOOLS PROJECT

The Accelerated Schools Project (ASP) was established in 1986–1987 with the launching of two pilot elementary schools serving high concentrations of at-risk students. Its goals were to eliminate remediation by using all of the schools' resources to accelerate the growth and development of all students in order to bring them into the academic mainstream by the end of elementary school (Levin, 1987). That is, the focus of Accelerated Schools is to advance the development of all children through using teaching and learning approaches that are usually reserved for gifted and talented students.

ASP has focused especially on schools with high concentrations of at-risk students, of whom large numbers had previously been relegated to remedial programs and special education as learning disability children. The project grew out of earlier research that had examined the demography of at-risk students and their educational prospects in conventional schools (Levin, 1986, 1987, 1988). It found that the predominant policy of tracking these students into remedial instruction characterized by drill and practice and associative learning had extremely deleterious consequences. At-risk children got further and further behind the educational mainstream the longer that they were in school, and many began to view school as punishing and arduous, even in the early elementary years. Out of this research came a quest for a different kind of school that would accelerate rather than remediate. Acceleration necessitates the remaking of the school in order to advance the academic and social development of children in at-risk situations, not slow it down. This meant creating a school in which all children were viewed as capable of benefiting from a rich instructional experience rather than relegating them to a watered-down one. It meant a school that creates powerful learning situations for all children, one that integrates curriculum, instructional strategies, and context (i.e., climate and organization) rather than providing piecemeal changes through new textbooks or instructional packages. It meant a school whose culture was transformed internally to encompass the needs of all students through creating a stimulating educational experience that builds on their identities and strengths.

Such transformation is neither simple nor swift. Schools are provided with training and follow-up experiences as part of a systematic process (Hopfenberg, Levin, & Associates, 1993). The training and follow-up activities require the participation of the full school staff, parents, and students (*Accelerated Schools* newsletter, 1994). A coach is trained to work with the school using constructivist activities that engage the members of the school community in problem-solving experiences that lead to a sequence of major activities that the school undertakes over subsequent months. The focus is on the school internalizing the Accelerated School philosophy and values through constructivist activities and school processes that lead to school change and the transformation of school culture (Finnan, 1994). Ultimately, these emerge in a school governance and decision-making process that focuses on the creation of powerful learning situations for all children. The details can be found in the *Accelerated Schools Resource Guide* (Hopfenberg et al., 1993). Through a particular governance structure and an inquiry approach to decision making, the school addresses its major problem areas in a way that will create powerful learning throughout the school.

Over the $7^1/_2$ years since the initiation of the two pilot schools, the Accelerated Schools Project has expanded considerably in the number of schools, coaches, and regional centers and in the depth and sophistication of the transformation process. In 1993–1994, the project encompassed over 500 elementary and middle schools in 33 states with a typical cost of about $30 per student. Some 137 coaches had been trained and were being mentored by the National Center for the Accelerated Schools Project through communication, site visits, and retreats. In addition, 10 regional centers had been established to work with schools and to train/co-train coaches with the National Center. The project had also initiated its first collaborative effort to transform an entire school district into an Accelerated School District where all schools would embrace the accelerated model in San Jose, California.

Evaluations of Accelerated Schools have shown substantial gains in student achievement, attendance, full inclusion of special needs children in the mainstream, parental participation, and numbers of students meeting traditional gifted and talented criteria. They have also shown reductions in the number of students repeating grades, student suspensions, and school vandalism (see, e.g., English, 1992; Knight & Stallings, 1994; Levin & Chasin, 1994; McCarthy & Still, 1993). These evaluations have included multi-year assessments in which Accelerated Schools have been compared with control schools (Knight & Stallings, 1994; McCarthy & Still, 1993).

ACCELERATED PRINCIPLES, VALUES, AND POWERFUL LEARNING

The Accelerated School is not just a collection of programs or an attempt to put together a school through piecemeal accumulation of different policies and practices. It is a set of practices based upon a coherent philosophy and principles. In this respect, inclusion is not an optional feature of an accelerated school but is embedded in the very structure and belief system of the school. The goal of the Accelerated School is to bring all students into a meaningful educational mainstream, to create for all children the dream school we would want for our own children. This is the guiding sentiment for the transformation of an Accelerated School, one that is embodied in its three central principles: 1) unity of purpose, 2) empowerment with responsibility, and 3) building on strengths.

Accelerated Schools Principles

Unity of Purpose *Unity of purpose* refers to the common purpose and practices of the school on behalf of all its children. Traditional schools separate children according to abilities, learning challenges, and other distinctions; staff are divided according to their narrow teaching, support, or administrative functions; and parents are usually relegated to only the most marginal of roles by the school in the education of their children. Accelerated Schools require that the schools forge a unity of purpose around the education of all students and all of the members of the school community, a living vision and culture of working together on behalf of all of the children. Strict separation of either teaching or learning roles works against this unity and results in different expectations for different groups of children. Accelerated Schools formulate and work toward high expectations for all children, and children internalize these high expectations for themselves. *Unity of purpose* means inclusion.

Empowerment with Responsibility Empowerment with responsibility refers to who makes the educational decisions and takes responsibility for their consequences. Traditional schools rely on higher authorities at school district and state levels as well as on the content of textbooks and instructional packages formulated by publishers who are far removed from schools. Staff at the school site have little discretionary power over most of the major curriculum and instructional practices of the school, and students and parents have almost no meaningful input into school decisions. In this respect, powerlessness leads to a feeling of exclusion in terms of the ability to influence the major dimensions of school life.

An Accelerated School requires that school staff, parents, and students take responsibility for the major decisions that will determine educational outcomes. That is, all constituents must participate, an all-encompassing principle of *inclusion* in daily school life. The school is no longer a place in which roles, responsibilities, practices, and curriculum content are determined by forces beyond the control of its members. In its daily operations, the school community hones its unity of purpose through making and implementing the decisions that will determine its destiny. At the same time, the school takes responsibility for the consequences of its decisions through continuous assessment and accountability, holding as its ultimate purpose its vision of what the school will become. This is accomplished through a parsimonious, but highly effective, system of governance and problem solving that ensures inclusion of students, staff, and parents in the daily life of the school.

Building on Strengths Traditionally, schools have been far more assiduous about identifying the weaknesses of their students than looking for their strengths. A focus on weakness or deficiencies leads naturally to organizational and instructional practices in which children are tracked according to common deficiencies. The logic is that "lower" groups cannot keep up with a curricular pace that is appropriate for higher groups. But Accelerated Schools begin by identifying strengths of participants and building on those strengths to overcome areas of weakness.

In this respect, all students are treated as gifted and talented students because the gifts and talents of each child are sought out and recognized. Such strengths are used as a basis for providing enrichment and acceleration. As soon as one recognizes that all students have strengths and weaknesses, a simple stratification of students no longer makes sense. Strengths include not only the various areas of intelligence identified by Gardner (1983) but also areas of interest, curiosity, motivation, and knowledge that grow out of the culture, experiences, and personalities of all children. Classroom themes can be those in which children show interest and curiosity and in which reciprocal teaching, cooperative learning, peer and cross-age tutoring, and individual and group projects can highlight the unique talents of each child in classroom and school activities. These group processes and the use of specialized staff can both recognize and build on the particular strengths and contributions of each child while providing assistance in areas of need within the context of meaningful academic work.

Accelerated Schools require that each child be fully included in the activities of the school while validating his or her strengths and addressing his or her areas of special need. This can be done in regular classrooms employing classroomwide and schoolwide curricular approaches that are based upon inclusion of every child in the central life of the school. It can be done not only with multiability grouping and multi-age grouping but also by recognizing that all children have different profiles of strengths that can be used to complement each other and be used to create strong teams that provide internal reinforcement among students.

It should also be noted that the process of building on strengths is not just limited to students. Accelerated Schools also build on the strengths of parents, teachers, and other school staff. Parents can be powerful allies if they are placed in productive roles and provided with the skills to work with their own children. Teachers bring gifts of insight, intuition, and organizational acumen to the instructional process, gifts that are often untapped by the mechanical curricula that are so typical of remedial programs. By acknowledging the strengths found among participants within the entire school community, all of the participants are expected to contribute to success.

Accelerated Schools Values

Accelerated Schools also acknowledge a set of values that permeate relationships and activities. These include the school as a center of expertise, equity, community, risk taking, experimentation, reflection, participation, trust, and communication. Virtually all of these are the values of inclusion, since the focus is on the inner power, vision, capabilities, and solidarity of the school community. But especially important are such values as equity: the view that the school has an obligation to all children to create for them the dream school that we would want for our own children. Such a school must treat children equitably and must address equitable participation and outcomes. The school is viewed as an overall community rather than as a building with many separate communities represented, although the cultures and experiences of different students are acknowledged and incorporated into the school experience. Addressing the needs of all children will require experimentation and risk taking, reflection, trust, and communication. Above all, the concept of unity of purpose is present in all of the values and practices of the school, a necessary approach to inclusion of all students in a common school dream.

Powerful Learning

The three principles and nine values of Accelerated Schools are all used to create what are called powerful learning situations (Hopfenberg et al., 1993, Chapters 6–10). A powerful learning situation is one that incorporates changes in school organization, climate, curriculum, and instructional strategies to build on the strengths of students, staff, and community to create an optimal learning situation. What is unique about this approach is that changes are not piecemeal but integrated around all aspects of the learning situation. This contrasts sharply with the usual attempts to transform schools through idiosyncratic reforms involving the ad hoc adoption of different curriculum packages, instructional practices, and organizational changes to address each perceived problem that the school faces. Over time, some of these are pruned, and others are added, without any attempt to integrate them into an overall philosophy and vision of the school. Powerful learning builds on the strengths of all community members and empowers them to be proactive learners by developing skills through intrinsically challenging activities that require both group work and individual endeavor.

Accelerated Schools also emphasize the connections between the big wheels of the school and the little ones. The big wheels refer to the overall school philosophy and change process that are shared collaboratively by all members of the school community. The small wheels refer to the informal innovations that grow out of participation by individuals or small groups in embracing the school's philosophy and change process. These little wheels result from the internalization of the school philosophy and change process into the belief system of school members, resulting in changes in their individual decisions and commitments in classrooms and in individual and group interactions.

THREE ILLUSTRATIONS

Thus far I have attempted to show that the entire framework of the Accelerated Schools concept and practices is based upon inclusion of all members of the community. The three guiding principles of Accelerated Schools, the underlying values, the focus on powerful learning, and the links between big wheels and small wheels provide an integrative and ubiquitous setting in which inclusion is foundational. In this section, I will provide a brief picture of three schools and how they transformed themselves from schools characterized by tracking, pullout of students for special services, and special day classes for handicapped students to full inclusion.

Thomas Edison Elementary School

Thomas Edison Elementary School in Sacramento, California, is a prototype of a school in a rapidly transforming neighborhood (Levin & Chasin, 1994; "Edison Accelerated School," 1994), a phenomenon that is quite common in California with its rapid influx of immigrants and rise in child poverty. In the fall of 1989, Edison had a total of 360 students, of which 36% were receiving public assistance under Aid to Families with Dependent Children (AFDC), and only English was spoken. Just 3 years later (1992–1993), the school's enrollment had grown by one third to 494 students, of which 80% were on AFDC; and 13 languages were spoken (Levin & Chasin, 1994).

In the earlier period, there was one self-contained classroom for children with severe learning disabilities, and other students with learning challenges were pulled out of their regular classrooms for services. As children from new language backgrounds were drawn into the school, they were provided with bilingual instruction in separate settings.

With the introduction of the Accelerated Schools process, the Edison community began to work on bringing specialists into regular classrooms to provide services to children within the context of their classroom projects and activities. Special-needs teachers and regular classroom teachers planned together to meet each child's needs, a practice that was embraced by the big wheels of school organization and inquiry. However, the special day class was still separated, although teachers began to introduce powerful learning approaches through the small wheels of the Accelerated Schools process.

By the beginning of the third year of ASP, the school began to focus on the full integration of the special day class into the life of the school. Using the inquiry process, the staff and parent representatives developed a collaborative approach in which all of the students in the self-contained class would be mainstreamed in regular classrooms. By January 1994, the new approach was implemented, and regular classroom teachers and specialists were working together. Early results have been very positive, although requiring continuous collaboration and inquiry to address challenges that have arisen. By the beginning of the third year of ASP, Thomas Edison had used the Accelerated Schools philosophy and practices to make the transition from traditional pullout programs and isolation of severely handicapped children to full inclusion of all children in the lifestream of the school.

Despite a larger student body with much higher concentrations of at-risk students, student suspensions have fallen; school vandalism has vanished; and student attendance, parent participation, and test scores have risen. Classrooms are buzzing with student projects, research, writing, discussions, and problem-solving activities for all students.

Samuel Mason Elementary School

Samuel Mason Elementary School ("Mason Elementary School," 1993) is located in one of the most inner-city neighborhoods of Boston, an area known for its poverty, gangs, and high crime. In 1990, Mason enrolled only 130 students and was scheduled to be closed because it could not attract more students under Boston's system of controlled choice. In 1991–1992, Mason launched its ASP program, and by 1993–1994 it enrolled 300 children, 11% above its capacity. In addition, it had as many as 60 students on waiting lists in some grades and had reduced its grade retentions from 25% of students to zero while increasing attendance by 10 percentage points. Test scores had also risen.

Early in its ASP adoption, Mason began to experiment with ways of providing a better school and improving learning opportunities for *all* children. Using its cadres and the inquiry method to create powerful learning situations, Chapter 1, special education, and regular classroom teachers began to plan shared curricular and instructional innovations for the first time. This resulted in special-needs teachers working with children directly in the classroom and collaborating with other teachers on a common set of educational experiences and expectations for all children. Starting with the early childhood program, Mason set up collaborative teams including the regular classroom teacher, a classroom aide, and special-needs teachers who took responsibility for particular classes. Even with students who ranged from those without special needs to those with mild and severe disabilities, the class was so successful that outsiders could not tell which students had special needs from observing class activities and participation. In subsequent years, other classes have been combined, bringing in not only the special-needs students but also their teachers. This had effectively reduced class size significantly in all of the grades, providing an incentive for teacher collaboration and the benefits of small class size and individual attention for all studens. Thus, the entire student body has benefited from full inclusion at Samuel Mason. As the principal, Mary Russo, has stated, "Becoming an Accelerated School has helped us become a multi-age, multi-ability, multi-neighborhood, multi-race, multi-class, multi-cultural school" (The Association of Retarded Citizens/ Texas, 1993).

North Middle School

North Middle School in Aurora, Colorado (adjoining Denver), has about 700 students of whom more than half are educationally at risk (The Association of Retarded Citizens/Texas, 1993). These numbers include 100 with mild to moderate disabilities. Prior to launching the Accelerated School process in the fall of 1992, North was facing a widening learning gap among its students, a rising teenage pregnancy rate, and other symptoms of a school that was becoming impacted increasingly by at-risk students. Over the 2 years that North has been an Accelerated School, its discipline problems have diminished, test scores have risen, student and parent participation has increased, and the entire school has taken on a new life. Classrooms vibrate with student enthusiasm over their challenging learning environments with thematic teaching across subjects and collaborative teaching and learning teams.

Prior to the advent of the Accelerated School, North employed pull-out programs for its students with learning disabilities and problem behavior. Under Accelerated Schools, the school began to address how it might fully integrate all students into all class activities and eliminate pull out. A long-term teacher-hiring strategy was adopted to seek dually certified teachers every time there is a staff opening. However, an immediate strategy was employed as well. Regular classroom teachers and special education teachers were combined into teams of two and three teachers to work with fully integrated groups of students. Members of the team plan together and consult on the needs of specific students through the use of a common planning period at each grade level. The result has been higher academic performance of special education and "regular" students as all classes pursue activities that were formerly reserved only for gifted and talented students. But, even more than this, the teachers have had to memorize who the "special education" kids are because it is not easy to differentiate them from other students.

CONCLUSION

The thrust of this work has been to argue for first establishing schools that embrace a profound philosophical commitment to a rich and empowering education for all students. Clearly, this must move beyond the slogans of the day that wind up on school pencils and on bulletin boards. It requires a deep transformational process that engages all members of the school community and creates new beliefs and practices that mirror the philosophy on a daily basis. Given this philosophical commitment and the demonstrated capacity to pursue it, schools will create their own unique solutions to equality and inclusion that are informed by their strengths, research, and the experiences of other schools. This is what we have learned from Accelerated Schools and their natural inclination to seek full inclusion as such schools develop and grow.

REFERENCES

The Association of Retarded Citizens/Texas. (1993, December). *Together inclusion works, 1*(3).
Cuban, L. (1984). *How teachers taught.* New York: Longmans.
Edison accelerated school: Creating a learning community. (1994, Winter). *Accelerated Schools, 3*(2), 4–9.
English, R.A. (1992). *Accelerated schools report.* Columbia: University of Missouri, Department of Educational and Counseling Psychology.
Finnan, C. (1994). School culture and educational reform: An examination of the accelerated schools project as cultural therapy. In G. Spindler & L. Spindler (Eds.), *Cultural therapy and culturally diverse classrooms* (pp. 137–156). Monterey Park, CA: Corwin Press.
Gardner, H. (1993). *Frames of mind.* New York: Basic Books.
Hopfenberg, W., Levin, H.M., & Associates. (1993). *The accelerated schools resource guide.* San Francisco: Jossey-Bass.
Knight, S., & Stallings, J. (1994). The implementation of the accelerated school model in an urban elementary school. In R. Allington & S.

Walmsley (Eds.), *No quick fix: Rethinking literacy programs in American elementary schools*. New York: Teachers College Press.

Levin, H.M. (1986). *Educational reform for disadvantaged students: An emerging crisis*. West Haven, CT: NEA Professional Library.

Levin, H.M. (1987). New schools for the disadvantaged. *Teacher Education Quarterly, 14*(4), 60–83.

Levin, H.M. (1988). *Towards accelerated schools*. New Brunswick, NJ: Center for Policy Research in Education, Rutgers–The State University.

Levin, H.M., & Chasin, G. (1994). Thomas Edison accelerated elementary school. In J. Oakes & K.H. Quartz (Eds.), *Creating new educational communities, schools, and classrooms where all children can be smart*. Chicago: University of Chicago Press.

Mason elementary school: Helping children beat the odds. (1993). *Accelerated Schools, 3*(1), 4–9.

McCarthy, J., and Still, S. (1993). Hollibrook accelerated elementary school. In J. Murphy & P. Hallinger (Eds.), *Restructuring schools* (pp. 63–83). Monterey Park, CA: Corwin Press.

INDEX

South Burlington School District,
    Vermont, 130
Southern Cayuga Central School
    District, New York, 122
Spatial intelligence, 357, 358
Special education
    appropriate services and, 277–278
    efficacy studies, 16
    school restructuring exclusion and,
        215–216
    separate, 1, 206–207
Special Education Programs, Office of
    (OSEP), U.S. Department of
    Education, 6
    private schools and appropriate
        services, 94
Specialized training time, 204–205
Spectrum Report, 362–364
Springfield Public Schools,
    Massachusetts, 195, 227
St. Cloud Community Schools,
    Minnesota, 137–138
Staff attitudes, 131–134
Staffing, school, 124–129, see also
    Personnel
Standardized testing, 74
Standards, high, for full inclusion, 103
State schools, special education, 73–74
States
    disabled student policies prior to
        1975, 264–266
    finance reform, special education,
        279–290
    inclusion policies, 104–113
    placement, special education, 5–6
"Stay put rule," 65
    inclusion limits and, 67
Story Telling and Retelling (STaR), 379
Strategic teacher, 126, 227
Strength-based design, 236–237
Strengths, building on, 393–394
Student, moving to adult, 238–239
Student-curriculum broker, 368–369
Students in inclusive education,
    response of, 149–151
Students served under IDEA, 4
Students supporting other students,
    160
Students without disabilities
    court decisions regarding, 87
    inclusion programs, effect on, 124,
        188–190, 204, 306
    special education consequences,
        31–32

Success for All, 231, 239, 375–383
Success from the start, achieving,
    239–240
Superintendent, role of, inclusive
    education, 134
Supportive learning style, 126
Supreme Court, U.S., 88
Surfside School, Brooklyn, New York,
    135
Suspensions, student, 392, 397
Syracuse University, merging of Special
    Education and Teaching and
    Leadership departments, 16

"Taken-for-granted" environment,
    322
Takhoma School District, Washington,
    168
TASH, on inclusive education, 175
Teacher-Led Computer Demonstration
    (TLC) project, 336–338, 343
    self-perceived learning competence
        and, 347
    technological gatekeepers and, 344
Teachers
    freedom to implement, inclusive
        education, 206
    individualized school and, 369–372
    preparation for inclusion, 205, 322
        PL 94-142 and, 15, 271
    role of, inclusive education, 136–139,
        394
    technology gatekeepers, 344–345
Team teaching, 125, 131
Technokids, 336–338
Technology, instructional, 102, 126,
    162–163, 329–352
    determination of appropriate,
        342–343
    diversity accommodation tools,
        332–333, 337
    essential tools, 346
    inclusion models, 333–339
    learning style accommodation, 333
Technology in the Classroom, ASHA
    study, 339–340
Technology integration coordinator,
    336–337
Temperament, human, aspects of, 237
Tests, 397
    ability, inadequacy of, 353–355
    culturally biased on disability basis,
        324